GREEN CAREERS
IN ENERGY

PETERSON'S

A **nelnet** COMPANY

About Peterson's

To succeed on your lifelong educational journey, you will need accurate, dependable, and practical tools and resources. That is why Peterson's is everywhere education happens. Because whenever and however you need education content delivered, you can rely on Peterson's to provide the information, know-how, and guidance to help you reach your goals. Tools to match the right students with the right school. It's here. Personalized resources and expert guidance. It's here. Comprehensive and dependable education content—delivered whenever and however you need it. It's all here.

For more information, contact Peterson's, 2000 Lenox Drive, Lawrenceville, NJ 08648; 800-338-3282 Ext. 54229.

Stephen Clemente, Managing Director, Publishing and Institutional Research; Bernadette Webster, Director of Publishing; Jill C. Schwartz, Editor; Ray Golaszewski, Manufacturing Manager; Linda M. Williams, Composition Manager; Practical Strategies, LLC: Contributing Researchers: Barbara Jani, Libby Romero; Contributing Writers: Margaret C. Moran, Judy Johnson, Rita A. Read

ISBN-13: 978-0-7689-2860-0
ISBN-10: 0-7689-2860-5

Printed in the United States of America

10 9 8 7 6 5 4 3 2 1   12 11 10

371.4
G

CONTENTS

CONTENTS

[f] www.facebook.com/green.series

A NOTE FROM THE PETERSON'S EDITORS

If you are a high school or college student thinking about your future—and the future of our planet— or if you are a career changer wondering what you need to do to get an energy-related job in today's new "green" economy, *Peterson's Green Careers in Energy* can offer you the information you need. Throughout the book, you will find details on numerous energy-related jobs and careers as well as programs offered at two-year and four-year colleges and universities and through trade unions and specialized organizations.

If, like most people, you need a better understanding of what being green or living a green lifestyle means and how to begin your search for a green job, you've come to the right place! In **What Does Being Green Mean?,** you'll find out why we're seeing an increase in the current interest in sustainability and what the New Energy for America Plan and the 2009 Stimulus Plan mean in terms of your green job search.

Next, **Essays on the Importance of Sustainability** features insightful and inspirational articles by individuals who are at the forefront of this exciting field:

- Mary Panks-Holmes, Director of Client Strategy at *Native*Energy
- Peter Buckland, Ph.D. candidate (Educational Theory and Policy) at Penn State University Park; president of 3e-coe (Environment-Ecology-Education in the College of Education)
- James W. DeHaven, Vice President of Economic & Business Development, Kalamazoo Valley Community College; Kalamazoo, Michigan
- Mary F.T. Spilde, President, Lane Community College, Eugene, Oregon
- Danny S. Growald, Vice-Chair of Princeton University's SURGE: Students United for a Responsible Global Environment

If you are seeking a professional or skilled job in the new green economy, check out **Part I (chapters 1–4)** for details on jobs in the energy, transportation, construction and building, and policy, analysis, advocacy, and regulatory affairs fields. You can search by field for information on job trends, career paths, earning potential, education/licensure requirements, and where to get additional information. Each job profile includes professional and trade associations that may have special interest groups or sections related to energy and sustainability. In addition, you'll find fascinating interviews with individuals in certain green careers. These folks offer great advice and insight, which is tremendously beneficial to anyone thinking about their particular field. Finally, as an added benefit, you will find links to videos on CareerOneStop.

org for many of the careers mentioned throughout these chapters—links that look like this:

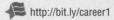 http://bit.ly/career1

CareerOneStop's Web site is sponsored by the U.S. Department of Labor, Employment and Training Administration. It offers career resources and workforce information to job seekers, students, businesses, and workforce professionals to foster talent development in a global economy.

To locate some of the great four-year and/or graduate programs or some of the outstanding two-year (including community colleges) and union programs, check out **Part II (chapters 5 and 6).** The colleges and universities profiled here support innovative programs in energy, have vibrant on-campus sustainability programs and organizations, and have made a commitment to making their campus communities sustainable. Both chapters highlight degrees offered, including distance learning opportunities, and green campus organizations and activities.

Don't want to leave your carbon footprint traveling to see colleges or universities and want to save some green in the process? Check out the videos and educational resources on YOUniversityTV. com. You'll find easy-to-use links to videos that look like this:

 http://bit.ly/collvid2

YOUniversityTV.com assists students with the college-selection process by providing access to videos and educational resources for colleges across the United States. YOUniversityTV.com is free-of-charge and does not receive compensation from any of the universities it features.

Chapter 7 features labor unions that offer energy-related apprenticeship and training programs. In **Chapter 8's State and Federal Workforce Training,** you'll discover what each state's One-Stop Career Center offers in terms of help with job search, resume writing, training programs, and

more. Simply find your state, and you'll uncover a wealth of information, including phone numbers and Web site.

In the **Appendixes,** you'll learn how to find and search "green" job boards and how to "green" your vocabulary—what all of the new terms actually mean. You'll also find a list of organizations in the United States and abroad that support sustainability through education, research, and activities.

Throughout the book, you'll find feature pages offering extra "green" tips and advice, with such topics as *The Future in Energy Careers, What is LEED?, Nanotechnologies: Promise or Peril?,* and *RecycleMania.* "About" boxes that are scattered throughout the chapters provide even more information and explanations to help you succeed on your way to a green job—and a green life.

Join Peterson's *Green Careers* conversation on Facebook® and Twitter™ at www.facebook.com/green.series and www.twitter.com/green_series. Peterson's resources are available to help you with your "green" job and college search.

Peterson's publishes a full line of books— education exploration, career preparation, test prep, and financial aid. Peterson's publications can be found at high school guidance offices, college libraries and career centers, and your local bookstore and library. Peterson's books are now also available as eBooks.

We welcome any comments or suggestions you may have about this publication. Your feedback will help us make educational dreams possible for you—and others like you.

Colleges and universities will be pleased to know that Peterson's helped you in your selection. Admissions and Sustainability Office staff members are more than happy to answer questions and help in any way they can. The editors at Peterson's wish you great success in your search for a great *green* career in energy!

WHAT IS THE
NEW GREEN ECONOMY?

Once upon a time, the only thing that was green was Kermit the Frog. Now, it seems as though everywhere you turn, all you see and hear is "green." Eat organically grown food. Use only low- or no-VOC paint. (What's VOC?) Trade in your gas-guzzler for a hybrid. Have a fuel-efficient car? Buy an even more fuel-efficient car. Wear clothes made from renewable sources such as cotton or bamboo. (Bamboo? For clothes?) Recycle your computer, your cell phone, and even your sneakers. On and on goes the list of do's and don'ts in this new sustainable, eco-friendly, twenty-first century. But what does it mean to you—the student, the worker, the consumer, and the citizen?

Why the Interest in Sustainability Now?

First, the fear of global warming and climate change as well as national security issues are driving the push to conserve energy and become less dependent on foreign oil. Second, the recession that began in 2007 turned the spotlight on the consumption patterns of Americans. Our savings rate had fallen into the negative zone as we borrowed against the equity in our homes to buy boats, electronics, the latest hot trends in clothes, gas-hungry SUVs, and crossovers—generally whatever we wanted until we reached our credit limits. And when we did, some of us just got another credit card. Whereas our great-grandparents may have darned a hole in a sock, shortened a hem on a dress, or had their shoes resoled, we just tossed out old items and bought new ones.

New Energy for America

Certainly a number of Americans did practice "recycle, reuse, reduce" since the first Earth Day in 1970, but the nation as a whole had not embraced the mantra of conservationists and environmentalists until the recent recession—which brings us to the third point. The election of Barack Obama in 2008 served to crystallize the need to do something about our profligate attitude toward the environment. As a candidate, President Obama had promised to reduce the nation's dependence on nonrenewable sources of energy and fight climate change. As President, he launched his "New Energy for America" program that is intended to

- "Chart a new energy future: . . . by embracing alternative and renewable energy, ending our addiction to foreign oil, addressing the global climate crisis, and creating millions of new jobs that can't be shipped overseas."

1

- "Invest in clean, renewable energy: To achieve our goal of generating 25 percent of our energy from renewable sources by 2025, we will make unprecedented investments in clean, renewable energy—solar, wind, biofuels, and geothermal power."
- "Fight climate change: We will invest in energy efficiency and conservation, two sure-fire ways to decrease deadly pollution and drive down demand. . . ."

The 2009 Stimulus Plan

Within a month of Obama's inauguration, Congress passed a $787-billion stimulus package, officially called the American Recovery and Reinvestment Act (ARRA) of 2009, to help the nation dig itself out of the recession. One goal of the act was to put the nation on the course to achieve the President's energy plan for the nation, including creating 3.5 million "green jobs." Among the programs included in the stimulus package were the following:

- $32 billion to transform the nation's energy transmission, distribution, and production system
- $6 billion to weatherize low-income homes
- $16 billion to repair and retrofit public housing for energy efficiency
- $30 billion for highway construction
- $31 billion to modernize federal and other public buildings for energy efficiency
- $19 billion for clean water, flood control, and environmental restoration
- $10 billion for transit and rail expansion
- $20 billion for health information technology
- $1.5 billion for biomedical research
- $3.95 billion for the Workforce Investment Act, which includes money available to community colleges for worker-training programs

- $25 billion in Recovery Zone bonds to states with high unemployment rates for job training, infrastructure construction and repair, and economic development
- $20 billion in tax incentives for installing solar and wind systems in homes and businesses

In July 2009, the President proposed another $12 billion to fund workforce training through the nation's network of community colleges. In his speech at Macomb Community College in Warren, Michigan, Obama said, "This is training to install solar panels and build those wind turbines and develop a smarter electricity grid. And this is the kind of education that more and more Americans are using to improve their skills and broaden their horizons." (http://www.whitehouse.gov/the_press_office/Remarks-by-the-President-on-the-American-Graduation-Initiative-in-Warren-MI/)

Focusing much of the stimulus package on energy conservation, infrastructure, and work force training has meant an immediate impact on people's lives. It has also helped to reorient our thinking about how the choices we make about food, clothing, housing, and the use of discretionary income affect others and the environment.

About Committing to Climate Change

". . . Colleges and universities must exercise their leadership in their communities and throughout society by modeling ways to eliminate global warming emissions, and by providing the knowledge and the educated graduates to achieve climate neutrality. . . ."
—The Signatories of the American College & University Presidents' Climate Commitment

2010 and Beyond

ARRA funding was structured so that grants to states and research institutes continued throughout 2010. Many of the awards went for development of renewable energy resources such as biofuel, wind, and solar power systems. The Department of Energy (DOE) also announced several loan guarantees in the millions and even a billion dollars to underwrite the construction of new power plants by private companies.

By investing in energy research, developing power systems based on that research, and then constructing devices and systems to enable consumers to tap into those power sources, the nation underscores its obligation to be a good steward of the environment, create jobs, and to expand the economy—a win-win for everyone, even the polar bears.

Where to Look for More Information

To find out more about federal energy programs, visit the U.S. Department of Energy, the Department of Transportation, and the Environmental Protection Agency Web sites:

> www.doe.gov
> www.dot.gov
> www.epa.gov

To find what your state is doing to reduce energy consumption and support the environment, go online to www.state.<insert state abbreviation>.us

For example for New Jersey, it would be:

> www.state.nj.us.

Check the state's home page as well as its environmental protection agency or department and its department of transportation.

How Green Is a Prospective Employer?

Today, just about any company that you interview with will say it is eco-conscious, but how do you know for sure? Here are some things to look for as you do your due diligence on prospective employers. Remember to look at the "small" picture—the daily culture of the company—not just the big picture, its social responsibility report.

1. Does the company have a social responsibility officer? Does the company issue a social responsibility report?

2. Does the company show up in the news as eco-friendly?

3. Depending on the type of company, what is its policy on carbon neutrality? How is it moving toward becoming carbon neutral?

4. If it has separate offices or manufacturing plants, what is the company's environmental policy toward new construction and/or toward retrofitting older sites?

5. If the company leases autos for employees, does it lease fuel-efficient ones?

6. If the company is in a suburban setting, does it encourage carpooling by setting aside special parking close to the building? Does it reimburse drivers of carpools for part of the mileage or tolls?

7. If the company is in a suburban setting with nearby train service, does it run a van or bus to meet trains to pick up and drop off employees?

8. What is the company's policy on telecommuting? What is its policy on flextime? Both cut down on auto emissions.

9. If there's a cafeteria, does it serve locally grown foods? Does it use paper, plastic, or ceramic dishes? Does it use metal or plastic utensils? What kind of take-out containers does it use?

10. What is the policy on printing e-mail? What is the policy on copying: single-sided or double-sided?

11. Does it have recycle bins for paper and plastic goods in convenient places for employees to use?

12. If the company is in retail sales, does it use paper or plastic bags? Does it encourage customers to use recyclable bags? How?

13. If it's a manufacturing company, what is its policy on the amount of packaging it uses for its products?

14. Does the company support green causes in its locations like the Great American Cleanup™? Does it have a foundation that makes grants to local environmental efforts?

ESSAYS ON THE IMPORTANCE OF SUSTAINABILITY

CULTIVATING AND NURTURING CHANGE

by Mary Panks-Holmes
Director of Client Strategy, *Native*Energy

Some Background

Environmental and social innovation. Preserving our natural resources. Biodiversity and ecological integrity. Nonpartisan camaraderie. Protecting our lakes and oceans. Health and wellness. Clean drinking water. Local farming. Renewable energy. Smarter, cleaner technology. A stronger sense of community. This is all part of what comes to mind when I think about sustainability.

In my last semester of college, I entered into the corporate world and became a national sales and marketing leader for a Fortune 500 company. It soon became clear to me that business as usual was not going to sustain, and if I was going to be a strategic growth professional, environmental and social responsibility needed to be the foundation that a successful business was built on. My journey started with the pleasurable experience of spending a few days with Former Vice President Al Gore and his phenomenal team at The Climate Project (TCP). The mission of TCP is to educate the public about the harmful effects of climate change and to work toward solutions at a grassroots level worldwide (www.theclimateproject.org). From there, I worked to establish strong affiliations with several international sustainability experts and pioneers in the industry who were able to provide me with unique insight and advantage, cut my teeth as an independent consultant, and eventually found what I call home, *Native*Energy. I met *Native*Energy through TCP, and for more than two years I admired them from afar. The opportunity presented itself for me to have a conversation with *Native*Energy about joining the team (*family*), and to this day it is the career choice I am most proud of, and grateful for. The firm's people and mission are making the world a better place and changing the way new renewable and carbon reduction projects are developed. And above all, they are genuine—the real deal. The experience has changed my life.

The Business of Energy: A Case Study

There are individuals and organizations in this field that are simply to be admired, and then there are those that are rock stars.

*Native*Energy was started by two guys in a garage a decade ago. Well, not a garage, but they did work out of their homes trying to help a Native American tribe develop a small wind project on its land. Since then, *Native*Energy has become a climate solutions innovator and recognized leader in the U.S. carbon market.

It is rightly admired for its distinctive "help build" model, which supports the construction of new smaller-scale wind farms, and other renewable generation and carbon-reduction projects. By helping to finance construction of Native American, family farm, and community-based projects, *Native*Energy and its customers help communities in need develop sustainable economies. Notable projects that *Native*Energy has helped build include the wind turbine on the Rosebud Sioux Reservation, the turbine that serves the Wray, Colorado, School District, and most recently the Greensburg Wind Farm in Kansas.

*Native*Energy works with a number of clients that are widely recognized as leaders in corporate social responsibility, like Green Mountain Coffee Roaster, Ben & Jerry's Homemade, Aveda, Timberland, and Stonyfield Farms. It has significant Native American ownership, providing tribes the ability to share in the business value that is being created by organizations' imaginative approach to climate solutions. And, as much as they might be too humble to admit, *Native*Energy and the people who make it what it is are more genuine and authentic than one could ever envision. They are changing the landscape. Literally.

The Importance of Sustainability

Social and environmental sustainability presents the most significant opportunity of our generation. It forces us to think differently about what it takes to be resilient over time. It drives us to learn from tomorrow and inspire change. Corporations are working to create strategies for becoming more sustainable. In my role as a sustainability strategist, I work with a team to analyze the type of energy that a company uses to power its operations, product design, and manufacturing. We look at where the energy comes from, how it is generated, and what limited natural resources are used in the process. We consider what the environmental and social impacts are. People do not typically think about this, but the energy we use has a social effect just as it has environmental effects. We work with organizations to create alternatives—renewable resources of energy, innovative ideas, new creative strategies that permanently alter the company's top and bottom lines, philosophy, and future.

Closing

According to Clean Edge's report *Clean Energy Trends 2010*, it is projected that solar, wind, and biofuels—the three benchmark technologies that totaled $124.8 billion in 2008 and grew 15.8 percent to $144.5 billion in 2009—will grow to $343.4 billion within a decade.

Corporations are investing in on-sight renewables, supporting clean energy projects that are located in the backyards of some of their supply chain members, and helping build new renewable generation and carbon reduction projects in at-risk communities. Clusters of family farms are benefitting from farm methane projects that help reduce operating costs and runoff. The stories are countless, and the list of benefits—social and environmental—is endless.

On a personal note...

Born and raised in Traverse City, Michigan, my family and I spent our summers tending to the garden, planting saplings and watering them at least twice a day, and enjoying Lake Michigan. As a young girl, it took me time to understand the purpose behind the amount of time and labor invested in growing trees. My father taught us that being a steward of the planet and appreciating and protecting our natural resources was noble. My mother instilled the values of being a nurturer and caretaker. Working in the sustainability field, energy in particular, has allowed me to cultivate change and facilitate the transformation of companies and communities. That is noble, and nurturing.

A couple of years ago when I was visiting my childhood home in Northern Michigan, I took the time to see how many of the trees we had planted when I was a young girl were still there. There were 400 still standing.

Join us. Work in our field. Be the next rock star.

Mary Panks-Holmes was born in Traverse City, Michigan, in 1972. Mary's childhood was split between the beach, the basketball court, and the floor of her father's business. Panks-Holmes attended DePaul University in Chicago, where she studied music and was a heptathlete. She soon returned to Michigan, then spent some time on the east coast studying industrial and organizational psychology and behavioral sciences. Course work failed to hold her attention, so she focused on her work and imaginative business practices. After ten years in the Fortune 500 and consulting, she joined NativeEnergy in 2009. Panks-Holmes's repertoire: Aspiring surfer; favors jeans, t-shirts, and flip flops. Certificate, Presidio Graduate School of Management's Climate Change Intensive. Volunteer, The Climate Project. Member, Surfrider Foundation. Mary currently lives in Chicago with her fabulous husband, and two beautiful Olde English Bulldogs.

EDUCATION AND ACTION TO ACHIEVE SUSTAINABILITY

by Peter Buckland, Ph.D. candidate,
Educational Theory and Policy, College of Education,
Penn State University Park

When it comes to sustainability, unsustainability, and "the green economy," we need to speak directly: defining economic success as unlimited consumption and production has led to a global economy that ignores the interdependent relationships between all life forms on the planet Earth. As the result of such an economic framework, the world is on the precipice of an ecological catastrophe. It is possible, within such an unrestrained system, for millions of pounds of garbage to stream into the ocean every hour. The result of this garbage flow is an infamous patchwork of trash twice the size of Texas in the North Pacific gyre. The multitude of organisms ingesting toxins in this gyre pass those same toxins onto animals higher in the food chain, like tuna and other predatory fish that humans eat.

Reflecting upon this and other ecological conditions, a tenth grader recently said to his mother, "Mom. Your generation has really screwed up the environment. What are you going to do about it?" It was this question that launched our club, and we hope to learn and unlearn our way as far out of it as we can—and lead others to "unscrew" it up as well.

Environment-Ecology-Education in the College of Education, or 3E-COE (http://3e-coe.blogspot.com/), is a group of current and future teachers working for sustainability. We view sustainability as John Ehrenfield does: "Sustainability is the possibility that humans and other life will flourish on Earth forever." Sustainability is not necessarily tied to governments, corporate wealth, global trade agreements, or "The Economy." Sustainability also cannot tie itself to a "Green Economy" in which people continue consuming as much as they want as long as they consume efficiently manufactured products. Sustainability, rightly understood, must centralize people's health and happiness in communities within bioregions integrated into Earth's awesomely complex patterns. We must use education and action to achieve this sustainability, a sustainability that provides bounty, a true richness of experience, and the possibility for flourishing.

Currently, we are working to convince individuals at Penn State to stop using 1.8 million single-use plastic water bottles each year. We should be responsibly drinking and maintaining healthy water here. Upon learning about the North Pacific trash continent, we scoured every source we could to remove the wool from our eyes and "solve for pattern," as farmer-philosopher-author Wendell Berry calls it. We must understand interconnected systems and solve problems without causing more problems.

The dominant economy driven by the expansion of consumption and production asks the following question: "How can someone make a lot of money by selling water?" Answer: "Single-use plastic water bottles."

www.facebook.com/green.series

From Fiji to India to Bolivia to Maine, water bottle corporations systematically undermine communities, economies, and watersheds. In the worst scenarios, companies collude with military dictatorships or desiccate aquifers that have sustained farmers for generations. In the United States, they take public water maintained at taxpayers' expense and mark it up hundreds or thousands of times. At Penn State, Aquafina® purchased from vending machines is 700 times more expensive than tap water. It is also much more wasteful.

It is now widely recognized that the plastic bottle's "life" cycle exemplifies anti-ecological engineering. Plastic water bottles generate mind-boggling quantities of solid pollutants, and only about 16 percent of them are ever recycled. Consider the following example. In a class of 20 students, each student consumes approximately 200 bottles of water per year, and they discard, on average, over 3,200 plastic bottles as pure waste. When you convert these figures with a U.S. population of more than 350 million, you end up with upwards of 58,000,000,000 wasted bottles, just for water alone.

Any "green economy" worth its name must solve for pattern. The question we stated earlier should be something like, "How do we maintain healthy water systems?" This question is holistic, fairly prioritizing economic, social, and ecological well-being. Its actual answer means working patiently with place-based natural systems, imitating them as best as we can, and maintaining healthy relationships with them to enrich people's communities and their economics.

At Penn State, we use well water from the Spring Creek watershed that is part of the Chesapeake Bay watershed. Our everyday water is connected to the Atlantic Ocean. Any decision we make at Penn State affects the whole system's health. Surely, flushing plastic bottles down that watershed degrades the Dauphin County farmers' life and the crabs' lives in the Chesapeake. We know that whatever we do, we have to push for reducing our footprint and reusing as many materials as possible. We have accomplished this with a pilot program in conjunction with the Office of Physical Plant and the support of awakened and awakening people.

Together, we have implemented bottle-filling stations on campus. These are inverted water fountains that easily fill bottles or cups with clean, clear, and cool drinking water. This solution can close most of the waste loops in our local piece of the capitalist water-distribution catastrophe. Every time you reuse a steel canteen, ceramic coffee mug, or bike bottle with one of these fountains, you eliminate demand for at least one more bottle, stop one more bottle from leeching into our common sink, and prevent about 800 grams of greenhouse gases from entering the atmosphere.

These stations, of course, are far from perfect. They cool water with electricity from a coal plant on campus, and the refrigerants in the machine are hydroflourocarbons, a greenhouse gas potentially hundreds of times more potent than carbon dioxide. This reinforces the enormous proportions of the consumptive dependence problem. But it is solvable.

In the end, we must reduce our economy. We must not just learn about reduction. If we want a verdant planet, then we will need to educate ourselves by unlearning the consumption economy and retool culture to live while using less. Only then, will we live in a truly green economy, and will humans and all life flourish on Earth.

_____

Peter Buckland is working on a Ph.D. in Educational Theory and Policy at Penn State where he focuses on sustainability in schools, philosophy of education, and the American controversy over teaching the theory of evolution. He is president of Environment-Ecology-Education in the College of Education (http://3e-coe.blogspot.com/), whose membership contributed to this essay. He also co-hosts Sustainability Now Radio, a call-in show focusing on sustainability (http://sustainabilitynowradio. blogspot.com). He has also served as the assistant to the Chair of the Pennsylvania Environmental Resource Consortium, a coalition of fifty-six Pennsylvania colleges and universities with some commitment to sustainability. In April 2010, he was awarded Penn State's Harold F. Martin Award for Teaching Excellence.

ESTABLISHING A WORLD-CLASS WIND TURBINE TECHNICIAN ACADEMY

by James W. DeHaven
Vice President of Economic & Business Development,
Kalamazoo Valley Community College

When Kalamazoo Valley Community College (KVCC) decided it wanted to become involved in the training of utility-grade technicians for wind-energy jobs, early on the choice was made to avoid another "me too" training course.

Our program here in Southwest Michigan, 30 miles from Lake Michigan, had to meet industry needs and industry standards.

It was also obvious from the start that the utility-grade or large wind industry had not yet adopted any uniform training standards in the United States.

Of course, these would come, but why should the college wait when European standards were solidly established and working well in Germany, France, Denmark, and Great Britain?

As a result, in 2009, KVCC launched its Wind Turbine Technician Academy, the first of its kind in the United States. The noncredit academy runs 8 hours a day, five days a week, for twenty-six weeks of intense training in electricity, mechanics, wind dynamics, safety, and climbing. The college developed this program rather quickly—in eight months—to fast-track individuals into this emerging field.

KVCC based its program on the training standards forged by the Bildungszentrum fur Erneuerebare Energien (BZEE)—the Renewable Energy Education Center.

Located in Husum, Germany, and founded in 2000, the BZEE was created and supported by major wind-turbine manufacturers, component makers, and enterprises that provide operation and maintenance services.

As wind-energy production increased throughout Europe, the need for high-quality, industry-driven, international standards emerged. The BZEE has become the leading trainer for wind-turbine technicians across Europe and now in Asia.

With the exception of one college in Canada, the standards are not yet available in North America. When Kalamazoo Valley realized it could be the first college or university in the United States to offer this training program—that was enough motivation to move forward.

For the College to become certified by the BZEE, it needed to hire and send an electrical instructor and a mechanical instructor to Germany for six weeks of "train the trainer." The instructors not only had to excel in their respective fields, they also needed to be able to climb the skyscraper towers supporting megawatt-class turbines—a unique combination of skills to possess. Truly, individuals who fit this job description don't walk through the door everyday—but we found them! Amazingly, we found a top mechanical instructor who was a part-time fireman and comfortable with tall ladder rescues and a skilled electrical instructor who used to teach rappelling off the Rockies to the Marine Corps.

In addition to employing new instructors, the College needed a working utility-grade nacelle that could fit in its training lab that would be located in the KVCC Michigan Technical Education Center. So one of the instructors traveled to Denmark and purchased a 300-kilowatt turbine.

Once their own training was behind them and the turbine was on its way from the North Sea, the instructors quickly turned to crafting the curriculum necessary for our graduates to earn both an academy certificate from KVCC and a certification from the BZEE.

Promoting the innovative program to qualified potential students across the country was the next step. News releases were published throughout Michigan, and they were also picked up on the Internet. Rather quickly, KVCC found itself with more than 500 requests for applications for a program built for 16 students.

Acceptance into the academy includes a medical release, a climbing test, reading and math tests, relevant work experience, and, finally, an interview. Students in the academy's pioneer class, which graduated in spring 2010, ranged in age from their late teens to early 50s. They hailed from throughout Michigan, Indiana, Ohio, and Illinois as well as from Puerto Rico and Great Britain.

The students brought with them degrees in marketing, law, business, science, and architecture, as well as entrepreneurial experiences in several businesses, knowledge of other languages, military service, extensive travel, and electrical, computer, artistic, and technical/mechanical skills.

Kalamazoo Valley's academy has provided some high-value work experiences for the students in the form of two collaborations with industry that has allowed them to maintain and/or repair actual utility-grade turbines, including those at the 2.5-megawatt size. This hands-on experience will add to the attractiveness of the graduates in the marketplace. Potential employers were recently invited to an open house where they could see the lab and meet members of this pioneer class.

The College's Turbine Technician Academy has also attracted a federal grant for $550,000 to expand its program through additional equipment purchases. The plan is to erect our own climbing tower. Climbing is a vital part of any valid program, and yet wind farms cannot afford to shut turbines down just for climb-training.

When the students are asked what best distinguishes the Kalamazoo Valley program, their answers point to the experienced instructors and the working lab, which is constantly changing to offer the best training experiences to the wind students.

Industry continues to tell us that community colleges need to offer fast-track training programs of this caliber if the nation is to reach the U.S. Department of Energy's goal of 20 percent renewable energy by 2030. This would require more than 1,500 new technicians each year.

With that in mind, KVCC plans to host several BZEE orientation programs for other community colleges in order to encourage them to consider adopting the European training standards and start their own programs.

Meanwhile, applications are continuing to stream in from across the country for the next Wind Turbine Technician Academy program at Kalamazoo Valley Community College.

James W. DeHaven is the Vice President for Economic & Business Development at Kalamazoo Valley Community College. He graduated from the Graduate School of Business at the University of Michigan. Prior to joining Kalamazoo Valley Community College in 2003, he served on its Board of Trustees for thirteen years. Among his current responsibilities at Kalamazoo Valley are its workforce development efforts, including the Wind Turbine Technician Academy.

A video about the program is available at http://www.mteckvcc.com/windtechacademy.html

ROLE OF COMMUNITY COLLEGES IN CREATING A WORKFORCE FOR THE GREEN ECONOMY

by Mary F.T. Spilde, President,
Lane Community College, Eugene, Oregon

Community colleges are expected to play a leadership role in educating and training the workforce for the green economy. Due to close connections with local and regional labor markets, colleges assure a steady supply of skilled workers by developing and adapting programs to respond to the needs of business and industry. Further, instead of waiting for employers to create job openings, many colleges are actively engaged in local economic development to help educate potential employers to grow their green business opportunities and to participate in the creation of the green economy.

As the green movement emerges there has been confusion about what constitutes a green job. It is now clear that many of the green jobs span several economic sectors such as renewable energy, construction, manufacturing, transportation, and agriculture. It is predicted that there will be many middle-skill jobs requiring more than a high school diploma but less than a bachelor's degree. This is precisely the unique role that community colleges play. Community colleges develop training programs, including pre-apprenticeship, that ladder the curriculum to take lower skilled workers through a relevant and sequenced course of study that provides a clear pathway to career track jobs. As noted in *Going Green: The Vital Role of Community Colleges in Building a Sustainable Future and Green Workforce,* community colleges are strategically positioned to work with employers to redefine skills and competencies needed by the green workforce and to create the framework for new and expanded green career pathways.

While there will be new occupations such as solar and wind technologists, the majority of the jobs will be in the energy management sector—retrofitting the built environment. For example, President Obama called for retrofitting more than 75 percent of federal buildings and more than 2 million homes to make them more energy-efficient. The second major area for growth will be the "greening" of existing jobs as they evolve to incorporate green practices. Both will require new knowledge, skills, and abilities. For community colleges, this means developing new programs that meet newly created industry standards and adapting existing programs and courses to integrate green skills. The key is to create a new talent pool of environmentally conscious, highly skilled workers.

The following two areas show remarkable promise for education and training leading to high wage/high demand jobs:

Efficiency and energy management: There is a need for auditors and energy efficiency experts to retrofit existing buildings. Consider how much built environment we have in this country, and it's not difficult to see that this is where the vast amount of jobs are now and will be in the future.

Greening of existing jobs: There are few currently available jobs that environmental sustainability will not impact. Whether it is jobs in construction, such as plumbers, electricians, heating and cooling technicians, painters, and building supervisors, or chefs, farmers, custodians, architects, automotive technicians, and interior designers, all will need to understand how to lessen their impact on the environment.

Lane Community College offers a variety of degree and certificate programs to prepare students to enter the energy efficiency fields.

Lane has offered an Energy Management program since the late 1980s—before it was hip to be green! Students in this program learn to apply basic principles of physics and analysis techniques to the description and measurement of energy in today's building systems, with the goal of evaluating and recommending alternative energy solutions that will result in greater energy efficiency and energy cost savings. Students gain a working understanding of energy systems in today's built environment and the tools to analyze and quantify energy efficiency efforts. The program began with an emphasis in residential energy efficiency/solar energy systems and has evolved to include commercial energy efficiency and renewable energy system installation technology.

The Renewable Energy Technician program is offered as a second-year option within the Energy Management program. Course work prepares students for employment designing and installing solar electric and domestic hot water systems. Renewable Energy students, along with Energy Management students, take a first-year curriculum in commercial energy efficiency giving them a solid background that includes residential energy efficiency, HVAC systems, lighting, and physics and math. In the second year, Renewable Energy students diverge from the Energy Management curriculum and take course work that starts with two courses in electricity fundamentals and one course in energy economics. In the following terms, students learn to design, install, and develop a thorough understanding of photovoltaics and domestic hot water systems.

Recent additions to Lane's offerings are Sustainability Coordinator and Water Conservation Technician degrees. Both programs were added to meet workforce demand.

Lane graduates find employment in a wide variety of disciplines and may work as facility managers, energy auditors, energy program coordinators, or control system specialists, for such diverse employers as engineering firms, public and private utilities, energy equipment companies, and departments of energy and as sustainability leaders within public and private sector organizations.

Lane Community College also provides continuing education for working professionals.

The Sustainable Building Advisor (SBA) Certificate Program is a nine-month, specialized training program for working professionals. It is designed to enable graduates to advise employers or clients on strategies and tools for implementing sustainable building practices. Benefits from participating in the SBA program often include saving long-term building operating costs, improving the environmental, social and economic viability of the region, reducing environmental impacts and owner liability, plus a chance to improve job skills in a rapidly growing field.

The Building Operators Certificate is a professional development program created by The Northwest Energy Efficiency Council. It is offered through the Northwest Energy Education Institute at Lane. The certificate is designed for operations and maintenance staff working in public or private commercial buildings. It certifies individuals in energy and resource-efficient operation of building systems at two levels: Level I - Building System Maintenance and Level II - Equipment Troubleshooting and Maintenance.

Lane Community College constantly scans the environment to assess workforce needs and develop programs that provide highly skilled employees. Lane, like most colleges, publishes information in its catalog on workforce demand and wages so that students can make informed decisions about program choice.

Green jobs will be a large part of a healthy economy. Opportunities will abound for those who take advantage of programs with a proven record of connecting with employers and successfully educating students to meet high skills standards.

Mary Spilde, has been president of Lane Community College in Eugene, Oregon, since August 2001. She joined Lane in 1995 as Vice President for Instructional Services. In 1997, she became VP for Instruction and Student Services. Prior to that, she served fifteen years at Linn-Benton Community College in Albany, Oregon, in positions that included dean of business, health, and training. Mary earned a bachelor's degree in business and social systems and a law degree from the University of Edinburgh, Scotland. She completed a master's in adult education and a doctorate in postsecondary education at Oregon State University.

Mary is past chair of the American Association of Community Colleges board of directors and serves on their Sustainability Task Force. She is a board member of the American Association of Colleges and Universities, the National Institute for Leadership Development, and the National Committee for Cooperative Education. Mary also serves on the steering committee for the American Presidents' Commitment to Climate Control, and she co-chairs Oregon's Post-Secondary Quality Education Commission. Mary is a former board member of the American Association of Women in Community Colleges and was president of that organization from 2002–2004.

Mary has a passion for learning about leadership and organizational change. She focuses much of her time and energy at Lane on leading and supporting initiatives that will develop a culture of innovation, achievement, and improvements in the learning environment.

THE FUTURE OF SUSTAINABILITY: REDEFINING THE AMERICAN DREAM

By Danny S. Growald
Vice-Chair of Princeton University's SURGE:
Students United for a Responsible Global Environment

These days, the easiest place to find "sustainability" is on the wrapper of your toilet paper. With that term highlighting the labels of pricey products as a marketing tool, reclining gracefully across eco-chic issues of fashion magazines, or silkscreened on the T-shirts of idealistic college students, it's hard to understand what sustainability really means.

Too often, sustainability appears little beyond the cause of wealthy environmentalists who can afford to worry more about whether the broccoli is organic and the deck wood forest-friendly than about how to put their kids through school. But viewed properly, sustainability represents a path to a future that's not only good for nature, but better for people and communities as well.

My own understanding of sustainability began in kindergarten, when my 6-year-old classmates and I chose "The Rainforest" as our theme of the month. We transformed the small classroom into a jungle—construction paper banana plants arched over the tables, blue carpets became an Amazon River of deadly piranhas and electric eels, and the whistle and hum of recorded rainforest noises entranced us into our daily nap.

Near the end of the month, a university professor and friend of my parents came to tell us about ethnobotany, the science of studying human uses of plants for food, medicine, and ritual. During a vivid slideshow, he told us of treading remote jungle paths in search of plants that might contain the chemicals to cure diabetes or cancer; of climbing giant trees to find new species of rare flowers; of the ancient knowledge and frightening magical powers of shamans and medicine men. Sitting in the darkened room with our tape of jungle sounds accompanying his narration, I was transfixed—it sounded like the height of adventure. But it was the conclusion that made the greatest impression on me: a final photo, not of vibrant greenery or the showy feathers of forest birds, but of a devastated landscape of smoke and jagged, charred stumps. The rainforest, the ethnobotanist told us, was being logged and burned to make way for cattle ranches and soybean plantations. Without the forests, we were losing the plants that might cure some of our most deadly diseases.

I was stunned. How could people be allowed to kill all those giant trees and the amazing creatures that lived beneath them? I resolved in that moment that I would devote my life to protecting the wild and beautiful wilderness my species was so carelessly destroying.

Until high school, my early concept of environmentalism was essentially this: people are destroying nature, nature is good, and so people must be the enemy. Sustainability, therefore, meant reducing our impact to essentially nothing, removing the human foot-print from the Earth. I demanded my parents buy Rainforest Crunch, a granola bar that donated a portion of profits to protecting rainforests. I chided classmates for not recycling paper and cans. I joined my high school environmental club and led projects to compost our cafeteria waste and run our buses on low-carbon biofuels. Yet the more I learned about both environmental and human problems, the more I began to realize that humans weren't going away and that focusing on the environment alone wouldn't lead to real solutions.

Kicking rural farmers out of newly created forest reserves without providing new incomes would create misery and poverty, and the logging of valuable mahogany trees would continue, except now in secrecy and with the aid of corruption and violence. As much as I wanted them to, my neighbors wouldn't buy less stuff if doing so would make their lives feel poorer. My parents wouldn't forego the long car trip if they couldn't go on vacation another way. My school wouldn't spend more on biodiesel if that meant cutting into the salaries of its employees. Something in my definition of sustainability had to shift.

As I entered college and threw myself into student organizing on climate change, the human element of sustainability became ever clearer. The breadth and importance of this new sustainability is epitomized in two stories I heard while working with other youth at the United Nations Climate Change negotiations in Copenhagen in December 2009.

Papa, a young environmentalist from Kenya, told me this story: "My friend Laiboni is a Maasai I met while holding a community theatre workshop on climate change. Last year he owned 450 head of cattle. But when the floods came, 200 of his cattle were washed away. We are sure they drowned. Immediately after, the rain disappeared. Then the sun came, and it was so hot that things dried up and there was no grass for the animals. Laiboni started moving towards the coast, but unfortunately there was no grass there. Beginning in March this year, Laiboni was selling his cattle at about $4 per head because they were in such poor health. Currently Laiboni doesn't run any animals at all."

Laiboni's story—one of poverty rapidly arising from environmental change—is being repeated across Africa and throughout the world. Human-caused climate change is already destroying livelihoods and lives and is leading to conflict over ever-diminishing resources. Sustainability in this context means reversing climate change and creating paths to economic development, paths that are resilient to social conflict and globalization, that promote equity, and that also minimize environmental decline. But sustainability isn't just a need of developing countries and farmers who depend on the rains—it's equally important much closer to home.

Danielle is a climate activist from Michigan: "My father is a union electrician and has been for the past thirty years. There have been fluctuations in the job market, but never as bad as this. He hasn't worked for two years. He spends his time trying to find other sorts of jobs to get by. There have been times when we've been close to losing our health care and house, and it's been hard for him because my brothers and I are away. My mom died a while ago, so it's only him. He wants a new job. He wants a green job, and he wants to keep working for his family. He's always been a supporter of American ingenuity and entrepreneurship. Passing domestic [climate change] legislation would stimulate the Michigan economy, give him a job again, and give me hope."

Responsible use and protection of the natural world is without question essential to sustainability. If we degrade our environment beyond its ability to provide us with clean air; clean water; productive oceans, soils, and forests; a livable temperature; and the inspiration we can gain from the millions of intricate and beautiful forms of life outside our own species, there is no question that anthropogenic climate change, toxic chemicals, and conflict over resources will destroy our way of life. But Danielle's story speaks to another side of sustainability, which anyone who has ever worked can relate to: the need for a secure, stable job that won't dissipate before the winds of Wall Street. Just as sustainability finds ways to use and respect the resources of nature over the long term, it also requires creating economic and social systems that allow us and our communities not only to live into the future, but to thrive.

That's the essence of my definition of sustainability: Not just living, but thriving. Not just an "environmental issue," but a human issue. And on both accounts, the power of the new sustainability has its potential to reshape the way we value our world.

The old American Dream envisions a big house with a white picket fence and an SUV in the yard. But there's a new American Dream, too, and it's one that values community, wellbeing, and happiness more than material goods. Thomas Jefferson didn't write "Life, Liberty, and the Pursuit of Stuff." He wrote "Life, Liberty, and the Pursuit of Happiness." Happiness—isn't that what we all strive for? Isn't that what we should be striving for?

Good jobs and a good income are necessary for freedom from worry and want. But the path to a good life is not based on money and consumption alone. The world we live in runs on high rates of consumption, from the social status that comes with big, oil-guzzling cars and all the latest gadgets to the fast returns sought by Wall Street speculators. The phrase is always more—more money, more possessions, more retreat into technology. With it comes more risk of losing your job when our consumption-driven economy crashes, more carbon pollution and environmental degradation, and more disconnection from nature and our communities.

Sustainability requires a fundamental shift in our values. From things to people; to relationships and the strength of community. A shift from quantity to quality of life. A re-valuation of our prosperity as individuals, communities, and nations in terms of wellbeing rather than gross domestic product.

This kind of sustainability doesn't mean moving to huts, wearing Birkenstocks, and living on handouts. In economic terms, it requires channeling the power of American ingenuity and entrepreneurship into creating new, more stable jobs in the rising clean economy, and replacing old ones that are tied directly to consumption and waste. This means insulating houses and workplaces to make them more efficient, building transmission lines and other infrastructure to support the development of decentralized renewable energy, growing more food and more happiness nearby, and shifting the emphasis from the international to the local. And it means using fewer, better, more local things when possible; using food, energy and materials more thoughtfully from distant industrial scales when necessary.

In social terms, the new sustainability is about the reinvigoration of communities—it's the reinstitution of lunch with the neighbors, unannounced. It's finding ways to grow our economy, our society, and our relationships from the ground up. By building trust and resilience through common activism and service, relocalizing ways to help those in need, innovating to return our energy and our jobs to our communities, and being thoughtful about our impact on the natural world, we have in our hands the opportunity to create a future that's more prosperous, happy, and just for all. We can build a world that thrives.

That's sustainability. That's a future worth fighting for. So let's get to work.

Danny Growald is a senior Ecology and Evolutionary Biology major at Princeton University and a 2010 Morris K. Udall Scholar. As the Vice-Chair and former Chair of the climate action group Princeton SURGE (Students United for a Responsible Global Environment), Danny led a strategic planning and restructuring process that allowed the group to expand and raise its targets, and has been deeply involved in building awareness, engagement, and activism on climate change. As a co-founder of Princeton's growing Social Entrepreneurship Initiative, he has focused on finding innovative ways to help others translate their passions into benefit for the world. Prior to his time at Princeton, Danny contributed to a Carnegie Trust UK discussion paper on the social impacts of climate change, and he designed an interactive art project at the Eden Project (in Cornwall, UK) that allowed over 10,000 participants to voice their perspectives about life on a warming globe. His current interests are in climate policy and developing strategic approaches to issues at the intersection of climate change, ecosystems, and human wellbeing. Danny is an avid backpacker, rock climber, cheddar cheese eater, and an artisan blacksmith.

HOW TO USE THIS GREEN CAREER GUIDE

Peterson's Green Careers in Energy contains a wealth of information for anyone interested in a career in green energy or an energy-related green industry. You will read about sixty-eight great green careers and the undergraduate, graduate, or training programs that can lead to these green careers. The following section details what you will find in each part of this book.

PART I: PROFESSIONAL AND SKILLED JOBS

Part I is divided into four chapters:
- Chapter 1: Energy Industry Jobs
- Chapter 2: Energy-Related Jobs in Transportation
- Chapter 3: Energy-Related Jobs in Construction & Building Operations
- Chapter 4: Energy-Related Jobs in Policy, Analysis, Advocacy, and Regulatory Affairs

The different jobs featured here represent a variety of interests, education, and training.

As you read through Part I, you will see that occupations may be designated as "Bright Outlook" and/or "Green New and Emerging" or "Green Enhanced-Skills" occupations. These are categories used by O*NET™, which stands for Occupational Information Network (O*NET), a joint effort of the U.S. Department of Labor/Employment and Training Administration (USDOL/ETA) and the North Carolina Employment Security Commission. "Bright Outlook" occupations are those that are expected to have a large number of new job openings, and "Green" jobs are those that require enhanced or new skill sets because technology, sustainability, and economic incentives are changing the nature of the occupation. The estimates of job growth and job opportunities between 2008 and 2018 are based on data and projections of the U.S. Bureau of Labor Statistics.

Details on industry overview, job trends, job duties, career paths, earning potential, education and licensure, and trade and professional organizations follow each job listed. Information on how the information was obtained for each of these sections—and what this data means to you as a job seeker—can be found at the beginning of Part I.

PART II: COLLEGES AND UNION ORGANIZATIONS WITH GREAT GREEN PROGRAMS

Chapters 5 and 6 describe innovative programs related to energy at both the undergraduate and graduate levels. Four-year colleges and universities are highlighted in Chapter 5. Chapter 6 features two-year schools. The programs were chosen to reflect a broad range of majors related to energy, all regions of the country, public and private schools, and large and small schools. The "Fast Facts" feature in each profile underscores on-campus sustainability programs, awards that schools have won, energy research facilities, and other notable highlights of the schools' efforts to be good citizens of the local and global communities.

Chapter 7 contains information on union-training programs, including apprenticeships for a variety of energy-related green jobs.

PART III: WORKFORCE TRAINING

Chapter 8 contains a list of the One-Stop Career Centers for training, job search, and career assistance information that are available in each of the fifty states and the District of Columbia. Under each state's name, you will find important contact information and a brief description of the job-related training services that each state offers.

PART IV: APPENDIXES

The appendixes in Part IV provide additional information that can help you in your search for a great green job. *Appendix A: Energy Jobs by Industry* is a handy tool to help you navigate the jobs listed in Chapters 1 through 4. In addition to the main job title, the alternate job titles and related careers for each job are included. *Appendix B: Green Job Boards* lists some job boards that specialize in green industry jobs. *Appendix C: "Green" Your Vocabulary for a Sustainable Future* provides a list with definitions of many of the terms that you will find on TV and Web sites and in magazines and newspapers that discuss the environment, sustainability, and renewable and alternative sources of energy. *Appendix D: Green Features in this Guide* provides an index of the interviews, feature articles, and "About" boxes that appear in this book, listed alphabetically and with page numbers.

SPECIAL FEATURES THROUGHOUT THIS GUIDE

All of the chapters in this guide also provide full-length features that offer tips on what you can do now to make a difference for the environment, where the greenest places are to live, how to find out if a potential employer is socially responsible, and how to dress fashionably in eco-friendly clothing, including clothes made from bamboo fiber (actually softer than rayon!). There are also features related specifically to energy, such as a description of the smart electric grid, how nanoscience may make a difference in reducing energy use, and some energy sectors to keep an eye on for jobs in the future.

Chapters 1 through 4 also have informational interviews. Each chapter has two interviews with practitioners of careers described in the chapter. For example, the interview in Chapter 2 is with a mechanical systems engineer. The subject of one of the interviews in Chapter 4 is a paralegal who works for a nonprofit environmental organization.

In addition, in shaded boxes throughout this guide, you will find useful information called "About . . ." that will help you find out what others are doing to live more eco-friendly lives and how to make your own life greener. Tips include where to recycle your old computer, cell phone, tennis balls, and even your sneakers; why you should be careful about how you fertilize your garden and lawn; and what community colleges, colleges, and universities are doing to commit to campus sustainability.

> **About the Talloires Declaration**
>
> In 1990, 35 university presidents met to discuss the university's role in environmental education and stewardship. The result was the Talloires Declaration, a commitment by higher educational institutions from around the world to promote awareness of environmental issues and to establish policies and programs to counter environmental problems.

Seven Steps to Landing Your Dream Job
By Rachel Gutter, Director of the Education Sector
U.S. Green Building Council

1. **Be willing to start at the bottom of the totem pole and work your way up.** Figure out where there are gaps in your knowledge base and/or resume and find a position that will allow you to fill them. If you can afford to take an unpaid internship at a place that will give you good access or relevant experience, do it—even if you have to live with your parents.

2. **Zero in on a few organizations or companies that most interest you and haunt their job pages.** Even in this economy, Washington, D.C., is always hiring ... eventually.

3. **Find a mentor who has your dream job and wow him or her.** If your mentor is your supervisor or someone else you work with, make yourself indispensable to him/her. If you don't work with him/her, try to do extra research or a side project to show how interested you are in the work he or she does. Shadow him/her for a week.

4. **Be persistent.** Always follow up. Always check back in. Always remind them you are still interested.

5. **Do your homework.** It's not so much about the job itself, it is about the culture of the organization. If you don't like the latter, you probably won't like the former.

6. **In the first few years of your career (not necessarily your first years of work experience, but your first years of work on a career track) you should work harder than you ever have and possibly harder than you ever will.**

7. **There's a lot more to life than work and it's always important to keep that in mind, even in Washington.** There is something to be said for having an employer that values personal sustainability.

PART I

PROFESSIONAL AND SKILLED JOBS

ABOUT PART I

The industries and sectors that are represented in Part I have a strong focus on clean energy. These are traditional ones that are being transformed by the new emphasis on clean technology and sustainability. Many of the jobs are also traditional jobs that have been "greened" to promote the factors that produce sustainability: efficient use of energy, renewable energy sources, and preservation and protection of the environment. Jobs also become "green" when they are performed for companies whose ultimate products promote sustainability.

HOW JOBS WERE SELECTED FOR INCLUSION

The jobs in Part I have been selected to represent a variety of interests and educational levels. Jobs in engineering, science, and technology are the most prevalent in industries that deal with energy. However, jobs have been included in public policy, advocacy, and regulatory affairs to show that you don't need a science, engineering, or technology background to be part of the greening of the U.S. economy. People with many different interests and backgrounds can find meaningful employment in work that is energy-related and environmentally friendly.

As you read through Part I, you will see that occupations may be designated as "Bright Outlook" and/or "Green New and Emerging" or "Green Enhanced-Skills" occupations. These are categories formulated by O*NET™, which stands for Occupational Information Network (O*NET), a joint effort of the U.S. Department of Labor/ Employment and Training Administration (USDOL/ETA) and the North Carolina Employment Security Commission. "Bright Outlook" occupations are those that are expected to have a large number of new job openings, and "Green Enhanced-Skills" jobs are those that require enhanced or new skill sets because technology, sustainability, and economic incentives are changing the nature of the occupation. The estimates of job growth and job opportunities between 2008 and 2018 are based on data and projections of the U.S. Bureau of Labor Statistics.

ABOUT THE LISTINGS

Here's what you need to know to navigate these chapters.

Energy Industry Overview

The Energy Industry Overview section describes overall trends in the industry. It also explains how developments in energy and the environment are changing the industry and providing new general job opportunities. The information is taken from a variety of sources, including the U.S. Department of Energy and trade associations.

Alternate Titles and Related Careers

Each occupation includes a list of alternate job titles and related careers that fall under that category. For example, a person looking for a job as an automotive engineer might find suitable jobs with titles such as hybrid powertrain development engineer or automotive power electronics engineer. These alternate titles were selected by reviewing O*NET's listing of reported alternate titles and also job boards.

Video Links

We've provided easy-to-use links that will take you directly to one of the many career videos from the One-Stop Career System Multimedia Career Video Library at CareerOneStop.org. The links will look like this:

 http://bit.ly/career1

Note that videos are not available for all jobs listed here. The videos come in QuickTime and Mpeg formats, with and without captions; download times may vary. CareerOneStop.org is sponsored by the U.S. Department of Labor/Employment and Training Administration.

Job Trends

The information on overall job trends is taken from the U.S. Bureau of Labor Statistics projections as reported on O*NET OnLine.

Nature of the Work

This section describes the kind of work that people in each occupation do. Most of the information is from O*NET OnLine, although some comes from the *Occupation Outlook Handbook* and from job boards. The section contains a listing of the duties performed by this occupation.

Career Path

To indicate progression through a career, entry-level jobs are usually noted as the basis for advancing to a particular occupation.

Earning Potential

Earning potential is given as median hourly wage and median annual wage and are from 2009 as noted. The information comes mainly from the Bureau of Labor Statistics as reported on O*NET. In a very few cases, wage data were not available and were taken from other sources.

Education/Licensure

Information about educational levels, certifications, and licenses, including the names of organizations that grant them, is provided here. These organizations often offer courses or materials to help prepare for the exams and professional development opportunities needed to maintain certification.

CHAPTER 1

ENERGY INDUSTRY JOBS

For More Information

Many of the organizations listed offer accreditation, professional development opportunities, and continuing education. Some offer certifications that are respected by employers and an advantage to job seekers. Most also contain information on their Web sites about careers in the field and many have job banks. Some have links to academic institutions with programs in the discipline.

ENERGY INDUSTRY OVERVIEW

The energy industry is expected to be a continual source of new jobs for many years. Energy demands continue to grow, but environmental sustainability is forcing the industry to look to renewable and alternative energy sources, such as biofuels, wind, solar, and geothermal power. Nuclear power is also being reconsidered as a way to reduce the nation's dependence on foreign oil and cut greenhouse gas emissions.

The U.S. Department of Energy's Alternative Fuels and Advanced Vehicles Data Center (www.afdc.energy/gov/afdc/fuels/index) states that there are more than a dozen alternative and advanced fuels in production or use today. Most are used in government-regulated or voluntary private fleets; for example, on college campuses. However, consumers are becoming more interested in energy efficiency and emissions reduction and as a result, automotive manufacturers are responding with vehicles that are powered by electric batteries, hybrid engines, biodiesel, and hydrogen-based fuel cells.

In addition to new sources of power to fuel vehicles, scientists and engineers are working on new ways to generate power for homes, schools, stores, office buildings, and factories. These new technologies include wind, solar, and geothermal power, as well as power generated from biomass processing and methane gas collection from landfills.

Development of these relatively new energy sources and refinement of older technologies such as clean coal and low-sulfur diesel are expected to create many new jobs. Research and development for clean technology will increase the number of professional and technical jobs, especially in engineering specialties.

JOBS PROFILED HERE

The following sectors and occupations are profiled in this chapter:

Biofuels
- Biofuels Processing Technician
- Biofuels Production Manager
- Biofuels Technology and Product Development Manager
- Biomass Plant Technician
- Biomass Production Manager
- Methane Capturing System Engineer

- Methane/Landfill Gas Collection System Operator
- Methane/Landfill Gas Generation System Technician

Electric Power
- Electric Power-Line Installer and Repairer
- Electric Power Plant Operator
- Energy Broker
- Power Plant Distributor and Dispatcher
- Smart Grid Engineer

Geothermal Power
- Geothermal Production Manager
- Geothermal Technician

Hydroelectric Power
- Hydroelectric Plant Technician
- Hydroelectric Production Manager
- Hydrologist

Nuclear Power
- Nuclear Engineer
- Nuclear Equipment Operations Technician
- Nuclear Power Reactor Operator

Solar Power
- Solar Energy Installation Manager
- Solar Energy Systems Engineer
- Solar Fabrication Technician
- Solar Photovoltaic Installer
- Solar Sales Representative and Assessor
- Solar Thermal Installer and Technician

Wind Power
- Wind Energy Engineer
- Wind Energy Operations Manager
- Wind Energy Project Manager
- Wind Turbine Machinist
- Wind Turbine Service Technician

KEY TO UNDERSTANDING THE JOB PROFILES

The job profiles are classified according to one or more of the following categories:

☼ Bright Outlook
🌐 Green Occupation

The classifications "Bright Outlook" and "Green Occupation" are taken from the National Center for O*NET Development's O*NET OnLine job site. O*NET, which is sponsored by the U.S. Department of Labor/Employment and Training Administration (USDOL/ETA), has broken green jobs into three categories:

- Green Increased-Demand occupations
  o These are occupations that are likely to see job growth, but the work and worker requirements are unlikely to experience significant changes.
- Green Enhanced-Skills occupations
  o These occupations are likely to experience significant changes in work and worker requirements. Workers may find themselves doing new tasks requiring new knowledge, skills, and credentials. Current projections do not anticipate increased demand for workers in these occupations, but O*NET notes that an increase is possible.
- Green New and Emerging occupations
  o These are new occupations—not growth in existing jobs—that are created as a result of activity and technology in green sectors of the economy.

BIOFUELS INDUSTRY

According to the Research and Markets report "Biofuels Production–Industry Profile," the biofuels industry in the United States grows at the rate of 25 to 50 percent a year. A study published by the National Biodiesel Board in 2006 estimated that the biodiesel sector alone could add 39,000 jobs worth $24 billion to the economy by 2015. The Renewable Fuels Association estimated in 2009 that ethanol fuel manufacture could add 1 million jobs to the economy and $1.6 trillion to the nation's GDP by 2022. These estimates include jobs added directly to the energy generation sector, as well as peripheral jobs such as parts fabricator for the energy sector and jobs like restaurant chef and store clerk in the general economy.

The major biofuels products currently produced are biodiesel and ethanol. However, new technologies are beginning to make other types of biofuels, such as biomass processing and methane/landfill gas collection and generation, more cost-efficient and -effective to develop. The commercialization of each new power source requires workers with specialized knowledge and skills.

Biofuels Processing Technician ☼🌐

This is both a "Bright Outlook" and "Green New and Emerging" occupation in the renewable energy generation sector of the economy. This job is the result of the development of the biofuels industry and the creation of unique work tasks that require new and unique worker requirements.

Job Trends

Because mass production of biofuels is so new, there are no reliable data on job growth for biofuels processing technicians. However, based on current evidence, the expectation is that the biofuels industry will grow and, thus, the need for this occupation will increase.

Nature of the Work

Biofuels processing technicians work in production plants that process feedstock into biofuels. Feedstock is the raw material that ferments or reacts to additives to produce biofuels. A biofuels technician might work for a company producing ethanol from sugarcane or diesel fuel from recycled grease.

According to O*Net, biofuels processing technicians

- Calculate, measure, load, or mix refined feedstock with additives in the fermentation or reaction process
- Operate the chemical processing equipment to control and adjust production
- Monitor the production process
- Operate equipment to extract biofuels products and secondary products or reusable fractions
- Calibrate the liquid flow devices and meters used in the processing, including fuel, chemical, and water meters
- Collect biofuels samples and perform routine lab tests or analyses to assess the biofuels quality
- Assess the quality of the biofuels additives for reprocessing
- Inspect biofuels plant or processing equipment regularly
- Measure and monitor raw biofuels feedstock

Career Path

According to the *Occupational Outlook Handbook,* the job is similar to that of a science or chemical processing control technician who works in manufacturing and focuses on quality assurance, monitoring product quality or production processes. Typically, entry-level positions require a high school diploma or GED and some formal postsecondary training, such as an associate degree. New employees work under an experienced technician and with experience may become supervisors themselves. To qualify for higher-level positions in the biofuels industry, at least a bachelor's degree is required.

Earning Potential

Median hourly wage (2009): $23.92

Median annual wage (2009): $49,760

This data is based on Bureau of Labor Statistics data for "Plant and System Operators, All Other."

Education/Licensure

Typically, entry-level jobs require a high school diploma or GED and some formal postsecondary training, such as an associate degree in process technology or some related science field. Technical and community colleges offer associate degree programs, and technical institutes offer certificate programs and associate degrees. However, the latter institutions offer less general education and less theory than community or technical colleges. Some jobs may provide one or two years of training for entry-level employees. The training may include on-the-job training and classroom instruction.

For More Information

Advanced Biofuels Association
1350 I Street, NW
Suite 510
Washington, DC 20005
202-747-0518
www.advancedbiofuelsassociation.com

American Coalition for Ethanol
5000 S. Broadband Lane
Suite 224
Sioux Falls, South Dakota 57108
605-334-3381
www.ethanol.org

Biotechnology Industry Organization
1201 Maryland Avenue, SW
Suite 900
Washington, DC 20024
www.bio.org

National Algae Association
4747 Research Forest Drive
Suite 180
The Woodlands, Texas 77381
936-321-1125
www.nationalalgaeassociation.com

National Biodiesel Board
605 Clark Avenue
P.O. Box 10-4898
Jefferson City, Missouri 65110-4898
800-841-5849
www.biodiesel.org

Renewable Fuels Association
One Massachusetts Avenue, NW
Suite 820
Washington, DC 20001
202-289-3835
www.ethanolrfa.org

Biofuels Production Manager ✿⑤

Alternate Titles and Related Careers
- Biodiesel Plant Manager
- Biodiesel Plant Operations Engineer
- Biodiesel Plant Superintendent
- Biodiesel Production Manager
- Biofuels Plant Manager
- Biofuels Plant Operations Engineer
- Biofuels Plant Superintendent
- Ethanol Production Manager
- Industrial Production Manager
- Quality Control Systems Manager

This is both a "Bright Outlook" and "Green New and Emerging occupation" in the renewable energy generation sector of the economy.

Job Trends

Because this occupation is so new, data collection is ongoing. However, as the biofuels industry expands, the need for managers to oversee the operations of plant manufacturing biofuels will grow as well.

Nature of the Work

Biofuels production managers manage the operations at biofuels power generation plants, planning, directing, and coordinating production activities of biofuels like ethanol and diesel fuels. Among their tasks are collecting and processing information on the plant's performance, diagnosing problems, and taking corrective actions. A manager may oversee an entire facility or parts of one, depending on the size of the facility.

According to O*NET, among the tasks that a biofuels production manager performs are the following:

- Adjust temperature, pressure, vacuum, level, flow rate, or transfer of biofuel to maintain processes at required levels
- Monitor meters, flow gauges, or other real-time data to ensure proper operation of production equipment, implementing corrective measures as needed
- Conduct cost, material, and efficiency studies for production plants or operations
- Prepare and manage budgets for a plant or unit
- Review logs, datasheets, and reports to ensure adequate production levels or to identify abnormalities with production equipment or processes
- Supervise production employees
- Confer with technical and supervisory personnel to report or resolve conditions affecting plant safety, operational efficiency, and product quality
- Draw samples of biofuels products or secondary by-products for quality control testing
- Monitor transportation and storage of flammable or other potentially dangerous feedstocks or products to ensure adherence to safety guidelines
- Ensure compliance with biofuels plant safety, environmental, and operational standards and regulations
- Provide training for new employees to improve biofuels plant safety or increase production
- Approve proposals for the acquisition, replacement, or repair of biofuels processing equipment or the implementation of new production processes

Career Path

Employers typically prefer candidates with college degrees for entry-level positions on the manager track. Those who enter directly from college or graduate school typically enter a company-sponsored training program. In larger companies, new employees may work in a variety of departments to become familiar with various operations. Some companies hire college graduates as first-line supervisors and promote them to management positions over time. Experience in some aspect of production operations is typically needed before advancement to upper-level management such as plant manager, superintendent, or vice president of operations.

Some industrial production managers do begin as production workers, advancing to supervisory positions after a number of years of experience, while earning a college degree and being selected for management.

Earning Potential

Median hourly wage (2009): $40.90

Median annual wage (2009): $85,080

(Based on industrial production managers' salaries)

Education/Licensure

Typically, for the biofuels production manager position, employers prefer to hire employees with a college degree in biotechnology, or chemical, electrical, mechanical, industrial technology, or industrial engineering from a school accredited by the Accreditation Board for Engineering and Technology (ABET).

As noted in the *Occupation Outlook Handbook,* some colleges and universities offer five-year programs that culminate in a master's degree in engineering. Some offer five- or six-year programs that include cooperative experience. Some four-year schools have arrangements with community colleges or liberal arts colleges that allow students to spend two or three years at the initial school and transfer for the last two years to complete their engineering degree.

All fifty states and the District of Columbia require engineers to be licensed as professional engineers (PE) if they serve the public directly. In most states, licensure requires graduation from a four-year engineering program accredited by ABET, four years of experience, and passing the state exam. Many engineers take the Fundamentals of Engineering portion of the exam upon graduation. They are then engineers in training (EIT). After obtaining appropriate work experience, they take the Principles and Practice of Engineering exam to complete their professional license. Most states recognize licenses from other states, as long as the requirements are the same or more stringent. Some states have continuing education requirements.

Some production managers earn certification to demonstrate their competency. The Association for Operations Management (APICS) offers the Certified in Production and Inventory Management (CPIM) certification that requires passing a series of exams that cover supply-chain management, resource planning, scheduling, production operations, and strategic planning. Successful candidates must renew their certifications every three years.

The American Society for Quality (ASQ) offers the Certified Manager of Quality/Organizational Excellence (CMQ/OE) credential. Candidates must have at least ten years of experience and pass an exam. To maintain the certification, candidates must take a certain number of professional development courses every three years.

For More Information

Accreditation Board for Engineering and
   Technology (ABET)
111 Market Place
Suite 1050
Baltimore, Maryland 21202
410-347-7700
www.abet.org

Advanced Biofuels Association
1350 I Street, NW
Suite 510
Washington, DC 20005
202-747-0518
www.advancedbiofuelsassociation.com

American Coalition for Ethanol
5000 S. Broadband Lane
Suite 224
Sioux Falls, South Dakota 57108
605-334-3381
www.ethanol.org

American Society for Quality (ASQ)
600 North Plankinton Avenue
Milwaukee, Wisconsin 53203
www.asq.org

Association for Operations Management (APICS)
8430 West Bryn Mawr Avenue
Suite 1000
Chicago, Illinois 60631
www.apics.org

Biotechnology Industry Organization
1201 Maryland Avenue, SW
Suite 900
Washington, DC 20024
www.bio.org

National Algae Association
4747 Research Forest Drive
Suite 180
The Woodlands, Texas 77381
936-321-1125
www.nationalalgaeassociation.com

National Biodiesel Board
605 Clark Avenue
P.O. Box 10-4898
Jefferson City, Missouri 65110-4898
800-841-5849
www.biodiesel.org

Renewable Fuels Association
One Massachusetts Avenue, NW
Suite 820
Washington, DC 20001
202-289-3835
www.ethanolrfa.org

About the Green Post Office

The U.S. Post Office operates more than 43,000 vehicles that are powered by alternative fuels: hybrid electric, electric, compressed natural gas, liquid propane gas, ethanol, biodiesel, and hydrogen fuel cells.

Biofuels Technology and Product Development Manager ☼⑤

Alternate Titles and Related Careers:

- Biodiesel Technology and Product Development Manager
- Engineering Manager

This is a "Bright Outlook" and "Green New and Emerging" occupation in the renewable energy generation sector of the economy.

Job Trends

The Bureau of Labor Statistics equates this job with the category of "Engineering Managers" and projects a growth rate of 3 to 6 percent overall.

In 2008, the category included 228,700 workers. However, the rate of job growth for biofuels technology and product development managers should parallel the growth of the biofuels industry itself. As a result, the number of biofuels technology and product development manager jobs should outpace the general category of engineering managers.

Nature of the Work

A biofuels technology and product development manager defines, plans, or executes research programs in biofuels. The goal of these programs is to evaluate alternative feedstock and process technologies to assess their commercial potential. Among the characteristics that a product development manager looks for in a potential biofuel are improved biomass yield, environmental adaptability, pest resistance, production efficiency, bioprocessing characteristics, or reduced environmental impacts.

According to O*NET, a biofuels technology and product development manager may perform any or all of the following tasks:

- Prepare, or oversee the preparation of, experimental plans for biofuels research or development
- Conduct research to breed or develop energy crops
- Oversee biofuels prototyping or development projects
- Propose new biofuels products, processes, technologies, or applications based on the findings from research projects
- Conduct experiments on biomass or pretreatment technologies
- Conduct experiments to test new or alternate feedstock fermentation processes
- Design chemical conversion processes, such as distillation, hydrogenation, and vegetable oil refining
- Design or conduct applied biofuels research projects on topics like transport,

thermodynamics, mixing, filtration, fermentation, extraction, and separation

- Design or execute solvent or product recovery experiments in laboratory or field settings
- Develop methods to estimate the efficiency of biomass pretreatments
- Develop methods to recover ethanol or other fuels from complex bioreactor liquid or gas streams
- Develop separation processes to recover biofuels
- Perform protein functional analysis and engineering for processing of feedstock and creation of biofuels
- Develop carbohydrates arrays and associated methods for screening enzymes involved in biomass conversion
- Prepare biofuels research and development reports for senior management or technical professionals
- Provide technical or scientific guidance to technical staff
- Develop computational tools or approaches to improve biofuels research and development activities
- Develop lab scale models of industrial scale processes such as fermentation

Career Path

Positions as biofuels technology and product development managers typically require at least a bachelor's degree in engineering, math, or science. Those with advanced technical knowledge and strong communication skills will be in the best position to become managers. Communication skills are important because managers need to be able to translate complex scientific work into language that nontechnical employees and company executives can understand. With experience, product managers may advance to progressively higher levels of management. Some product managers may choose to go into technical sales.

Earning Potential

Median hourly wage (2009): $56.25

Median annual wage (2009): $117,000

Education/Licensure

Biofuels technology and product development managers typically need at least a bachelor's degree, and some may enter the workforce with a master's or PhD. Some product development managers may choose to earn a master's in business administration (MBA) as a way to further their career. A product manager with an undergraduate degree in engineering may choose instead to earn a master's degree in engineering management (MEM). Some employers may pay for some or all of the cost of advanced degrees. Some may even offer degree programs onsite.

An engineering degree should be from an institution accredited by the Accreditation Board for Engineering and Technology (ABET). Some colleges and universities offer five-year programs that culminate in a master's degree in engineering. Some offer five- or six-year programs that include cooperative experience. Some four-year schools have arrangements with community colleges or liberal arts colleges that allow students to spend two or three years at the initial school and transfer for the last two years to complete their engineering degree.

All fifty states and the District of Columbia require engineers to be licensed as professional engineers (PE) if they serve the public directly. In most states, licensure requires graduation from a four-year engineering program accredited by ABET, four years of experience, and passing the state exam. Many engineers take the Fundamentals of Engineering portion of the exam upon graduation. They are then engineers in training (EIT). After obtaining appropriate work experience, they take the Principles and Practice of Engineering exam to complete their professional license. Most states recognize licenses from other states, as long as the requirements are the same or more stringent. Some states have continuing education requirements.

For More Information

Accreditation Board for Engineering and
    Technology (ABET)
111 Market Place
Suite 1050
Baltimore, Maryland 21202
410-347-7700
www.abet.org

Advanced Biofuels Association
1350 I Street, NW
Suite 510
Washington, DC 20005
202-747-0518
www.advancedbiofuelsassociation.com

American Coalition for Ethanol
5000 S. Broadband Lane
Suite 224
Sioux Falls, South Dakota 57108
605-334-3381
www.ethanol.org

Biotechnology Industry Organization
1201 Maryland Avenue, SW
Suite 900
Washington, DC 20024
www.bio.org

National Algae Association
4747 Research Forest Drive
Suite 180
The Woodlands, Texas 77381
936-321-1125
www.nationalalgaeassociation.com

National Biodiesel Board
605 Clark Avenue
P.O. Box 10-4898
Jefferson City, Missouri 65110-4898
800-841-5849
www.biodiesel.org

Renewable Fuels Association
One Massachusetts Avenue, NW
Suite 820
Washington, DC 20001
202-289-3835
www.ethanolrfa.org

About Biomass

California alone estimates that it could generate enough electricity for about two million homes from the 60 million tons of biomass that its residents produce each year.

Biomass Plant Technician ☼ ⏻

Alternate Title and Related Career
  • Assistant Plant Technician, Biomass

This is a "Bright Outlook" and "Green New and Emerging" occupation in the renewable energy generation field. It requires new types of skills in the workforce.

Job Trends

The Bureau of Labor Statistics includes this occupation in the "Plant and Systems Operators, All Others" category. Like the biofuels processing technician occupation, data collection for job growth is still underway on this job. However, based on current evidence, the expectation is that the biomass power generation sector of the biofuels industry will grow, and, thus, the need for this occupation will increase.

Nature of the Work

A biomass plant technician controls and monitors production processes within the power-generation plant. The technician also performs routine maintenance and makes minor repairs to the mechanical, electronic, and electrical equipment. In order to perform the job, the biomass plant technician must be able to read and interpret instruction manuals and technical drawings related to the equipment and processes employed in the plant. The biomass being processed may be wood; waste such as manure, grasses; or refuse materials such as inedible plant stalks.

According to O*NET, among the tasks that the biomass plant technician may perform are the following:

- Measure and monitor raw biomass feedstock
- Assess the quality of the feedstock
- Calculate, measure, load, or mix the biomass feedstock
- Operate valves, pumps, engines, or generators to control and adjust production
- Calibrate liquid flow devices or meters
- Inspect biomass power plant or processing equipment, recording or reporting damage and mechanical problems
- Operate biomass fuel-burning boiler or biomass fuel gasification system equipment in accordance with specifications or instructions
- Operate equipment to heat biomass and to start, stop, or regulate biomass-fueled generators, generator units, boilers, engines, or auxiliary systems
- Operate high-pressure steam boiler or water chiller equipment for electrical cogeneration operations
- Preprocess feedstock to prepare for biochemical or thermochemical production processes
- Record or report operational data such as readings on meters, instrument, and gauges
- Ensure that work areas are in compliance with safety regulations
- Manage parts and supply inventories

Career Path

The job is similar to that of a science or chemical processing control technician who works in manufacturing and focuses on quality assurance by monitoring product quality or production processes. Typically, entry-level positions require a high school diploma or GED and some formal postsecondary training such as an associate degree. New employees work under an experienced technician and with experience may become supervisors themselves. To qualify for higher-level positions in the biomass industry, at least a bachelor's degree is required.

Earning Potential

Median hourly wage (2009): $23.92

Median annual wage (2009): $49,760

Education/Licensure

Typically, entry-level jobs require a high school diploma or GED, and some formal postsecondary training such as an associate degree in process technology or some related science field. Technical and community colleges offer associate degree programs in specific technologies. Technical institutes offer certificate programs and associate degrees, but these institutions offer less general education and less theory than community or technical colleges.

For More Information

Advanced Biofuels Association
1350 I Street, NW
Suite 510
Washington, DC 20005
202-747-0518
www.advancedbiofuelsassociation.com

Biomass Power Association
100 Middle Street
P.O. Box 9729
Portland, Maine 04104-9729
202-429-4929
www.biomass.org

Renewable Fuels Association
One Massachusetts Avenue, NW
Suite 820
Washington, DC 20001
202-289-3835
www.ethanolrfa.org

About Global Warming and Biomass

As they grow, plants use and store carbon dioxide (CO_2), which is released when the plant material is burned or decays. By replanting the same crops, the new plants use the CO_2 produced when the previous crop cycle was burned or decayed. Using and replanting biomass helps close the CO_2 cycle.

Biomass Production Manager ✿🌐

Alternate Titles and Related Careers
- Biomass Operations Manager
- Biomass Plant Engineer
- Biomass Plant Manager
- Biomass Plant Operations Engineer
- Biomass Plant Superintendent
- Industrial Production Manager
- Quality Control Systems Manager

This is a "Bright Outlook" and "Green New and Emerging" occupation in the renewable energy generation sector of the green economy.

Job Trends

Because this occupation is so new, data collection is ongoing. However, as the generation of electricity from biomass production grows, the need for managers to oversee the operations of biomass production facilities can be expected to grow as well.

Nature of the Work

Biomass production managers manage the operations at biomass power-generation plants, planning, directing, and coordinating power-generation activities. They oversee biomass plant or substation operations and all maintenance, repair, and testing activities. They also supervise operations and maintenance staffs. The biomass being processed may be wood, waste, grasses, or refuse materials like inedible plant stalks.

According to O*NET, the tasks that the biomass production manager may perform include the following:
- Conduct field inspections of biomass plants, stations, or substations to ensure normal and safe operating conditions
- Monitor the operating status of biomass plants by observing control system parameters, distributed control systems, switchboard gauges, dials, and other indicators
- Evaluate power production or demand trends to identify opportunities for improved operations
- Inspect biomass gasification processes, equipment, and facilities for ways to maximize capacity and minimize operating costs
- Plan and schedule biomass deliveries, ash removal, and regular maintenance
- Prepare and manage plant budgets
- Prepare reports on operations, status, maintenance, etc.
- Review biomass operations performance specifications to ensure compliance with regulatory requirements
- Review logs, datasheets, and reports to ensure adequate production levels and safe production environments or to identify

abnormalities with power production equipment or processes

- Adjust equipment controls to generate specified amounts of electrical power
- Compile and record operational data
- Manage parts and supply inventories

Career Path

This occupation is similar to industrial production managers, and employers typically prefer candidates with college degrees for entry-level position on the manager track. Those who enter directly from college or graduate school typically enter a company-sponsored training program. In larger companies, new employees may work in a variety of departments to become familiar with various operations. Some companies hire college graduates as first-line supervisors and promote them to management positions over time. Experience in some aspect of production operations is typically needed before advancement to upper-level management such as plant manager, superintendent, or vice president of operations.

Some industrial production managers do begin as production workers, advancing to supervisory positions while earning a college degree and being selected for management.

Earning Potential

Median hourly wage (2009): $40.90

Median annual wage (2009): $85,080

Education/Licensure

Typically, for the production manager position, employers prefer to hire employees with a college degree in biotechnology or chemical, mechanical, electrical, industrial technology, or industrial engineering from an institution accredited by the Accreditation Board for Engineering and Technology (ABET).

Some colleges and universities offer five-year programs that culminate in a master's degree in engineering. Some offer five- or six-year programs that include cooperative experience. Some four-year schools have arrangements with community colleges or liberal arts colleges that allow students to spend two or three years at the initial school and transfer for the last two years to complete their engineering degree.

All fifty states and the District of Columbia require engineers to be licensed as professional engineers (PE) if they serve the public directly. In most states, licensure requires graduation from a four-year engineering program accredited by ABET, four years of experience, and passing the state exam. Many engineers take the Fundamentals of Engineering portion of the exam upon graduation. They are then engineers in training (EIT). After obtaining appropriate work experience, they take the Principles and Practice of Engineering exam to complete their professional license. Most states recognize licenses from other states, as long as the requirements are the same or more stringent. Some states have continuing education requirements.

Some production managers earn certification to demonstrate their competency. The Association for Operations Management (APICS) offers the Certified in Production and Inventory Management (CPIM) certification that requires passing a series of exams that cover supply-chain management, resource planning, scheduling, production operations, and strategic planning. Successful candidates must renew their certifications every three years.

The American Society for Quality (ASQ) offers the Certified Manager of Quality/Organizational Excellence (CMQ/OE) credential. Candidates must have at least ten years of experience and pass an exam. To maintain the certification, candidates must take a certain number of professional development courses every three years.

For More Information

Accreditation Board for Engineering and
    Technology (ABET)
111 Market Place
Suite 1050
Baltimore, Maryland 21202
410-347-7700
www.abet.org

Advanced Biofuels Association
1350 I Street, NW
Suite 510
Washington, DC 20005
202-747-0518
www.advancedbiofuelsassociation.com

American Society for Quality (ASQ)
600 North Plankinton Avenue
Milwaukee, Wisconsin 53203
www.asq.org

Association for Operations Management (APICS)
8430 West Bryn Mawr Avenue
Suite 1000
Chicago, Illinois 60631
www.apics.org

Biomass Power Association
100 Middle Street
P.O. Box 9729
Portland, Maine 04104-9729
202-429-4929
www.biomass.org

Biotechnology Industry Organization
1201 Maryland Avenue, SW
Suite 900
Washington, DC 20024
www.bio.org

Renewable Fuels Association
One Massachusetts Avenue, NW
Suite 820
Washington, DC 20001
202-289-3835
www.ethanolrfa.org

About Waste-Based Energy

As landfill waste decomposes, it produces methane and other gases. According to the Environmental Industry Associations (EIA), more than 75 percent of the methane could be used for "green energy," either to generate electricity or piped directly to factories, schools, government buildings, and other facilities for heating and cooling.

Methane Capturing System Engineer ⊛

Alternate Titles and Related Careers

- Landfill Gas Engineer
- Senior Landfill Specialist
- Project Engineer

This is a "Green New and Emerging" occupation in the methane, or landfill gas (LFG), collection and generation sector of the green renewable energy economy.

Job Trends

Data is being collected on this occupation, but as the methane gas collection and power generation industry expands, the need for people to research, design, and take landfill facilities through the government permit process will be needed.

Nature of the Work

A methane capturing systems engineer designs and oversees the construction of landfill gas systems. This individual is responsible for the planning, design, permitting, and building of LFG control and recovery systems of existing and new landfill facilities.

Among the tasks that the methane capturing engineer may perform are the following:

- Design LFG collection networks and erosion and sediment control structures
- Conduct line of site analysis, engineering analysis, and calculations during landfill permitting

- Conduct landfill expansion feasibility studies and prepare reports
- Prepare construction drawings and specs
- Provide construction management
- Conduct statistical analysis of groundwater monitoring data
- Ensure compliance with federal and state laws, regulations, and policies
- Monitor government laws, regulations, and policies for updates

Career Path

An undergraduate degree in environmental, chemical, geological, or civil engineering is generally required for this position, plus typically a minimum of two to five years' experience. More senior-level responsibilities require more experience. Areas of experience may include landfill, landfill gas, or subslab methane mitigation systems design. In time, a methane capturing system engineer may move into executive positions or start a consulting business.

Earning Potential

Median hourly wage (2009): $36.82

Median annual wage (2009): $76,590

(Based on earnings for civil engineers)

Education/Licensure

An undergraduate degree in environmental, chemical, geological, or civil engineering from an engineering school accredited by the Accreditation Board for Engineering and Technology (ABET) is preferred.

Some colleges and universities offer five-year programs that culminate in a master's degree in engineering. Some offer five- or six-year programs that include cooperative experience. Some four-year schools have arrangements with community colleges or liberal arts colleges that allow students to spend two or three years at the initial school

and transfer for the last two years to complete their engineering degree.

All fifty states and the District of Columbia require engineers to be licensed as professional engineers (PE) if they serve the public directly. In most states, licensure requires graduation from a four-year engineering program accredited by ABET, four years of experience, and passing the state exam. Many engineers take the Fundamentals of Engineering portion of the exam upon graduation. They are then engineers in training (EIT). After obtaining appropriate work experience, they take the Principles and Practice of Engineering exam to complete their professional license. Most states recognize licenses from other states as long as the requirements are the same or more stringent. Some states have continuing education requirements.

For More Information

Accreditation Board for Engineering and
    Technology (ABET)
111 Market Place
Suite 1050
Baltimore, Maryland 21202
410-347-7700
www.abet.org

Environmental Industry Associations (EIA)
4301 Connecticut Avenue, NW
Suite 300
Washington, DC 20008
202-244-4700
www.environmentalistseveryday.org

Solid Waste Association of North America
    (SWANA)
1100 Wayne Avenue
Silver Spring, Maryland 20910
301-585-2898
www.swana.org

About LFG as a Reality

By the end of 2009, the U.S. Environmental Protection Agency estimated that there were 509 Landfill Gas (LFG) collection and generation projects operating in forty-six states. These produce 1,563 megawatts of electricity annually and 304 million standard cubic feet of LFG for heating and cooling. Government agencies such as NASA; educational institutions such as the University of New Hampshire and UCLA; and corporations such as BMW, General Motors, and Honeywell use LFG.

Methane/Landfill Gas Collection System Operator ✿⑤

Alternate Titles and Related Careers

- Gas Operations Manager
- Gas Plant Manager
- Gas Plant Supervisor
- Landfill Gas Operations Manager
- Landfill Manager

This is a "Bright Outlook" and "Green New and Emerging" occupation in the renewable energy generation sector of the economy.

Job Trends

Because this occupation is so new, data collection is ongoing. However, as the methane/landfill gas (LFG) collection and generation industry expands, the need for managers to oversee LFG operations will grow as well.

Nature of the Work

A methane/landfill gas collection system operator has direct daily responsibility for the operation, maintenance, and repair of LFG projects. This includes supervision of landfill, well field, and other site employees. The duties of a methane/landfill gas collection system operator extend to maintaining daily logs, determining service priorities, and ensuring compliance with all reporting requirements. Duties may also include overseeing the construction of landfill gas collection systems.

According to O*NET, a methane/landfill gas collection system operator may perform any of the following tasks:

- Monitor and control liquid or gas landfill extraction systems
- Oversee gas collection landfill operations including leachate and gas management
- Evaluate LFG gas collection service requirements to meet operational plans and productivity goals
- Optimize gas collection landfill operational costs and productivity consistent with safety and environmental rules and regulations
- Develop or enforce procedures for normal operations, start-up, or shut-down of methane gas collection systems
- Inspect landfill or conduct site audits to ensure adherence to safety and environmental regulations
- Maintain records to demonstrate compliance with safety and environmental laws, regulations, and policies
- Monitor gas collection systems emissions data
- Monitor landfill permit requirements for updates
- Prepare soil reports as required by regulatory or permitting agencies
- Operate computerized control panels to manage gas compression operations
- Prepare and manage budgets
- Read meters, gauges, or automotive recording devices at specified intervals to verify gas collection systems operating conditions
- Diagnose or troubleshoot gas collection equipment and programmable logic controller (PLC) systems

- Prepare reports on landfill operations and gas collection system productivity or efficiency
- Track volume and weight of landfill waste

Career Path

Employers typically prefer candidates with college degrees for entry-level position on the manager track. Those who enter directly from college or graduate school typically enter a company-sponsored training program. Some companies hire college graduates as first-line supervisors and promote them to management positions over time. Experience in some aspect of production operations is typically needed before advancement to upper-level management such as plant manager, superintendent, or vice president of operations.

Some industrial production managers begin as production workers, advancing to supervisory positions while earning a college degree and being selected for management training.

Earning Potential

Median hourly wage (2009): $40.90

Median annual wage (2009): $85,080

Education/Licensure

Typically, for the production manager position, employers prefer to hire employees with a college degree in biotechnology, industrial technology, or chemical, electrical, or mechanical engineering from a school accredited by the Accreditation Board for Engineering and Technology (ABET).

Some colleges and universities offer five-year programs that culminate in a master's degree in engineering. Some offer five- or six-year programs that include cooperative experience. Some four-year schools have arrangements with community colleges or liberal arts colleges that allow students to spend two or three years at the initial school and transfer for the last two years to complete their engineering degree.

All fifty states and the District of Columbia require engineers to be licensed as professional engineers (PE) if they serve the public directly. In most states, licensure requires graduation from a four-year engineering program accredited by ABET, four years of experience, and passing the state exam. Many engineers take the Fundamentals of Engineering portion of the exam upon graduation. They are then engineers in training (EIT). After obtaining appropriate work experience, they take the Principles and Practice of Engineering exam to complete their professional license. Most states recognize licenses from other states, as long as the requirements are the same or more stringent. Some states have continuing education requirements.

Some industrial production managers earn certification to demonstrate their competency. The Association for Operations Management (APICS) offers the Certified in Production and Inventory Management (CPIM) certification that requires passing a series of exams that cover supply-chain management, resource planning, scheduling, production operations, and strategic planning. Successful candidates must renew their certifications every three years.

The American Society for Quality (ASQ) offers the Certified Manager of Quality/Organizational Excellence (CMQ/OE) credential. Candidates must have at least ten years of experience and pass an exam. To maintain the certification, candidates must take a certain number of professional development courses every three years.

For More Information

Accreditation Board for Engineering and Technology (ABET)
111 Market Place
Suite 1050
Baltimore, Maryland 21202
410-347-7700
www.abet.org

American Society for Quality (ASQ)
600 North Plankinton Avenue
Milwaukee, Wisconsin 53203
www.asq.org

Association for Operations Management (APICS)
8430 West Bryn Mawr Avenue
Suite 1000
Chicago, Illinois 60631
www.apics.org

Environmental Industry Associations (EIA)
4301 Connecticut Avenue, NW
Suite 300
Washington, DC 20008
202-244-4700
www.environmentalistseveryday.org

Solid Waste Association of North America
   (SWANA)
1100 Wayne Avenue
Silver Spring, Maryland 20910
301-585-2898
www.swana.org

About Nebraska's Use of Wind Power

Much of what we hear about new energy sources relates to funding to develop these sources, but Nebraska is using the revenue from leasing more than 1 million acres of state-owned land to solar- and wind-power companies to fund performance pay for the state's teachers.

Methane/Landfill Gas Generation System Technician ✿ ⑤

Alternate Titles and Related Careers

- Gas Operations Specialist
- Gas Plant Technician
- Methane Capturing System Installer ⑤
- Methane/Landfill Gas Collection System Technician

This is a "Bright Outlook" and "Green New and Emerging" occupation in the renewable energy-generation sector of the economy.

Job Trends

Data is being collected on this occupation, but as the methane gas collection and power generation industry expands, the need for people to monitor, operate, and maintain LFG collection components and controls should increase as well.

Nature of the Work

Methane/landfill gas generation system technicians monitor, operate, and maintain landfill gas collection components including collection and power generation systems. They are also responsible for monitoring, operating, and maintaining environmental monitoring and control systems at landfill sites.

Among the tasks that methane/landfill gas generation system technicians may perform are the following, according to O*NET:

- Perform routine maintenance and minor repairs, including repairing or replacing gas piping
- Balance individual gas extraction wells at landfill gas facilities
- Diagnose and troubleshoot problems with methane or landfill gas collection systems
- Measure landfill gas vegetative covering, installing additional covering as required
- Measure liquid levels in landfill gas extraction wells

- Monitor landfill well fields periodically to ensure proper functioning and performance, adjusting monitoring equipment as needed
- Prepare and submit compliance, operation, and safety forms or reports
- Record and maintain log of well-head gauge pressure reading
- Verify that well field monitoring data conforms to applicable regulations
- Monitor landfill gas perimeter probes to identify landfill gas migration
- Perform landfill surface scans to determine overall effectiveness of the site
- Trace electrical circuitry for landfill gas buildings to ensure compliance of electrical systems with applicable codes or laws

Career Path

The job is similar to that of a science or chemical processing control technician who works in manufacturing and focuses on quality assurance, monitoring product quality or production processes. New employees work under an experienced technician and with experience may become supervisors themselves. To qualify for higher-level positions, at least a bachelor's degree is required.

Earning Potential

Median hourly wage (2009): $23.92

Median annual wage (2009): $49,760

This data is based on Bureau of Labor Statistics data for "Plant and System Operators, All Other."

Education/Licensure

Typically entry-level positions require a high school diploma or GED and some formal post-secondary training such as an associate degree. Technical and community colleges offer associate degree programs and technical institutes offer certificate programs and associate degrees. However, the latter institutions offer less general education and less theory than community or technical colleges. New employees may also undergo a one- or two-year training program, which includes on-the-job training and classroom instruction.

For More Information

Environmental Industry Associations (EIA)
4301 Connecticut Avenue, NW
Suite 300
Washington, DC 20008
202-244-4700
www.environmentalistseveryday.org

Solid Waste Association of North America (SWANA)
1100 Wayne Avenue
Silver Spring, Maryland 20910
301-585-2898
www.swana.org

ELECTRIC POWER INDUSTRY

As the Department of Energy's (DOE) Web site says, "America—and much of the world—is becoming increasingly electrified." Using 3.8 trillion kilowatt hours, the United States is the largest consumer of electric power in the world. China ranks second with 2.8 trillion kilowatt hours, and Russia is a distant third consuming 985 billion kilowatt hours (all statistics from 2007).

The majority of U.S. electricity is produced by burning coal, an abundant and low-cost source of energy. Natural gas, nuclear power, biofuels, solar, and wind power are other sources of electric power currently used or under development in the United States. The DOE estimates that 90 percent of the new power plants built over the next twenty years will be natural gas plants.

Because of the growing need for electricity, jobs in the electric power industry are expected to grow. Because of the efforts to reduce the environmental impact of the methods we use to generate electricity, it's also a green sector of the energy industry.

Electric Power-Line Installer and Repairer 💲

Alternate Titles and Related Careers

- Electrical Lineworker
- Journeyman Lineman
- Lineman
- Power Lineman

This is a "Green Increased-Demand" occupation, which means that while there will be additional job openings because of the greening of the economy, there will be no new skill requirements for workers.

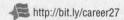 http://bit.ly/career27

Job Trends

The Bureau of Labor Statistics projects a 3 to 6 percent growth rate for this occupation between 2008 and 2018, which translates into 45,500 jobs. However, as the population continues to increase and new power sources come on-line, the occupation may see a faster growth rate.

Nature of the Work

An electrical power-line installer and repairer installs or repairs cables and wires used in electric power systems. They are the workers who install and maintain the power grid. In addition to stringing lines, installers may also erect utility poles and light- and heavy-duty transmissions towers and dig trenches to lay cable underground. They must be able to use digger derricks, augurs, cranes, power equipment, and hand tools, including splicers and soldering irons.

Following safety practices and procedures is a high priority for this occupation because of the potential hazards that power-line installers/repairers encounter on the job. Those who work on long-distance transmission lines work with high-voltage electricity, which is hundreds of thousands of volts. The lines that feed electricity to homes and businesses within an area may be less than

10,000 volts—but still deadly. Because of safety precautions, fatalities are rare according to the *Occupational Outlook Handbook.*

Line workers who maintain the interstate power grid work in crews that travel to work locations throughout a large region to maintain transmission lines and towers. Those who work for localities work mainly with lower-voltage distribution lines, maintaining equipment like transformers, voltage regulators, and switches. They may also work on traffic lights and streetlights.

About a New Certification Program

The National Cable Splicing Certification Board (NCSCB) is developing a Cable Splicing Certification. NCSCB is working in cooperation with the National Joint Apprenticeship and Training Committee (NJATC), several unions, and a number of companies involved in electric power to develop the certification. Check the NCSCB Web site for information about when the program will be operational, www.njatc.org/cert.

According to O*NET, an electrical power-line installer and repairer may perform any or all of the following tasks:

- Open switches and attach grounding devices to remove electrical hazards from disturbed or fallen lines or to facilitate repairs
- Climb poles or use truck-mounted buckets to access equipment
- Place insulating or fireproofing materials over conductors and joints
- Install, maintain, and/or repair electrical distribution and transmission systems
- Identify defective sectionalizing devices, circuit breakers, fuses, voltage regulators, transformers, switches, relays, or wiring, using wiring diagrams and electrical testing instruments

- Inspect and test power lines and auxiliary equipment to locate and identify problems, using reading and testing instruments
- String wire conductors and cables between poles, towers, trenches, pylons, and buildings, setting lines in place and using winches to adjust tension
- Test conductors, according to electrical diagrams and specifications, to identify corresponding conductors and to prevent incorrect connections
- Replace or straighten damaged poles
- Install watt-hour meters and connect service drops between power lines and consumers' facilities
- Trim trees that could be hazardous to the functioning of cables or wires
- Attach cross-arms, insulators, and auxiliary equipment to poles prior to installing them
- Splice or solder cables together or to overhead transmission lines, customer service lines, or street light lines
- Cut and peel lead sheathing and insulation from defective or newly installed cables and conduits prior to splicing
- Clean, cover with tin, and splice corresponding conductors by twisting ends together or by joining ends with metal clamps and soldering connections

Career Path

Entry-level line workers generally begin with classroom training and an apprenticeship under the supervision of experienced workers. Their first jobs may be tree trimming and ground work. As they continue their training, entry-level workers are given more advanced tasks such as stringing cable and performing service installations. Over time, they advance to more complex assignments and become responsible for increasingly larger portions of the network.

After three to five years of work, qualified line workers reach the journeyman level. A journeyman line worker can do most tasks without supervision. At this point, they have enough experience to move to another company if they choose. After a number of years of experience, an electrical power-line installer/repairer may become a first-line supervisor or a trainer.

Earning Potential

Median hourly wage (2009): $27.24

Median annual wage (2009): $56,670

Education/Licensure

Typically, entry-level workers are required to have a high school diploma or equivalent. Basic knowledge of algebra and trigonometry, as well as reading and writing skills, are important. Technical knowledge of electricity gained through military service, vocational programs, or community college work can be helpful in being hired, but is rarely a requirement.

Many community colleges offer programs in electricity. Some work with local companies to offer one-year certificates that emphasize hands-on fieldwork. More advanced two-year associate degree programs provide students with a broader knowledge of the subject. However, much of the training for line installers/repairers is on the job. Often, entry-level employees must complete a formal apprenticeship program or other employer training.

Apprenticeship programs can last up to five years and combine on-the-job training with formal classroom instruction. They are typically administered jointly by the employer and the local union representing the workers. Safety regulations strictly define the training and educational requirements for apprentice electrical line installers, but licensure is not required. There are six recognized apprenticeships associated with electrical power-line installer and repairer: cable installer-repairer, cable splicer, line erector, line maintainer, line repairer, and troubleshooter II.

For More Information

American Public Power Association (APPANET)
1875 Connecticut Avenue, NW
Suite 1200
Washington, DC 20009-5715
www.appanet.org

Center for Energy Workforce Development
  (CEWD)
701 Pennsylvania Avenue, NW
Washington, DC 20004-2696
www.cewd.org

International Brotherhood of Electrical Workers
  (IBEW)
900 Seventh Street, NW
Washington, DC 20001
www.ibew.org

National Joint Apprenticeship and Training
  Committee (NJATC)
301 Prince Georges Boulevard
Suite D
Upper Marlboro, Maryland 20774
www.njatc.org

Electric Power Plant Operator ⊛

Alternate Titles and Related Careers
- Auxiliary Operator
- Control Center Operator
- Control Operator
- Control Room Operator
- Operations and Maintenance Gas Turbine Technician
- Operations and Maintenance Technician (O&M Technician)
- Plant Control Operator
- Unit Operator

This is a "Green Enhanced-Skills" occupation in the energy and carbon capture and storage, green construction, and renewable energy generation sectors of the green economy. Those who wish to enter this field will need new skills, knowledge, and credentials to perform new tasks associated with new technologies.

Job Trends

In 2008, about 35,400 people were employed as power plant operators. The Bureau of Labor Statistics sees little or no change in the total number of jobs, but expects that job opportunities will be excellent between 2008 and 2018 for several reasons. First, a large number of workers will be retiring. Second, the demand for energy is expected to increase because of the growing population. Third, recent legislation allows for the construction of new power plants.

The exception to the slow growth of power plant operator jobs is in the nuclear power industry where nuclear power reactor operators will see a 19 percent growth in job opportunities between 2008 and 2018.

In an effort to counter the expected large number of power plant operators retiring, some utilities have established education programs at community colleges and high schools to train new operators. Potential power plant operators need strong technical and mechanical skills and an understanding of science and math.

Nature of the Work

Power plant operators control, operate, and maintain the machinery that generates electric power. The machinery includes boilers, turbines, generators, and auxiliary equipment such as pumps, fans, compressors, condensers, feedwater heaters, filters, and chlorinators. According to O*NET, power plant operators may perform any of the following tasks:
- Monitor and inspect power plant equipment and indicators to detect operating problems
- Adjust controls to generate specified electrical power or to regulate the flow of power between generating stations and substations

- Operate or control power generating equipment using control boards or semiautomatic equipment
- Regulate equipment operations and conditions based on data from recording and indicating instruments or from computers
- Take readings from charts, meters, and gauges at established intervals and take corrective steps as necessary
- Start or stop generators and other power plant equipment and connect or disconnect equipment from circuits
- Inspect records and logbook entries and communicate with other plant personnel to assess equipment operating status
- Control and maintain auxiliary equipment to supply water, fuel, lubricants, air, and auxiliary power
- Communicate with systems operators to regulate and coordinate transmission loads and frequencies and line voltages
- Record and compile operational data
- Collect oil, water, and electrolyte samples for lab analysis
- Make adjustments and minor repairs and report the need for major repairs
- Control generator output to match the phase, frequency, and voltage of electricity supplied to panels
- Place standby emergency electrical generators online in emergencies and monitor the temperature, output, and lubrication of the system
- Receive outage calls and call in necessary personnel during power outages and emergencies
- Examine and test electrical power distribution machinery and equipment
- Clean, lubricate, and maintain equipment to prevent equipment failure or deterioration
- Replenish electrolytes in batteries and oil in voltage transformers and reset tripped electric relays

Career Path

Most entry-level jobs begin with classroom instruction followed by a period as helpers or laborers. Workers advance to more responsible positions over time as they become familiar with the plant operations. Typically, there are three to five classifications of worker, based on experience. Each level has its own training requirements, mandatory waiting times, and exams. Over time, with training and experience, workers can advance to shift supervisor, trainer, or consultant.

Energy companies usually promote from within. Most workers advance by moving up within the same company or by moving from one plant to another within the same company. Advancing by moving from company to company can be difficult because of the different systems used by different companies.

Power plant operators are subject to random drug and alcohol tests.

Earning Potential

Median hourly wage (2009): $29.04

Median annual wage (2009): $60,400

Education/Licensure

Entry-level jobs in a power plant require a high school diploma. Those with college or vocational school degrees have an advantage both in hiring and in advancement. New employees undergo a combination of on-the-job training and classroom instruction that lasts for several years.

Power plant operators are required to take a certain number of hours of training annually. This includes training on plant simulators to reproduce real-world situations that operators could encounter at their plants.

Licensing requirements vary by state and by specific job functions. In some states, power plant operators are licensed as firemen or engineers.

For More Information

American Public Power Association (APPANET)
1875 Connecticut Avenue, NW
Suite 1200
Washington, DC 20009-5715
www.appanet.org

American Solar Energy Society (ASES)
2400 Central Avenue
Suite A
Boulder, Colorado 80301
303-443-3130
www.ases.org

American Wind Energy Association
1501 M Street, NW
Suite 1000
Washington, DC 20005
202-383-2500
www.awea.org

Center for Energy Workforce Development
    (CEWD)
701 Pennsylvania Avenue, NW
Washington, DC 20004-2696
www.cewd.org

International Brotherhood of Electrical Workers
    (IBEW)
900 Seventh Street, NW
Washington, DC 20001
www.ibew.org

Solar Electric Power Association
1220 19th Street, NW
Suite 401
Washington, DC 20036-2405
www.solarelectricpower.org

Solar Energy Industries Association
805 15th Street, NW
Washington, DC 20005
202-682-0556
www.seia.org

Energy Broker ☼ ⊕

Alternate Titles and Related Careers

- Account Executive: Energy Sales
- Energy Consultant
- Energy Sales Consultant
- Energy Sales Representative

This is a "Bright Outlook" and "Green New and Emerging" occupation in the energy trading sector of the financial services industry. Although included under the electricity industry, energy brokers may also work in the natural gas and propane/liquid fuels sectors.

Job Trends

The Bureau of Labor Statistics includes this occupation in "Sales Representatives, Services, All Other" and rates the category as having a 14 to 19 percent growth rate between 2008 and 2018. This is faster than average for all occupations.

Energy deregulation, which began in the late 1990s, created this job by creating competition among companies to sell energy to consumers—residential and commercial. Under energy deregulation, states decide if they want to allow consumers to choose from whom they buy their power. They can choose to keep their current utility or buy from a new supplier that has bought the power from a power-generation company. The power is delivered over existing power lines by a third-party distributor, which charges a fee to its competitor for the service. As the companies that produce power proliferate, the need for energy brokers as intermediaries to buy power from generation companies and sell it to consumers should grow as well.

Nature of the Work

Energy brokers buy and sell energy for customers. They buy from energy generators and sell to consumers. The goal is to help consumers realize savings from energy deregulation by creating a competitive marketplace. Each company tries to provide the best pricing terms and conditions for consumers, while making a profit.

Among the tasks that an energy broker who interacts with consumers performs are the following, according to O*NET:

- Contact prospective buyers or sellers of power to arrange transactions
- Create product packages based on assessment of customers' or potential customers' needs
- Educate customers and answer questions related to the buying or selling of energy, energy markets, or alternative energy sources
- Explain contract and related documents to customers
- Analyze customer bills and utility rate structures to select optimal rate structures for customers

About Federal Clean Energy Resources

EREN stands for Efficiency and Renewable Energy Network, the U.S. Department of Energy's Web site on renewable energy issues. Visit www.eren.gov to see what the network has to offer. Also check out the National Renewable Energy Laboratory at www.nrel.org for information about alternative energy research studies. The Green Power Network at http://apps3.eere.energy.gov is the U.S. Department of Energy's Web site for information on green power markets, green power providers, products, consumer protection issues, and policies.

Energy brokers who deal with purchasing energy from electric power companies or natural gas and propane/liquid gas providers may perform the following tasks:

- Contact prospective buyers or sellers of power to arrange transactions
- Purchase or sell energy or energy derivatives for customers

- Explain contract and related documents to customers
- Forecast energy supply and demand to minimize the cost of meeting load demands and to maximize the value of supply resources
- Negotiate prices and contracts for energy sales or purchases
- Price energy based on market conditions
- Develop and deliver proposals or presentations on topics such as the purchase and sale of energy
- Facilitate the delivery or receipt of wholesale power or retail load scheduling
- Monitor the flow of energy in response to changes in consumer demand

Career Path

After a probationary period with greater supervision, an entry-level energy broker will work on his/her own. Advancement typically takes the form of being assigned to a larger account or territory, where commissions are likely to be greater. Brokers with good sales records and leadership ability may advance to higher level positions, such as sales supervisor, district manager, territory manager, or vice president of sales. Some may become sales trainers working with new employees on selling techniques and company policies. Others may strike out on their own as independent sales agents or consultants.

Earning Potential

Median hourly wage (2009): $23.76

Median annual wage (2009): $49,410

Education/Licensure

Those engaged in financial sales (energy derivatives) require a bachelor's degree in business, finance, accounting, or economics. A master's in business (MBA) can be helpful for advancement. For other energy brokers, there is no formal educational requirement. Regardless of educational background, factors such as communication skills, the ability to sell, and knowledge of the products are key components for success.

Some states such as Massachusetts require licensing of energy brokers. Energy brokers who deal in derivatives must register with the Financial Industry Regulatory Authority (FINRA) and comply with exam and licensing requirements.

The Association of Energy Engineers (AEE) offers the Certified Energy Procurement Professional (CEP) program for energy brokers. The American Public Power Association offers the e-Learning course "Solving Your Customer's Energy Concerns" as initial training or a refresher.

For More Information

American Public Power Association (APPANET)
1875 Connecticut Avenue, NW
Suite 1200
Washington, DC 20009-5715
www.appanet.org

Association of Energy Engineers (AEE)
4025 Pleasantdale Road
Suite 420
Atlanta, Georgia 30340
770-447-5083
www.aeecenter.org

Electric Power Supply Association (EPSA)
1401 New York Avenue, NW
11th Floor
Washington, DC 20005-2110
www.epsa.org

Financial Industry Regulatory Authority (FINRA)
1735 K Street, NW
Washington, DC 20006
www.finra.org

National Energy Marketers Association (NEMA)
3333 K Street, NW
Suite 110
Washington, DC 20007
202-333-3288
www.energymarketers.com

Security Industries and Financial Markets Association (SIFMA)
120 Broadway
35th Floor
New York, New York 10271-0080
212-313-1200
AND
1101 New York Avenue, NW
Washington, DC 20005
202-962-7300
www.sifma.org

Power Plant Distributor and Dispatcher 🌏

Alternate Titles and Related Careers
- Control Area Operator
- Control Operator
- Distribution Operations Supervisor
- Distribution System Operator
- Electric System Operator
- Load Dispatcher
- Power System Dispatcher
- Power System Operator
- System Operator
- Transmission System Operator

This is a "Green Increased-Demand" occupation in the renewable energy generation sector. In addition to new energy sources like wind and solar, this sector also includes traditional sources undergoing significant green technological changes.

Job Trends

In 2008, about 10,000 people were employed as power distributors and dispatchers. The Bureau of Labor Statistics sees little or no change in the total number of jobs, but expects that job opportunities will be excellent between 2008 and 2018 for several reasons. First, a large number of workers will be retiring. Second, the demand for energy is expected to increase because of the growing population. Third, recent legislation allows for the construction of new power plants.

The exception to the slow growth of power plant operator jobs is in the nuclear power industry where nuclear power reactor operators will see a 19 percent growth in job opportunities between 2008 and 2018.

In an effort to counter the expected large number of retirements, some utilities have established education programs at community colleges and high schools to train new power plant dispatchers and distributors. To be successful, candidates need strong technical and mechanical skills and an understanding of science and math.

Nature of the Work

Power distributors and dispatchers coordinate, regulate, or distribute electricity or steam. They control the flow of electricity as it travels through the network of transmission lines that reach from the power plant to industrial plants and substations and from there through distribution lines to residential users. They work in power plants and in substations and team with engineers, planners, field personnel, control room operators, and other utility workers to perform their jobs.

Among the duties that power dispatchers and distributors have are the following, according to O*NET:

- Respond to emergencies such as transformer failures and route current around affected areas
- Prepare switching orders that isolate areas without causing power outages
- Control, monitor, or operate equipment that regulates or distributes electricity or steam, using data from instrument readings or computers
- Monitor and record switchboard and control board readings to ensure that electrical or steam distribution equipment is operating properly
- Direct personnel engaged in controlling and operating distribution equipment and machinery

- Distribute and regulate the flow of power between entities such as generating stations, substations, distribution lines, and users, keeping track of the status of circuits and connections
- Track conditions that could affect power needs like changes in weather and adjust equipment accordingly
- Calculate and determine load estimates or equipment requirements to determine required control settings
- Manipulate controls to adjust and activate power distribution equipment and machines
- Record and compile operational data
- Accept and implement energy schedules
- Inspect equipment to ensure that specifications are met and to detect any defects
- Repair, maintain, and clean equipment and machinery

Career Path

Power distributors and dispatchers work for utility companies, nonutility power-generation companies, and companies that access the power grid directly. Most entry-level jobs begin with classroom instruction followed by a period as helpers or laborers. Workers advance to more responsible positions over time as they become familiar with the plant operations. Typically, there are three to five classifications of worker, based on experience. Each level has its own training requirements, mandatory waiting times, and exams. Over time, with training and experience, workers can advance to shift supervisor, trainer, or consultant.

Energy companies usually promote from within. Most workers advance by moving up within the same company or by moving from one plant to another within the same company. Advancing by moving from company to company can be difficult because of the different systems used by different companies.

Earning Potential

Median hourly wage (2009): $32.21

Median annual wage (2009): $66,990

Education/Licensure

Entry-level jobs require a high school diploma. Those with college or vocational school degrees have an advantage both in hiring and in advancement. New employees undergo a combination of on-the-job training and classroom instruction that lasts for several years. In addition, power plant operators are required to take a certain number of hours of training annually. This includes training on plant simulators to reproduce real-world situations that operators could encounter at their plants.

Licensing requirements for power plant distributors and dispatchers vary by state and by specific job functions. If their jobs could affect the power grid, they must be certified by the North American Energy Reliability Corporation, which offers the System Operator Certification Program that includes four specialized exams: Reliability Operator, Balancing and Interchange Operator, Transmission Operator, and Balancing, Interchange, and Transmission Operator.

For More Information

American Public Power Association (APPANET)
1875 Connecticut Avenue, NW
Suite 1200
Washington, DC 20009-5715
www.appanet.org

American Solar Energy Society (ASES)
2400 Central Avenue
Suite A
Boulder, Colorado 80301
303-443-3130
www.ases.org

American Wind Energy Association (AWEA)
1501 M Street, NW
Suite 1000
Washington, DC 20005
202-383-2500
www.awea.org

Center for Energy Workforce Development (CEWD)
701 Pennsylvania Avenue, NW
Washington, DC 20004-2696
www.cewd.org

International Brotherhood of Electrical Workers (IBEW)
900 Seventh Street NW
Washington, DC 20001
www.ibew.org

North American Energy Reliability Corporation (NERC)
116-390 Village Boulevard
Princeton, New Jersey 08540-5721
609-452-8060
www.nerc.com

Solar Electric Power Association (SEPA)
1220 19th Street, NW
Suite 401
Washington, DC 20036-2405
www.solarelectricpowcr.org

Solar Energy Industries Association (SEIA)
805 15th Street, NW
Washington, DC 20005
202-682-0556
www.seia.org

About New Degree Programs in Smart Grid Engineering

In 2010, the federal government allocated $100 million in American Recovery and Reinvestment Act (ARRA) funding to fifty-four colleges and universities to develop courses in clean energy and smart grid engineering. The three-year program will result in new courses to strengthen existing engineering programs and create master's programs and undergraduate and graduate certifications as well as workforce training programs. Some programs will be delivered online. Among the schools that received funding were Penn State, Syracuse University, and Washington State University.

Smart Grid Engineer

Alternate Titles and Related Careers:

- Distribution Engineer–Smart Grid Protection
- Electrical Engineer ⊕
- Lead Smart Grid Test Engineer
- Senior Engineer, Smart Grid AMR/AMI (Automated Meter Reading/Advanced Metering Infrastructure)
- Smart Grid Software Engineer
- Smart Grid Test Engineer
- Systems Engineer
- Transmission Services Engineer

A smart grid engineer is a relatively new engineering specialty. Electrical engineering is a good basis, and O'NET classifies that as a "Green Enhanced-Skills" occupation.

Job Trends

While the Bureau of Labor Statistics projects little or no change in job growth for electrical engineers between 2008 and 2018, the demand for engineers who can design, develop, and monitor the smart grid will grow. The federal government's $100 million investment in education for clean technology and smart grid training is evidence of the importance of this work to the nation's future.

Nature of the Work

In general, an electrical engineer designs, develops, tests, or supervises the manufacture and installation of electrical equipment, components, or systems. A smart grid engineer, according to a review of job boards, applies engineering principles to the modernization and functioning of the nation's electric power grid. The work may involve advance sensing and control; integration of renewable energy sources; systems stability; intelligent agents; distributed computing; electrical, mechanical, and information systems integration; enterprise information architecture, cyber security, and information modeling.

A smart grid engineer may:

- Monitor the electric power infrastructure and delivery system to identify and solve problems
- Design and develop new electric power generation, delivery, and utilization systems

Those involved in software development for the electric power system may:

- Develop adaptors and interfaces for smart grid applications for utility customers
- Develop and execute test plan strategies for integrated systems in the power distribution sector
- Develop validation and verification procedures

General engineering tasks that a smart grid engineer might perform, based on the O*NET profile of the electrical engineering occupation, are the following:

- Design, implement, maintain, and improve electrical instruments, equipment, facilities, components, products, and systems
- Direct and coordinate manufacturing, construction, installation, maintenance, support, documentation, or testing activities

to ensure compliance with specifications, codes, and customer requirements

- Perform detailed calculations to compute and establish manufacturing, construction, and installation standards and specifications
- Oversee project production to assure projects are completed satisfactorily, on time, and within budget
- Plan and implement research methodology and procedures
- Develop budgets
- Compile data and write reports regarding existing and potential engineering studies and projects
- Plan layout of electric power generation plants and distribution lines and stations
- Inspect completed installations and observe operations to ensure conformance to design and equipment specifications and compliance with operational and safety standards
- Conduct field surveys and study maps, graphs, diagrams, and other data to identify and correct power system problems
- Assist in developing capital project programs for new equipment and major repairs
- Collect data relating to commercial and residential development, population, and power system interconnection to determine operating efficiency of electrical systems

Career Path

At the minimum, a bachelor's degree is needed for an entry-level position. Some jobs may require a graduate degree. As engineers gain experience, they become specialists and advance into positions where they supervise a team of engineers and other staff members. Some eventually become managers or move into sales jobs where their technical background is particularly useful. Some go on to earn a master's in business administration (MBA) to prepare them for high-level managerial positions. Others go into consulting.

Earning Potential

Median hourly wage (2009): $39.96

Median annual wage (2009): $83,110

(Based on electrical engineer's salaries)

Education/Licensure

One route to becoming a smart grid engineer is a degree in electrical engineering, Other relevant degrees are systems engineering, power systems engineering, and civil engineering. Some jobs may require a degree in computer software engineering.

For entry-level positions, a bachelor's degree in engineering from a college or university program that is accredited by the Accreditation Board for Engineering and Technology (ABET) is required. In some cases, engineers with degrees in one type of engineering may qualify for jobs in other areas of engineering. Smart grid engineering is one such occupation, because of the lack of degree programs in smart grid engineering.

Some colleges and universities offer five-year programs that culminate in a master's degree. Some offer five- or six-year programs that include cooperative experience. Some four-year schools have arrangements with community colleges or liberal arts colleges that allow students to spend two or three years at the initial school and transfer for the last two years to complete their engineering degree.

All fifty states and the District of Columbia require engineers to be licensed as professional engineers (PE) if they serve the public directly. In most states, licensure requires graduation from a four-year engineering program accredited by ABET, four years of experience, and passing the state exam. Many engineers take the Fundamentals of Engineering portion of the exam upon graduation. They are then engineers in training (EIT). After obtaining appropriate work experience, they take the Principles and Practice of Engineering exam to complete their professional license. Most states recognize licenses from other states, as long as the requirements are the same or more stringent. Some states have continuing education requirements.

The International Council on Systems Engineering (INCOSE) offers a Systems Engineering Professional Certification program that involves three levels: Associate Systems Engineering Professional for entry-level systems engineers, Certified Systems Engineering Professional at the next level, and Expert Systems Engineering Professional at the senior level.

About Electric Grid Efficiency

The U.S. Department of Energy estimates that if the present power grid were just 5 percent more efficient, the savings in fuel and greenhouse gas emissions would be comparable to permanently eliminating these emissions from 53 million cars.

For More Information

Accreditation Board for Engineering and
    Technology (ABET)
111 Market Place
Suite 1050
Baltimore, Maryland 21202
410-347-7700
www.abet.org

American Public Power Association (APPANET)
1875 Connecticut Avenue, NW
Suite 1200
Washington, DC 20009-5715
www.appanet.org

American Society for Engineering Education
    (ASEE)
1818 N Street, NW
Suite 600
Washington, DC 20036-2479
202-331-3500
www.asee.org

Institute of Electrical and Electronics Engineers
    (IEEE)
445 Hoes Lane
Piscataway, New Jersey 08854-4141
732-981-0060
www.ieee.org

International Council on Systems Engineering
    (INCOSE)
7670 Opportunity Road
Suite 220
San Diego, California 92111-2222
800-366-1164
www.incose.org

National Society of Professional Engineers
    (NSPE)
1420 King Street
Alexandria, Virginia 22314
703-684-2800
www.nspe.org

Power & Energy Working Group
www.incose/org/practice/techactivities/wg/pande/

GEOTHERMAL POWER

The Geothermal Energy Association (GEA) announced that the geothermal power industry grew at a rate of 26 percent in 2009. The association reported that 188 new projects were begun in fifteen states during the year. They will add over 7,000 megawatts of power annually to the nation's capacity, which translates into serving 7.6 million new customers. The American Recovery and Reinvestment Act (ARRA) through the U.S. Department of Energy has funneled $600 million into 135 new research projects in twenty-five states. Most of the nation's geothermal reserves are in the western states and Hawaii, so that's where the jobs are.

Geothermal Production Manager ☼ ⊕

Alternate Titles and Related Careers
- Geothermal Electrical Engineer
- Geothermal Operations Engineer
- Geothermal Operations Manager
- Geothermal Project Manager
- Geothermal Resource Manager

This is both a "Bright Outlook" and "Green New and Emerging" occupation in the renewable energy generation sector of the economy.

Job Trends

Because this occupation is so new, data collection is ongoing. However, as the geothermal energy sector increases its capacity, the need for managers to oversee the operations of plants producing geothermal power will grow as well.

Nature of the Work

Geothermal engineers manage operations at geothermal power-generation facilities. They maintain and monitor geothermal plant equipment for efficient and safe plant operations. Among the tasks that a geothermal production manager performs are the following, according to O*NET:
- Inspect geothermal plant or injection fields to verify proper operation of equipment
- Oversee geothermal plant operations, maintenance, and repairs to ensure compliance with applicable standards or regulations
- Supervise employees in geothermal power plants or well fields
- Develop operating plans and schedules
- Develop or manage budgets
- Identify and evaluate equipment, procedural, or conditional inefficiencies involving geothermal plant systems
- Identify opportunities to improve plant electrical equipment, controls, or process control methodologies
- Negotiate interconnection agreements with other utilities
- Obtain permits for constructing, upgrading, or operating geothermal power plants
- Perform or direct the performance of preventive maintenance on plant equipment
- Prepare environmental permit applications or compliance reports
- Record, review, or maintain daily logs, reports, maintenance, and other records
- Troubleshoot and make minor reports to plant instrumentation or electrical systems
- Conduct well field site assessments
- Select and implement corrosion control or mitigation systems for geothermal plants

Career Path

Employers typically prefer candidates with college degrees for entry-level positions on the manager track. Those who enter directly from college or graduate school typically enter a company-sponsored training program. In larger companies, new employees may work in a variety of departments to become familiar with various operations. Some companies hire college graduates as first-line supervisors and promote them to management positions over time. Experience in some aspect of production operations is typically needed before advancement to upper-level management such as plant manager, superintendent, or vice president of operations.

About Checking CSR

Check a prospective employer's Web site for information on how it views its responsibilities to the environment, its customers, and its employees. Timberland, for example, has a section on its home page titled "Corporate Social Responsibility." Be prepared to ask the Human Relations interviewer questions that you want answered about how well the company "walks the talk."

Some industrial production managers begin as production workers, advancing to supervisory positions after a number of years while earning a college degree and then being selected for management.

Earning Potential

Median hourly wage (2009): $40.90

Median annual wage (2009): $85,080

(Based on industrial production managers' salaries)

Education/Licensure

Typically, employers prefer to hire employees for the production manager position with a bachelor's degree in electrical, mechanical, chemical, industrial technology, or industrial engineering from an institution accredited by the Accreditation Board for Engineering and Technology (ABET).

As noted in the *Occupation Outlook Handbook,* some colleges and universities offer five-year programs that culminate in a master's degree in engineering. Some offer five- or six-year programs that include cooperative experience. Some four-year schools have arrangements with community colleges or liberal arts colleges that allow students to spend two or three years at the initial school and transfer for the last two years to complete their engineering degree.

All fifty states and the District of Columbia require engineers to be licensed as professional engineers (PE) if they serve the public directly. In most states, licensure requires graduation from a four-year engineering program accredited by ABET, four years of experience, and passing the state exam. Many engineers take the Fundamentals of Engineering portion of the exam upon graduation. They are then engineers in training (EIT). After obtaining appropriate work experience, they take the Principles and Practice of Engineering exam to complete their professional license. Most states recognize licenses from other states, as long as the requirements are the same or more stringent. Some states have continuing education requirements.

Some production managers earn certification to demonstrate their competency. The Association for Operations Management (APICS) offers the Certified in Production and Inventory Management (CPIM) certification that requires passing a series of exams that cover supply chain management, resource planning, scheduling, production operations, and strategic planning. Successful candidates must renew their certifications every three years.

The American Society for Quality (ASQ) offers the Certified Manager of Quality/Organizational Excellence (CMQ/OE) credential. Candidates must have at least ten years of experience and pass an exam. To maintain the certification, candidates must take a certain number of professional development courses every three years.

For More Information

Accreditation Board for Engineering and
    Technology (ABET)
111 Market Place
Suite 1050
Baltimore, Maryland 21202
410-347-7700
www.abet.org

American Society for Quality (ASQ)
600 North Plankinton Avenue
Milwaukee, Wisconsin 53203
www.asq.org

Association for Operations Management (APICS)
8430 West Bryn Mawr Avenue
Suite 1000
Chicago, Illinois 60631
www.apics.org

Geothermal Energy Association (GEA)
209 Pennsylvania Avenue, SE
Washington, DC 20003
202-454-5261
www.geo-energy.org

Geothermal Heat Pump Consortium (GHPC)
1050 Connecticut Avenue, NW
Suite 1000
Washington, DC 20036
888-255-4436
www.geoexchange.org

Geothermal Resources Council (GRC)
2001 Second Street
Suite 5
Davis, California 95617
www.geothermal.org

International Ground Source Heat Pump
Association (IGSHPA)
374 Cordell South
Stillwater, Oklahoma 74078
405-744-5175
www.igshpa.okstate.edu

Geothermal Technician ☼ ⊕

Alternate Title and Related Career
- Geothermal Installer

This is a "Bright Outlook" and "Green New and Emerging" occupation in the renewable energy generation sector. Geothermal technicians will also find work in green construction.

Job Trends

The Bureau of Labor Statistics equates this occupation with "Installation, Maintenance, and Repair Workers, All Other" and estimates an average rate of growth of 7 to 13 percent for the category. However, two factors may increase the rate of growth for geothermal technicians: the investment in geothermal research and ultimately power-generation plants and the growth of geothermal technology for home heating.

Nature of the Work

Geothermal technicians monitor and control operating activities at geothermal power generation facilities and perform maintenance and repairs as necessary. They may also install, test, and maintain residential and commercial geothermal heat pumps. Their areas of responsibilities include geothermal heating, air-conditioning, and hot water utilities in new construction and retrofits.

According to O*NET, geothermal technicians who work in geothermal power plants may perform the following tasks:
- Identify and correct malfunctions of geothermal plant equipment, electrical systems, instrumentation, or controls
- Monitor and adjust operations of the geothermal power plant equipment or systems
- Adjust power production systems to meet load and distribution demands
- Maintain, calibrate, or repair plant instrumentation, control, and electronic devices in geothermal plants
- Apply coating or operate system to mitigate corrosion of geothermal plant equipment or structures
- Collect and record data associated with geothermal power plants or well fields
- Install and maintain geothermal plant electrical protection equipment
- Prepare and maintain logs, reports, or other documentation of work performed
- Test water sources for factors such as flow volume and contaminant presence

Geothermal technicians who install residential or commercial geothermal systems may perform the following functions:
- Install, maintain, or repair ground or water source-coupled heat pumps to heat and cool residential or commercial building air or water
- Calculate heat loss and heat gain factors for residential properties to determine heating and cooling required by installed geothermal systems

- Design and lay out geothermal heat systems according to property characteristics, heating an cooling requirements, piping and equipment requirements, applicable regulations, or other factors
- Determine the type of geothermal loop system most suitable to a specific property and its heating and cooling needs
- Perform pre- and post-installation pressure, flow, and related tests of vertical and horizontal loop piping
- Dig trenches for system piping to appropriate depths and lay piping in trenches
- Backfill piping trenches to protect pipes from damage
- Prepare newly installed geothermal heat systems for operation by flushing, purging, or other actions
- Identify equipment options, such as compressors, and make appropriate selections
- Install and maintain geothermal system instrumentation or controls
- Place geothermal system pipes in bodies of water, weighting them to allow them to sink into position
- Verify that piping placed in bodies of water is situated to prevent damage to aquaculture and away from potential sources of harm
- Integrate hot water heater systems with geothermal heat exchange systems
- Prepare and maintain logs, reports, or other documentation of work performed
- Test water sources for factors such as flow volume and contaminant presence

Career Path

Typically, technicians begin as helpers working under the supervision of experienced employees. Several months or even a year of on-the-job training may be required to move to the next level of responsibility. Workers may advance through several levels of experience and responsibility to become supervisors themselves. In time, some geothermal technicians start their own businesses installing residential and commercials systems or consulting with homeowners and businesses.

Earning Potential

Median hourly wage (2009): $17.08

Median annual wage (2009): $35,520

Education/Licensure

Most employers prefer entry-level workers to have high school diplomas or the equivalent. Typically, workers in geothermal power plants undergo on-the-job training working under experienced technicians.

The same is true for technicians who work as commercial and residential installers of geothermal systems. States and municipalities may require licensing as plumbers, electricians, or HVAC (heating, ventilation, air-conditioning) installers.

Some community colleges and a variety of for-profit institutes and training providers are now offering short-course training opportunities for geothermal technicians. Some of these are online courses.

The International Ground Source Heat Pump Association (IGSHPA), in partnership with the HeatSpring Learning Institute, offers the Accredited Geothermal Installer Certification. HeatSpring also offers an online Entry Level Geothermal Professional Certificate. The Green Building Certification Institute, affiliated with the U.S. Green Building Council, offers LEED (Leadership in Energy and Environmental Design) credentials in green building that are applicable for geothermal technicians.

For More Information

Geothermal Energy Association (GEA)
209 Pennsylvania Avenue, SE
Washington, DC 20003
202-454-5261
www.geo-energy.org

Geothermal Heat Pump Consortium (GHPC)
1050 Connecticut Avenue, NW
Suite 1000
Washington, DC 20036
888-255-4436
www.geoexchange.org

Geothermal Resources Council (GRC)
2001 Second Street
Suite 5
Davis, California 95617
www.geothermal.org

HeatSpring Learning Institute
220 Concord Avenue
Cambridge, Massachusetts 02138
800-393-2044
www.heatspring.com

International Ground Source Heat Pump
    Association (IGSHPA)
374 Cordell South
Stillwater, Oklahoma 74078
405-744-5175
www.igshpa.okstate.edu

U.S. Green Building Council (USGBC)
2101 L Street, NW
Suite 500
Washington, DC 20037
800-795-1747 (toll-free)
www.usgbc.org

HYDROELECTRIC POWER

Hydroelectric power, a clean renewable energy source, uses the force of moving water to turn turbines and generate electricity. Conventional sources of water power are reservoirs, run-of-river, and pumped storage. Today, there are also four types of new hydro power: hydrokinetic, wave energy, tidal energy, and constructed waterways. Currently, the Department of Energy states that hydropower generates more electricity than any other renewable energy source. The National Hydropower Association, quoting a research study, estimates that, if further developed, hydropower can create 1.4 million jobs by 2025.

Hydroelectric Plant Technician ✿⊛

Alternate Titles and Related Careers.
- Controls and Electrical Technician (ICE Technician)
- Hydroelectric Plant Installation Technician
- Instrumentation Technician

This is a "Bright Outlook" and "Green New and Emerging" occupation in the renewable energy-generation sector.

Job Trends

Data is still being collected on this occupation, but because it is considered part of the new green economy, job opportunities should expand as investments in hydroelectric power increases.

Nature of the Work

Hydroelectric plant technicians monitor and control activities associated with hydropower generation. They monitor equipment operation and performance and make necessary adjustments to ensure that the plant operates at an optimal level of performance. Among the equipment that they work with are turbines, pumps, valves, relays, voltage regulators, generators, air compressors, switch gears, meters, electric control boards, and battery banks.

According to O*NET, among the tasks that hydroelectric plant technicians perform are the following:

- Start, adjust, and stop generating units, operating valves, gates, or auxiliary equipment in hydroelectric power generating plants
- Communicate status of hydroelectric operating equipment to dispatchers or supervisors
- Implement load and switching orders in accordance with specifications or instructions
- Inspect water-powered electric generators and auxiliary equipment to verify proper operation and to determine maintenance or repair needs
- Identify and address malfunctions of equipment
- Install and calibrate electrical and mechanical equipment
- Operate high-voltage switches and related devices in hydropower stations
- Operate hydroelectric plant equipment
- Maintain, test, and repair or replace hydroelectric plant electrical, mechanical, and electronic equipment
- Change oil, hydraulic fluid, or other lubricants to maintain condition of equipment
- Connect metal parts or components by welding, soldering, riveting, bolting, bonding, or screwing
- Cut, bend, or shape metal for applications, using equipment such as hydraulic benders and pipe threaders
- Erect scaffolds, platforms, or hoisting frames to access plant machinery or infrastructure for repair or replacement
- Perform preventive or corrective containment and cleanup measures to prevent environmental contamination
- Perform tunnel or field inspections of hydroelectric plant facilities or resources
- Take readings and record data such as water levels, temperatures, and flow rates
- Maintain logs, reports, work requests, and records

Career Path

Most entry-level jobs begin with classroom instruction and then a period of time working under experienced technicians. Workers advance to more responsible positions as they become familiar with the plant operations. There may also be additional training as workers advance up the job ladder. Over time, with training and experience, workers can advance to shift supervisor, trainer, or consultant.

Typically, energy companies promote from within. Most workers advance by moving up within the same company or by moving from one plant to another within the same company.

Earning Potential

Median hourly wage (2009): $23.92

Median annual wage (2009): $49,760

(Based on Bureau of Labor Statistics data for "Plant and System Operators, All Other)"

Education/Licensure

Typically, entry-level jobs require a high school diploma or GED and some formal postsecondary training, which may include an apprenticeship with on-the-job training and classroom instruction, a certificate, or an associate degree in a related field such as electronics or instrumentation technology.

Technical and community colleges offer associate degree programs and certifications, and technical institutes may also offer both. However, the latter institutions offer less general education and less theory than community or technical colleges. Depending on the institution and the course of study, a program may last a few weeks or up to two years for an associate degree.

Licensing requirements vary by state and by specific job functions. Some states require that electricians be licensed.

For More Information

American Public Power Association (APPANET)
1875 Connecticut Avenue, NW
Suite 1200
Washington, DC 20009-5715
www.appanet.org

Electric Power Supply Association (EPSA)
1401 New York Avenue, NW
11th Floor
Washington, DC 20005-2110
www.epsa.org

National Hydropower Association (NHA)
25 Massachusetts Avenue, NW
Suite 450
Washington, DC 20001
202-682-1700
www.hydro.org

Northwest Hydroelectric Association (NWHA)
P.O. Box 2517
Clackamas, Oregon 97015
503-545-9420
www.nwhydro.org

Hydroelectric Production Manager ☼⊕

Alternate Titles and Related Careers
- Engineer Manager
- Engineer Supervisor
- Hydroelectric Operations Supervisor
- Operations Manager
- Plant Manager

This is a "Bright Outlook" and "Green New and Emerging" occupation in the renewable energy-generation sector of the economy.

Job Trends

Data is still being collected on this occupation. However, as investments and interest in harnessing the nation's water resources to provide clean, reliable energy increase, the need for hydroelectric production managers should also increase.

Nature of the Work

Hydroelectric production managers manage operations at hydroelectric power-generation facilities. They monitor equipment to ensure that plants run safely and efficiently and are in conformance with regulations or required standards. They monitor and inspect facilities such as switchyards, control houses, and relay houses and equipment such as hydro-turbines, generators, and control systems.

Among the tasks that hydroelectric production managers may perform are the following, according to O*NET:
- Direct operations, maintenance, or repair of hydroelectric power facilities
- Check hydroelectric operations for compliance with prescribed operating limits, such as loads, voltages, temperatures, lines, and equipment
- Inspect hydroelectric facilities and equipment for normal operation and adherence to safety standards
- Create and enforce hydrostation voltage schedules
- Operate energized high- and low-voltage hydroelectric power transmission system substations according to procedures and safety requirements
- Perform or direct preventive or corrective containment and cleanup to protect the environment

- Plan and coordinate hydroelectric production operations to meet customer requirements
- Plan or manage hydroelectric plant upgrades
- Respond to problems related to rate payers, water users, power users, government agencies, educational institutions, and other private and public power resource interests
- Develop and implement projects to improve efficiency, economy, or effectiveness of hydroelectric plant operations
- Develop or implement policy evaluation procedures for hydroelectric generation activities
- Identify and communicate power system emergencies
- Supervise hydropower plant equipment installations, upgrades, or maintenance
- Provide technical direction in the erection and commissioning of hydroelectric equipment and supporting electrical or mechanical systems
- Develop or review budgets, annual plans, power contracts with other public or private utilities, power rates, standing operating procedures, power reviews, or engineering studies
- Maintain records of hydroelectric facility operations, maintenance, or repairs

Career Path

Employers typically prefer candidates with college degrees for entry-level positions on the manager track. Those who enter directly from college or graduate school typically enter a company-sponsored training program. In larger companies, new employees may work in a variety of departments in a company to become familiar with various operations. Some companies hire college graduates as first-line supervisors and promote them to management positions over time. Experience in some aspect of production operations is typically needed before advancement to upper-level management

such as plant manager, superintendent, or vice president of operations.

Some industrial production managers do begin as production workers, advancing to supervisory positions after a number of years of experience, while earning a college degree and being selected for management.

Earning Potential

Median hourly wage (2009): $40.90

Median annual wage (2009): $85,080

(Based on "Industrial Production Managers")

Education/Licensure

The majority of industrial production managers have either an associate degree or a bachelor's degree. Only about a quarter have only a high school diploma or less. Typically, for a production manager position, employers prefer to hire employees with a college degree in electrical, mechanical, industrial technology, or industrial engineering from a school accredited by the Accreditation Board for Engineering and Technology (ABET).

As noted in the *Occupation Outlook Handbook,* some colleges and universities offer five-year programs that culminate in a master's degree in engineering. Some offer five- or six-year programs that include cooperative experience. Some four-year schools have arrangements with community colleges or liberal arts colleges that allow students to spend two or three years at the initial school and transfer for the last two years to complete their engineering degree.

All fifty states and the District of Columbia require engineers to be licensed as professional engineers (PE) if they serve the public directly. In most states, licensure requires graduation from a four-year engineering program accredited by ABET, four years of experience, and passing the state exam. Many engineers take the Fundamentals of Engineering portion of the exam upon graduation.

They are then engineers in training (EIT). After obtaining appropriate work experience, they take the Principles and Practice of Engineering exam to complete their professional license. Most states recognize licenses from other states, as long as the requirements are the same or more stringent. Some states have continuing education requirements.

Some production managers earn certification to demonstrate their competency. The Association for Operations Management (APICS) offers the Certified in Production and Inventory Management (CPIM) certification that requires passing a series of exams that cover supply-chain management, resource planning, scheduling, production operations, and strategic planning. Successful candidates must renew their certifications every three years.

The American Society for Quality (ASQ) offers the Certified Manager of Quality/Organizational Excellence (CMQ/OE) credential. Candidates must have at least ten years of experience and pass an exam. To maintain the certification, candidates must take a certain number of professional development courses every three years.

For More Information

Accreditation Board for Engineering and
    Technology (ABET)
111 Market Place
Suite 1050
Baltimore, Maryland 21202
410-347-7700
www.abet.org

American Public Power Association (APPANET)
1875 Connecticut Avenue, NW
Suite 1200
Washington, DC 20009-5715
www.appanet.org

American Society for Quality (ASQ)
600 North Plankinton Avenue
Milwaukee, Wisconsin 53203
www.asq.org

Association for Operations Management (APICS)
8430 West Bryn Mawr Avenue
Suite 1000
Chicago, Illinois 60631
www.apics.org

Electric Power Supply Association (EPSA)
1401 New York Avenue, NW
11th Floor
Washington, DC 20005-2110
www.epsa.org

National Hydropower Association (NHA)
25 Massachusetts Avenue, NW
Suite 450
Washington, DC 20001
202-682-1700
www.hydro.org

Northwest Hydroelectric Association (NWHA)
P.O. Box 2517
Clackamas, Oregon 97015
503-545-9420
www.nwhydro.org

Hydrologist ⚡

Alternate Titles and Related Careers

- Dam Designer
- Hydraulic Engineer
- Hydrologic Engineer
- Project Manager—Hydro Licensing and Water Resources
- Senior Hydrologist
- Supervisory Civil Engineer/Hydrologist

This is a "Green Increased-Demand" occupation in the environment protection and research, design, and consulting services sectors of the economy. The occupation also has applications in the hydro-electric power sector.

 http://bit.ly/career30

Job Trends

The hydrologist category is projected to have faster than average growth between 2008 and 2018. This rate of 14 to 19 percent translates into 3,800 job openings. In 2008, according to the Bureau of Labor Statistics, 49 percent of hydrologists were employed at some level of government and 46 percent in professional, scientific, and technical services.

According to the *Occupational Outlook Handbook,* the need for energy sources, environmental protection, and responsible land and water management is driving the growth. Many hydrologists work in the area of environmentalism. They evaluate building sites for potential geologic hazards such as floods and landslides, study hazardous waste sites to determine the effect of pollutants, and consult on enforcement of government regulations related to clean water, rising sea levels, and deteriorating coastlines. Some hydrologists work in jobs related to the hydroelectric power industry.

About Geologists

Geologists, like hydrologists, study the composition, structure, and physical characteristics of the Earth. Petroleum geologists explore the subsurface of oceans or land as they look for oil and natural gas deposits. If the price of oil remains high, the *Occupational Outlook Handbook* projects that petroleum geologists will remain in demand. It suggests that those who can speak foreign languages and are willing to live abroad will have excellent prospects.

Nature of the Work

Hydrologists study the quantity, distribution, circulation, and physical properties of underground and surface water and the water cycle. Among the topics that they study are the form and intensity of precipitation, its rate of infiltration into the soil, its movement through the Earth, and its return to the ocean and atmosphere. Depending on the job level, hydrologists may coordinate and supervise the work of professional and technical staff, including research assistants, technologists, and technicians.

According to O*NET, hydrologists may perform the following tasks:

- Design and conduct scientific hydrogeological investigations to ensure that accurate and appropriate information is available for use in water resource management decisions
- Measure and graph phenomena like lake levels, stream flows, and changes in water volumes
- Answer questions and provide technical assistance and information to contractors or the public regarding issues such as well drilling, code requirements, hydrology, and geology
- Install, maintain, and calibrate instruments like those that monitor water levels, rainfall, and sediments
- Evaluate data and provide recommendations regarding the feasibility of municipal projects, such as hydroelectric power plants, irrigation systems, flood warning systems, and waste treatment facilities
- Design civil works associated with hydrographic activities and supervise their construction, installation, and maintenance
- Review applications for site plans and permits and recommend approval, denial, modification, or further investigative action
- Evaluate research data in terms of its impact on issues such as soil and water conservation, flood control planning, and water supply forecasting
- Monitor the work of well contractors, exploratory borers, and engineers and enforce rules regarding their activities
- Draft final reports describing research results

Hydrologists who work on environmental issues including hazardous waste and waste water may also:

- Prepare hydrogeologic evaluations of known or suspected hazardous waste sites and land treatment and feedlot facilities
- Study public water supply issues, including flood and drought risks, water quality, wastewater, and impacts on wetland habitats
- Collect and analyze water samples as part of field investigations or to validate data from automatic monitors
- Apply research findings to help minimize the environmental impacts of pollution, waterborne diseases, erosion, and sedimentation
- Investigate complaints or conflicts related to the alteration of public waters, gathering information, recommending alternatives, informing participants of progress, and preparing draft orders
- Conduct research and communicate information to promote the conservation and preservation of water resources
- Administer programs designed to ensure the proper sealing of abandoned wells

Career Path

Entry-level jobs in government or industry for hydrologists often are in field exploration or as research assistants or lab technicians. As hydrologists gain experience, they take on more complex assignments with less supervision. In time, they may become project leaders, program managers, or senior researchers. Some may move up to higher-level management positions where responsibilities increasingly involve scheduling and budgeting.

Earning Potential

Median hourly wage (2009): $35.42

Median annual wage (2009): $73,670

Education/Licensure

Typically, entry-level hydrology jobs require a master's degree in engineering from a school accredited by the Accreditation Board for Engineering and Technology (ABET). A degree in hydrology is not widespread, but some offer concentrations in hydrology. A degree in civil engineering, geosciences, or geology can also be a good foundation for a career in hydrology.

As noted in the *Occupation Outlook Handbook,* some colleges and universities offer five-year programs that culminate in a master's degree in engineering. Some offer five- or six-year programs that include cooperative experience. Some four-year schools have arrangements with community colleges or liberal arts colleges that allow students to spend two or three years at the initial school and transfer for the last two years to complete their engineering degree.

All fifty states and the District of Columbia require engineers to be licensed as professional engineers (PE) if they serve the public directly. In most states, licensure requires graduation from a four-year engineering program accredited by ABET, four years of experience, and passing the state exam. Many engineers take the Fundamentals of Engineering portion of the exam upon graduation. They are then engineers in training (EIT). After obtaining appropriate work experience, they take the Principles and Practice of Engineering exam to complete their professional license. Most states recognize licenses from other states, as long as the requirements are the same or more stringent. Some states have continuing education requirements.

Some states require that hydrologists who offer their services to the public be licensed. Licensing requirements vary by state, but generally a candidate for a license must have attained a certain educational level plus a certain number of years of experience, and pass an exam.

For More Information

Accreditation Board for Engineering and
 Technology (ABET)
111 Market Place
Suite 1050
Baltimore, Maryland 21202
410-347-7700
www.abet.org

American Geological Institute
4220 King Street
Alexandria, Virginia 22302-1502
703-379-2480
www.agiweb.org

NUCLEAR POWER INDUSTRY

The United States has 104 nuclear reactors operating in thirty-one states. The 1979 accident at Three Mile Island nuclear power plant stalled nuclear power development in the United States for close to three decades. However, the need for clean energy has created renewed interest in this sector of the energy industry. But to expand the number of nuclear plants in operation, a new workforce of nuclear engineers and technicians must be trained. In 2008, the U.S. Congress, through the Nuclear Regulatory Commission (NRC), provided $15 million to support education in nuclear science, engineering, and related trades. The goal of the funding is to develop a workforce that can design, construct, operate, and regulate nuclear facilities and the handling of nuclear materials safely.

According to Samuel W. Bodman, Secretary of Energy under President George W. Bush, the "building of a new nuclear plant creates, on average more than 1400" construction jobs and at the peak level of building, 2400 jobs. "The operation of a nuclear plant generates 400 to 700 permanent jobs, and these jobs pay, on average, 36 percent more than average salaries in the local area." There are also the indirect, or secondary, jobs that are created in an area as a result of the

plant being built, as well as the federal, state, and local tax payments that are estimated to be $95 million annually.

Nuclear Engineer

Alternate Titles and Related Careers
- Criticality Safety Engineer
- Engineer
- Generation Engineer
- Nuclear Design Engineer
- Nuclear Licensing Engineer
- Nuclear Process Engineer
- Nuclear Reactor Engineer
- Resident Inspector
- System Engineer

This is a "Green Enhanced-Skills" occupation in the governmental and regulatory administration and research, design, and consulting services sectors of the economy. There are also opportunities in the renewable energygeneration sector.

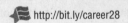 http://bit.ly/career28

Job Trends

The Bureau of Labor Statistics estimates 5,400 job openings between 2008 and 2018. This is rated an average rate of growth at 7 to 13 percent. About 42 percent of nuclear engineers work for utilities; 34 percent for professional, scientific, and technical services; and 13 percent for government.

The United States has not built any new nuclear power plants for almost thirty years. However, nuclear power is considered by many to be a viable way to curb carbon emissions from energy generation. The Obama administration committed to making nuclear power one of the solutions for reducing greenhouse gases. In 2010, for example, the U.S. Department of Energy announced loan guarantees of up to $8.33 billion to a consortium of three power companies to build and operate two nuclear power plants in Georgia. Increased interest in nuclear power will spur demand for nuclear engineers to research and develop new designs for reactors and to work in those plants.

Nature of the Work

Nuclear engineers conduct research on nuclear engineering problems or apply the principles and theory of nuclear science to problems concerned with the release, control, and utilization of nuclear energy and with nuclear waste disposal. They research and develop the processes, instruments, and systems used to derive benefits from nuclear energy and radiation. Nuclear engineers who work in the power industry may work on the nuclear fuel cycle or on the development of fusion energy. The nuclear fuel cycle is the production, handling, and use of nuclear fuel and the safe disposal of waste produced by the generation of nuclear energy.

Because of the presence of radioactive material and the potential for harm if it falls into the wrong hands, nuclear power plant and transmission stations have very strict security guidelines for employees.

The following are among the tasks that a nuclear engineer in the power-generation energy industry may perform, according to O*NET:

- Monitor nuclear facility operations to identify any design, construction, or operation practices that violate safety regulations and laws or that could jeopardize the safety of operations
- Examine accidents to obtain data that can be used to design preventive measures
- Initiate corrective actions or order plant shutdowns in emergency situations
- Recommend preventive measures to be taken in the handling of nuclear technology, based on data obtained from operations monitoring or from evaluation of test results
- Write operational instructions to be used in nuclear plant operation and nuclear fuel and waste handling and disposal

- Direct operating and maintenance activities of operational nuclear power plants to ensure efficiency and conformity to safety standards
- Prepare construction project proposals that include cost estimates and discuss proposals with interested parties such as vendors, contractors, and nuclear facility review boards
- Design and oversee construction and operation of nuclear reactors and power plants and nuclear fuels reprocessing and reclamation systems

Nuclear engineers engaged in research in the nuclear power-generation industry may:

- Perform experiments that will provide information about acceptable methods of nuclear material usage, nuclear fuel reclamation, and waste disposal
- Design and develop nuclear equipment such as reactor cores, radiation shielding, and associated instrumentation and control mechanisms
- Conduct tests of nuclear fuel behavior and cycles and performance of nuclear machinery and equipment, to optimize performance of existing plants
- Synthesize analyses of test results, and use the results to prepare technical reports of findings and recommendations
- Analyze available data and consult with other scientists to determine parameters of experimentation and suitability of analytical models
- Design and direct nuclear research projects to discover facts, to test or modify theoretical models, or to develop new theoretical models or new uses for current models

Career Path

A master's degree is required for many jobs in nuclear engineering. Typically, entry-level engineers work as assistant engineers under the supervision of experienced engineers. They may also be required to take additional class work. As they gain knowledge and experience, they are given more complex tasks and greater responsibility and independence. Over time, they may become senior engineers and supervise a staff or team of engineers and technicians. Eventually, some will move into higher-level management and become executives.

Earning Potential

Median hourly wage (2009): $46.59

Median annual wage (2009): $96,910

Education/Licensure

A bachelor's degree is the minimum requirement for entry-level jobs, but a master's degree from a school accredited by the Accreditation Board for Engineering and Technology (ABET) is required for many nuclear engineering jobs. As noted in the *Occupation Outlook Handbook,* some colleges and universities offer five-year programs that culminate in a master's degree in engineering. Some offer five- or six-year programs that include cooperative experience. Some four-year schools have arrangements with community colleges or liberal arts colleges that allow students to spend two or three years at the initial school and transfer for the last two years to complete their engineering degree.

All fifty states and the District of Columbia require engineers to be licensed as professional engineers (PE) if they serve the public directly. In most states, licensure requires graduation from a four-year engineering program accredited by ABET, four years of experience, and passing the state exam. Many engineers take the Fundamentals of Engineering portion of the exam upon graduation. They are then engineers in training (EIT). After obtaining appropriate work experience, they take the Principles and Practice of Engineering exam to complete their professional license. Most states recognize licenses from other states, as long as the requirements are the same or more stringent. Some states have continuing education requirements.

The Nuclear Regulatory Commission (NRC) provides training for its employees, and the nuclear industry provides training for employees of nuclear power plants.

For More Information

Accreditation Board for Engineering and
    Technology (ABET)
111 Market Place
Suite 1050
Baltimore, Maryland 21202
410-347-7700
www.abet.org

American Nuclear Society (ANS)
555 North Kensington Avenue
La Grange Park, Illinois 60526
www.ans.org

Nuclear Energy Institute (NEI)
1776 I Street, NW
Suite 400
Washington, DC 20006-3708
202-739-8000
www.nei.org

U.S. Nuclear Regulatory Commission (NRC)
Washington, DC 20555-0001
800-368-5642
www.nrc.gov

Nuclear Equipment Operations Technician ⑤

Alternate Titles and Related Careers

- Auxiliary Operator
- Licensed Nuclear Operator
- Nuclear Auxiliary Operator
- Nuclear Equipment Operator

- Nuclear Plant Equipment Operator
- Nuclear Station Plant Equipment Operator
- Radiation Protection Technician (RPT)
- Systems Operator

This is a "Green Enhanced-Skills" occupation in the renewable energy generation sector of the economy.

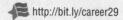 http://bit.ly/career29

Job Trends

In 2008, there were 6,000 workers employed as nuclear technicians, and the projected rate of job growth would add 2,800 openings between 2008 and 2018. This growth rate of 7 to 13 percent is about average for all occupations. They will be needed to monitor the current aging nuclear reactors, to research future advances in nuclear power, and to work in new nuclear plants if current plans to build them are realized.

The United States has not built any new nuclear power plants for almost thirty years. However, nuclear power is considered by many to be a viable way to curb carbon emissions from energy generation. The Obama administration committed to making nuclear power one of the solutions for reducing greenhouse gases. In 2010, for example, the U.S. Department of Energy announced loan guarantees of up to $8.33 billion to a consortium of three power companies to build and operate two nuclear power plants in Georgia. Increased interest in nuclear power will spur demand for nuclear engineers to research and develop new designs for reactors and to work in those plants.

Nature of the Work

Nuclear equipment operation technicians operate the equipment use for the release, control, and utilization of nuclear energy to assist scientists in laboratory and production activities. Because of the presence of radioactive material and the potential for harm if it falls into the wrong hands, nuclear power plant and transmission stations have very strict security guidelines for employees.

According to O*NET, nuclear equipment operation technicians may perform the following duties:

- Modify, devise, and maintain equipment used in operations
- Set control panel switches, according to standard procedures, to route electric power from sources and direct particle beams through injector units
- Submit computations to supervisors for review
- Calculate equipment operating factors, such as radiation times, dosages, temperatures, gamma intensities, and pressures, using standard formulas and conversion tables
- Perform testing, maintenance, repair, and upgrading of accelerator systems
- Monitor instruments, gauges, and recording devices in control rooms during operation of equipment, under direction of nuclear experimenters
- Write summaries of activities and record experimental data, such as accelerator performance, systems status, particle beam specification, and beam conditions obtained

For those working with nuclear materials, it is especially important to follow policies and procedures for radiation workers in order to ensure their own safety and that of other employees. One of the duties of a nuclear equipment operation technician is to warn maintenance workers of radiation hazards and direct workers to leave hazardous areas.

Career Path

Most employers prefer applicants with two years of specialized postsecondary training or an associate degree in applied science or a science-related technology. Typically, entry-level jobs for technicians are trainee positions. They begin work under the supervision of a scientist or engineer or more experienced technician. As they gain experience, technicians are given more complex responsibility and more independence. In time, some technicians become supervisors. Those with bachelor's degrees may be promoted to professional-level jobs with experience or a graduate degree.

Earning Potential

Median hourly wage (2009): $32.37

Median annual wage (2009): $67,340

Education/Licensure

Forty-six percent of nuclear technicians have a bachelor's degree or higher in nuclear engineering, engineering, engineering technology, or a related science. Thirty-five percent have some college education, typically, an associate degree in a technical discipline. Entry-level employees also receive on-the-job training.

For More Information

American Nuclear Society (ANS)
555 North Kensington Avenue
La Grange Park, Illinois 60526
www.ans.org

Nuclear Energy Institute (NEI)
1776 I Street, NW
Suite 400
Washington, DC 20006-3708
202-739-8000
www.nei.org

U.S. Nuclear Regulatory Commission (NRC)
Washington, DC 20555-0001
800-368-5642
www.nrc.gov

Nuclear Power Reactor Operator ✪

Alternate Titles and Related Careers

- Control Room Supervisor
- Nuclear Control Operator
- Nuclear Control Room Nonlicensed Operator
- Nuclear Control Room Operator
- Nuclear Operator
- Nuclear Plant Operator (NPO)
- Nuclear Power Reactor Operation
- Nuclear Station Operator
- Reactor Operator (RO)
- Unit Reactor Operator

This is a "Green Enhanced-Skills" occupation in the renewable energy generation sector of the economy.

Job Trends

This occupation is expected to grow at a faster-than-average rate of 14 to 19 percent, between 2008 and 2018, which translates into 2,700 jobs. In 2008, there were 5,000 employees in this category.

The United States has not built any new nuclear power plants for almost thirty years. However, nuclear power is considered by many to be a viable way to curb carbon emissions from energy generation. The Obama administration committed to making nuclear power one of the solutions for reducing greenhouse gases. In 2010, for example, the U.S. Department of Energy announced loan guarantees of up to $8.33 billion to a consortium of three power companies to build and operate two nuclear power plants in Georgia. Increased interest in nuclear power will spur demand for nuclear engineers to research and develop new designs for reactors and to work in those plants.

Nature of the Work

Nuclear power reactor operators control and operate nuclear reactors. Reactor operators must be licensed by the Nuclear Regulatory Commission

(NRC). At least one senior operator must be on duty during each shift at a reactor to act as plant supervisor. Nuclear power plant and transmission stations have very strict security guidelines for employees because of the potential for harm if the nuclear material falls into the wrong hands.

Among the duties that nuclear power reactor operators may perform, according to O*NET, are the following:

- Adjust controls according to standard procedures to position rod and to regulate flux level, reactor period, coolant temperature, and rate of power flow
- Monitor all systems for normal running conditions, performing activities such as checking gauges to assess output or the effects of generator loading on other equipment
- Implement operational procedures such as those controlling start-up and shut-down activities
- Monitor and operate boilers, turbines, wells, and auxiliary power plant equipment
- Respond to system or unit abnormalities, diagnosing the cause, and recommending or taking corrective action
- Note malfunctions of equipment, instruments, or controls, and report these conditions to supervisors
- Dispatch orders and instructions to coordinate auxiliary equipment operation
- Record operating data
- Participate in nuclear fuel element handling activities, such as preparation, transfer, loading, and unloading
- Conduct inspections and operations outside of control rooms as necessary
- Authorize maintenance activities on units and changes in equipment and system operational status
- Direct reactor operators in emergency situations, in accordance with emergency operating procedures

Nuclear power reactor operators are subject to random drug and alcohol tests and must pass a medical exam every two years.

Career Path

Most nuclear power reactor operators begin as equipment or auxiliary operators with on-the-job training. While working under more experienced workers, they learn the basics of plant operations. With experience and further training, they may sit for the NRC licensing exam for reactor operator. Over time, they may become senior reactor operators with responsibility for all the controls in a reactor's control room.

Earning Potential

Median hourly wage (2009): $34.93

Median annual wage (2009): $72,650

Education/Licensure

Typically, nuclear power reactor operators have bachelor's degrees in engineering or the physical sciences from a school accredited by the Accreditation Board of Engineering Technology (ABET). As noted in the *Occupation Outlook Handbook,* some colleges and universities offer five-year programs that culminate in a master's degree in engineering. Some offer five- or six-year programs that include cooperative experience. Some four-year schools have arrangements with community colleges or liberal arts colleges that allow students to spend two or three years at the initial school and transfer for the last two years to complete their engineering degree.

Nuclear reactor operators must be licensed by the Nuclear Regulatory Commission (NRC) and pass periodic qualifying exams also conducted by the NRC. The purpose of the testing is to ensure that the operators have maintained their skill level and can respond to various situations that evaluate their knowledge of the power plant and the interaction of its various components.

Training for nuclear power plant operator includes simulator and on-the-job training, classroom instruction, and individual study. Before beginning training, a nuclear power plant operator must have three years of power plant experience. At least one of those three years must be at the nuclear power plant where the operator is to be licensed; six months should be as a non-licensed operator at the plant. Training generally takes at least one year, after which the worker must take an NRC-administered written examination and operating test.

To maintain their licenses, reactor operators must pass an annual practical plant-operating exam and a biennial written exam administered by their employers. Reactor operators can upgrade their licenses to the senior-reactor-operator level after a year of licensed experience at the plant by taking another examination given by the NRC.

Individuals with a bachelor's degree in engineering or the equivalent may apply for senior operator's licenses directly if they have three years of nuclear power plant experience, with at least six months at the site. Although waivers are possible, generally, licensed nuclear power reactor operators and senior operators have to pass a new written exam and operating test administered by the NRC if they transfer from one facility to another.

For More Information

Accreditation Board for Engineering and
    Technology (ABET)
111 Market Place
Suite 1050
Baltimore, Maryland 21202
410-347-7700
www.abet.org

American Nuclear Society (ANS)
555 North Kensington Avenue
La Grange Park, Illinois 60526
www.ans.org

Nuclear Energy Institute (NEI)
1776 I Street, NW
Suite 400
Washington, DC 20006-3708
202-739-8000
www.nei.org

U.S. Nuclear Regulatory Commission (NRC)
Washington, DC 20555-0001
800-368-5642
www.nrc.gov

SOLAR POWER

Solar power can be generated either directly by capturing the sun's energy with photovoltaic (PV) cells, or by using the sun's energy to boil water that is then used to provide power. The latter is called solar thermal or concentrated power (CSP), and PV cells are what cover solar panels. As part of the American Recovery and Reinvestment Act (ARRA), the federal government invested $62 million over five years in research and development of CSP systems.

Solar Energy Installation Manager ✪ ⑤

Alternate Titles and Related Careers
- Foreman
- Project Manager

This is a "Bright Outlook" and "Green New and Emerging" occupation in renewable energy generation.

Job Trends

This occupation is expected to grow at a faster-than-average rate of 14 to 19 percent between 2008 and 2018. The expansion of the solar photovoltaic and CSP sectors is driving this growth. The Bureau of Labor Statistics groups this occupation in the category of "First-Line Supervisors/Managers."

Nature of the Work

Solar energy installation managers direct work crews that install residential or commercial solar photovoltaic or thermal systems. They estimate materials, equipment, and personnel needs for residential and commercial solar installation projects. Among the tasks that solar energy installation managers may perform, according to O*NET, are the following:

- Assess potential solar installation sites to determine feasibility and design requirements
- Plan and coordinate installations of photovoltaic (PV) solar and solar thermal systems to ensure conformance to codes
- Prepare solar installation project proposals, quotes, budgets, or schedules
- Evaluate subcontractors or subcontractor bids for quality, cost, and reliability
- Supervise solar installers, technicians, and subcontractors for solar installation projects to ensure compliance with safety standards
- Monitor work of contractors and subcontractors to ensure projects conform to plans, specifications, schedules, or budgets
- Perform start-up of systems for testing or customer implementation
- Assess system performance or functionality at the system, subsystem, and component levels
- Coordinate or schedule building inspections for solar installation projects
- Develop and maintain system architecture, including all piping, instrumentation, or process flow diagrams
- Identify means to reduce costs, minimize risks, or increase efficiency of solar installation projects
- Provide technical assistance to installers, technicians, or other solar professionals in areas such as solar electric systems, solar thermal systems, electrical systems, and mechanical systems

Career Path

New employees begin work as helpers to experienced solar panel installers. Over time they take on more responsibility on projects and work their way up to installation manager.

Over time, some experienced installation managers may move into sales, and others may become consultants to homeowners or businesses interested in converting to solar power. Some may start their own solar panel or thermal installation companies. Coursework in management, accounting, and marketing can be useful for new business owners.

Earning Potential

Median hourly wage (2009): $28.04

Median annual wage (2009): $58,330

Education/Licensure

About 60 percent of first-line managers have a high school diploma or less. Thirty percent have some college, and 10 percent have a bachelor's degree or higher.

Community colleges, technical colleges, and vocational institutes, as well as private, for-profit training organizations offer training for a variety of solar PV and thermal degrees and certificates. The North American Board of Certified Energy Practitioners offers both the Solar Thermal Installer Certificate and the Photovoltaic Installer Certification. These can be useful in demonstrating an individual's competence in the field.

For More Information

American Solar Energy Society (ASES)
2400 Central Avenue
Suite A
Boulder, Colorado 80301
303-443-3130
www.ases.org

North American Board of Certified Energy
Practitioners (NABCEP)
634 Plank Road
Suite 102
Clifton Park, New York 12065
800-654-0021
www.nabcep.org

Solar Electric Power Association (SEPA)
1220 19th Street, NW
Suite 401
Washington, DC 20036-2405
202-857-0898
www.solarelectricpower.org

Solar Industries Association (SEIA)
575 7th Street, NW
Suite 400
Washington, DC 20009
202-682-0556
www.seia.org

Solar Living Institute (SLI)
13771 South Highway 101
P.O. Box 836
Hopland, California 95449
707-472-2450
www.solarliving.org

Solar Energy Systems Engineer ☼🌎

Alternate Titles and Related Careers
- Commercial Project Engineer
- Director of Engineering and Operations
- Principal Electrical Engineer—Solar PV
- Principal Systems Engineer—Solar Systems
- PV Power Systems Engineer
- Senior Renewable Energy Systems Engineer—Solar
- Solar Energy Engineer
- Solar Energy Systems Design Engineer
- Solar PV Systems Engineer
- Solar PV Utility Manager
- Solar Systems Designer

This is a "Bright Outlook" and "Green New and Emerging" occupation in the renewable energy generation sector of the economy.

Job Trends

The Bureau of Labor Statistics projects an average growth rate of 7 to 13 percent for the engineering category. However, as a "Bright Outlook" occupation, solar energy systems engineers should see expanded job opportunities.

Nature of the Work

Solar energy systems engineers conduct engineering site audits to collect structural, electrical, and related site information. This information is used to design solar hot water and space heating systems for new and existing residential, commercial, and industrial structures. In the design process, solar energy systems engineers apply knowledge of structural energy requirements, local climates, solar technology, and thermodynamics.

According to O*NET, solar energy systems engineers may perform the following job tasks:
- Design or coordinate design of photovoltaic (PV) or solar thermal systems, including system components
- Create plans for solar energy system development, monitoring, and evaluation activities
- Perform computer simulation of solar photovoltaic (PV) generation system performance or energy production to optimize efficiency
- Develop design specifications and functional requirements for residential, commercial, or industrial solar energy systems or components
- Create electrical single-line diagrams, panel schedules, or connection diagrams for solar electric systems using computer-aided design (CAD) software
- Create checklists for review or inspection of completed solar installation projects

- Provide technical direction or support to installation teams during installation, start-up, testing, system commissioning, or performance monitoring
- Develop standard operation procedures and quality or safety standards for solar installation work
- Design or develop vacuum tube collector systems for solar applications
- Perform thermal, stress, or cost reduction analyses for solar systems
- Review specifications and recommend engineering or manufacturing changes to achieve solar design objectives
- Test or evaluate photovoltaic (PV) cells or modules

Career Path

As engineers gain experience, they become specialists and advance into positions where they supervise a team of engineers and other staff. Some eventually become managers or move into sales jobs where their technical background is particularly useful. Some go on to earn a master's in business administration (MBA) to prepare them for higher level managerial positions.

Earning Potential

Median hourly wage (2009): $43.06

Median annual wage (2009): $89,560

(Based on "Engineers, All Other")

Education/Licensure

Typically, this occupation requires an engineering degree from a college or university accredited by the Accreditation Board of Engineering and Technology (ABET). Typically, a degree in electrical engineering is preferred for a solar energy systems engineer position. However, a degree in a related technical field may also be acceptable.

Some colleges and universities offer five-year programs that culminate in a master's degree. Some

offer five- or six-year programs that include cooperative experience. Some four-year schools have arrangements with community colleges or liberal arts colleges that allow students to spend two or three years at the initial school and transfer for the last two years to complete their engineering degree.

All fifty states and the District of Columbia require engineers to be licensed as professional engineers (PE) if they serve the public directly. In most states, licensure requires graduation from a four-year engineering program accredited by ABET, four years of experience, and passing the state exam. Many engineers take the Fundamentals of Engineering portion of the exam upon graduation. They are then engineers in training (EIT). After obtaining appropriate work experience, they take the Principles and Practice of Engineering exam to complete their professional license. Most states recognize licenses from other states, as long as the requirements are the same or more stringent. Some states have continuing education requirements.

For More Information

Accreditation Board for Engineering and Technology (ABET)
111 Market Place
Suite 1050
Baltimore, Maryland 21202
(410) 347-7700
www.abet.org

American Solar Energy Society (ASES)
2400 Central Avenue
Suite A
Boulder, Colorado 80301
303-443-3130
www.ases.org

Solar Electric Power Association (SEPA)
1220 19th Street, NW
Suite 401
Washington, DC 20036-2405
202-857-0898
www.solarelectricpower.org

Solar Industries Association (SEIA)
575 7th Street, NW
Suite 400
Washington, DC 20009
202-682-0556
www.seia.org

Solar Living Institute (SLI)
13771 South Highway 101
P.O. Box 836
Hopland, California 95449
707-472-2450
www.solarliving.org

Solar Fabrication Technician ⊕

Alternate Titles and Related Careers
- Journeyman Sheetmetal Worker
- PV Fabrication and Testing Technician
- Sheet Metal Apprentice
- Sheet Metal Layout Mechanic
- Sheet Metal Mechanic
- Sheet Metal Worker

This job is not classified by the Bureau of Labor Statistics, but it is similar to the job of a sheet metal worker, which in general is a "Green Enhanced-Skills" occupation in green construction, manufacturing, and renewable energygeneration sectors of the economy. The occupation fits into the first two categories because a sheet metal worker may be involved in the installing of green technology into new and existing construction or in the industrial manufacture of green technology.

Job Trends

Sheet metal worker is rated as having a slower-than-average job growth of 3 to 6 percent between 2008 and 2018. Total projected job openings are 51,700. A solar fabrication technician builds large solar collector arrays. As the solar power industry grows, the need for skilled workers for this occupation should also grow.

According to the *Occupational Outlook Handbook,* job prospects should be especially good for sheet metal workers with apprenticeship training and a welding certification.

Nature of the Work

Solar fabrication technicians create large solar panel arrays for commercial entities such as public utilities. The solar panels on sun farms are the work of solar fabrication technicians. These technicians do not work on residential structures and do not do any of the wiring involved in setting up the solar panel arrays. Metal steel, copper sheet metal, tubing, and pipefittings are typical materials used in the job.

The work may involve setting up and operating fabricating machines to cut, bend, and straighten sheet metal. They also shape metal over anvils, blocks, or forms using a hammer. Some sheet metal workers operate soldering and welding equipment to join sheet metal parts, inspecting, assembling, and smoothing seams and joints of burred surfaces. Sheet metal workers must be able to read and follow blueprints, drawings, templates, and written and oral instructions and convert blueprints into shop drawings. They must be able to use calculators, scribes, dividers, squares, rulers, calipers, scales, and micrometers, as well as power equipment such as drills, soldering irons, and riveters.

According to O*NET, the following are the tasks that a sheet metal worker may perform:
- Determine project requirements including scope, assembly sequences, and required methods and materials
- Lay out, measure, and mark dimensions and reference lines on material
- Maneuver completed units into position for installation
- Install assemblies in supportive frameworks
- Select gauges and types of sheet metal or nonmetallic material according to the product specifications

- Drill and punch holes in metal, for screws, bolts, and rivets
- Fasten seams and joints together
- Fabricate or alter parts at construction sites
- Maintain equipment, making repairs and modifications when necessary
- Transport prefabricated parts to construction sites for assembly and installation
- Develop and lay out patterns that use materials most efficiently, using computerized metalworking equipment to experiment with different layouts
- Inspect individual parts, assemblies, and installation for conformance to specifications and building codes

Career Path

Becoming a solar fabrication technician typically requires work experience in the building trades or some type of formal training. Experienced fabricators may advance to supervisory jobs. In time, they may become building inspectors on job sites or quality control inspectors within manufacturing plants. They may also go into business for themselves as solar installation contractors.

Earning Potential

Median hourly wage (2009): $19.54

Median annual wage (2009): $40,640

Education/Licensure

Typically, a high school diploma or equivalent is required for entry-level workers. Individuals new to solar panel fabrication typically have construction training and work experience. They may be graduates of a vocational or technical school or an on-the-job apprenticeship.

The Fabricators & Manufacturers Association, Intl (FMA) offers a Precision Sheet Metal Operator (PSMO) Certificate. FMA also offers online webinars and courses.

For More Information

American Solar Energy Society (ASES)
2400 Central Avenue
Suite A
Boulder, Colorado 80301
303-443-3130
www.ases.org

Fabricators & Manufacturers Association, Intl (FMA)
833 Featherstone Road
Rockford, Illinois 61107
888-394-4362
www.fmanet.org

Sheet Metal Workers International Association (SMWIA)
1750 New York Avenue, NW
6th Floor
Washington, DC 20006
www.smwia.org

Solar Electric Power Association (SEPA)
1220 19th Street, NW
Suite 401
Washington, DC 20036-2405
202-857-0898
www.solarelectricpower.org

Solar Industries Association (SEIA)
575 7th Street, NW
Suite 400
Washington, DC 20009
202-682-0556
www.seia.org

Solar Living Institute (SLI)
13771 South Highway 101
P.O. Box 836
Hopland, California 95449
707-472-2450
www.solarliving.org

Solar Photovoltaic Installer ✿⊛

Alternate Titles and Related Careers
- Solar Field Service Technician
- Solar Installation Electrician
- Solar Installation Technician Commercial
- Solar Installation Technician Residential
- Solar and PV Installation Roofer

This is a "Bright Outlook" and "Green New and Emerging" occupation in the renewable energy-generation sector of the economy.

Job Trends

The statistics are based on the Bureau of Labor's category of "Construction and Related Workers, All Other," which projects an average growth rate of 7 to 13 percent for this category between 2008 and 2018. This translates into 26,600 new employees overall. However, as a "Bright Outlook" occupation in the renewable energy sector, it may require more workers more quickly than anticipated.

Nature of the Work

Solar photovoltaic installers assemble, install, or maintain solar photovoltaic (PV) systems on roofs or other structures in compliance with site assessments and schematics. These systems may include solar collectors, concentrators, pumps, and fans. In the course of their jobs, solar photovoltaic installers may work with modules, arrays, batteries, power conditioning equipment, safety systems, structural systems, and weather sealing.

Their work may include measuring, cutting, assembling, and bolting structural framing and solar modules. They may also perform minor electrical work such as current checks.

According to O*NET, solar photovoltaic installers may perform the following duties:
- Diagram layouts and locations for photovoltaic (PV) arrays and equipment, including existing building or site features
- Examine designs to determine current requirements for all parts of the photovoltaic (PV) system electrical circuit
- Identify electrical, environmental, and safety hazards associated with photovoltaic (PV) installations
- Identify installation locations with proper orientation, area, solar access, or structural integrity for photovoltaic (PV) arrays
- Identify methods for laying out, orienting, and mounting modules or arrays to ensure efficient installation, electrical configuration, or system maintenance
- Assemble solar modules, panels, or support structures
- Install photovoltaic (PV) systems in accordance with codes and standards using drawings, schematics, and instructions
- Determine appropriate sizes, ratings, and locations for all system overcurrent devices, disconnect devices, grounding equipment, and surge suppression equipment
- Determine connection interfaces for additional subpanels or for connecting photovoltaic (PV) systems with utility services or other power-generation sources
- Determine photovoltaic (PV) system designs or configurations based on factors such as customer needs, expectations, and site conditions
- Perform routine photovoltaic (PV) system maintenance and balance of systems equipment
- Activate photovoltaic (PV) systems to verify system functionality and conformity to performance expectations
- Apply weather sealing to array, building, or support mechanisms
- Check electrical installation for proper wiring, polarity, grounding, or integrity of terminations
- Identify and resolve any deficiencies in photovoltaic (PV) system installation or materials

- Install module array interconnect wiring, implementing measures to disable arrays during installation
- Install required labels on solar system components and hardware
- Measure and analyze system performance and operating parameters to assess operating condition of systems or equipment
- Program, adjust, or configure inverters and controls for desired set points and operating modes
- Select mechanical designs, installation equipment, or installation plans that conform to environmental, architectural, structural, site, and code requirements
- Test operating voltages to ensure operation within acceptable limits for power-conditioning equipment, such as inverters and controllers
- Visually inspect and test photovoltaic (PV) modules or systems
- Compile or maintain records of system operation, performance, and maintenance
- Demonstrate system functionality and performance, including start-up, shut-down, normal operation, and emergency or bypass operations
- Determine materials, equipment, and installation sequences necessary to maximize installation efficiency

Career Path

Entry-level solar photovoltaic technicians begin work under the supervision of more experienced workers. Over time, they are given more complex work and more independence in accomplishing it. Some become supervisors or become electrical inspectors. Others start their own businesses as consultants or as solar panel installation contractors.

Earning Potential

Median hourly wage (2009): $16.34

Median annual wage (2009): $33,980

Education/Licensure

Entry-level jobs in construction typically require a high school diploma or equivalent and generally start workers as laborers, helpers, or apprentices. Skilled occupations such as solar photovoltaic technician require classroom instruction and on-the-job training that may be gotten by attending a technical or trade school, participating in an apprenticeship, or taking part in an employer-provided training program. Some community colleges, technical schools and institutes, and trade associations offer short-term online training programs.

Apprenticeships are administered by local employers, trade associations, and trade unions and provide the most thorough training. Typically, they last between three and five years and combine on-the-job training and 144 hours or more of related classroom instruction for each year of the program. The Independent Electrical Contractors (IEC) operates apprenticeship training programs for individuals wishing to become electricians, as does the International Brotherhood of Electrical Workers (IBEW).

Solar power training certification is currently voluntary, but some states are looking into requiring it. The North American Board of Certified Energy Practitioners (NABCEP) provides the Solar Photovoltaic Installer Certification program. Most states require licensing for electricians.

For More Information

American Solar Energy Society (ASES)
2400 Central Avenue
Suite A
Boulder, Colorado 80301
303-443-3130
www.ases.org

Independent Electrical Contractors (IEC)
4401 Ford Avenue
Suite 1100
Alexandria, Virginia 22303
703-549-7351
www.ieci.org

International Brotherhood of Electrical Workers
   (IBEW)
900 Seventh Street, NW
Washington, DC 20001
202-833-7000
www.ibew.org

North American Board of Certified Energy
   Practitioners (NABCEP)
634 Plank Road
Suite 102
Clifton Park, New York 12065
800-654-0021
www.nabcep.org

Solar Electric Power Association (SEPA)
1220 19th Street, NW
Suite 401
Washington, DC 20036-2405
202-857-0898
www.solarelectricpower.org

Solar Industries Association (SEIA)
575 7th Street, NW
Suite 400
Washington, DC 20009
202-682-0556
www.seia.org

Solar Living Institute (SLI)
13771 South Highway 101
P.O. Box 836
Hopland, California 95449
707-472-2450
www.solarliving.org

Solar Sales Representative and Assessor ☼ 🌐

Alternate Titles and Related Careers

- Account Manager
- Assistant Sales Manager
- Director, Regional Sales
- Independent Sales Representative, Solar
- Outside Solar Energy Sales Representative
- Outside Solar Sales Representative
- Outside Sales Representative, Residential Solar
- PV Sales Representative, Commercial
- Senior Account Executive
- Solar Account Executive
- Solar PV Sales Representative

This is a "Bright Outlook" and "Green New and Emerging" occupation in the renewable energy generation sector of the economy. The term "outside," also called "field sales," means that the sales job requires traveling to customers' sites rather than phone sales, which is also known as "inside" sales.

Job Trends

Using information for "Sales Representatives, Wholesale and Manufacturing, Technical and Scientific Products" as the basis, the Bureau of Labor Statistics projects an average growth of 7 to 13 percent for this category. This translates into 42,000 estimated job openings between 2008 and 2018 for all technical and scientific salespeople. However, as a "Bright Outlook" occupation in the renewable energy generation sector, it may see faster growth and a greater expansion of job opportunities. Job prospects will be best for those with a college degree, the appropriate technical experience, and an outgoing personality with good communication skills.

Nature of the Work

Sales representatives may work for large manufacturers or wholesalers, or in the case of solar sales representatives/assessors, they may work for small companies that install the end product—solar panels or solar thermal systems. In the distribution chain, the small company that does the installation is probably visited by a sales representative from a manufacturer of solar panels who wants the installer to buy panels only from his/her employer. Some sales representatives who have been successful working for manufacturers or wholesalers may start their own independent agencies and represent several different manufacturers or wholesalers. Regardless of for whom the sales representative works, the goal is the same: to convince the customer to buy from the sales representative.

Solar sales representatives and assessors contact new or existing customers to determine their solar equipment needs. They analyze, or assess, the site and suggest systems or equipment and estimate the costs for purchase and installation. It is important that they stay current with the latest products and trends in the industry as well as the changing needs of the marketplace.

According to O*NET, a solar sales representative and assessor may perform the following tasks:

- Develop marketing or strategic plans for sales territories
- Generate solar energy customer leads to develop new accounts
- Assess sites to determine suitability for solar equipment
- Calculate potential solar resources or solar array production for a particular site, considering issues such as climate, shading, and roof orientation
- Gather information from prospective customers to identify their solar energy needs
- Select solar energy products, systems, or services for customers based on electrical energy requirements, site conditions, price, or other factors

- Create customized energy management packages to satisfy customer needs
- Prepare proposals, quotes, contracts, or presentations for potential solar customers
- Provide customers with information such as quotes, orders, sales, shipping, warranties, credit, funding options, incentives, or tax rebates
- Prepare or review detailed design drawings, specifications, or lists related to solar installations
- Provide technical information about solar power, solar systems, equipment, and services to potential customers or dealers
- Demonstrate use of solar and related equipment to customers or dealers

Career Path

While sales jobs in general do not have formal educational requirements, technical and scientific product sales jobs typically require a degree. A beginning salesperson may ride along with an experienced sales representative for a short period to become familiar with the product line, how customers react to the product, and the questions they ask.

Promotion typically means taking on bigger accounts or a larger territory. Individuals with good sales records and leadership abilities may advance to management jobs such as sales supervisor, district manager, or vice president of sales. Some may move into other areas of the business such as marketing and advertising or become trainers for new sales employees. Others may start their own businesses as independent representatives.

Earning Potential

Median hourly wage (2009): $34.30

Median annual wage (2009): $71,340

(Based on "Sales Representatives, Wholesale and Manufacturing, Technical and Scientific Products")

Education/Licensure

Typically, technical and scientific sales jobs require a degree. Some employers may accept an associate degree, and others may require a bachelor's degree in a technical or scientific discipline. New employees typically undergo training on the product they will sell. Companies also train all sales personnel on a new product as it is introduced. In addition, sales representatives may attend seminars and webinars on sales techniques.

There are no licensing requirements for this occupation, but the Manufacturer's Representatives Education Research Foundation offers two certifications, the Certified Professional Manufacturers' Representative (CPMR) and the Certified Sales Professional (CSP). The North American Board of Certified Energy Practitioners (NABCET) is working on a Photovoltaic Technical Sales Certification program.

For More Information

American Solar Energy Society (ASES)
2400 Central Avenue
Suite A
Boulder, Colorado 80301
303-443-3130
www.ases.org

Manufacturers' Agents National Association (MANA)
16A Journery
Suite 200
Aliso Viejo, California 92656-3317
877-626-2776
www.manaonline.org

Manufacturer's Representatives Education Research Foundation (MRERF)
8329 Cole Street
Arvada, Colorado 80005
303-463-1801
www.mrerf.org

North American Board of Certified Energy Practitioners (NABCEP)
634 Plank Road
Suite 102
Clifton Park, New York 12065
800-654-0021
www.nabcep.org

Solar Electric Power Association (SEPA)
1220 19th Street, NW
Suite 401
Washington, DC 20036-2405
202-857-0898
www.solarelectricpower.org

Solar Industries Association (SEIA)
575 7th Street, NW
Suite 400
Washington, DC 20009
202-682-0556
www.seia.org

Solar Living Institute (SLI)
13771 South Highway 101
P.O. Box 836
Hopland, California 95449
707-472-2450
www.solarliving.org

Solar Thermal Installer and Technician ✿ⓢ

Alternate Titles and Related Careers
- Solar Field Service Technician
- Solar Installation Technician Commercial
- Solar Installation Technician Residential

These two jobs are "Bright Outlook" and "Green New and Emerging" occupations in the renewable energy generation sector of the economy.

Job Trends

The statistics are based on the Bureau of Labor's category of "Construction and Related Workers, All Other," which projects an average growth rate of 7 to 13 percent for this category between 2008 and

2018. This translates into 26,600 new employees overall. However, as a "Bright Outlook" occupation in the renewable energy sector, the solar thermal installer and technician jobs may require more workers more quickly than anticipated.

Nature of the Work

Solar thermal installers install energy systems designed to collect, store, and circulate solar-heated water for residential, commercial, or industrial use. Solar thermal technicians repair these systems.

Both occupations deal with piping, water heaters, valves, tanks, pipefittings, and auxiliary equipment. Solar thermal installers and technicians work with soldering equipment, pipe cutters, acetylene torches, wire brushes, sand cloths, plastic glue, brackets, and struts. They have to be able to read manufacturer specifications as well as flow meters and temperature and pressure gauges.

According to O*NET, solar thermal installers may perform the following tasks:

- Design active direct or indirect, passive direct or indirect, or pool solar systems
- Apply operation or identification tags or labels to system components, as required
- Assess collector sites to ensure structural integrity of potential mounting surfaces or the best orientation and tilt for solar collectors
- Connect water heaters and storage tanks to power and water sources
- Determine locations for installing solar subsystem components
- Fill water tanks and check for leaks
- Identify plumbing, electrical, environmental, or safety hazards associated with solar thermal installations
- Install circulating pumps; copper or plastic plumbing; flat-plat, evacuated glass, or concentrating solar collectors; heat exchangers and heat exchanger fluids;

monitoring system components; and plumbing
- Install solar collector mounting devices on tile, asphalt, shingle, or built-up gravel roofs, using appropriate materials and penetration methods
- Install solar thermal system controllers and sensors
- Test operation or functionality of mechanical, plumbing, electrical, and control systems
- Apply ultraviolet radiation protection to prevent degradation of plumbing
- Apply weather seal, such as pipe flashings and sealants, to roof penetrations and structural devices
- Cut, miter, and glue piping insulation to insulate plumbing pipes and fittings
- Demonstrate start-up, shut-down, maintenance, diagnostic, and safety procedures to thermal system owners
- Solar thermal technicians specifically perform routine maintenance or repairs to restore solar thermal systems to baseline operating conditions.

Career Path

Entry-level solar thermal installers begin work under the supervision of more experienced workers. Over time, they are given more complex work and more independence in accomplishing it. After several years of experience installing thermal systems, the installer may become a technician. Installers and technicians with more experience may become supervisors. Others start their own businesses as consultants or as solar panel installation and service contractors.

Earning Potential

Median hourly wage (2009): $16.34

Median annual wage (2009): $33,980

Education/Licensure

Entry-level jobs in construction typically require a high school diploma or equivalent and generally start workers as laborers, helpers, or apprentices. Skilled occupations such as solar thermal installer and technician require classroom instruction and on-the-job training that may be acquired by attending a community college or technical or trade school, participating in an apprenticeship, or taking part in an employer-provided training program. Some community colleges, technical schools and institutes, and trade associations offer short-term online training programs.

Apprenticeships are administered by local employers, trade associations, and trade unions and provide the most thorough training. Typically, they last between three and five years and combine on-the-job training and 144 hours or more of related classroom instruction for each year of the program. The Independent Electrical Contractors (IEC) operates apprenticeship training programs for individuals wishing to become electricians, as does the International Brotherhood of Electrical Workers (IBEW). Most states require licensing for plumbers and electricians.

Solar power training certification is currently voluntary, but some states are looking into requiring it. The North American Board of Certified Energy Practitioners (NABCEP) provides the Solar Thermal Installer Certification program.

For More Information

American Solar Energy Society (ASES)
2400 Central Avenue
Suite A
Boulder, Colorado 80301
303-443-3130
www.ases.org

North American Board of Certified Energy Practitioners (NABCEP)
634 Plank Road
Suite 102
Clifton Park, New York 12065
800-654-0021
www.nabcep.org

Solar Electric Power Association (SEPA)
1220 19th Street, NW
Suite 401
Washington, DC 20036-2405
202-857-0898
www.solarelectricpower.org

Solar Industries Association (SEIA)
575 7th Street, NW
Suite 400
Washington, DC 20009
202-682-0556
www.seia.org

Solar Living Institute (SLI)
13771 South Highway 101
P.O. Box 836
Hopland, California 95449
707-472-2450
www.solarliving.org

WIND POWER

According to the Department of Energy's Wind and Water Program, the cost of producing electricity using wind power has dropped from $0.80 per kilowatt hour to $0.05 to $0.08 today. Thirty-six states have commercial wind energy systems. As part of the American Recovery and Reinvestment Act (ARRA), the federal government committed to $117 million in loan guarantees for a wind energy project in Hawaii. The goal is to supply 70 percent of the state's energy by 2030 and displace nearly 160 million pounds of carbon dioxide produced by the state's current petroleum-powered electricity grid. This was just one of several multimillion- and billion-dollar federal loan guarantees to jump start clean energy projects.

Wind Energy Engineer ✿⊛

Alternate Titles and Related Careers
- Civil Engineer, Wind Energy
- Electrical Engineer, Wind Farm
- Wind Energy Electrical Engineer
- Wind Farm Design Manager
- Wind Farm Electrical Systems Designer
- Wind Projects Development Engineer (Civil)

This is a "Bright Outlook" and "Green New and Emerging" occupation in the renewable energy generation sector.

Job Trends

The Bureau of Labor Statistics projects an average growth rate of 7 to 13 percent for the engineering category. However, as a "Bright Outlook" occupation, wind energy engineers should see expanded job opportunities.

Nature of the Work

Wind energy engineers design underground or overhead wind farm collector systems. Part of their job includes preparing and developing site specifications. Among the tasks that wind energy engineers perform, according to O*NET, are the following:

- Create models to optimize the layout of wind farm access roads, crane pads, crane paths, collection systems, substations, switchyards, or transmission lines
- Create or maintain wind farm layouts, schematics, or other visual documentation for wind farms
- Develop active control algorithms, electronics, software, electromechanical, or electrohydraulic systems for wind turbines
- Develop specifications for wind technology components, such as gearboxes, blades, generators, frequency converters, and pad transformers

- Direct balance of plant (BOP) construction, generator installation, testing, commissioning, or supervisory control and data acquisition (SCADA) to ensure compliance with specifications
- Monitor wind farm construction to ensure compliance with regulatory standards or environmental requirements
- Analyze operation of wind farms or wind farm components to determine reliability, performance, and compliance with specifications
- Provide engineering technical support to designers of prototype wind turbines
- Oversee the work activities of wind farm consultants or subcontractors
- Test wind turbine components, using mechanical or electronic testing equipment
- Test wind turbine equipment to determine effects of stress or fatigue
- Perform root cause analysis on wind turbine tower component failures
- Investigate experimental wind turbines or wind turbine technologies for properties such as aerodynamics, production, noise, and load
- Recommend process or infrastructure changes to improve wind turbine performance, reduce operational costs, or comply with regulations
- Write reports to document wind farm collector system test results

About Federal Initiatives in Wind Power
Visit www.windpoweringamerica.gov for an overview of the federal government's support of wind energy. The goals of the initiative are to target regional economic development, enlarge the nation's power-generation options, protect the environment, and increase U.S. energy and national security.

Career Path

As engineers gain experience, they become specialists and advance into positions where they supervise a team of engineers and other staff. Some eventually become managers or move into sales jobs where their technical background is particularly useful. Some go on to earn a master's in business administration (MBA) to prepare them for higher level managerial positions.

Earning Potential

Median hourly wage (2009): $43.06

Median annual wage (2009): $89,560

(Based on "Engineers, All Other")

Education/Licensure

Typically, this occupation requires an engineering degree from a college or university accredited by the Accreditation Board of Engineering and Technology (ABET). The specialty desired for a particular job, such as civil or electrical engineering, depends on the main duties of the job. A degree in a related engineering or technical field may also be acceptable.

Some colleges and universities offer five-year programs that culminate in a master's degree. Some offer five- or six-year programs that include cooperative experience. Some four-year schools have arrangements with community colleges or liberal arts colleges that allow students to spend two or three years at the initial school and transfer for the last two years to complete their engineering degree.

All fifty states and the District of Columbia require engineers to be licensed as professional engineers (PE) if they serve the public directly. In most states, licensure requires graduation from a four-year engineering program accredited by ABET, four years of experience, and passing the state exam. Many engineers take the Fundamentals of Engineering portion of the exam upon graduation. They are then engineers in training (EIT). After obtaining appropriate work experience, they take the Principles and Practice of Engineering exam to complete their professional license. Most states recognize licenses from other states, as long as the requirements are the same or more stringent. Some states have continuing education requirements.

For More Information

Accreditation Board for Engineering and
    Technology (ABET)
111 Market Place
Suite 1050
Baltimore, MD 21202
(410) 347-7700
www.abet.org

American Wind Energy Association (AWEA)
1501 M Street, NW
Suite 1000
Washington, DC 20005
202-383-2500
www.awea.org

National Wind Coordinating Collaborative
    (NWCC)
1255 23rd Street, NW
Suite 875
Washington, DC 20037
202-965-6398
www.nationalwind.org

Utility Wind Integration Group (UWIG)
P.O. Box 2787
Reston, Virginia 20195
703-860-5160
www.uwig.org

World Wind Energy Association (WWEA)
Charles-de-Gaulle Strasse 5
53113 Bonn
Germany
www.wwindea.org

Wind Energy Operations Manager ☼ ⊕

Alternate Titles and Related Careers

- Assistant Operations Manager
- Assistant Site Manager
- Operations Manager
- Wind Farm Site Manager
- Wind Power Plant Project Engineer
- Wind Project Site Manager
- Wind Site Manager

This is a "Bright Outlook" and "Green New and Emerging" occupation that is part of the renewable energy generation sector of the economy.

Job Trends

The Bureau of Labor Standards category of "Managers, All Other" is estimated to experience an average growth rate of 7 to 13 percent between 2008 and 2018. This translates into 297,500 job openings for the entire category. The number of job openings for wind energy operations managers will depend on how quickly the wind energy sector expands. As a "Bright Outlook" occupation, job prospects should be good.

Nature of the Work

Wind energy operations managers oversee all the elements of a wind field operation, which includes personnel, maintenance, budgeting, and planning and scheduling. The wind field operation includes such site assets as turbine towers, transformers, electrical collector systems, and roadways.

Among the tasks that a wind energy operations manager may perform are the following:

- Establish goals, objectives, or priorities for wind field operations
- Oversee the maintenance of wind field equipment or structures
- Supervise employees or subcontractors to ensure quality of work or adherence to safety regulations or policies

- Develop processes and procedures for wind operations, including transitioning from construction to commercial operations
- Develop relationships and communicate with customers, site managers, developers, land owners, authorities, utility representatives, and residents
- Estimate costs associated with operations, including repairs and preventive maintenance
- Prepare wind field operational budgets
- Negotiate or review and approve wind farm contracts
- Recruit or select wind operations employees, contractors, or subcontractors
- Monitor and maintain records of daily facility operations and operations records, such as work orders, site inspection forms, or other documentation
- Manage warranty repair or replacement services
- Oversee the ordering of parts, tools, or equipment needed to maintain, restore, or improve wind field operations
- Provide technical support to wind field customers, employees, or subcontractors.
- Track and maintain records for wind operations, such as site performance, downtime events, parts usage, and substation events
- Train, or coordinate the training of, employees in operations, safety, environmental issues, or technical issues

Career Path

Most entry-level jobs begin with classroom instruction followed by a period as helpers or laborers. Workers advance to more responsible positions over time as they become familiar with the plant operations. Over time, with training and experience, workers can advance to shift supervisor, trainer, or consultant. Wind energy operations managers may enter the management track as assistant or junior operations managers and work their way up to higher level management.

Earning Potential

Median hourly wage (2009): $44.52

Median annual wage (2009): $92,600

Education/Licensure

Typically, wind energy operations manager positions are filled by individuals with bachelor's degrees, though some employers may prefer advanced degrees and some may accept associate degrees for junior or assistant operations manager positions. The degrees are typically in an engineering specialty or a related technical field. An engineering degree should be from an institution accredited by the Accreditation Board for Engineering and Technology (ABET).

As noted in the *Occupation Outlook Handbook,* some colleges and universities offer five-year programs that culminate in a master's degree in engineering. Some offer five- or six-year programs that include cooperative experience. Some four-year schools have arrangements with community colleges or liberal arts colleges that allow students to spend two or three years at the initial school and transfer for the last two years to complete their engineering degree.

All fifty states and the District of Columbia require engineers to be licensed as professional engineers (PE) if they serve the public directly. In most states, licensure requires graduation from a four-year engineering program accredited by ABET, four years of experience, and passing the state exam. Many engineers take the Fundamentals of Engineering portion of the exam upon graduation. They are then engineers in training (EIT). After obtaining appropriate work experience, they take the Principles and Practice of Engineering exam to complete their professional license. Most states recognize licenses from other states as long as the requirements are the same or more stringent. Some states have continuing education requirements.

States may require licensing of wind energy operations managers. Requirements vary by state.

For More Information

Accreditation Board for Engineering and Technology (ABET)
111 Market Place
Suite 1050
Baltimore, Maryland 21202
410-347-7700
www.abet.org

American Wind Energy Association (AWEA)
1501 M Street, NW
Suite 1000
Washington, DC 20005
202-383-2500
www.awea.org

National Wind Coordinating Collaborative (NWCC)
1255 23rd Street, NW
Suite 875
Washington, DC 20037
202-965-6398
www.nationalwind.org

Utility Wind Integration Group (UWIG)
P.O. Box 2787
Reston, Virginia 20195
703-860-5160
www.uwig.org

World Wind Energy Association (WWEA)
Charles-de-Gaulle Strasse 5
53113 Bonn
Germany
www.wwindea.org

Wind Energy Project Manager ✿⑤

Alternate Titles and Related Careers

- Director of Wind Development
- Projects Development Director
- Project Manager, Development
- Senior Wind Energy Consultant
- Wind Project Developer

This is a "Bright Outlook" and "Green New and Emerging" occupation in the renewable energy generation sector of the economy.

Job Trends

The Bureau of Labor Statistics classifies this occupation as part of "Managers, All Other" and estimates an average growth rate of 7 to 13 percent for the category. This translates into 297,500 jobs overall between 2008 and 2018. The number of positions available for wind energy project manager will depend on how quickly the market moves to expanding wind power.

Nature of the Work

Wind energy project managers lead or manage the development and evaluation of potential wind energy business opportunities. Activities include overseeing environmental studies, permitting of sites, and development of proposals. A project manager may also manage the construction of the wind power-generation site.

According to O*NET, among the tasks that a wind energy project manager may perform are the following:

- Create wind energy project plans, including project scope, goals, tasks, resources, schedules, costs, contingencies, and other project information
- Prepare, or assist in the preparation of, applications for environmental, building, or other required permits
- Coordinate or direct development, energy assessment, engineering, or construction activities to ensure that wind project needs and objectives are met
- Develop scope of work for wind project functions, such as design, site assessment, environmental studies, surveying, and field support services
- Manage wind project costs to stay within budget limits
- Prepare wind project documentation, including diagrams or layouts
- Provide technical support for the design, construction, or commissioning of wind farm projects
- Provide verbal or written project status reports to project teams, management, subcontractors, customers, or owners
- Review civil design, engineering, or construction technical documentation to ensure compliance with applicable government or industrial codes, standards, requirements, or regulations
- Review or evaluate proposals or bids to make recommendations regarding awarding of contracts
- Update schedules, estimates, forecasts, or budgets for wind projects
- Lead or support negotiations involving tax agreements or abatements, power purchase agreements, land use, or interconnection agreements
- Manage site assessments or environmental studies for wind fields
- Prepare requests for proposals (RFPs) for wind project construction or equipment acquisition
- Supervise the work of subcontractors or consultants to ensure quality and conformance to specifications or budgets

Career Path

A wind energy project manager may begin in the technical side of the industry or in the administrative/financial side and gain experience in various facets of the business. As individuals gain experience, they move into more complex assignments with more responsibility and independence. Promotion to higher levels of management may come by moving from company to company, gaining experience and a wider view of the industry with each move. Ultimate jobs are vice president, president, chief executive officer (CEO), or chief financial officer (CFO).

Earning Potential

Median hourly wage (2009): $44.52

Median annual wage (2009): $92,600

Education/Licensure

A bachelor's degree is required for this job and an advanced degree is a plus. The degree could be in engineering or a related technical field, economics, accounting, finance, or business, especially a master's in business administration (MBA). If the degree is in engineering, it should be from an institution accredited by the Accreditation Board for Engineering and Technology (ABET).

As noted in the *Occupation Outlook Handbook,* some colleges and universities offer five-year programs that culminate in a master's degree in engineering. Some offer five- or six-year programs that include cooperative experience. Some four-year schools have arrangements with community colleges or liberal arts colleges that allow students to spend two or three years at the initial school and transfer for the last two years to complete their engineering degree.

All fifty states and the District of Columbia require engineers to be licensed as professional engineers (PE) if they serve the public directly. In most states, licensure requires graduation from a four-year engineering program accredited by ABET, four years of experience, and passing the state exam. Many engineers take the Fundamentals of Engineering portion of the exam upon graduation. They are then engineers in training (EIT). After obtaining appropriate work experience, they take the Principles and Practice of Engineering exam to complete their professional license. Most states recognize licenses from other states, as long as the requirements are the same or more stringent. Some states have continuing education requirements.

For More Information

Accreditation Board for Engineering and Technology (ABET)
111 Market Place
Suite 1050
Baltimore, Maryland 21202
410-347-7700
www.abet.org

American Wind Energy Association (AWEA)
1501 M Street, NW
Suite 1000
Washington, DC 20005
202-383-2500
www.awea.org

National Wind Coordinating Collaborative (NWCC)
1255 23rd Street, NW
Suite 875
Washington, DC 20037
202-965-6398
www.nationalwind.org

Utility Wind Integration Group (UWIG)
P.O. Box 2787
Reston, Virginia 20195
703-860-5160
www.uwig.org

World Wind Energy Association (WWEA)
Charles-de-Gaulle Strasse 5
53113 Bonn
Germany
www.wwindea.org

Wind Turbine Machinist ⊕

Alternate Titles and Related Careers
- Gear Machinist
- Machine Operator
- Machine Repair Person
- Machinist
- Maintenance Specialist
- Set-Up Machinist
- Tool Room Machinist
- Utility Operator

This is a "Green Enhanced-Skills" occupation in manufacturing and renewable energy generation. A wind turbine machinist is a manufacturing job that benefits the energy sector.

Job Trends

This occupation is one for which data is still being collected, but as a green occupation, job growth may be anticipated.

Nature of the Work

Machinists support metalworking projects from planning and fabrication through assembly, inspection, and testing, using knowledge of machine functions, metal properties and mathematics. They set up and operate a variety of machine tools to produce precision parts and instruments, in this case, wind turbine components. Knowledge of math and computer numerically controlled (CNC) machine tools can be important in this field. Among the tools that a machinist uses are lathes, milling machines, shapers, and grinders.

Among the tasks that a wind turbine machine may perform are the following from O*NET:
- Study sample parts, blueprints, drawings, and engineering information to determine methods and sequences of operations needed to fabricate products and to determine product dimensions and tolerances

- Calculate dimensions and tolerances using knowledge of mathematics and instruments such as micrometers and vernier calipers
- Select the appropriate tools, machines, and materials to be used in preparation of machinery work
- Align and secure holding fixtures, cutting tools, attachments, accessories, and materials onto machines
- Machine parts to specifications
- Monitor the feed and speed of machines during the machining process
- Set up, adjust, and operate all basic machine tools and many specialized or advanced variation tools to perform precision machining operations
- Measure, examine, and test completed units to detect defects and ensure conformance to specifications
- Set controls to regulate machining or enter commands to retrieve, input, or edit computerized machine control media
- Maintain industrial machines, applying knowledge of mechanics, shop mathematics, metal properties, layout, and machining procedures
- Observe and listen to operating machines or equipment to diagnose machine malfunctions and to determine need for adjustments or repairs
- Check work pieces to ensure that they are properly lubricated and cooled
- Lay out, measure, and mark metal stock to display placement of cuts
- Confer with engineering, supervisory, and manufacturing personnel to exchange technical information
- Program computers and electronic instruments
- Operate equipment to verify operational efficiency
- Clean and lubricate machines, tools, and equipment to remove grease, rust, stains, and foreign matter

- Design fixtures, tooling, and experimental parts to meet special engineering needs
- Evaluate experimental procedures, and recommend changes or modifications for improved efficiency and adaptability to setup and production
- Confer with numerical control programmers to check and ensure that new programs or machinery will function properly, and that output will meet specifications
- Establish work procedures for fabricating new structural products, using a variety of metalworking machines
- Fit and assemble parts to make or repair machine tools
- Set up and operate metalworking, brazing, heat-treating, welding, and cutting equipment
- Dismantle machines or equipment, using hand tools and power tools, to examine parts for defects and replace defective parts where needed
- Install repaired parts into equipment or install new equipment
- Prepare working sketches for the illustration of product appearance
- Test experimental models under simulated operating conditions for such purposes as development, standardization, and feasibility of design
- Install experimental parts and assemblies such as hydraulic systems, electrical wiring, lubricants, and batteries into machines and mechanisms

Career Path

Entry-level employees begin as helpers or learners under the supervision of skilled machinists. As new employees gain experience, they may advance to machine operators, machine setters, team leaders, and supervisor. With additional time on the job, some may be promoted to a management position.

Earning Potential

Median hourly wage (2009): $18.10

Median annual wage (2009): $37,650

Education/Licensure

Machinists receive training through apprenticeship programs, vocational schools, or community or technical colleges, as well as on the job. A high school diploma or equivalent is required for entry-level positions, although more and more machinists are earning associate degrees. Many machinists begin their careers as machine setters, operators, or tenders and work their way up, taking classes to advance. Most acquire their skills through a combination of classroom and on-the-job training.

Some machinists learn their trade through formal apprenticeship programs that also combine shop training and classroom instruction. These programs may last up to four years while the apprentice is working and being paid. Apprenticeship programs are often taught in cooperation with local community colleges or vocational-technical schools, employers, and appropriate unions.

Completing a recognized certification program offered by for-profit training companies, state apprenticeship boards, and colleges provides a machinist with better career opportunities. State apprenticeship programs may offer journeyworker certification upon completion of the program.

The National Tooling and Machining Association (NTMA) has launched a workforce development program, Precision Jobs for American Manufacturing, to increase the number of trained machinists for the nation's manufacturing jobs, which includes energy, green, and infrastructure industries.

For More Information

American Wind Energy Association (AWEA)
1501 M Street, NW
Suite 1000
Washington, DC 20005
202-383-2500
www.awea.org

National Tooling and Machining Association
(NTMA)
9300 Livingston Road
Fort Washington, Maryland 20744
800-248-6862
www.ntma.org

National Wind Coordinating Collaborative
(NWCC)
1255 23rd Street, NW
Suite 875
Washington, DC 20037
202-965-6398
www.nationalwind.org

Precision Machined Products Association
(PMPA)
6700 West Snowville Road
Brecksville, Ohio 44141-3292
440-526-5803
www.pmpa.org

Utility Wind Integration Group (UWIG)
P.O. Box 2787
Reston, Virginia 20195
703-860-5160
www.uwig.org

World Wind Energy Association (WWEA)
Charles-de-Gaulle Strasse 5
53113 Bonn
Germany
www.wwindea.org

Wind Turbine Service Technician ☼ ⊕

Alternate Titles and Related Careers

- Lead Wind Technician
- Lead Wind Turbine Technician
- Senior Wind Plant Technician
- Wind Services Technician
- Wind Turbine Technician

This is a "Bright Outlook" and "Green New and Emerging" occupation in the renewable energy generation sector of the economy.

Job Trends

Wind turbine service technician is included in the Bureau of Labor Statistics "Installation, Maintenance, and Repair Workers, All Other" category. The category is estimated to grow at an average rate of 7 to 13 percent. However, as a "Bright Outlook" occupation in the green energy sector, wind turbine service technician job opportunities may expand more quickly as the nation's investment in wind power grows.

Nature of the Work

Wind turbine service technicians inspect, diagnose, adjust, or repair wind turbines. They perform maintenance on the wind turbine equipment, including resolving electrical, mechanical, and hydraulic malfunctions. A technician must be in good physical condition because he or she may need to climb the wind turbine tower.

According to O*NET, a wind turbine service technician's job duties may include the following:

- Inspect or repair fiberglass turbine blades
- Troubleshoot or repair mechanical, hydraulic, or electrical malfunctions related to variable pitch systems, variable speed control systems, converter systems, or related components
- Diagnose problems involving wind turbine generators or control systems

- Perform routine maintenance on wind turbine equipment, underground transmission systems, wind field substations, or fiberoptic sensing and control systems
- Start or restart wind turbine generator systems to ensure proper operations
- Test electrical components of wind systems with devices such as voltage testers, multimeters, oscilloscopes, infrared testers, and fiberoptic equipment
- Test structures, controls, or mechanical, hydraulic, or electrical systems according to test plans and in coordination with engineers
- Assist in assembly of individual wind generators or construction of wind farms
- Collect turbine data for testing or research and analysis
- Maintain tool and spare parts inventories required for repair, installation, or replacement services
- Train end-users, distributors, installers, or other technicians in wind commissioning, testing, or other technical procedures

Career Path

Entry-level wind turbine service technicians begin work under the supervision of more experienced workers. Several months or even a year of on-the-job training may be required to move to the next level of responsibility. Workers may advance through several levels of experience and responsibility to become supervisors themselves. Others start their own businesses as consultants or service contractors.

Earning Potential

Median hourly wage (2009): $17.08

Median annual wage (2009): $35,520

Education/Licensure

Entry-level jobs typically require a high school diploma or equivalent and generally start workers as laborers, helpers, or apprentices. Skilled occupations such as wind turbine technician typically require classroom instruction and on-the-job training that may be had by attending a community college or technical or trade school, participating in an apprenticeship, or taking part in an employer-provided training program. Apprenticeships are administered by local employers, trade associations, and trade unions and provide the most thorough training, which combines on-the-job training and classroom instruction while working and being paid.

Some jobs such as "wind technician, electrical specialist" may require an electrician's license, depending on the state.

The North American Board of Certified Energy Practitioners (NABCEP) is working on a Professional Small Wind Energy System Installer certification program for those who install wind systems that are less than 100 kilowatts in size.

For More Information

American Wind Energy Association (AWEA)
1501 M Street, NW
Suite 1000
Washington, DC 20005
202-383-2500
www.awea.org

National Wind Coordinating Collaborative (NWCC)
1255 23rd Street, NW
Suite 875
Washington, DC 20037
202-965-6398
www.nationalwind.org

North American Board of Certified Energy
  Practitioners (NABCEP)
634 Plank Road
Suite 102
Clifton Park, New York 12065
800-654-0021
www.nabcep.org

Utility Wind Integration Group (UWIG)
P.O. Box 2787
Reston, Virginia 20195
703-860-5160
www.uwig.org

World Wind Energy Association (WWEA)
Charles-de-Gaulle Strasse 5
53113 Bonn
Germany
www.wwindea.org

The Future in Energy Careers

The development of alternative and renewable energy generation is moving very quickly with new occupations being invented seemingly overnight. Here are a few jobs with too little information to include in this book at this point in time, but that anyone interested in working in the green energy field should keep an eye on.

CARBON MARKET 🌐
- Carbon capture and sequestration systems installer
- Carbon credit trader/broker
- Carbon trading analyst

All three are classified as occupations in the carbon trading and storage sector of the green energy economy. O*NET categorizes them as "Green New and Emerging" occupations.

Carbon capture and sequestration is the process by which excess carbon dioxide is removed from the air and stored underground. It is one solution that is being studied for solving climate change. In December 2009, the U.S. Department of Energy (DOE) announced a $3.18 billion investment in research to accelerate the development of carbon capture and storage technologies for coal. Earlier in the year, the DOE had announced the construction of a coal-fueled, near-zero emissions power plant in Illinois to establish the feasibility of producing electricity from coal while capturing and sequestering the carbon dioxide generated in the process. If successful, this research should lead to more such power plants and more jobs.

Carbon credit trader and carbon trading analyst refer to the occupations of individuals involved in the cap-and-trade systems for carbon credits. Cap-and-trade is a government-established system of pollution credits based on the amount of air pollution created in a region. The credits enable a company that doesn't use all of its pollution credits to sell unused ones to companies that pollute more than the credits allotted to them by the government.

While the cap-and-trade Acid Rain Program has been around since the 1990s, a national system for carbon credits is part of President Barack Obama's energy policy. However, a voluntary market already existed. It traded 100 million dollars' worth of credits for 23 million metric tons of carbon dioxide in 2007. If a federal program becomes law or the voluntary efforts intensify, the U.S. job market for carbon credit traders and analysts—those who buy and sell carbon credits on carbon trading exchanges—will grow.

HYDROGEN POWER

Another category of occupations to keep in mind is hydrogen energy. Hydrogen power is green power because it produces no greenhouse gas emissions—only hot air and water vapor. Potential occupations in this green industry sector include

- Hydrogen power plant installer
- Hydrogen plant operator
- Hydrogen plant operations manager

Hydrogen power generation jobs haven't been included in the Bureau of Labor Statistics reports or the O*NET system yet, probably because there are so few hydrogen power plants. The first hydrogen power plant in Scandinavia became operable in 2007. It produces electricity and steam for a chemical plant. In 2009, Enel, an Italian energy company, completed the first phase of the first hydrogen power plant in Italy. The plant receives its hydrogen as a by-product of the production process of a nearby petrochemical factory. Ultimately, the plant will provide electricity to 20,000 households.

The DOE's Hydrogen and Clean Coal Fuel Program supports research, development, and demonstration of innovative technologies to produce, deliver, store, and use hydrogen as a power source. In November 2009, the DOE signed an agreement with Hydrogen Energy California LLC (HECA) to build a hydrogen-powered electric generating facility that includes carbon capture and storage. The plant, to be built in Kern County, California, won't be operable until 2016, but it is expected to sequester 2 million tons of CO_2 annually while providing power to customers.

Private companies are also slowly investing in hydrogen power plants. For example, in mid-2009, Jetstream Wind signed on to develop the first sustainable zero-emissions hydrogen power plant. The plant in New Mexico will use power generated from renewable resources such as wind and solar power to produce hydrogen. As more research is conducted and pilot plants are built and are successful at creating affordable power, more jobs in all areas of hydrogen power generation will be built.

CONCENTRATING SOLAR POWER (CSP)

The U.S. Department of Energy is working with a dozen entities to develop storage solutions, manufacturing approaches, and new system concepts for large-scale concentrating solar power (CSP) plants. These plants require large tracts of land to house the parabolic troughs used to generate the power from the sun and the storage facilities for energy reserves. A 250-megawatt plant with six hours of storage requires nearly three square miles of land. Potential sites will be located in the Southwest. The goal is to make CSP a competitive source of power in the United States by 2020. Even before then, solar thermoelectric plant/CSP plant operators and solar power plant technicians will be needed.

How Smart Grid Technology Works

In October 2009, President Barack Obama committed $3.4 billion in government grants to 100 "smart grid" projects, with the goal of modernizing the nation's aging electric power grid. The funds were aimed not only at making the electricity-generating grid more efficient, but also at accommodating the expanding use of renewable energy technologies, such as wind and solar power. After award recipients match these grants, the total funding for the initiative tops $8 billion. In making the announcement, the President said that our electricity grid "runs on century-old technology." The goal of a smart grid, he pointed out, is to give consumers control over their energy use and costs, and to drive wind and solar power development and other clean-energy technologies.

The country's current electric power grid incorporates more than 9,200 electric generating units, more than 1 million megawatts of generating capacity, and more than 300,000 miles of transmission lines. Even as massive as it is, the grid has not kept pace with the increasing demand for electricity fueled by population growth, larger homes and TVs, and more air conditioning and computers. Demand has surpassed transmission growth by nearly 25 percent every year since 1982. Even the small percentage of outages and interruptions that occur today costs the United States at least $150 billion annually—or $500 for every American.

The DOE has identified the following seven characteristics of a smart grid:
1. It is self-healing from power disturbances.
2. It enables active participation by consumers in "demand response" programs.
3. It operates resiliently against physical or cyber attacks.
4. It provides quality power for twenty-first-century needs.
5. It accommodates all generation and storage options.
6. It enables new products, services, and markets to function.
7. It optimizes utility assets and operational efficiency using sensors.

How do we do create a smart power grid? Primarily by transforming the current centralized power grid into a more consumer-interactive system. In part, this involves applying the ideas and technologies to the field of utilities and electric generation that made the growth of the Internet possible. Among these concepts are:
- *Advanced Metering Infrastructure:* This technology allows utilities to detect problems and fix them more rapidly than current technology allows, and it also helps consumers use electricity more efficiently. In what's called a demand response system, real-time price signals are relayed from utilities to consumers via "smart" home controls in thermostats, washers, dryers, and refrigerators. The devices process price data based on the consumer's wishes, which have been programmed into the devices, and distribute power accordingly.
- *Visualization Technology:* This technique is already used by utilities to monitor peak load times and plan load growth. A next-generation version called VERDE (Visualizing Energy Resources Dynamically on Earth), under development at the Oak Ridge National Laboratory, will provide utilities with a "picture" over vast reaches of the grid by integrating real-time sensor data, weather data, and grid modeling with geographical information. Utilities can

view the national grid, then switch in seconds to areas as small as street-level neighborhoods. Information about power outages and quality can be conveyed more rapidly than in the current system, thus increasing grid efficiency. VERDE aims to build a platform based on Google Earth that will allow it to use content generated by Google's users.

The smart grid isn't just about efficiency. Most of today's power-generating capacity relies on fossil fuels. To satisfy the increasing demand for power and reduce carbon dioxide emissions at the same time, a smart grid must generate power sustainably and economically. But many renewable energy sources, including solar and wind power, provide energy intermittently and at varying levels, or they don't deliver power at times of peak demand, when emissions can be far higher than average. Smart-grid technologies such as demand response will enable the country's power grid to absorb fluctuations in renewable energy supply and create a more sustainable system overall.

A fully engaged smart grid will be characterized by a two-way flow of information and electricity and will be capable of monitoring power plants, customer preferences, even individual appliances for peak efficiency and sustainability—and it's not that far off.

How Being Green Works for **Erik Limpaecher, Entrepreneur**

Erik Limpaecher, 31, is an entrepreneur, electrical engineer, and the director of research and development (R&D) for a company that develops power converters. The company, located in Princeton, New Jersey, is based on an idea that Limpaecher and two fellow students developed in his dorm room during his senior year of college. Limpaecher co-founded the company after winning first place with this idea in the 2001 Princeton University Business Plan Competition. Limpaecher has been working in the green technology for nine years. Here, Limpaecher takes voltage measurements inside his company's prototype Demand Response Inverter (DRI), a new product that shifts power consumption from peak demand to off-peak times. His company is working with the military on ways to use this product at remote posts in Iraq and Afghanistan, which could reduce the need for U.S. soldiers and Marines to participate in dangerous fuel convoys.

Describe your job, including common daily tasks and long-term projects that you have worked on or are working on now. What, specifically, about your job makes it green?

Our company develops power converters, which are the "glue" between the power grid and any type of power source or load. For example, a power converter takes direct current (DC) from a solar panel, wildly varying alternating current (AC) power from a spinning wind turbine, or DC from a battery bank. It converts those varying energy sources into smooth, controlled, fixed-frequency AC power for use in homes, factories, and on the utility power grid. We specialize in converters in the 5-kilowatt (kW) to 1-megawatt (MW) range. Our standard 100-kW product is about the size of a refrigerator.

The design of these boxes requires a wide variety and depth of engineering and technical skills. . . . As director of research and development, I am responsible for the technical execution of these product development efforts (except some of the assembly and test work). This includes developing the specifications and designs of new products together with our customers. Our customers include solar system integrators, wind turbine and battery manufacturers, and military system integrators. We also work with government funding agencies, such as the Department of Energy, the Navy, and the Army.

Our company also performs fundamental research into new power conversion technologies and new system designs. Our goal is to eventually integrate these new ideas into commercial and military products. For my position, this means developing proposals for new research programs for the U.S. Department of Defense and Department of

Energy and on the technical execution of awarded contracts.

Our company has worked on some exciting projects recently. We just finished developing a variable speed motor controller for use on Navy ships. . . . It has the potential to reduce fuel consumption for large Navy ships, reducing annual fuel costs by an estimated $1 million to $5 million per ship.

For the past year we've been selling a new Demand Response Inverter (DRI), which combines power from solar panels, batteries, the utility power grid, motor loads, generators, and neighborhood and factory power grids. Using intelligent controls and a communication interface to the local utility company, the DRI shifts power consumption from peak demand times (when electricity is most expensive and the power grid is overloaded) to off-peak times (when electricity is least expensive). This will allow end users to reduce their energy bills while also reducing fuel and maintenance costs for the big utility power producers.

We're working with the Army and Marines to use this same commercial technology to reduce the fuel needs on remote posts. Currently, attacks on fuel convoys result in about 15 percent of the casualties in Iraq and Afghanistan. Remote bases, however, waste much of this fuel because generators must constantly be idled so that power is always available without delay. The DRI would be able to blend power from a variety of sources, such as ruggedized solar panels and local intermittent power grids, and provide storage from batteries for emergency situations. The end result would be significantly reduced fuel consumption from generators, reduced fuel costs for the U.S. taxpayer, and a reduced need for U.S. soldiers and Marines to participate in dangerous fuel convoys.

We recently started working on a unique power converter, which will be the main gateway into a new high-voltage DC transmission system in Alaska. Currently, the remote villages and towns in that state are completely disconnected from the power grid, so they generate all of their own power and must have diesel fuel flown in during the warm season.

Why/how did you decide to work in a green industry?

My father, Dr. Rudy Limpaecher, a Ph.D. in plasma physics, worked on the Star Wars missile defense program during the Cold War. . . . To solve [certain] issues, he taught himself power electronics and started to innovate in that field.

I was an electrical engineering major and in 1998, which was my sophomore year in college I worked with my father to patent his latest idea, a new power conversion technology known as AC-link™. My senior year, 2001, was the year of the California energy crisis. . . . With encouragement from one of my electrical engineering professors, Ed Zschau, I wrote a business plan based on the AC-link™ technology. My idea was to start a company that would apply this technology to products that would improve energy reliability and power quality. Later ideas we developed also applied the technology to energy efficiency and the integration of renewable energy sources, such as wind and solar. I took a reduced course load during the spring semester of my senior year so that I could work on developing the AC-link™ control system in my dorm room. Together with some of my engineering classmates, including Darren Hammell and Mark Holveck, we entered the plan into the Princeton Business Plan Competition and performed some additional market research. With a first-place win under our belt, Ed introduced us to Greg Olsen, a wildly successful dot.com entrepreneur (and the third private "space tourist" to fly to the International Space Station).

An hour after the graduation ceremony ended, I received an e-mail from Greg saying that he wanted to invest in my idea. Within a month, the money was in the new company's account. My co-founders and I continued to work in my dorm room, but eventually moved into an incubator space across the street from Princeton University. Nine years later, we're a multi-million-dollar company with over 30 employees. . . . We have an incredibly smart, innovative, and hard-working group of engineers, technicians, and staff. We definitely have been lucky with the timing of our business and the quality of people we've been able to attract.

How did you prepare for your current position?

My electrical engineering degree provided the basis for all my work. I also received a minor in finance. Having exposure to basic accounting principles has been incredibly useful in running the business. Most of my experience since college has been gained simply through "trial by fire" on the job.

Which aspect of your education and/or training do you think has been the most helpful and/or useful to you? Why?

An engineering degree is a prerequisite for professional employment in the green economy. Power electronics, electrical, and mechanical engineering majors are in the greatest demand in my industry. Computer science, civil, materials, physics, and chemistry majors also have their particular niches. Since the industry is capital-intensive and much of the market still depends on government subsidies and incentives, it's

valuable to have a finance background if you want to work on the business side.

Do you find that the skills and/or knowledge required for your job continue to evolve? If so, what have you done to keep up-to-date?

The key has been to listen to mentors, hire energetic and skilled employees, use experienced contractors with unique technical skills, and find the highest-quality and most responsive suppliers. I've taken some additional online courses in product development and technical project management, as well as some on-site training in "soft skills" to improve my management skills. I strongly urge professionals to enroll in online or local continuing education courses on an ongoing basis. Trade conferences and trade journals are the best resources for staying up-to-date on the latest industry trends and developments.

The best way, by far, to stay up-to-date is to simply pick up the phone. In most cases, the engineering questions and problems that people face have already been answered in some manner by someone else. I've found that experts are more than happy to share a couple minutes of their time to answer a few focused questions.

How have continuing education and/or training impacted the way you do your job?

Being successful in an innovative field is all a matter of developing constructive habits and knowing how to simplify a problem to its fundamentals. Continuing education has helped by giving me some additional tools to help develop good habits and learning more efficient ways to distill a problem.

What is the most rewarding part of your work, and what do you find to be the most challenging?

Seeing a team of engineers and technicians that I've organized and managed successfully execute a challenging technical development program is by far the most rewarding part of my work. Seeing a product—which my team and I have spent hundreds of hours and many late nights developing—installed at a customer's site is also incredibly rewarding.

Those things that are most rewarding are also the most difficult. As a startup company grows quickly, as is happening with many companies in the green energy space, it is incredibly challenging to keep the team working efficiently despite the various personalities, new employees coming onboard, competing work priorities, nascent processes, and long work hours. In a growing, fledgling marketplace, countless risks can derail a product on its way to the market: unclear specifications, buggy software, engineering design oversights, high materials costs, fundamental technology challenges, late supplier deliveries and manufacturing errors, insufficient testing, changing customer priorities, or project team turnover.

What advice would you give to people interested in pursuing your career?

For people still in school, start by learning the fundamentals with an engineering degree and some training in finance and accounting. Apply for summer internships at a small company working on green technology in your area. Don't just work at any company—ask questions about their business plans, their staff's technical strength, and their historical performance. Volunteer to take on additional assignments instead of waiting for someone to hand you more responsibility. Invite the engineers and managers to breakfast or lunch to have an informal setting in which you can ask them about their work, find out where else you could contribute, and learn about the industry. Get exposure to all areas of the business by volunteering to help prepare marketing materials, project proposals, technical reports, and technical documentation.

If you're already in the working world, are looking to transition into this field, and your training is in an unrelated area, take evening or online courses and cross-train in an applicable engineering specialty. Once you're ready, attend one or two industry trade shows in order to get exposure to a wide variety of companies and get face time with some of their employees. Look for articles written by the company's employees in trade magazines or technical journals, and then e-mail or mail them some thoughtful feedback to demonstrate your ability to contribute. Pick up the phone, show up at their front desk, write letters, and—in any other way possible—show your strong interest to get into this field and contribute to the company's success.

For those with a bright idea looking to start their own business, start small and start today. Write a business plan and look for local investors to get you some modest seed funding. Avoid venture capitalists (at least for your first three rounds of funding), and avoid investors who don't have relevant industry connections or a track record of entrepreneurship success. Be tactical, not strategic: think in six-month to one-year increments, not grand five- or ten-year plans. On the business side, make profitability your holy grail. And on the technical side, show measurable progress through incremental product releases.

How Being Green Works for Newt Loken, Solar Contractor

Newt Loken, 51, is a solar contractor located in Eugene, Oregon. Loken specializes in the design and installation of solar thermal (hot water) and solar electric systems and is licensed as a journeyman installer for both technologies. Loken owns a company that is licensed to install these systems in Oregon. He has been working in this green industry for the past twenty-five years.

Here, Loken works with Kim McBride, a journeyman electrician, to install a solar electric panel on the roof of Mohawk High School for a 'Solar in the Schools' student-education program in Marcola, Oregon.

Describe your job, including common daily tasks and long-term projects that you have worked on or are working on now. What, specifically, about your job makes it green?

Planning is an important part of each job. We ensure that the design is complete and that there are no outstanding details. We also make sure that the permit and utility incentive paperwork is complete so that we have all of the necessary approvals. State approval is a given and done at a later time, assuming all guidelines are followed. Most of our journeymen are also project leaders on more involved or difficult jobs, and they take responsibility for the overall process.

When connecting with my co-workers on the day of a job, I try to offer my input when it is helpful. However, most know the solar [routine]. The first thing we must do on any job is to identify the job and material requirements. Then, my co-workers and I load the van with the necessary materials. When we arrive at the job, I make sure that everyone understands the orientation and layout of the project. Then, I plan the approach with my apprentice or fellow journeyman, prep and stage materials, and get down to installing the functional sculpture of the racking, solar array, and piping and balance of the system, which can be either solar thermal or solar electric (photovoltaic). These system installs have a similar approach with many common design parameters, but they are very different technologies for gathering solar energy. One is hydronic, or water-based, and the other is an electric-based solar-energy-gathering technology.

When working on a solar installation project, it is important to protect yourself and your fellow workers first. Always work smart and safe. Protecting the house or building you are working on is also imperative. The benefits of energy savings can be significantly compromised if damage is done to the building or if longevity is compromised in any way. "Measure twice and cut or drill once" is an old saying that still rings true. It is equally important to install quality products using best industry practices that will ensure a long [product] life and lead to years of clean energy production.

A typical residential installation usually takes from one to three days with a crew of two or three, depending upon complexity and size. Once the installation is complete, we clean up the work site and organize our materials for the next day. I update the customer on our progress and complete the necessary paperwork, such as materials used and material stocking needs. When I get back to the office, I update my records regarding phase of completion and address any other issues that have come up during the day

I was in the field for 10 years on a regular basis, but now I only go out occasionally to help on commercial solar thermal and residential solar electric installations. My role now is more that of oversight/coordinator/manager. Because of that, an important part of my job is pricing jobs. This requires finalizing the conceptual design with a computer-aided design (CAD) program, making requests for material quotes to suppliers, calculating all necessary materials costs, and estimating labor needs with a spreadsheet. I also conduct site visits to almost all jobs. This is typically necessary before I can quote each job, but it is not always necessary for new construction if drawings are available and the site is known to have a good solar window. Assessing the quality of the solar window, or what we call the TSFR, the total solar resource fraction, is also necessary. This TSRF is a combination of factors and includes the system performance impact of shading at the future array location, as well as the tilt and orientation of the array. The tools and methods used basically quantify your available solar resource when compared to a perfect site in your location.

My job is a green job for a simple reason: the work that I do helps people cut energy use, thereby conserving natural resources and diminishing the impact of overuse.

Renewable energy and efficient technologies combine to make dramatic savings when applied in combination. For example, we installed a solar thermal array for a four-story mixed-use building with storefronts at the base level and thirty-five apartments above. This solar thermal system contains twelve collectors and utilizes two pumps and a heat exchanger that relays the solar heat from the solar loop to a 700-gallon solar tank. Here, it will preheat the water for distribution to the individual water heaters in each unit. During the summer, solar water temperatures will reach 160 degrees. In winter months, the cold city water temperature of 50° F may reach between 60° F and 100° F, depending upon weather conditions. When combined with energy-efficient showerheads and cold-water washing, it will result in a solar savings fraction of 50 percent to 60 percent. This is the percentage of the conventional gas or electric energy displaced by solar. It will reduce operating costs, make affordable housing more affordable, and keep our planet more livable as well.

Why/how did you decide to work in a green industry?

I first became interested in the environment as a young boy. . . . I grew up in Ann Arbor [Michigan], which at the time was a hotbed of environmentalism. I think that I was more aware of my biosphere and my place in it than most kids my age because of this. Ann Arbor was a great place to be an amateur stream ecologist at age 12. We lived near the edge of town, and the area was transitioning from a farm and natural area into subdivisions. . . . I didn't recognize all of the raw materials, understand where they came from, or grasp the deeper science of building at the time, but I did become familiar with the anatomy of building. I learned that it's all about details.

As a kid, I also became an expert at taking things apart and reassembling them. These two interests converged as I grew up . . . I realized that our technological world needed to be taken apart, modified, corrected, and put back together. In my teens, I realized that I could study green technology, and this would allow me to combine my interest in mechanical things . . . with my love of nature.

How did you prepare for your current position?

To be a solar installer, you must be physically fit and enjoy the physical challenge. Over the years, I have accumulated physical skills from sports, especially gymnastics. You also need a good academic background, particularly in math. Science is also helpful. As for my formal education, college programs specifically for solar applications were not common in the late 1970s, so a patchwork of classes and on-the-job experience have helped me gain the knowledge I needed to work in this field. After classes in energy, physics, math, and architecture at the University of Michigan in Ann Arbor, where I graduated with a bachelor of science in natural resources, I realized I knew concepts, but I was lacking real hands-on skills to do what I wanted: design and build.

To broaden my education, I attended several workshops in Michigan that focused on how to build solar thermal and solar electric panels. . . . In 1980, I attended my first owner/builder school—the Shelter Institute in Bath, Maine—for three weeks to pick up some needed hands-on skills. Their Design/Build class was attractive to me because of its combination of design skills and craftsmanship. . . .

I discovered Colorado Mountain College, which had a solar retrofitting program at its Carbondale, Colorado, campus. Colorado was then—and still is—among the most progressive solar states, so I enrolled in classes and prepared to move. This program had stimulating classes in construction, passive solar design, and solar hot water systems. I was also able to work for a local solar/radiant heat/and energy-efficiency contractor to gain more real-world experience, and I was a volunteer in the building of the Rocky Mountain Institute.[1] I visited the Solar Energy Research Institute (SERI), which is now known as the National Renewable Energy Laboratory (NREL), in Golden, Colorado, and researched available solar water-heating systems. This gave me even further insight into available technology, concept development, government-funded research, and solar energy's practical applications.

Which aspect of your education and/or training do you think has been the most helpful and/or useful to you? Why?

The most helpful aspects of my education were a solid base of mathematics, specifically geometry, and physics. Learning scientific methods, especially in labs, has sharpened my process and troubleshooting skills. Classes in computer spreadsheets and CAD drawing are a must, but a basic class in architectural hand drawing and perspective drawing helps to communicate ideas quickly with simple tools such as the pen or pencil and paper.

Also helpful are the many inspiring talks and lectures I have attended. The global overview of our energy and environmental problems and the numerous solutions these speakers offer have been helpful in focusing my efforts and commitment toward the details of renewable energy implementation, some of which can be tedious.

Do you find that the skills and/or knowledge required for your job continue to evolve? If so, what have you done to keep up-to-date?

You must follow developments in multiple areas of knowledge when you work in the solar industry. These include industry codes (electric, plumbing, or solar specific), technological updates or advancements on existing products or techniques, the introductions of new technologies that require new methods, and utility and government incentive program changes in both technical requirements and process- and form-related procedures. Many resources—such as books, journals, and national and regional conferences—exist to help you stay abreast of the changes. There are also technical forums sponsored by industry associations, distributors, manufacturers, and local utilities or union halls. Visiting organizational Web sites or taking online classes can be a good option for interested people.

How have continuing education and/or training impacted the way you do your job?

Continuing education is both interesting and necessary. We all get into ruts and need to climb out and take a look around. In doing this, we refresh some of the ideas, skills, or technical know-how necessary to do our jobs. Continuing education comes in a wide variety of offerings. Solar energy licensing is somewhat new, so the Joint Apprenticeship Training Committee for our two renewable energy specialty licenses in Oregon (solar electric and solar thermal) has compiled a list of approved classes that we can take. Some of these classes are Internet-based. Distributors often hold technical forums with classes for their dealers that are taught by equipment manufacturers. Occupational Safety and Health Administration (OSHA) training is a requirement for any trade. On-the-job safety should be integral to the goals of the job, so this training should be high on the list.

Other continuing education may be broader and include specific training in a software design program, a drawing program, or perhaps a class in ENERGY STAR, or Earth Advantage®2 programs or LEED (Leadership in Energy and Environmental Design) accreditation.

What is the most rewarding part of your work, and what do you find to be the most challenging?

Encouraging and advising our customers on their best route to an energy-efficient and solar-powered future is very rewarding. So is turning on another solar system and watching the first surge of directly captured energy from the sun pass through on its way to work. Customers also enjoy seeing this, and this helps them have an absolute awareness that their system is indeed functioning.

A day in the field isn't necessarily easy work. It can be very satisfying if approached with a good attitude. We hear back from the field crew regarding new methods they've found that make things a little easier. "Field intelligence" implies these [workers] are in a constant process of design/build iterations. However, teamwork can be difficult, and . . . how we approach one another can be either divisive and challenging or inclusive and nonjudgmental. Active listening helps build our team. Being part of a team that's taken a project, especially a complex one, smoothly from design concept to function is very satisfying. It's often a learning adventure along the way, and it's hard to beat the satisfaction of reaching the goal as a group.

What advice would you give to people interested in pursuing your career?

Seek out events like energy fairs and conferences where you can get a broad orientation to the field. At these events, you can track down training programs that suit the area you want to focus on. Short classes—from hours to days—are available. These allow you to get an inside view of the profession as a whole, or of a particular specialty, so you can see how it would suit you. Longer programs are a bigger investment and should be carefully assessed. Also, be careful to find out what licensing or certifications will be necessary and ensure that your specific training program can help you accomplish this. Some programs are more about concept and design, while others are apprenticeships that include learning and paid work. Research carefully. Then, don't forget the practical skills and know-how. These make for better installers, designers, and engineers.

---

[1] *The nonprofit Rocky Mountain Institute, founded in Snowmass, Colorado, in 1982, addresses challenges and searches for solutions related to energy and resources.*

[2] *Earth Advantage® is the Northwestern U.S.'s premier green building program.*

CHAPTER 2

ENERGY-RELATED JOBS IN TRANSPORTATION

TRANSPORTATION INDUSTRY OVERVIEW

Growing transportation needs and environmental concerns will generate job opportunities for professionals who plan, design, and build transportation systems and new energy-efficient cars, trucks, buses, trains, ships, and airplanes. New and more stringent environmental regulations place increasing demands on transportation systems. Existing vehicles and fleets must be upgraded to be more energy-efficient and meet stricter emissions standards. Between 2012 and 2016, passenger vehicles will have to achieve 35.5 miles per gallon. Demand is also growing for vehicles that use alternative fuels.

In addition, new openings are expected in areas of transportation that are less energy-intensive, such as rail and water. According to the National Railway Labor Conference, the industry is hiring thousands of new employees to meet the growing needs of railway traffic.

A review of the nation's infrastructure showed a huge need for replacing and upgrading the nation's highway, bridge, and tunnel system. The Federal Highway Administration authorized almost 6,000 projects in response to the American Recovery and Reinvestment Act of 2009 (ARRA). A portion of the ARRA funding was earmarked for on-the-job training/support services projects.

Growing transportation needs and environmental concerns will generate jobs in the area of public transportation systems. In addition, there will be job opportunities for skilled workers to convert buses, trucks, and other motorized equipment for greater fuel efficiency and to build and expand public transportation systems.

In addition to jobs that relate directly to increasing energy efficiency or reducing environmental pollution, which are called green industries, there will also be jobs created because of the "greening of an industry." As a result of increased spending and employment in industries like construction, job opportunities will be created in transportation. More operators will be needed to haul all kinds of building supplies, from pallets of insulation for residential retrofitting to giant steel beams for new or replacement bridges. Wind turbines and solar panels, too, will need to be hauled from manufacturing plants to installation sites.

JOBS PROFILED HERE

The following sectors and occupations are profiled in this chapter:

Vehicle Design, Development, Manufacture, and Maintenance

- Automotive Engineer
- Automotive Engineering Technician
- Automotive Specialty Technician

- Diesel Service Specialist
- Electromechanical Engineering Technologist
- Mechatronics Engineer
- Mechanical Engineer
- Mechanical Engineering Technologist
- Nanosystems Engineer
- Nanotechnology Engineering Technologist/ Nanotechnology Engineering Technician

Fuel Cell Development and Applications

- Fuel Cell Engineer
- Fuel Cell Technician

Transportation Systems

- Civil Engineer
- Supply Chain Manager
- Transportation Engineer
- Transportation Planner

Vehicle and Transit System Operations

- Truck Driver, Heavy and Tractor-Trailer
- Dispatcher
- Freight Forwarder

KEY TO UNDERSTANDING THE JOB PROFILES

The job profiles are classified according to one or more of the following categories:

☼ Bright Outlook
🌎 Green Occupation

The classifications "Bright Outlook" and "Green Occupation" are taken from the National Center for O*NET Development's O*NET OnLine job site. O*NET, which is sponsored by the U.S. Department of Labor/Employment and Training Administration (USDOL/ETA), has broken green jobs into three categories

- Green Increased-Demand occupations
  - o These are occupations that are likely to see job growth, but the work and worker requirements are unlikely to experience significant changes.
- Green Enhanced-Skills occupations
  - o These occupations are likely to experience significant changes in work and worker requirements. Workers may find themselves doing new tasks requiring new knowledge, skills, and credentials. Current projections do not anticipate increased demand for workers in these occupations, but O*NET notes that an increase is possible.
- Green New and Emerging occupations
  - o These are new occupations—not growth in existing jobs—that are created as a result of activity and technology in green sectors of the economy.

Video Links

We've provided easy-to-use links that will take you directly to a particular career video from the One-Stop Career System Multimedia Career Video Library at CareerOneStop.org. The links will look like this:

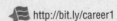 http://bit.ly/career1

Note that videos are not available for all jobs listed here. The videos come in QuickTime and Mpeg formats, with and without captions; download times may vary. CareerOneStop.org is sponsored by the U.S. Department of Labor/Employment and Training Administration.

VEHICLE DESIGN, DEVELOPMENT, MANUFACTURE, AND MAINTENANCE

Motor vehicle and parts manufacturing is one of the largest employers in the nation—even after the bailout of the big three automakers in 2009. About 9,000 businesses manufacture motor vehicles and parts. The growing interest in hybrid and electric vehicles is powering the demand for those with professional degrees in the design and development of these alternative-fuel–powered vehicles and for skilled workers to produce them. Maintaining these vehicles also requires specialized skills. In addition, new secondary industries, such as electric battery manufacturers and chains of battery-charging stations, will develop to provide products related to motor vehicles.

Automotive Engineer ☼ ⑤

Alternate Job Titles and Related Careers

- Automotive Power Electronics Engineer
- Powertrain Control Systems and Software Engineer
- Hybrid Powertrain Development Engineer
- Diesel Retrofit Designer
- Electrical Engineer
- Electronics Engineer
- Emissions Researcher
- Mechanical Engineer
- Quality Engineers

This is both a "Bright Outlook" and "Green New and Emerging" occupation in the transportation sector and the research, design, and consulting services sectors of the economy.

 http://bit.ly/career1

Job Trends

The technology behind the development of motor vehicles is changing as a result of environmental concerns and regulations related to fuel efficiency and air quality standards. According to the U.S. Bureau of Labor's *Career Guide to Industries,* the acceptance by the public of more fuel-efficient vehicles such as hybrid-electric cars is pushing experimentation with electric cars and vehicles powered by alternative fuels.

The *Career Guide* also notes that engineers are the single largest sector of professionals in the motor vehicle industry. The Bureau of Labor Statistics projects the need between 2008 and 2018 for 75,700 new mechanical engineers, of which automotive engineers are a subset. The growth rate is slower than the average of all job categories, however, ranging from 3 percent to 6 percent, but as both a "Bright Outlook" and a "Green New and Emerging" occupation, this may underestimate actual growth. While jobs in the auto industry have long been concentrated in Michigan, Indiana, and Ohio, companies experimenting with alternative-fuel–powered vehicles are springing up in other states.

About UPS

Early in 2009, UPS began testing a hydraulic hybrid truck. The project, in cooperation with the Environmental Protection Agency, could cut UPS's per-lifetime cost of a truck by $50,000 and cut carbon dioxide emissions by 30 percent or more. The truck uses a diesel engine in combination with a hydraulic fluid pump.

Nature of the Work

In general, automotive engineers develop new or improved designs for engines, transmissions, brakes, suspension, and other mechanical and electrical components of motor vehicles and oversee the building and testing of these designs. Using computers and simulation models, instruments, and tools, engineers test their designs to determine whether they meet cost, safety, performance, and quality specifications. Some automotive engineers are involved in the design and testing of vehicles, others focus on the performance, durability, and speed of vehicles, and a third category of automotive engineers develop the manufacturing processes for building vehicles.

In general, automotive engineers design control systems for automotive energy management and emissions management as well as for factors such as safety and performance. They design or analyze systems in areas such as aerodynamics, alternate fuels, hybrid power, brakes, transmission, steering, safety, and diagnostics.

Depending on their engineering specialty, engineers with mechanical engineering backgrounds work on designs for engines, transmissions, and other working parts. Electrical and electronics engineers design electrical and electronic systems, as well as industrial robot control systems used to assemble vehicles.

According to O*NET's survey of incumbents in the occupation, automotive engineers may perform the following specific tasks:

- Design automobile systems, components, control systems, or algorithms
- Build models for algorithm and control feature verification testing
- Conduct or direct testing
- Conduct automotive design review
- Develop engineering specifications and cost estimates for automotive design concepts
- Develop or integrate vehicle control feature requirements
- Perform failure, variation, or root cause analysis
- Develop new techniques and methods for production
- Provide technical direction to other engineers or engineering support personnel
- Conduct research studies to develop new concepts
- Coordinate production activities with other units in the manufacturing process
- Develop or implement operating methods and procedures

- Establish quality control and production standards
- Ensure quality and adherence to government regulations during manufacturing

Career Path

As automotive engineers gain experience, they may become specialists or advance into positions where they supervise a team of engineers and other staff members. Some eventually become managers. Some go on to earn a master's in business administration (MBA) degree to prepare for high-level managerial positions. Some move into technical sales.

Earning Potential

Median hourly wage (2009): $37.03

Median annual wage (2009): $77,020

Education/Licensure

For entry-level positions, a bachelor's degree in engineering from a college or university program that is accredited by the Accreditation Board for Engineering and Technology (ABET) is required. In some cases, engineers with degrees in one type of engineering may qualify for jobs in other areas of engineering.

Some colleges and universities offer five-year programs that culminate in a master's degree. Some offer five- or six-year programs that include cooperative experience. Some four-year schools have arrangements with community colleges or liberal arts colleges that allow students to spend two or three years at the initial school and transfer for the last two years to complete their engineering degree.

All fifty states and the District of Columbia require engineers to be licensed as professional engineers (PE) if they serve the public directly. In most states, licensure requires graduation from a four-year engineering program accredited by ABET, four years of experience, and passing the state exam. Many engineers take the Fundamentals of Engineering portion of the exam upon graduation.

They are then engineers in training (EIT). After obtaining appropriate work experience, they take the Principles and Practice of Engineering exam to complete their professional license. Most states recognize licenses from other states, as long as the requirements are the same or more stringent. Some states have continuing education requirements.

The Society of Automotive Engineers (SAE) offers professional development courses in classrooms and via Webcasts and online courses. Continually updating skills is important to keep up with developments in technology. For example, SAE offers the following certificate programs: Fundamentals of Drivetrain Systems, Diesel Technology, and Vehicle Dynamics.

For More Information

Accreditation Board for Engineering and
   Technology (ABET)
111 Market Place
Suite 1050
Baltimore, Maryland 21202
410-347-7700
www.abet.org

American Society of Mechanical Engineers
   (ASME)
3 Park Avenue
New York, New York 10016-5990
800-843-2763 (toll-free)
www.asme.org

Institute of Electrical and Electronic Engineers
   (IEEE)
3 Park Avenue
New York, New York 10016-5902
646-742-0371
www.ieee.org

National Society of Professional Engineers
   (NSPE)
1420 King Street
Alexandria, Virginia 22314
703-684-2800
www.nspe.org

Society of Automotive Engineers (SAE)
400 Commonwealth Drive
Warrendale, Pennsylvania 15096-0001
724-776-4841
www.sae.org

Automotive Engineering Technician ☼ 🌐

Alternate Job Titles and Related Careers
- Automotive Testing Technician
- Electrical Engineering Technician
- Engineering Technician
- Aeronautical and Aerospace Engineering Technician

Automotive engineering technician is considered a "Bright Outlook" and "Green New and Emerging" occupation according to the Bureau of Labor Statistics. It will have an impact on increasing energy efficiency and reducing the environmental impact of the transportation industry.

 http://bit.ly/career2

Job Trends

According to the Bureau of Labor Statistics, there were 46,000 mechanical engineering technicians in 2008, of which automotive engineering technicians are a subset. Based on current projections, there will be openings for 8,700 engineering technicians by 2018. However, as both a "Bright Outlook" and a "Green New and Emerging" occupation, there may be a large number of openings in this subset in the future.

About Recharging Those Electric Cars

Did you ever wonder how electric car owners would recharge their car batteries? San Francisco has one answer. The city building code now includes wiring for car chargers in all new buildings. Start-up companies are working on establishing car battery recharging stations in California and metropolitan areas in other parts of the country where the new electric battery-powered cars are being introduced.

Nature of the Work

Creativity and knowledge of computer programs may be the two most important talents that an engineering technician can possess. Creativity is important because automotive engineering technicians assist engineers in design work, and much of engineer technicians' work is done by computer. Computers are especially important in automotive engineering because of their use in analysis, design, manufacturing, and operations. Automotive engineering technicians must be proficient in using computers for constructing prototypes, setting up databases, recording data, and analyzing it. They are also expected to have some knowledge of operations, maintenance, and manufacturing.

Automotive engineering technicians work under the supervision of engineers. According to O*NET, technicians may perform the following tasks:

- Create prototypes for testing
- Conduct tests of automotive systems or component performance
- Document test results with cameras, spreadsheets, or other tools
- Analyze test data
- Recommend product or component design improvements based on tests
- Calibrate, maintain, and repair test equipment
- Monitor computer-controlled test equipment

Career Path

The *Occupational Outlook Handbook* notes that opportunities are best for those who possess an associate degree or other postsecondary training in engineering technology. Engineering technicians usually begin their careers working under an experienced technician or technologist, or an engineer. Over time, engineering technicians take on more responsibility with less supervision. In time, they may become supervisors.

Earning Potential

Median hourly wage (2009): $23.54

Median annual wage (2009): $48,970

Education/Licensure

Typically, entry-level positions require an associate degree or other postsecondary training. Students interested in this career should begin by taking math and science courses in high school to prepare them for postsecondary course work.

Community colleges, technical institutes, extension divisions of colleges and universities, and public and private vocational-technical schools often offer degree programs and certification training for automotive engineering technicians. Technical institutes offer less general education and less theory than community or technical colleges. However, they tend to focus more on intensive technical training and may be part of a community college or state university system.

The Accreditation Board for Engineering and Technology (ABET) accredits two-year associate degree programs in engineering technology. Typically, ABET requires that these programs include at least college algebra and trigonometry, and one or two basic science courses.

For More Information

Accreditation Board for Engineering and
   Technology (ABET)
111 Market Place
Suite 1050
Baltimore, Maryland 21202
410-347-7700
www.abet.org

Society of Automotive Engineers (SAE)
400 Commonwealth Drive
Warrendale, Pennsylvania 15096-0001
724-776-4841
www.sae.org

Automotive Specialty Technician ✿⊛

Alternate Job Titles and Related Careers

- Electric Vehicle Electrician
- Electric Vehicle Conversion Specialist
- Automotive Master Mechanic ✿
- Automotive Service Technician and
  Mechanic ✿
- Air Conditioning Technician (A/C
  Technician)
- Alignment Specialist
- Automobile Radiator Mechanic
- Automotive-Cooling-System Diagnostic
  Technician
- Automotive Technician (Auto Technician)
- Automotive Technician Specialist
- Brake Technician/Brake Repairer
- Carburetor Mechanic
- Drivability Technician
- Front-End Mechanic
- Fuel-Injection Servicer
- Spring Repairer
- Tune-Up Mechanic
- Trim Technician
- Undercar Specialist

A "Bright Outlook" occupation, this field is considered one of the "Green Enhanced-Skills" categories in transportation.

 http://bit.ly/career-3

Job Trends

In 2008, the general category of automotive
service technicians and mechanics had 764,000
employees. While currently considered to have a
slower-than-average job growth of 3 to 6 percent,
the automotive specialty technician subcategory is
considered to have a "bright outlook." Even with
the current projected growth rate, the automotive
service technician and mechanic category is estimated to have 181,700 job openings between 2008
and 2018.

Specialties such as electric vehicle electrician
and electric vehicle conversion specialist may
drive added growth. These two specialties will
become increasingly important as Americans begin
replacing cars powered by the traditional internal
combustion engine with electric battery-powered
vehicles. It is possible that mechanics working
on electric-powered cars may need to be licensed
electricians.

Nature of the Work

Automotive specialty technicians must be able
to perform routine maintenance, repair systems,
troubleshoot problems, and install equipment and
wiring. Unlike car mechanics of earlier decades,
automotive specialty technicians repair only one
system or component of a vehicle, such as brakes
or the air conditioning system. They must have
knowledge of the practical applications of engineering science and technology, computers and
electronics, and math. If a technician wishes to
move up to management or to open a shop, he or
she must also have knowledge of customer service,
finance, and sales and marketing and the ability to
use computer software such as customer invoicing
programs.

In terms of skills, automotive specialty technicians
must have arm-hand steadiness, manual dexterity,
control precision, finger dexterity, hearing sensi-
tivity, good near vision, and the ability to filter out
distractions and concentrate on the task at hand.

They must also be good at gathering information through observation, recording data, solving problems, and decision making.

About Renting Cars

Whether renting for business or vacation, go green in your rental car. Hertz® was the first to introduce fuel-efficient rentals, and Enterprise Rent-A-Car has the biggest fleet of fuel-efficient cars.

Depending on a technician's specialty, specific tasks include the following according to O*NET:

- Use electronic test equipment to locate and correct problems in fuel, ignition, or emissions systems
- Compile estimates of repair costs
- Repair, overhaul, and adjust systems or components
- Test electronic computer components
- Tune engines to ensure proper and efficient functioning
- Install and repair air conditioners
- Install service components such as compressors, condensers, or controls
- Repair, replace, and adjust defective carburetor parts and gasoline filters
- Replace defective mufflers and tailpipes

Career Path

Most jobs require training in vocational schools and on-the-job training or an associate degree. After two years of supervised experience and possibly an apprenticeship program, automotive specialty technicians are given more responsibility and work on their own. Over time, with additional experience and training, they may become supervisors or service managers.

Retail trade like auto repair departments in auto dealerships and auto maintenance and repair shops employs 41 percent of automotive specialty technicians. About 16 percent are self-employed. The remainder works in other services and industries, such as car rental companies. Government also employs automotive specialty technicians to maintain their fleets.

Earning Potential

Median hourly wage (2009): $17.03

Median annual wage (2009): $35,420

Electric vehicle technician and electric vehicle conversion specialist may make $22 to $26 an hour.

Education/Licensure

Technicians in the automotive specialty field require either formal training through a vocational school with on-the-job experience or an associate degree from a community college, technical institute, vocational-technical school, or technical college. Electric vehicle technician and electric vehicle conversion specialist require an associate degree.

Even with a degree, automotive specialty technicians typically need one to two years of on-the-job experience and informal training under the supervision of experienced workers. Depending on the specialty, the technician may be required to enter an apprenticeship program.

The National Automotive Technicians Education Foundation (NATEF) evaluates "technician training programs against standards developed by the automotive industry" and recommends qualifying programs for accreditation. Accredited programs include those on brakes, electrical/electronic systems, engine performance, engine repair, heating and air condition, and suspension and steering.

The school accreditation is carried out by the National Institute for Automotive Service Excellence (ASE), which also offers certification programs for automotive service and repair professionals. Among the certifications that are possible are Alternate Fuels, Electronic Diesel Engine Diagnosis Specialist, Advanced Engine Performance Specialist, Automobile Service

Consultant, Automobile/Light Truck, Damage Analysis and Estimating Certification, School Bus, Transit Bus, Undercar Specialist, and Medium/Heavy Truck.

Automotive Youth Educational Systems (AYES) has developed National Apprenticeship Guidelines for its automotive technician specialist training programs, which are administered by a partnership that includes auto manufacturers, auto dealerships, and high schools and vocational schools.

The changes in the design and operation of motor vehicles and the push for alternative fuel sources will require continual upgrading of skills and knowledge in the future.

For More Information

Automotive Youth Educational Systems (AYES)
(For high school stuents)
50 W. Big Beaver
Suite 145
Troy, Michigan 48084
248-526-1750
www.ayes.org

Accrediting Commission of Career Schools and Colleges of Technology (ACCSCT)
2101 Wilson Boulevard
Suite 302
Arlington, Virginia 22201
703-247-4212
www.accsct.org

National Automotive Technicians Education Foundation (NATEF)
101 Blue Seal Drive SE
Suite 101
Leesburg, Virginia 20175
703-669-6650
www.natef.org

National Institute for Automotive Service Excellence (ASE)
101 Blue Seal Drive SE
Suite 101
Leesburg, Virginia 20175
703-669-6600
www.ase.org

Diesel Service Specialist

Alternate Job Titles and Related Careers

- Bus and Truck Mechanics and Diesel Engine Specialist
- Certified Mechanic
- Commercial Transport Mechanic
- Diesel Engine Mechanic
- Diesel Mechanic
- Diesel Retrofit Installer
- Diesel Retrofit Manufacturing Plant Worker
- Diesel Technician
- Fleet Mechanic
- Heavy Duty Mechanic
- Heavy Equipment Service Mechanic
- Heavy Equipment Service Technician
- Journeyman Bus Mechanic
- Medium/Heavy Truck Mechanic
- Mobile Equipment Mechanic
- Transit Mechanic
- Transportation Mechanic
- Aircraft and Avionics Equipment Mechanic
- Aircraft and Avionics Equipment Service Technician

There are as many specialties as there are kinds of vehicles powered by diesel engines.

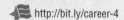 http://bit.ly/career-4

Job Trends

According to the *Occupational Outlook Handbook,* employment opportunities for diesel engine specialists and mechanics, including bus and truck mechanics, are expected to increase 6 percent by 2018, slower than average for all occupations. The increase would amount to about 14,900 more jobs in the general category.

However, the need to retrofit existing engines to meet new environmental emissions standards and pollution regulations is a source of the potential growth. Job candidates who have completed formal training programs should have very good opportunities. The California Economic Development

Department predicts nearly 4,000 new jobs just in California by 2016.

According to a study released in 2010 by the Center for American Progress, the Natural Resources Defense Council, and the United Autoworkers, close to 12 percent of all passenger cars and light trucks produced in 2020 will be powered by diesel engines; this represents a 450 percent increase over 2008 actual levels and also signifies the need for more diesel service specialists/mechanics.

Nature of the Work

Diesel service technicians and mechanics adjust, diagnose, repair, and overhaul buses, trucks, locomotives, automobiles, and heavy equipment that have diesel engines. Diesel technicians usually specialize in either light vehicles like automobiles or heavy vehicles like trucks and buses. Because diesel engines often outlast gasoline engines, retrofitting these engines with filters and controls to comply with environmental and pollution standards is often part of the job. Increasing use of microprocessor controls requires mechanics to use computers to diagnose and solve engine problems.

About Airline Emissions

The European Union has adopted a standard that requires air carriers to cut emissions from their planes or begin buying carbon permits in 2012 as part of the EU's cap-and-trade program to reduce greenhouse gases.

Career Path

Experienced diesel service mechanics and technicians specialize by acquiring additional certifications. Some may become supervisors or service managers. Some become sales representatives, and others may open their own shops.

Earning Potential

Median hourly wage (2009): $19.35

Median annual wage (2009): $40,250

Education/Licensure

Job opportunities are best for those who have completed formal training programs. Many community colleges and vocational or trade schools offer training programs in diesel engine repair. These programs may lead to a two-year associate degree or to certification. Some mechanics learn the trade on the job. After three or four years of experience, they advance to the journey level. Employers often send technicians and mechanics to classes offered by manufacturers to learn the latest technology.

Certification is not required. However, national certification is the standard and improves opportunities to get a job and to advance. The National Institute for Automotive Service Excellence (ASE) offers certification for ASE Master Technician (automotive, bus, medium/heavy truck) and ASE Master Medium/Heavy Vehicle Technician. The latter has several specializations including diesel engines and heating, ventilation, and air conditioning. The "Truck Equipment Specialist" certification includes specialization in electrical/electronic systems and auxiliary power systems. These certifications require a combination of education, experience, and passing a series of tests. Technicians and mechanics must recertify every five years by taking the appropriate tests.

The National Automotive Technicians Education Foundation (NATEF) evaluates training programs and certifies the programs for ASE certification training. The Association of Diesel Specialists provides hands-on training seminars at the entry and continuing education levels.

For More Information

Accrediting Commission of Career Schools and
    Colleges of Technology (ACCSCT)
2101 Wilson Boulevard
Suite 302
Arlington, Virginia 22201
703-247-4212
www.accsct.org

Association of Diesel Specialists
400 Admiral Boulevard
Kansas City, Missouri 64106
816-285-0810
www.diesel.org

Diesel Technology Forum
5291 Corporate Drive
Suite 102
Frederick, Maryland 21703
301-668-7230
www.dieselforum.org

National Automotive Technicians Education
Foundation (NATEF)
101 Blue Seal Drive SE
Suite 101
Leesburg, Virginia 20175
703-669-6650
www.natef.org

National Institute for Automotive Service
Excellence (ASE)
101 Blue Seal Drive SE
Suite 101
Leesburg, Virginia 20175
703-669-6600
www.asecert.org

Electromechanical Engineering Technologist ☼ ⊕

Alternate Job Titles and Related Careers
- Electromechanical Technician
- Electrical Engineering Technician
- Electronic Engineering Technician
- Mechanical Engineering Technician
- Mechatronics Technician

This is both a "Bright Outlook" and a "Green New and Emerging" occupation in manufacturing and research, design, and consulting.

Job Trends

About 77,000 people worked as engineering technicians in 2008, and 18,500 job openings are projected between then and 2018. This rate of 3 to 6 percent is considered slower than average, but electromechanical engineering technologist is considered a "Green New and Emerging" occupation, which should result in a higher growth rate. Generally, electromechanical engineering technologists work in manufacturing and research, design, and consulting services.

Nature of the Work

Electromechanical engineering combines electrical-electronics and mechanical engineering principles and is an important specialty in highly automated manufacturing, production, and assembly plant processes. Some electromechanical engineering technologists work under engineers to help design, develop, test, and manufacture electronic and computer-controlled mechanical systems. Others operate these systems in manufacturing plants.

About Biotech in Your Garden

Biotech is not just bioengineered food. That organic fertilizer you use in your garden may have been bioengineered. Check out products like Dr. Earth's line of organic plant fertilizers.

According to O*NET, the following are among the many tasks that electromechanical engineering technologists perform:

- Collaborate with engineers to implement electromechanical designs in various settings
- Analyze engineering designs or logical and digital circuitry, motor controls, instrumentation, and data acquisition for implementation into new or existing systems
- Produce electrical, electronic, and mechanical drawings, and other related documents
- Translate electromechanical drawings into design specifications
- Consult with machinists and technicians to ensure that electromechanical equipment and systems meet design specifications

- Install and program computer hardware and machine and instrumentation software in microprocessor-based systems
- Select and use laboratory, operational, and diagnostic techniques and test equipment to assess electromechanical circuits, equipment, processes, systems, and subsystems
- Select electromechanical equipment, materials, components, and systems to meet functional specifications
- Fabricate mechanical, electrical, and electronic components and assemblies
- Establish and maintain inventory, records, and documentation systems
- Modify, maintain, and repair components, equipment, and systems
- Specify, coordinate, and conduct quality-control and quality-assurance programs and procedures

Career Path

Electromechanical engineering technologists work under the supervision of engineers. As they become more experienced, electromechanical technologists become involved in more difficult projects with less supervision. Some will eventually become supervisors themselves.

Earning Potential

Median hourly wage (2009): $27.66

Median annual wage (2009): $57,530

Education/Licensure

A two-year associate degree is preferred. The Technology Accreditation Commission of the Accreditation Board for Engineering and Technology (ABET) accredits two-year associate-degree programs in engineering technology. Typically, ABET requires that these programs include at least college algebra and trigonometry and one or two basic science courses. Graduates of these programs are considered to have an acceptable level of competence.

Degree and certificate programs are offered at community colleges, public and private technical institutes, and vocational-technical schools. Technical institutes offer less general education and less theory than community or technical colleges. However, they tend to focus more on intensive technical training, and may be part of a community college or state university system. Some four-year colleges offer bachelor's degrees in electromechanical engineering technology, but graduates of these programs usually work as engineers.

For More Information

Accreditation Board for Engineering and
     Technology (ABET)
111 Market Place
Suite 1050
Baltimore, Maryland 21202
410-347-7700
www.abet.org

American Society of Mechanical Engineers
     (ASME)
3 Park Avenue
New York, New York 10016-5990
800-843-2763
www.asme.org

Institute of Electrical and Electronic Engineers
     (IEEE)
3 Park Avenue
New York, New York 10016-5902
646-742-0371
www.ieee.org

Society of Automotive Engineers (SAE)
400 Commonwealth Drive
Warrendale, Pennsylvania 15096-0001
724-776-4841
www.sae.org

Society of Manufacturing Engineers (SME)
1 SME Drive
Dearborn, Michigan 48121
800-733-4763
www.sme.org

Mechatronics Engineer ⚙️🌐

Alternate Job Titles and Related Careers

- Computer Hardware Engineering
- Controls Engineer
- Electromechanical Engineer
- Manufacturing Engineer
- Mechanical Design Engineer
- Mechanical Modeling and Simulation Manager
- Powertrain Simulation Engineer
- Systems Engineer
- Technical Engineer

This is both a "Bright Outlook" and a "Green New and Emerging" occupation. In addition to the automotive industry, any industry that uses technology is a possible option for mechatronics engineers, but especially manufacturing and research, design, and consulting services.

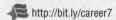 http://bit.ly/career7

Job Trends

Many jobs include mechatronics, but most job titles don't, so you have to look at the industry and type of work that is required. Electrical, mechanical, and computer software jobs often include "mechatronics" in the job description.

The Bureau of Labor Statistics groups mechatronics engineers in the category "All other engineers" to distinguish them from the other sixteen categories of engineers, such as civil, mechanical, and electrical. According to the Bureau of Labor's 2008 survey, 183,000 engineers worked in this "all other" category. The growth rate is estimated to be about average at 7 to 13 percent between 2008 and 2018. However, as an emerging green occupation, the percentage for mechatronics engineers may be higher.

Nature of the Work

A relatively new discipline, mechatronics engineering began as the combining of mechanics and electronics. Today, it unites knowledge from the disciplines of mechanical engineering, electronic engineering, computer hardware and software engineering, control engineering, and systems design engineering. It combines a variety of cutting-edge technologies, including robotics, automation systems, and micro electromechanical systems. Among the topics taught in a mechatronics program are modeling and design, systems integration, intelligent control, robotics, motion control, vibration and noise control, automotive systems, and manufacturing.

Mechatronics engineers design automation, intelligent systems, smart devices, and industrial systems controls for the automotive industry and other manufacturing industries. O*NET lists the following as among the tasks that mechatronics engineers perform:

- Design advanced precision equipment and mechatronics components
- Upgrade existing devices by adding mechatronic elements
- Conduct studies to determine feasibility, costs, or performance benefits of new mechatronic equipment
- Create embedded software design programs
- Fabricate mechanical models and tolerance analyses to simulate mechatronic design concepts
- Design advanced electronic control systems for mechanical systems and engineering systems for the automation of industrial tasks
- Design, develop, or implement control circuits and algorithms for electromechanical and pneumatic devices or systems
- Identify and select appropriate materials for mechatronic system designs
- Implement and test design solutions
- Analyze existing development or manufacturing procedures and recommend changes and improvements

- Create design documents for parts, assemblies, or finished products
- Oversee the work of contractors and suppliers

Career Path

As mechatronics engineers gain experience, they advance into positions where they supervise a team of engineers and other staff members. Some eventually become managers. Some go on to earn a Master of Business Administration (MBA) degree to prepare them for higher-level managerial and executive positions.

Earning Potential

Median hourly wage (2009): $43.06

Median annual wage (2009): $89,560

Education/Licensure

A bachelor's degree is necessary for entry-level positions from a college or university program that is accredited by the Accreditation Board for Engineering and Technology (ABET). In relation to other engineering degrees, few colleges have degrees in mechatronics engineering, but this should change as demand grows. As with other specialties, engineers with other engineering degrees may qualify for jobs in mechatronics engineering.

Some colleges and universities offer five-year programs that culminate in a master's degree. Some offer five- or six-year programs that include cooperative experience. Some four-year schools have arrangements with community colleges or liberal arts colleges that allow students to spend two or three years at the initial school and transfer for the last two years to complete their engineering degree.

All fifty states and the District of Columbia require engineers to be licensed as professional engineers (PE) if they serve the public directly. In most states, licensure requires graduation from a four-year engineering program accredited by ABET, four years of experience, and passing the state exam. Many engineers take the Fundamentals of Engineering portion of the exam upon graduation. They are then engineers in training (EIT). After obtaining appropriate work experience, they take the Principles and Practice of Engineering exam to complete their professional license. Most states recognize licenses from other states, as long as the requirements are the same or more stringent. Some states have continuing education requirements to maintain engineering licenses.

For More Information

Accreditation Board for Engineering and
    Technology (ABET)
111 Market Place
Suite 1050
Baltimore, Maryland 21202
410-347-7700
www.abet.org

American Society of Mechanical Engineers
    (ASME)
3 Park Avenue
New York, New York 10016-5990
800-843-2763
www.asme.org

Institute of Electrical and Electronic Engineers
    (IEEE)
3 Park Avenue
New York, New York 10016-5902
646-742-0371
www.ieee.org

Society of Automotive Engineers (SAE)
400 Commonwealth Drive
Warrendale, Pennsylvania 15096-0001
724-776-4841
www.sae.org

Society of Manufacturing Engineers (SME)
1 SME Drive
Dearborn, Michigan 48121
800-733-4763
www.sme.org

Mechanical Engineer 🜨

Alternate Job Titles and Related Careers
- Electromechanical Engineer
- Lead Mechanical Engineer
- Lead Process Engineer
- Mechanical Handling Engineer
- Process Design Engineer
- Project Manager
- Projects Control Manager

In addition to manufacturing, a number of jobs in the field of mechanical engineering are in oil and natural gas development, an important area for environmental impact. This is a "Green Enhanced-Skills" occupation.

 http://bit.ly/career6

Job Trends

An emerging trend in the new green economy is to retool U.S. manufacturing. For example, manufacturing plants that built gasoline-powered cars and trucks can be modified to produce hybrid vehicles and factories that previously made auto components can be modified to make wind turbine components. These modifications require mechanical engineers to design the products and the processes and equipment to manufacture them.

The Bureau of Labor Statistics predicts that growth in mechanical engineering will be 6 percent through 2018, which is slower than the average for all occupations, but still amounts to 14,400 new openings. This slow growth is tied to a decline in the manufacturing industry. Nevertheless, because there were about 238,700 mechanical engineering jobs in 2008, mechanical engineering still ranks as one of the top 50 occupations with the most openings that requires a bachelor's degree. It can also be the basis for jobs in green industries such as motor vehicle manufacturing.

Nature of the Work

Mechanical engineering is a broad discipline concerned with power and energy and how these are transmitted, converted, controlled, and utilized effectively in mechanical devices. Mechanical engineers design, develop, and manufacture all types of mechanical devices, including tools, engines, turbines, generators, and robots. They design and manufacture heating, ventilation, and cooling systems used in residential and commercial buildings, and they also design biomedical devices like artificial joints. In designing a product, engineers must consider a wide variety of factors such as cost, safety, performance, appearance, reliability, ergonomics, recyclability, energy efficiency, and environmental impact. Computer simulation and modeling are important tools in the design process.

Mechanical engineers are an important part of the transportation industry. Existing forms of transportation must be continuously improved or replaced. Mechanical engineers design and manufacture all types of vehicles, including the powertrain and components for hybrid and alternative-fuel automobiles and trucks. They also develop the software that controls electromechanical systems in vehicles and design energy-efficient engines for buses and trains. Fuel efficiency, by-products of fuel consumption, and environmental impact are critical factors that mechanical engineers address in their work.

Mechanical engineers also work in many other industries that affect the environment, including advanced manufacturing, aerospace, agricultural production, biomedical, construction, energy, geospatial technology, and nanotechnology. In all these industries, energy efficiency and environmental impact are factors.

About Infrastructure Management

One key to reducing energy use and greenhouse gases is smart infrastructure. This is a system of wireless sensors and analytic and visualization software that can result in the more efficient management of everything from commuter traffic to the nation's electric grid.

Career Path

As mechanical engineers gain experience, they may become specialists or advance into positions where they supervise a team of engineers and other staff members. Some eventually become managers. Some go on to earn an MBA degree to prepare them for high-level managerial positions. Some move into technical sales.

Earning Potential

Mean hourly wage (2009): $37.03

Mean annual wage (2009): $77,020

Education/Licensure

For entry-level positions, a bachelor's degree in engineering from a college or university program that is accredited by the Accreditation Board for Engineering and Technology (ABET) is required. In some cases, engineers with degrees in one type of engineering may qualify for jobs in other areas of engineering. Most colleges and universities offer mechanical engineering degrees.

Some colleges and universities offer five-year programs that culminate in a master's degree. Some offer five- or six-year programs that include cooperative experience. Some four-year schools have arrangements with community colleges or liberal arts colleges that allow students to spend two or three years at the initial school and transfer for the last two years to complete their engineering degree.

All fifty states and the District of Columbia require engineers to be licensed as professional engineers (PE) if they serve the public directly. In most states, licensure requires graduation from a four-year engineering program accredited by ABET, four years of experience, and passing the state exam. Many engineers take the Fundamentals of Engineering portion of the exam upon graduation. They are then engineers in training (EIT). After obtaining appropriate work experience, they take the Principles and Practice of Engineering exam to complete their professional license. Most states recognize licenses from other states as long as the requirements are the same or more stringent. Some states have continuing education requirements.

The American Society of Mechanical Engineers (ASME) offers a number of specialized certifications, short courses, Internet seminars, and online courses. The Society of Automotive Engineers (SAE) offers professional development courses in classrooms and via Webcasts and online courses. Continually updating skills is important to keep up with developments in technology.

For More Information

Accreditation Board for Engineering and
    Technology (ABET)
111 Market Place
Suite 1050
Baltimore, Maryland 21202
410-347-7700
www.abet.org

American Society of Mechanical Engineers
    (ASME)
3 Park Avenue
New York, New York 10016-5990
800-843-2763 (toll-free)
www.asme.org

National Society of Professional Engineers
    (NSPE)
1420 King Street
Alexandria, Virginia 22314
703-684-2800
www.nspe.org

Society of Automotive Engineers (SAE)
400 Commonwealth Drive
Warrendale, Pennsylvania 15096-0001
724-776-4841
www.sae.org

Mechanical Engineering Technologist ✿ ⑤

Alternate Job Titles and Related Careers

- Design Engineer
- Engineering Fitter (Machine Fitter)
- Engineering Lab Technician
- Engineering Technician
- Engineering Technical Analyst
- Equipment Engineer
- Mechanical Engineering Designer
- Mechanical Engineering Technician
- Metal Turner
- Operations Mechanic
- Process Technician
- Research and Development Technician
- Toolmaker

This is both a "Bright Outlook" and a "Green New and Emerging" occupation. It is found mainly in manufacturing and in research, design, and consulting services.

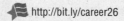 http://bit.ly/career26

Job Trends

The Bureau of Labors Statistics lists 77,000 workers employed as engineering technologists/technicians in 2008, and projects 18,500 job openings between 2008 and 2018. This is slower than average at 3 to 6 percent, although as a "Green New and Emerging" occupation, the mechanical engineering technologist occupation may experience higher job growth.

Nature of the Work

According to O*NET, mechanical engineering technologists apply engineering theory and technical skills to support mechanical engineering activities. These include the generation, transmission, and use of mechanical and fluid energy. Mechanical engineering technicians assist mechanical engineers in designing, testing, and analyzing equipment and production processes. One of their functions in the automotive industry is to set up the test equipment for automobile crash tests.

Among the tasks that mechanical engineering technologists may perform are the following:

- Assemble or disassemble mechanical systems
- Assist engineers to design, develop, test, or manufacture industrial machinery, consumer products, or equipment
- Test machines, components, materials, or products to determine characteristics such as performance, strength, and response to stress
- Prepare specifications, designs, or sketches
- Oversee, monitor, and inspect mechanical installations or construction projects
- Apply testing or monitoring apparatus
- Conduct failure analyses, document the results, and recommend corrective actions
- Design specialized or customized equipment, machines, or structures
- Provide technical support to other employees regarding mechanical design, fabrication, testing, or documentation
- Perform routine maintenance on equipment
- Prepare cost and materials estimates and project schedules
- Prepare equipment inspection schedules, reliability schedules, work plans, and other records

Career Path

Mechanical engineering technologists work under the supervision of engineers. As they become more experienced, they become involved in more difficult projects with less supervision. Some will eventually become supervisors themselves.

Earning Potential

Median hourly wage (2009): $27.66

Median annual wage (2009): $57,530

Education/Licensure

To get ahead in the field, an associate degree is desirable. A number of community colleges, technical institutes, extension divisions of colleges and universities, and public and private vocational-technical schools offer degree and certification programs to train mechanical engineering technologists. Technical institutes offer less general education and less theory than community or technical colleges. However, they tend to focus more on intensive technical training and may be part of a community college or state university system.

The Technology Accreditation Commission of the Accreditation Board for Engineering and Technology (ABET) accredits two-year associate-degree programs in engineering technology. Typically, ABET requires that these programs include at least college algebra and trigonometry and one or two basic science courses. Graduates of these programs are considered to have an acceptable level of competence.

The National Institute for Certification in Engineering Technologies (NICET) provides certification for industrial instrumentation.

For More Information

Accreditation Board for Engineering and
  Technology (ABET)
111 Market Place
Suite 1050
Baltimore, Maryland 21202
410-347-7700
www.abet.org

American Society of Certified Engineering
  Technicians (ASCET)
P.O. Box 1536
Brandon, Missouri 39043
601-824-8991
www.ascet.org

American Society of Mechanical Engineers
  (ASME)
3 Park Avenue
New York, New York 10016-5990
800-843-2763 (toll-free)
www.asme.org

National Institute for Certification in Engineering
  Technologies (NICET)
1420 King Street
Alexandria, Virginia 22314
888-476-4238
www.nicet.org

National Society of Professional Engineers
  (NSPE)
1420 King Street
Alexandria, Virginia 22314
703-684-2800
www.nspe.org

Nanosystems Engineer ☼⑤

Alternate Job Titles and Related Careers

- Metamaterials Scientist
- Nanotechnology Engineer
- Nanotechnology Researcher

This "Bright Outlook" and "Green New and Emerging" occupation is found in the green economy sectors of manufacturing and research, design, and consulting services.

Job Trends

Nanosystems engineers are grouped as part of the "All other engineers" category by the Bureau of Labor Statistics; 183,000 engineers fit this category in 2008. The growth rate for this category is projected to be average, 7 to 13 percent, which will result in an estimated 50,200 job openings between 2008 and 2018. However, external circumstances are driving the nanotechnology industry, and job growth for nanosystems engineers may be higher.

The federal government alone is funneling close to $2 billion into nanotechnology research and development. In 2008, the United States as a whole invested $5.7 billion in nanotechnology. Much of it ends up as grants to universities to conduct research. One reason for the recent push for more money for research and development in nanoscience is the 2010 report by the President's Council of Advisors on Science and Technology that while U.S. public and private investment in nanotechnology grew by 18 percent between 2003 and 2008, funding outside the United States grew by 27 percent. As a result, the competition from other nations has increased dramatically. In order to maintain the nation's initial lead in nanotechnology research and development, the Council advocated greater funding and also recommended a greater emphasis on commercializing new nanotech products. Both additional funding and the need to bring applications to market quickly will undoubtedly require more workers proficient in the knowledge and skills needed for nanotechnology.

Nature of the Work

Nanotechnology is the science and technology of building devices from single atoms and molecules. It is the engineering of functional systems at a molecular scale. Nanosystems engineers or nanotechnology engineers use the principles of nanoscale physics and electrical, chemical, and biological engineering. Their work involves designing, developing, and supervising the production of materials, devices, and systems of unique molecular or macromolecular compositions. They conduct research on a variety of nanotechnology topics, including heat-transfer, hybrid systems, and nanocomposites.

Among the tasks that a nanosystems engineer performs are the following, according to O*NET:

- Conduct research
- Create designs or prototypes for nanosystems applications
- Design or engineer nanomaterials, nanodevices, nano-enabled products, and nanosystems using CAD software
- Coordinate or supervise the work of suppliers and vendors in the design, building, and testing of devices
- Design or conduct tests of new products, processes, or systems
- Engineer production processes for specific applications
- Prepare invention disclosures and patent applications

- Identify new applications for existing nanotechnologies
- Provide technical guidance and support to customers
- Write proposals for funding and reports
- Supervise technologists and technicians conducting nanotechnology research or production

Career Path

As nanotechnology engineers gain experience, they become specialists and advance into positions where they supervise a team of engineers and other staff members. Some eventually become managers. Some go on to earn an MBA degree to prepare them for higher level managerial positions. Some continue their education by obtaining graduate degrees in engineering that enable them to move into executive positions in industry and government.

Earning Potential

Median hourly wage (2009): $43.06

Median annual wage (2009): $89,560

About Nanotechnology Funding

The National Nanotechnology Initiative (NNI) is a federally funded effort to support research "applications in nanotechnology that will lead to a revolution in technology and industry that benefits society." In the 2011 federal budget, the agencies working with nanotechnology asked for $1.8 billion for nanotechnology research and development; this doesn't include the money that corporations and other institutions are spending on nanoscience research. NNI is the central point for all federal agencies dealing with nanotechnology. For more information, check out www.nano.gov.

Education/Licensure

Nanotechnology is relatively new, and it is not a single discipline, but an interdisciplinary and multidisciplinary field. According to the National Nanotechnology Initiative, few colleges and universities currently offer a degree in nanotechnology. However, many research universities offer courses in the field and also undergraduate experiences through their interdisciplinary centers. Each summer, the National Nanofabrication Infrastructure Network offers a Research Experience of Undergraduates Program (NNIN REU). Engineering and science students with an interest in nanotechnology and who will not be graduating before August of that year are eligible. Visit www.nnin.org/nnin_reu.html for more information.

When looking for programs, check out degree programs in applied science. You may find courses in nanotechnology, nanosystems, nanoscience, or even a concentration in the field.

For entry-level positions, a bachelor's degree in engineering from a college or university program that is accredited by the Accreditation Board for Engineering and Technology (ABET) is required. Some colleges and universities offer five-year programs that culminate in a master's degree. Some offer five- or six-year programs that include cooperative experience. Some four-year schools have arrangements with community colleges or liberal arts colleges that allow students to spend two or three years at the initial school and transfer for the last two years to complete their engineering degree.

All fifty states and the District of Columbia require engineers to be licensed as professional engineers (PE) if they serve the public directly. In most states, licensure requires graduation from a four-year engineering program accredited by ABET, four years of experience, and passing the state exam. Many engineers take the Fundamentals of Engineering portion of the exam upon graduation. They are then engineers in training (EIT). After obtaining appropriate work experience, they take the Principles and Practice of Engineering exam to complete their professional license. Most states recognize licenses from other states, as long as the requirements are the same or more stringent. Some states have continuing education requirements.

For More Information

Accreditation Board for Engineering and
  Technology (ABET)
111 Market Place
Suite 1050
Baltimore, Maryland 21202
410-347-7700
www.abet.org

American Chemical Society (ACS)
1155 Sixteenth Street, NW
Washington, DC 20036
800-227-5558 (toll-free)
www.acs.org

American Society of Mechanical Engineers
  (ASME)
3 Park Avenue
New York, New York 10016-5990
800-843-2763 (toll-free)
www.asme.org
  (See Nanotechnology Institute of ASME
  International
  www.nanotechnologyinstitute.org)

American Society of Precision Engineering
  (ASPE)
P.O. Box 10826
Raleigh, North Carolina 27604-0826
919-839-8039
www.aspe.net

Institute of Electrical and Electronic Engineers
  (IEEE)
3 Park Avenue
New York, New York 10016-5902
646-742-0371
www.ieee.org
  (See IEEE Nanotechnology Council
  http://ewh.ieee.org/tc/nanotech/)

Materials Research Society
506 Keystone Drive
Warrendale, Pennsylvania 15086-7537
724-779-3003
www.mrs.org

Society of Manufacturing Engineers (SME)
1 SME Drive
Dearborn, Michigan 48121
800-733-4763 (toll-free)
www.sme.org

Nanotechnology Engineering Technologist ☼⑨

Nanotechnology Engineering Technician ☼⑨

Alternate Job Title and Related Career

- Nanotechnology Machinist

Both the nanotechnology engineering technologist and technician positions are "Bright Outlook" and "Green New and Emerging" occupations.

Job Trends

The outlook for both nanotechnology engineering technicians and technologists is similar. In 2008, the Bureau of Labor Statistics counted 77,000 employees in the "All other engineering technicians, except drafters," with a slower-than-average growth rate of 3 to 6 percent. This translates into about 18,500 job openings for this category between 2008 and 2018. However, both nanotechnology engineering technicians and technologists are listed as "Bright Outlook" occupations, meaning they may see greater job growth than projected.

The federal government alone is funneling close to $2 billion into nanotechnology research and development. In 2008, the United States as a whole invested $5.7 billion in nanotechnology. Much of it ends up as grants to universities to conduct research. One reason for the recent push for more money for research and development in nanoscience is the President's Council of Advisors on Science and Technology's 2010 report, which stated that while U.S. public and private investment in nanotechnology grew by 18 percent between 2003 and 2008, funding outside the United States grew by 27 percent. As a result, the competition from other nations has increased dramatically. In order to maintain the nation's initial lead in nanotechnology research and development, the Council advocated greater funding and also recommended a greater emphasis on commercializing new nanotech products. Both additional funding and the need to bring applications to market quickly will undoubtedly require more workers proficient in the knowledge and skills needed for nanotechnology.

Nature of the Work

Nanotechnology is the science and technology of building devices from single atoms and molecules. It is the engineering of functional systems at a molecular scale. Nanosystems/nanotechnology engineers use the principles of nanoscale physics and electrical, chemical, and biological engineering. Nanotechnology engineering technologists and technicians assist engineering staff and have different duties.

Nanotechnology engineering technologists implement production processes for nanoscale design. O*NET lists the following tasks as ones that a nanotechnology engineering may perform:

- Design or conduct experiments in collaboration with scientists or engineers
- Implement new or enhanced methods and processes for the processing, testing, or manufacturing of nanotechnology materials or products
- Inspect or measure thin films of nanotubes, polymers, or inorganic coatings
- Produce images and measurements
- Collect and compile nanotechnology research and engineering data
- Develop or modify laboratory experimental techniques for nanoscale use

- Prepare capability data, training materials, or other documentation for transfer of processes to production
- Contribute to grant proposals and patent applications
- Install nanotechnology production equipment at customer sites
- Supervise or provide technical direction to technicians engaged in nanotechnology research or production

Nanotechnology engineering technicians operate commercial-scale production equipment to produce, test, and modify nanotechnology materials, devices, and systems. They must assemble the components and conduct experiments. Among the job duties that O*NET lists for this classification are the following:

- Assist scientists, engineers, and technologists in processing or characterizing materials according to physical and chemical properties
- Calibrate nanotechnology equipment
- Measure or mix chemicals or compounds following formulas and instructions
- Monitor equipment during operation to ensure adherence to specifications for such characteristics as pressure and temperature
- Perform functional tests of nano-enhanced assemblies, components, or systems
- Inspect work products to ensure quality and adherence to specifications
- Produce detailed images and measurements
- Record test results and maintain accurate records
- Repair processing or test equipment
- Track inventory and supplies

Career Path

The nanotechnology engineering technologist occupation requires more skills and has higher-level responsibilities than a nanotechnology engineering technician. A technologist may have technicians reporting to him or her. Both require at least an associate degree.

Earning Potential

The earning potential for both occupations is similar.

Median hourly wage (2009): $27.66

Median annual wage (2009): $57,530

Education/Licensure

Because of the relative newness of the nanotechnology field, not many community colleges, technical institutes, extension divisions of colleges and universities, and public and private vocational-technical schools offer degree and certification programs to train nanotechnology engineering technologists or technicians. When you are looking for programs, look for those in applied science with a concentration in nanotechnology, nanoscale, or nanoscience.

The Technology Accreditation Commission of the Accreditation Board for Engineering and Technology (ABET) accredits two-year associate-degree programs in engineering technology. Typically, ABET requires that these programs include at least college algebra and trigonometry and one or two basic science courses. Graduates of these programs are considered to have an acceptable level of competence.

For More Information

Accreditation Board for Engineering and
     Technology (ABET)
111 Market Place
Suite 1050
Baltimore, Maryland 21202
410-347-7700
www.abet.org

American Chemical Society (ACS)
1155 Sixteenth Street, NW
Washington, DC 20036
800-227-5558 (toll-free)
www.acs.org

American Society of Certified Engineering
Technicians (ASCET)
P.O. Box 1536
Brandon, Missouri 39043
601-824-8991
www.ascet.org

American Society of Mechanical Engineers
(ASME)
3 Park Avenue
New York, New York 10016-5990
800-843-2763 (toll-free)
www.asme.org
(See Nanotechnology Institute of ASME
International
www.nanotechnologyinstitute.org)

American Society of Precision Engineering
(ASPE)
P.O. Box 10826
Raleigh, North Carolina 27604-0826
919-839-8039
www.aspe.net

Institute of Electrical and Electronic Engineers
(IEEE)
3 Park Avenue
New York, New York 10016-5902
646-742-0371
www.ieee.org
(See IEEE Nanotechnology Council
http://ewh.ieee.org/tc/nanotech/)

Materials Research Society
506 Keystone Drive
Warrendale, Pennsylvania 15086-7537
724-779-3003
www.mrs.org

Society of Manufacturing Engineers (SME)
1 SME Drive
Dearborn, Michigan 48121
800-733-4763 (toll-free)
www.sme.org

Nanotechnologies: Promise or Peril

Nanoscience, the study of matter on the atomic and molecular scale, is considered by many to be the foundation of the new industrial revolution. Products made by nanotechnology include processors for computers, wireless keyboard mice, more efficient solar panels, and an antibacterial mobile phone, all of which you might expect from a science with the word "technology" in it. But nanotechnology engineers have also developed such things as antibacterial pet products, ski wax, hair dryers, air purifiers, insulation, skin cream, sunscreen, and sunglasses—in fact, more than 1,000 consumer products to date.

Automotive companies have also been conducting research to find ways to use nanotechnology in their motor vehicles. In 2001, Toyota began using nanocomposite material for a bumper design. The nanocomposite makes the bumper 60 percent lighter than traditional bumpers and twice as resistant to denting and scratching. Toyota also began using plastics in the interiors of its Lexus HS hybrid that are produced from plants using nanotechnology. Toyota claims this lowers carbon dioxide emissions by 33 percent "from the time the raw materials are grown until they are disposed of."

In 2002, General Motors introduced nanocomposite material on the step assist of GMC Safari and Chevrolet Astro vans. In 2004, GM introduced nanocomposits on the exterior side molding of its Chevrolet Impala. GM's 2005 Hummer H2 SUT used nanocomposite material in its cargo bed. This lightweight material reduces the overall weight of vehicles, and thereby has the potential to reduce fuel consumption.

Ford has a goal of improving the fuel efficiency of its vehicles by 40 percent by 2020. It plans to achieve this by using nanotechnology. Ford scientists and engineers are working to develop paints, light metals, plastics, and catalysts to produce lighter cars and trucks. They have already achieved weight and fuel savings with their reengineered aluminum engine technology using nanoscience and are looking at new energy storage solutions for alternative power sources.

A number of companies have developed products for car maintenance, including motor oil, glass cleaner, wheel cleaner, brake dust shield, and car polish. At least one tire company has developed a tire using nanotechnology, which makes tires lighter and longer lasting.

According to the Project on Emerging Nanotechnologies, as of 2009, nanotechnology research and development was being conducted at 182 government labs and universities and more than 1,000 companies and other organizations in the United States. Every state and the District of Columbia had at least one group working on nanotechnology. California, Massachusetts, New York, and Texas each had seventy-five or more centers. The top metropolitan centers with thirty or more groups working in nanotechnology in order were Boston, Massachusetts; San Francisco, California; San Jose, California; Raleigh, North Carolina; Middlesex-Essex, Massachusetts; and Oakland, California.

There is worry that nanotechnologies come with risks. Concerned scientists point to potential risks to the environment, as well as to public health and safety because so little is known about long-term exposure to nanoengineered substances. There are also social and ethical implications of nanotechnology.

For more information on nanotechnologies, their potential benefits, their risks, and current developments, including companies with nanotechnology research and development programs, visit the Web site for The Project on Emerging Nanotechnologies, a collaboration of the Woodrow Wilson International Center for Scholars in Washington, D.C., and The Pew Charitable Trusts, www.nanotechproject.org.

FUEL CELL DEVELOPMENT AND APPLICATIONS

Fuel Cell Engineer ✿🌐

Alternate Job Titles and Related Careers

- Battery Product Development Specialist
- Fuel Cells Application Engineer
- Lithium Ion Battery Cathode Materials Specialist
- Mechanical Engineer
- Structural Analysis Engineer

This is considered a "Green New and Emerging" occupation that requires special skills. Employment opportunities are generally in research, design, and consulting services and in the transportation industry.

Job Trends

The Bureau of Labor Statistics groups fuel cell engineers in the category of mechanical engineers. Based on 2008 employment numbers, Bureau of Labor Statistics projects a growth rate for jobs in this category of 3 to 6 percent, which is slower than average. It counted 239,000 mechanical engineers in 2008 and projected job openings of 75,700 by 2018. However, fuel cell engineer is a "Bright Outlook" and "Green New and Emerging" occupation, which means that greater growth is anticipated, but not yet quantifiable based on the current number of employees. In a survey of the automotive field, Arthur D. Little, an international consulting company, projected that every 1,000 megawatts of power creates 5,000 jobs in this industry. Note that these jobs will include not only fuel cell engineers and technicians, but also nontechnical employees ranging from human resources managers to truck drivers.

About Fuel Cell Development and Application

Fuel cells are placed in this chapter because of their potential for transportation uses. Fuel cells are already being used to power NASA's space shuttle and such ordinary products as vacuum cleaners and highway signs. Fuel cells have been installed in hospitals, police stations, wastewater treatment plants, and cell phone and radio towers. Today, the push is on to develop fuel cell applications that will power cars and other motor vehicles for longer distances. The U.S. Department of Energy is projecting that by 2040, fuel cell power will have displaced the internal combustion engine for autos and light trucks, saving the United States as much as 11 million barrels of oil a day. It is predicted that cars run by fuel cells will be 2.5 times as energy-efficient as those powered by the internal combustion engine.

Nature of the Work

In general, engineers develop cost-efficient solutions to problems. In the transportation industry, fuel cell engineers design, evaluate, modify, and construct fuel cell components and systems that use new technologies to solve the problem of how to power motor vehicles by means other than internal combustion engines. Fuel cell engineers must be proficient in the use of a variety of software, simulation, and modeling programs.

Among specific tasks for fuel cell engineers, according to O*NET, are the following, depending on level of experience:

- Design fuel cell systems, subsystems, stacks, assemblies, or components
- Recommend or implement changes to fuel cell system design
- Design or implement fuel cell testing or development programs
- Prepare test stations, instrumentation, or data acquisition systems for use in specific tasks

- Plan or conduct experiments to validate new materials, optimize startup protocols, reduce conditioning time, or examine contaminant tolerance
- Analyze test data and conduct post-service and failure analyses
- Calculate the efficiency and power output of a fuel cell system or process
- Develop fuel cell materials and fuel cell test equipment
- Integrate electric drive subsystems with other vehicle systems
- Manage hybrid system architecture for fuel cell battery hybrids
- Fabricate prototypes of fuel cell components, assemblies, stacks, or systems
- Simulate or model fuel cell, motor, or other system information using simulation software programs
- Plan or implement cost reduction or production improvement projects in collaboration with other engineers, suppliers, support personnel, or customers

Career Path

As fuel cell engineers gain experience, they may advance into positions where they supervise a team of engineers and other staff members. Some eventually become managers. Some go on to earn an MBA degree to prepare them for high-level managerial positions. Some continue their engineering education by obtaining graduate degrees in engineering that enable them to move into executive positions in industry and government.

Earning Potential

Median hourly wage (2009): $37.03

Median annual wage (2009): $77,020

Education/Licensure

For entry-level positions as a fuel cell engineer, a bachelor's degree in engineering or mechanical engineering from a college or university program that is accredited by the Accreditation Board for Engineering and Technology (ABET) is required. In some cases, engineers with degrees in one type of engineering may qualify for jobs in other areas of engineering. However, a number of colleges and universities are now offering engineering concentrations or engineering degrees specifically related to fuel cell technology.

Some colleges and universities offer five-year programs that culminate in a master's degree. Some offer five- or six-year programs that include cooperative experience. Some four-year schools have arrangements with community colleges or liberal arts colleges that allow students to spend two or three years at the initial school and transfer for the last two years to complete their engineering degree.

All fifty states and the District of Columbia require engineers to be licensed as professional engineers (PE) if they serve the public directly. In most states, licensure requires graduation from a four-year engineering program accredited by ABET, four years of experience, and passing the state exam. Many engineers take the Fundamentals of Engineering portion of the exam upon graduation. They are then engineers in training (EIT). After obtaining appropriate work experience, they take the Principles and Practice of Engineering exam to complete their professional license. Most states recognize licenses from other states, as long as the requirements are the same or more stringent. Some states have continuing education requirements to maintain engineering licenses.

Continuing education is critical for fuel cell engineers to keep up with the latest innovations in their field.

About the 2010 Olympics

The 30-foot-tall, lighted Olympic Rings in the harbor of Vancouver, British Columbia, during the 2010 Olympics were powered by hydrogen fuel cells, The Vancouver transit network uses twenty buses powered by fuel cells.

For More Information

Accreditation Board for Engineering and
    Technology (ABET)
111 Market Place
Suite 1050
Baltimore, Maryland 21202
410-347-7700
www.abet.org

American Society of Mechanical Engineers
    (ASME)
3 Park Avenue
New York, New York 10016-5990
800-843-2763 (toll-free)
www.asme.org

California Fuel Cell Partnership (CaFCP)
3300 Industrial Boulevard
Suite 1000
West Sacramento, California 95691
916-371-2870
www.fuelcellspartnership.org

Electric Drive Transportation Association (EDTA)
1101 Vermont Avenue, NW
Suite 401
Washington, DC 20005
202-408-0774
www.electricdrive.org

National Hydrogen Association
1211 Connecticut Avenue, NW
Suite 600
Washington, DC 20036-2701
202-223-5547
www.hydrogenassociation.org

Society of Automotive Engineers (SAE)
400 Commonwealth Drive
Warrendale, Pennsylvania 15096-0001
724-776-4841
www.sae.org

U.S. Fuel Cell Council (USFCC)
1625 K Street, NW
Suite 725
Washington, DC 20006
202-293-5500
www.usfcc.com

Fuel Cell Technician ☼ ⑤

Alternate Job Titles and Related Careers
- Fuel Cell Field Technician
- Fuel Cell Maintenance Technician
- Fuel Cell Manufacturing Technician
- Laboratory Technician: Test Monitor

Fuel cell technician is both a "Bright Outlook" and a "Green New and Emerging" occupation. The major industry sector is transportation.

Job Trends

In 2008, the Bureau of Labor Statistics counted 77,000 employees in the category of "all other engineering technicians, except drafters" and rated the job growth rate for this category as slower than average at 3 to 6 percent. The 2018 projection shows job openings of 18,500 positions for this category of engineering technician. However, fuel cell engineering technician is considered a "Green New and Emerging" occupation and may have a higher percentage of growth, much like its professional counterpart, fuel cell engineer.

Nature of the Work

Fuel cell technicians work under fuel cell engineers in research facilities, whether research centers or for manufacturing companies, to build and test fuel cells. They may also work in the manufacturing plants that assemble fuel cells for commercial use, or they may become fuel cell field technicians that install, operate, and maintain fuel cell installations like cell phone towers.

Fuel cell technicians working in labs to develop fuel cells have the following tasks, according to O*NET:
- Test fuel cells or fuel cell stacks
- Fabricate prototypes
- Calibrate equipment used for fuel cell testing and troubleshoot any problems with the equipment
- Document and maintain fuel cell test data

- Analyze fuel cell test data
- Build or test electrical systems and test power plant systems
- Recommend improvements to fuel cell design and performance

Career Path

Opportunities are best for those who possess an associate degree or a postsecondary training certificate in fuel cell engineering technology. Technicians usually begin their careers working under an experienced technician or technologist, or an engineer. Over time, fuel cell technicians take on more responsibility with less supervision. In time, they become supervisors, managing their own projects, reporting out the data, and recommending design changes.

Earning Potential

Median hourly wage (2009): $27.66

Median annual wage (2009): $57,530

Education/Licensure

To get ahead in the field, an associate degree is desirable. A number of community colleges, technical institutes, extension divisions of colleges and universities, and public and private vocational-technical schools offer degree and certification programs to train fuel cell technicians. Technical institutes offer less general education and less theory than community or technical colleges. However, they tend to focus more on intensive technical training and may be part of a community college or state university system. Most of these programs are located in states that are actively seeking to exploit their alternate fuel resources.

The National Alternative Fuels Training Center, which is based at West Virginia University, provides training programs at sites across the country for those interested in becoming trained technicians in fuel cell technology. Course offerings are also available online. Topics include hydrogen-powered vehicles, fuel cells and fuel cell vehicles, light-duty natural gas vehicles, and propane vehicle training, as well as biodiesel fuels and battery-powered electric vehicles.

For More Information

National Alternative Fuels Training Center (NAFTC)
Ridgeview Business Park
1100 Frederick Lane
Morgantown, West Virginia 26508
304-293-7882
www.naftc.wvu.edu

California Fuel Cell Partnership (CaFCP)
3300 Industrial Boulevard
Suite 1000
West Sacramento, California 95691
916-371-2870
www.fuelcellspartnership.org

Electric Drive Transportation Association (EDTA)
1101 Vermont Avenue, NW
Suite 401
Washington, DC 20005
202-408-0774
www.electricdrive.org

National Hydrogen Association
1211 Connecticut Avenue, NW
Suite 600
Washington, DC 20036-2701
202-223-5547
www.hydrogrenassociation.org

Society of Automotive Engineers (SAE)
400 Commonwealth Drive
Warrendale, Pennsylvania 15096-0001
724-776-4841
www.sae.org

U.S. Fuel Cell Council (USFCC)
1625 K Street, NW
Suite 725
Washington, DC 20006
202-293-5500
www.usfcc.com

TRANSPORTATION SYSTEMS

Civil Engineer ☼⑨

Alternate Job Titles and Related Careers

- City Engineer
- Civil Engineering Manager
- Design Engineer
- Geotechnical Engineer
- Project Engineer
- Project Manager
- Railroad Design Consultant
- Research Hydraulic Engineer
- Structural Engineer
- Water/Wastewater Engineer

This is both a "Bright Outlook" and a "Green Enhanced-Skills" occupation. Civil engineers will find employment in green construction, renewable energy generation, and research, design, and consulting services.

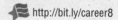 http://bit.ly/career8

Job Trends

According to the *Occupational Outlook Handbook,* employment in civil engineering is expected to grow by 20 percent or more between 2008 and 2018. This is much faster than the average for all occupations. It ranked number 21 on the list of the top 50 occupations requiring at least a bachelor's degree with the most openings through 2018. As a "Bright Outlook" occupation, civil engineering is expected to grow rapidly, with a potential for large numbers of job openings.

Environmental regulations and considerations increase the demand by requiring more engineers to expand existing transportation systems or to design and build new systems. Engineers are also needed to repair existing roads and bridges.

Nature of the Work

Civil engineers plan, design, and oversee the construction and maintenance of building structures and facilities, including pipelines and power plants, and roads, railroads, airports, bridges, harbors, channels, dams, water and sewage systems, and waste disposal units. As a result, civil engineers need a wide knowledge base including engineering and technology, design, building and construction, math, physics, transportation, public safety and security, law and government, and computers and electronics. As a "Green Enhanced-Skills" occupation, civil engineering may require new tasks, skills, knowledge, and credentials going forward.

O*NET lists the following duties that civil engineers may perform:

- Manage and direct staff and the construction, operations, or maintenance activities at a project site
- Provide technical advice regarding design, construction, or program modifications and structural repairs
- Inspect project sites to monitor progress and conformance to design specifications and safety and sanitation standards
- Estimate quantities and costs
- Test soils and materials to determine adequacy and strength of foundations, concrete, asphalt, or steel
- Plan and design transportation or hydraulic systems and structures
- Analyze survey reports, maps, drawings, blueprints, aerial photography, and other topographical or geologic data to plan projects
- Prepare or present public reports on such topics as bid proposals and environmental impact statements
- Direct or participate in surveying
- Conduct studies on traffic patterns or environmental conditions to identify engineering problems and assess potential impact of projects

Knowledge and understanding of the National Environmental Policy Act (NEPA) and context-sensitive solutions (CSS) and how they are applied in the transportation sector are beneficial to job seekers.

Career Path

As civil engineers gain experience, they become specialists and advance into positions where they supervise a team of engineers and other staff members. Some eventually become managers. Some go on to earn an MBA degree to prepare them for higher-level managerial positions. Some civil engineers continue their education by obtaining graduate degrees in engineering that enable them to move into executive positions in industry and government.

Earning Potential

Median hourly wage (2009): $36.82

Median annual wage (2009): $76,590

Education/Licensure

For entry-level positions, a bachelor's degree in civil engineering from a college or university program that is accredited by the Accreditation Board for Engineering and Technology (ABET) is required. In some cases, engineers with degrees in one type of engineering may qualify for jobs in other areas of engineering. Most colleges and universities offer transportation engineering as a specialty in civil engineering.

Some colleges and universities offer five-year programs that culminate in a master's degree. Some offer five- or six-year programs that include cooperative experience. Some four-year schools have arrangements with community colleges or liberal arts colleges that allow students to spend two or three years at the initial school and transfer for the last two years to complete their engineering degree.

All fifty states and the District of Columbia require engineers to be licensed as professional engineers (PE) if they serve the public directly. In most states, licensure requires graduation from a four-year engineering program accredited by ABET, four years of experience, and passing the state exam. Many engineers take the Fundamentals of Engineering portion of the exam upon graduation. They are then engineers in training (EIT). After obtaining appropriate work experience, they take the Principles and Practice of Engineering exam to complete their professional license. Most states recognize licenses from other states, as long as the requirements are the same or more stringent. Some states have continuing education requirements.

The Transportation Professional Certification Board (TPCB) of the Institute of Transportation Engineers (ITE) offers certifications in planning and traffic control.

The National Institute for Certification in Engineering Technologies (NICET) offers certification programs in bridge safety inspection, highway construction, highway design, highway materials, highway surveys, highway traffic operations, and highway system maintenance and preservation.

For More Information

Accreditation Board for Engineering and
   Technology (ABET)
111 Market Place
Suite 1050
Baltimore, Maryland 21202
410-347-7700
www.abet.org

American Society of Civil Engineers
Transportation and Development Institute
1801 Alexander Bell Drive
Reston, Virginia 20191-4400
800-548-2723 (toll-free)
www.asce.org

Institute of Transportation Engineers
1099 14th Street, NW
Suite 300 West
Washington, DC 20005-3438
202-289-0222
www.ite.org

National Institute for Certification in Engineering
    Technologies (NICET)
1420 King Street
Alexandria, Virginia 22314
888-476-4238 (toll-free)
www.nicet.org

National Society of Professional Engineers
    (NSPE)
1420 King Street
Alexandria, Virginia 22314
703-684-2800
www.nspe.org

Supply Chain Manager ☼ ⊛

Alternate Titles and Related Careers
- Logistics Analyst ☼ ⊛
- Logistics Engineer ☼ ⊛
- Logistics Manager ☼ ⊛
- Demand Planner
- Project Manager
- Supply Chain Analyst
- Vendor Manager
- Inventory Analyst
- Senior Consultant
- International Logistics Manager
- Master Production Scheduler
- Purchasing Manager
- Sourcing Manager
- Transportation Manager
- Director of Operations
- Director of Transportation
- Vice President of Global Logistics
- Vice President of Supply Chain
  Management

This occupation is considered a "Green New and Emerging" occupation with the potential for increasing efficiency and reducing environmental impact in the transportation sector of the economy.

Job Trends

The current number of "all other managers" according to the Bureau of Labor Statistics is put at 898,000. The category is expected to grow at an average rate of 7 to 13 percent by 2018. The total job openings are projected to be 297,500 by 2018. However, the job of supply chain manager is considered a green job with a bright outlook, so it may result in an increased job growth.

Nature of the Work

According to the Council of Supply Chain Management Professionals, supply chain managers are involved in every aspect of the business process, including "planning, purchasing, production, transportation, storage and distribution, and customer service . . . . These managers are the 'glue' that connects the different parts of the organization."

Supply chain managers direct or coordinate production, purchasing, warehousing, distribution, or financial forecasting services and activities. Their goal is to limit costs and improve accuracy, customer service, and safety. Depending on their positions and responsibilities, their duties include the movement, storage, processing, and inventory of finished goods. It is the supply chain manager's involvement in the movement and storage of goods that especially impacts energy use.

> ### About Supply Chains and Energy Use
> According to the Supply-Chain Council (SCC), 90 percent of the total costs for energy, oil, and gas companies comes from the supply chain. In 2010, SCC launched a working group to define supply-chain benchmarks to guide decision making related to these industries.

Supply chain managers may perform the following tasks as listed on O*NET:

- Design and implement supply chains
- Develop procedures to coordinate the supply chain with other aspects of a business, such as production schedules and financial goals
- Manage activities related to purchasing, materials planning, inventory control, warehousing, or receiving
- Develop procedures or systems for evaluating and selecting suppliers
- Analyze data and evaluate supplier performance and procurement programs against that data
- Analyze inventories to reduce inventory shelf-life, reduce waste, or optimize customer service
- Establish performance metrics to measure and evaluate supply chain factors like cost and quality
- Design and execute warehousing plans for materials or finished goods

Career Path

More than half of all current supply chain managers are self-employed. About 11 percent are employed by government entities, and the remaining 32 percent work in a variety of industries that rely on the movement of goods. These include manufacturers, retailers, transportation companies, third-part logistics firms, and service firms.

Entry-level jobs in supply management are supervised by senior managers. After four years or so, workers may move up to middle management positions and supervise others. The top job after 11+ years is a senior-level position such as Vice President of Global Logistics.

Earning Potential

Median hourly wage (2009): $44.52

Median annual wage (2009): $92,600

About Greening the Supply Chain

In 2010, Walmart® announced plans to reduce greenhouse gas emissions from its worldwide supply chain by 20 million metric tons by 2015. Walmart claims this is equivalent to the annual emissions of 3.5 million cars. Walmart and its suppliers will work on ways to reduce the energy used in sourcing, manufacturing, packaging, and shipping goods to Walmart warehouses and from warehouses to stores.

Education/Licensure

Most supply chain managers hold a bachelor's or higher in business, finance, or an engineering field. Some colleges and universities also confer degrees in supply chain management, operations management, and similarly titled degrees. Look for this career to require continuing education as the green economy impacts the supply chains and worker requirements.

The American Society of Transportation and Logistics (ASTL) offers certification programs for "Professional Designation in Logistics and Supply Chain Management (PLS)" and "Certified in Transportation and Logistics."

The Association for Operations Management (APICS, Advancing Productivity, Innovation, and Competitive Success) offers two certification programs: "Certified in Production and Inventory Management" and "Certified Supply Chain Professional." There are also certification maintenance programs available from APICS.

The Institute for Supply Management (ISM) offers two certification programs: "Certified in Professional Supply Management" and "Certified Purchasing Manager." The International Society of Logistics (SOLE) has a four-step certification program that moves from Demonstrated Logistician through Demonstrated Senior Logistician to Demonstrated Master Logistician and finally to Certified Master Logistician.

The Supply-Chain Council (SCC) offers the SCOR-Professional certification program for those already working in the field and the SCOR-Scholar certification program for students studying the field in colleges and universities.

The Council for Supply Chain Management Professionals (CSCMP) and other organizations provide a number of online courses for continuing education in this field.

For More Information

American Society of Transportation and Logistics (ASTL)
PO Box 3363
Warrenton, Virginia 20188
202-580-7270
www.astl.org

Association for Operations Management (APICS)
8430 West Bryn Mawr Avenue
Suite 1000
Chicago, Illinois 60631
800-444-2742
www.apics.org

Council of Supply Chain Management Professionals (CSCMP)
333 East Butterfield Road
Suite 140
Lombard, Illinois 60148
630-574-0985
http://cscmp.org

Institute for Supply Management (ISM)
PO Box 22160
Tempe, Arizona 85285-2160
800-888-6276 (toll-free)
www.ism.ws/

International Society of Logistics (SOLE)
810 Professional Place
Suite 111
Hyattsville, Maryland 20785
301-459-8446
www.sole.org

National Industrial Transportation League (NITL)
1799 North Moore Street
Suite 1900
Arlington, Virginia 22209
703-524-5011
www.nitl.org

Supply-Chain Council (SCC)
1400 Eye St., NW
Suite 1050
Washington, DC 20005
202-962-0440
www.supply-chain.org

Warehousing Education and Research Council
1100 Jorie Boulevard
Oak Brook, Illinois 60523
630-990-0001
www.werc.org

Transportation Engineer ☼ ⑤

Alternate Job Titles and Related Careers
- Highway Engineer
- Traffic Engineer

This is a "Bright Outlook" and a "Green New and Emerging" occupation. In addition to the transportation industry, transportation engineers work in research, design, and consulting services.

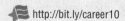 http://bit.ly/career10

Job Trends

According to the *Occupational Outlook Handbook,* employment in civil engineering, of which transportation engineering is a subset, is expected to grow by 20 percent or more. This is much faster than the average for all occupations. Civil engineering is ranked number 21 on the list of the top 50 occupations, requiring at least a bachelor's degree, with the most openings through 2018.

Environmental regulations and considerations increase the demand by requiring more engineers to expand existing transportation systems or to design and build new systems. Engineers are also needed to repair existing roads and bridges. An aspect of the greening of the transportation industry is the generation of activities that either increase efficiency and/or reduce the environmental impact of transportation including trucking, mass transit, and freight rail.

Nature of the Work

Transportation engineering is a specialty of civil engineering that deals with all aspects of transportation, such as airports, commuter rail systems, freight, traffic flow, highways, streets, bridges, drainage structures, and roadway lighting. They are even concerned with pedestrians and bicyclists.

Among a transportation engineer's job duties are the following, according to O*NET:

- Design and prepare plans for new transportation systems or parts of systems
- Supervise the maintenance or repair of transportation systems or system components
- Analyze environmental impact statements for transportation projects
- Review development plans to determine potential traffic impact
- Check construction plans, design calculations, or cost estimates
- Direct the surveying, staking, and laying out of construction projects
- Investigate or test specific construction project materials to determine compliance
- Inspect completed projects to ensure safety and compliance
- Investigate traffic problems and recommend improvements to traffic flow and safety
- Model transportation scenarios to evaluate impacts of activities or identify possible solutions to transportation problems
- Participate in contract bidding, negotiation, and administration
- Plan alteration and modification of existing transportation structures to improve safety or function

- Prepare final project layout drawings, budgets, schedules, and specifications
- Evaluate transportation systems, traffic control devices, lighting systems, to determine need for modification or expansion
- Prepare administrative, technical, or statistical reports on traffic-operation issues
- Prepare data, maps, or other information for public hearings and meetings

Transportation engineers must also be knowledgeable about state and federal construction policy. Knowledge and understanding of the National Environmental Policy Act (NEPA) and context-sensitive solutions (CSS) and how they are applied in the transportation sector are beneficial to job seekers.

Career Path

As transportation engineers gain experience, they become specialists and advance into positions where they supervise a team of engineers and other staff members. Some eventually become managers. Some go on to earn an MBA degree to prepare them for higher-level managerial positions. Some transportation engineers continue their education by obtaining graduate degrees in engineering that enable them to move into executive positions in industry and government.

Earning Potential

Median hourly wage (2009): $36.82

Median annual wage (2009): $76,590

Education/Licensure

For entry-level positions, a bachelor's degree in engineering from a college or university program that is accredited by the Accreditation Board for Engineering and Technology (ABET) is required. In some cases, engineers with degrees in one type of engineering may qualify for jobs in other areas of engineering. Most colleges and universities offer transportation engineering as a specialty in civil engineering.

Some colleges and universities offer five-year programs that culminate in a master's degree. Some offer five- or six-year programs that include cooperative experience. Some four-year schools have arrangements with community colleges or liberal arts colleges that allow students to spend two or three years at the initial school and transfer for the last two years to complete their engineering degree.

All fifty states and the District of Columbia require engineers to be licensed as professional engineers (PE) if they serve the public directly. In most states, licensure requires graduation from a four-year engineering program accredited by ABET, four years of experience, and passing the state exam. Many engineers take the Fundamentals of Engineering portion of the exam upon graduation. They are then engineers in training (EIT). After obtaining appropriate work experience, they take the Principles and Practice of Engineering exam to complete their professional license. Most states recognize licenses from other states, as long as the requirements are the same or more stringent. Some states have continuing education requirements.

The Transportation Professional Certification Board (TPCB) of the Institute of Transportation Engineers (ITE) offers certifications as "Professional Transportation Planner" and "Professional Transportation Engineer."

The National Institute of Certification for Engineering Technologies offers certification programs in bridge safety inspection, highway construction, highway design, highway materials, highway surveys, highway traffic operations, and highway system maintenance and preservation

For More Information

Accreditation Board for Engineering and
    Technology (ABET)
111 Market Place
Suite 1050
Baltimore, Maryland 21202
410-347-7700
www.abet.org

American Society of Civil Engineers
Transportation and Development Institute
1801 Alexander Bell Drive
Reston, Virginia 20191-4400
800-548-2723 (toll-free)
www.asce.org

Institute of Transportation Engineers
1099 14th Street, NW
Suite 300 West
Washington, DC 20005-3438
202-289-0222
www.ite.org

National Institute for Certification in Engineering
    Technologies (NICET)
1420 King Street
Alexandria, Virginia 22314
888-476-4238 (toll-free)
www.nicet.org

National Society of Professional Engineers
    (NSPE)
1420 King Street
Alexandria, Virginia 22314
703-684-2800
www.nspe.org

Transportation Planner ☼🌍

Alternate Job Titles

- Aviation Planner
- Campus Transportation Planner
- Environmental Planner
- Transportation Environmental Planner
- Transit Operations Analyst
- Urban and Regional Planner
- Urban Planner

This occupation is both a "Bright Outlook" and a "Green New and Emerging" occupation. Transportation planners can find work in government and regulatory administration and research, design, and consulting services as well as the transportation industry.

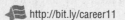 http://bit.ly/career11

Job Trends

The Bureau of Labor Statistics lists the category of "social scientists and related workers, all other" as having a 20 percent or higher growth rate between 2008 and 2018. This is much faster than the average of all other occupations. Planners with master's degrees and good computer skills, including modeling and geographic information systems (GIS) skills, will have the best opportunities in all sectors of transportation environmental planning.

Growth in transportation planning results from population increases, particularly in rapidly expanding communities that need streets and other services. Currently, 68 percent of planners are employed in local governments. Only 21 percent are employed in private companies that provide architectural, engineering, and related services. However, employment in this sector is expected to increase faster than government employment, especially in firms that provide technical services. Transportation planners also work in construction and emerging geospatial industries.

Nature of the Work

Transportation planners are a subset of urban and regional planners and specialize in the environmental aspects of transportation planning. According to a salary survey by the American Planning Association, 26 percent specialize in transportation and 25 percent in environmental and natural resources. Because transportation systems affect the environment in numerous ways, the two areas are often part of the same job. Specifically, transportation engineers gather, compile, and analyze data to study the use and operation of transportation systems. This information includes land use policies, environmental impact of projects, and long-range planning needs.

Among the job duties of transportation planners are the following, based on O*NET's survey of job holders in this classification:

- Define regional or local transportation planning problems and priorities
- Recommend transportation system improvements or projects
- Analyze and interpret data from traffic modeling software, geographic information systems (GIS), associated databases, and traffic counting programs
- Analyze transportation-related consequences of federal and state legislative proposals
- Collaborate with engineers to research, analyze, or resolve complex transportation design issues
- Design transportation surveys and computer models for transportation planning issues and direct urban counting programs
- Develop or test new methods and models of transportation analysis
- Develop design ideas for new or improved transport infrastructure
- Review development plans for transportation systems effects, infrastructure requirements, and compliance
- Prepare reports and recommendations on transportation planning and environmental documents including environmental impact statements
- Prepare documents for project approvals and permits
- Prepare or review engineering studies or specifications
- Participate in public meetings or hearings
- Represent jurisdictions in the approval process for land development

Transportation environmental planners develop systems that balance a variety of transportation modes, including private cars, bicycles, pedestrians, and public transportation. Some transportation planners work for universities where they are responsible for the university's vehicle fleet and may have to develop plans for alternate transportation, such as carpools or bicycle sharing. On campus, pedestrian traffic and safety are extremely important considerations. Aviation planners develop master plans for airports and conduct assessments of noise and environmental impact.

In all cases, transportation planners must consider the environmental implications of transportation systems. Knowledge and understanding of the National Environmental Policy Act (NEPA) and context-sensitive solutions (CSS) and how they are applied in the transportation sector are beneficial to job seekers.

Career Path

As planners gain experience, they advance to more independent assignments and gain greater responsibility in areas like policy and budget planning. They may become senior planners or community-planning directors, where they meet with officials and supervise a staff. Often, advancement is to a larger jurisdiction with greater responsibilities and more difficult problems. In larger jurisdictions, they may advance to bureau chief or community development director.

Earning Potential

Median hourly wage (2009): $33.59

Median annual wage (2009): $69,860

Education/Licensure

Generally, a master's degree in urban and regional planning from an accredited program is required. The Planning Accreditation Board accredits college and university programs. Its Web site includes links to schools with accredited planning programs. Master's degrees in related fields, such as geography, urban design, urban studies, economics, or business, may be acceptable for many planning jobs. For transportation environmental planning, a bachelor's or master's degree in civil or environmental engineering may also be acceptable.

A few schools offer a bachelor's degree in urban and regional planning. Graduates of these programs qualify for some entry-level jobs, but they may have limited opportunities for advancement.

Only two states currently have requirements for licensing planners. New Jersey requires that planners pass two exams to qualify for a license. One exam tests general planning knowledge, and the other tests knowledge of New Jersey laws. Michigan requires community planners to register, and the registration is based on passing state and national exams and on professional experience.

Even though most states do not have requirements for certification, many communities do. The preferred certification is from the American Institute of Certified Planners (AICP), the professional institute of the American Planning Association. The AICP certification is based on education, experience, and passing an exam. Maintaining certification requires professional development on a two-year cycle.

For More Information

American Planning Association
1776 Massachusetts Avenue, NW
Suite 400
Washington, DC 20036-1904
202-872-0611
www.planning.org

Association of Collegiate Schools of Planning
6311 Mallard Trace
Tallahassee, Florida 32312
850-385-2054
www.acsp.org

VEHICLES AND TRANSIT SYSTEM OPERATIONS

In 2008, the Bureau of Labor Statistics counted 40,900 trucking companies handling long-distance transportation of goods and 29,400 companies engaged in the local transport of goods. Long-distance trucking carries goods between distant locations and sometimes between the United States and Canada or Mexico. Long-haul trucking and associated transportation sectors, such as rail systems, play a large role in the use of nonrenewable energy sources.

Truck Driver, Heavy and Tractor-Trailer ✿⑤

Alternate Job Titles and Related Careers

- Delivery Driver
- Feeder Driver
- Flatbed Truck Driver
- Industrial Truck and Tractor Operator ✿ ⑤
- Long-Haul Driver
- Over-the-Road Driver (OTR Driver)
- Road Driver
- Truck Driver, Light and Delivery Services ✿ ⑤

This is a "Bright Outlook" and a "Green Enhanced-Skills" occupation in the transportation sector.

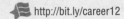 http://bit.ly/career12

Job Trends

The general category of "truck drivers, heavy and tractor-trailer" had close to 1.8 million workers in 2008. The Bureau of Labor Statistics projects 291,900 job openings between 2008 and 2018. Several of the related jobs in this category are "Bright Outlook" and "Green Enhanced-Skills" occupations, so job growth may be greater than the 7 to 13 percent projected by the Bureau.

Nature of the Work

A heavy-truck, long-haul, or tractor-trailer driver transports and delivers goods, livestock, or materials in liquid, loose, or packaged form in trucks that have a capacity of more than three tons. Drivers may be required to unload the cargo or to use automated routing equipment. Several kinds of technology are used in trucking including databases, inventory management software, and route navigation software.

Among the job tasks of a trucker are the following, according to O*NET:

- Follow appropriate safety procedures for transporting dangerous goods
- Check vehicles to ensure they are in good working order
- Maintain logs of working hours and vehicle service and repairs
- Read bills of lading to determine assignment details and verify instructions and routes for deliveries
- Check load-related documentation to ensure completeness and accuracy
- Obtain receipts and signatures for delivered goods and collect payment if required
- Drive trucks to weigh stations before and after loading and along routes to document weights and to comply with state regulations
- Check conditions of trailers after contents have been unloaded to ensure there is no damage
- Perform basic vehicle maintenance
- Follow any special cargo-related procedures, such as checking refrigeration systems

Federal regulations require alcohol and drug testing by employers as a condition of employment and then random checks while they are on duty. A driver cannot have been convicted of a felony involving the use of a motor vehicle or a crime involving drugs, driving under the influence of drugs or alcohol, refusing to submit to an alcohol test required by a state or its implied consent laws or regulations, leaving the scene of a crime, or causing a fatality through negligent operation of a motor vehicle. For interstate trucking, a driver must be 21 years of age.

Career Path

Most truck drivers are employed along major interstate highways or in large metropolitan areas where trucking, retail, and wholesale companies concentrate. Although most new truck drivers are assigned to regular driving jobs, some start as extra drivers substituting for regular drivers who are ill or on vacation. An extra driver doesn't get a regular route until an opening occurs. Over time, truck drivers advance to jobs with higher wages, preferred schedules, or better working conditions. Drivers with good safety records earn more than newer drivers. Drivers who work on local delivery routes may advance to driving heavy or specialized trucks such as concrete mixers or transfer to long-distance routes. Some truck drivers become dispatchers or managers.

Some long-haul drivers buy or lease trucks and go into business for themselves as owner-operators. Courses in accounting, business, and business math, as well as experience driving a truck and knowledge of truck mechanics, are needed for an owner-operator to be successful. About 8 percent of all truck drivers are self-employed.

Earning Potential

Median hourly wage (2009): $18.14

Median annual wage (2009): $37,730

Companies typically pay long-haul drivers by the mile with bonuses for drivers who save the company money. Local truck drivers are generally paid by the hour, making extra for overtime.

Education/Licensure

A majority of drivers have a high school diploma, GED, or less, and about a quarter have some post-baccalaureate education. Many trucking companies prefer high school graduates. Operation of trucks with a gross weight of more than 26,000 pounds or carrying hazardous materials or oversized loads requires a commercial driver's license (CDL). Training for the CDL is available from private and public vocational-technical schools that offer driver-training courses in how to handle large vehicles on crowded streets and heavy traffic, and how to inspect trucks and freight for compliance with state and federal regulations.

The Professional Truck Driver Institute (PTDI) certifies driver-training courses at truck driver training schools that meet industry standards and Federal Highway Administration guidelines for training tractor-trailer drivers.

Only a standard driver's license from the state in which a driver lives is required for operating all other trucks.

Once hired, drivers usually have to participate in a training program given by their new employers. These programs are brief—a day or two at most—of classroom instruction. Often, the training also includes riding along with an experienced driver employee for a period of time.

The American Trucking Association (ATA) offers an endorsement program in hazardous materials.

For More Information

American Trucking Association (ATA)
950 North Glebe Road
Suite 210
Arlington, Virginia 22203
www.truckline.com

International Brotherhood of Teamsters (IBT)
25 Louisiana Avenue, NW
Washington, DC 20001
www.teamster.org

Professional Truck Driver Institute (PTDI)
555 E. Braddock Road
Alexandria, Virginia 22314
www.ptdi.org

> ### About Used Sports Equipment
> Check www.sportsgift.com for information on how to recycle used athletic equipment such as baseballs, basketballs, soccer balls, volleyballs, cleats, and shin guards. Sports Gifts donates the equipment to some 40,000 children worldwide. Play on a team? Team uniforms and coaching equipment are also gladly received.

Dispatcher 🌐

Alternate Job Titles and Related Careers
- Aircraft Dispatcher
- Airline Flight Dispatcher
- Bus Dispatcher
- City Dispatcher
- Dispatch Manager
- Dispatch Supervisor
- Dispatcher
- Motor Coach Supervisor
- Rail Operations Controller
- School Bus Dispatcher
- Train Dispatcher
- Truck Dispatcher

This is a "Green Increased-Demand" occupation in transportation and warehousing and in administration and support services. Public safety dispatchers (police, fire, and ambulance), also known as 911 operators, are a separate category of dispatcher.

 http://bit.ly/career13

Job Trends

According to the *Occupational Outlook Handbook,* there will be 40,300 job openings for dispatchers between 2008 and 2018, which will arise as current dispatchers retire or move to other jobs. Candidates who have the required skills to work the increasingly complex equipment involved in the dispatcher's job will have the best chances of finding employment.

As more people switch from driving cars to using public transportation and mass transit, the need for dispatchers to manage schedules for trains and buses is expected to increase. Depending on the dispatcher's job, one duty might be to plan the most efficient routes. In 2008, 41 percent of dispatchers worked in transportation and warehousing, 10 percent worked in administration and support services, and the remainder worked in a variety of industries, including construction and government.

Nature of the Work

Dispatchers schedule and dispatch vehicles, equipment, and workers. Most use computer-assisted systems. They maintain records and logs of activities and are responsible for all communications within their assigned areas. They also monitor equipment and personnel and are in charge of having equipment repaired.

Dispatchers can specialize in different types of vehicles or jobs.

- Aircraft flight dispatchers, also known as airline flight dispatchers, work for airlines and are responsible for all flights, both passenger and cargo. Their duties include planning the most efficient flight route, monitoring the plane while it's in the air, and ensuring that the aircraft and crew meet federal qualifications and regulations.
- Bus dispatchers work for local or long-distance bus companies and school districts and are responsible for scheduling, arranging repairs, and maintaining service.
- Train dispatchers are responsible for train schedules, locations of trains on tracks, and positions of switches.
- Truck dispatchers work for trucking companies and plan routes, schedule pickups and deliveries of freight, and schedule drivers.

Career Path

Dispatchers who work for large companies, such as an airline or urban bus company, may become shift supervisors or, in time, managers. Those who work for small companies will find little advancement.

Earning Potential

(Not including fire, police, and ambulance dispatchers)

Mean hourly wage (2009): $16.58

Mean annual wage (2009): $34,480

Education/Licensure

Dispatchers generally learn the skills they need on the job working under the supervision of an experienced person. A high school diploma or GED is required. Persons with more experience and computer skills will have better job opportunities. Many states require specific certifications or training. In some locales, community colleges provide the training, which usually involves instruction in the latest technology and the use of computers to aid in dispatching.

The major rail companies train employees at the Railroad Education and Development Institute in Atlanta, Georgia, and the National Academy of Railroad Sciences (NARS) in Overland Park, Kansas.

The Federal Aviation Administration (FAA) licenses and certifies aircraft flight dispatchers.

For More Information

Airline Dispatchers Federation (ADF)
2020 Pennsylvania Avenue, NW
Suite 821
Washington, DC 20006
800-676-2685 (toll-free)
www.dispatcher.org

American Train Dispatchers Association, Member
    AFL-CIO Transportation Trades Department
4239 West 150th Street
Cleveland, Ohio 44135
216-251-7984

www.atdd.homestead.com

National Business Aviation Association (NBAA)
Schedulers and Dispatchers Committee
1200 18th Street
Suite 400
Washington, DC 20036
202-783-9000
www.nbaa.org

National Railway Labor Conference (NRLC)
1901 L Street, NW, Suite 500
Washington, DC 20036
202-862-7200
www.raillaborfacts.org

Freight Forwarder ☼🌐

Alternate Titles and Related Careers

- Cargo Agent
- Documentation Clerk
- Drop Shipment Clerk
- Forwarder
- Forwarding Agent
- Freight Agent
- Freight Broker
- Intermodal Dispatcher
- International Coordinator
- Load Planner
- Logistics Coordinator
- Logistics Service Representative
- Ship Broker

This is a "Bright Outlook" and a "Green New Emerging" occupation in the transportation industry.

 http://bit.ly/career14

Job Trends

In 2008, the Bureau of Labor Statistics counted 86,000 cargo and freight agents of which freight forwarder is a subset. The projected rate of job growth is 20 percent or higher, much faster than average. This would result in an estimated 40,300 new jobs between 2008 and 2018. As a "Green New Emerging" occupation, freight forwarders may see a greater increase. For one thing, the increase in online shipping aids growth in this occupation, as does the overall growth of the economy and international trade.

Nature of the Work

Freight forwarders research rates, routings, and modes of transportation for shipment of products taking into consideration regulations affecting the international movement of any cargo. They also make arrangements for additional services such as storage and inland transportation.

Freight forwarders do the following tasks, according to O*NET:

- Determine efficient and cost-effective methods of moving goods
- Select shipment routes, based on the type of goods being shipped, transit times, or security needs
- Inform clients of shipping options, timelines, transfers, and regulations
- Reserve necessary space on ships, aircraft, trains, or trucks
- Arrange for delivery or storage of goods at destinations
- Verify adherence of documentation to customs, insurance, and regulatory requirements and complete shipping documents and customs paperwork
- Consolidate loads with common destinations to reduce costs to individual shippers
- Negotiate rates with cargo carriers and prepare invoices and cost quotations
- Obtain or arrange for cargo insurance

- Maintain records of goods dispatched and received
- Monitor and record locations of goods in transit
- Clear goods through customs, arranging for applicable duties and taxes
- Make arrangements with customs brokers to facilitate the passage of goods through customs
- Assist clients in obtaining insurance reimbursement for lost or damaged cargo
- Provide shipment status notification to exporters, consignees, and insurers
- Keep up-to-date on relevant legislation, political situations, or other factors that could affect freight shipping

About Reducing Energy for Ocean Shipping

Maersk, the Danish shipping company, adopted a new slow boat protocol in 2008. Instead of getting cargo to ports as fast as possible, the company cut the top cruising speed of its ships in half, thereby cutting fuel use, greenhouse gas emissions, and costs to its customers. The company reduced energy usage by as much as 30 percent on major routes.

Many freight forwarders work for transportation intermediary companies. Depending on the type of freight that a company ships, it is licensed by a different federal agency. The Federal Motor Carrier Safety Administration (FMCSA) licenses companies that serve as freight agents in the trucking industry. The Transportation Security Administrator (TSA) licenses companies that serve the airfreight industry; these companies must register as indirect air carriers. Transportation intermediary companies that serve the ocean transportation sector must register as either a nonvessel operating common carrier (NVOCC) or a freight forwarder with the Federal Maritime Commission.

Much of the business is done by computer, so freight forwarders need to be comfortable with a variety of software programs. They must also be able to input, file, and maintain records.

Career Path

Advancement is limited, but some agents become team leaders or switch to other jobs in the same company. Some may move to higher paying transportation industry jobs. To become self-employed as transportation intermediary broker or start a business, a person must obtain a license from the appropriate federal agency.

Earning Potential

Median hourly wage (2009): $17.77

Median annual wage (2009): $36,960

Education/Licensure

Many jobs are entry level, and most require a high school diploma. Slightly less than half of all employed cargo and freight agents had high school diplomas in 2008, and approximately the same percentage had some college. The remainder had at least a bachelor's degree. There is usually informal on-the-job training for new employees.

The Transportation Intermediaries Association (TIA) offers a "Certified Transportation Broker" program. The National Customs Brokers and Forwarders Association of America, Inc. (NCBFAA) offers the "Certified Customs Specialist Certification Program" and the "Certified Export Specialist Certification Program."

The American Society of Transportation and Logistics (ASTL) offers an entry-level certification "Certified in Transportation and Logistics" program. To qualify, a person may have either an undergraduate degree or three years of experience.

For More Information

American Society of Transportation and Logistics (ASTL)
P.O. Box 3363
Warrenton, Virginia 20188
202-580-7270
www.astl.org

National Customs Brokers and Forwarders Association of America, Inc. (NCBFAA)
1200 18th Street, NW
Suite 901
Washington, DC 20036
202-466-0222
www.ncbfaa.org

Transportation Intermediaries Association (TIA)
1625 Prince Street
Suite 200
Alexandria, Virginia 22314
www.tianet.org

About Buying Online

The Green Design Institute at Carnegie Mellon University studied the buying habits on buy.com. The institute reported that online ordering resulted in 35 percent less energy and carbon emissions. Instead of a product being shipped from a distribution center to a warehouse and then to the store, it was shipped directly to the customer from the distribution center. When you factor in the amount of energy and carbon emissions saved by customers driving to a bricks-and-mortar store to buy the product, the savings increase.

How Being Green Works for
David Loper, Alternative Fuel Specialist

David W. Loper, 54, works as an alternative fuel specialist/service manager for an equipment distributor in Forest Park, Georgia, working with vehicles that operate on either compressed natural gas (CNG) or propane. Loper has been doing environmentally green work for more than nine years. Here he is programming a vehicle's fuel gauge so that it will recognize CNG.

Describe your job, including common daily tasks and long-term projects that you have worked on or are working on now. What, specifically, about your job makes it green?

The company that I work for has been a family-owned business since 1919. My job is to keep the shop busy, open and close repair orders, bring in new business, and utilize the technicians' skills.

We offer preventive maintenance and parts for bucket trucks, aerial lifts, and digger derricks. As part of my job, I perform American National Standards Institute (ANSI) inspections required by the Occupational Safety and Health Administration (OSHA), dielectric testing, and repairs. I perform the complete rebuilding and overhaul of lift equipment, and I also convert cars and trucks to operate on alternative fuels, such as compressed natural gas (CNG) and propane. There is a lot of similarity in working on high-pressure hydraulics and installing high-pressure fuel systems on cars. Both utilize much of the same shop equipment, and special tools and training are required for both.

My job is green because every vehicle that we convert runs much cleaner than those that use petroleum fuels. This lessens our dependence on foreign and domestic oil.

Why/how did you decide to work in a green industry?

After working seven years for a local Caterpillar® dealer, I was introduced to alternative systems that allowed diesel engines to operate on either CNG or LNG, which is liquefied natural gas. Understanding the many benefits of converting heavy-duty engines to using alternative fuels, I pursued a career in that industry. In 2001, I took a job selling liquefied natural gas fuel systems. I've also sold compressed natural gas cylinders and natural gas conversion systems.

How did you prepare for your current position?

I do not have a degree in any one area. I have training in mechanical engineering, LNG and CNG certificates, along with sales training and computer skills. I've been involved with Clean Cities–Atlanta for several years and currently serve as a board member.

Which aspect of your education and/or training do you think has been the most helpful and/or useful to you? Why?

My mechanical and technical engine knowledge and sales experience have been the most beneficial and helpful in working in the alternative fuel industry.

Do you find that the skills and/or knowledge required for your job continue to evolve? If so, what have you done to keep up-to-date?

Of course, all of us need to continually learn new things. I subscribe to several alt-fuel magazines and take advantage of all training opportunities. The companies that I have worked for have had in-house training.

How have continuing education and/or training impacted the way you do your job?

Training is helpful, but hands-on experience is the best teacher to me.

What is the most rewarding part of your work, and what do you find to be the most challenging?

It's rewarding to see a finished converted vehicle and just knowing that we are moving away from the use of oil and toward a clean, renewable fuel. It is distressing to know that the United States is way behind many other countries when it comes to using alternative fuels.

What advice would you give to people interested in pursuing your career?

Enter this industry [alternative fuels] at any level, and keep your options open. Keep as informed as possible about the direction of this industry.

How Being Green Works for Charles Westra, Mechanical Systems Engineer

Charles Westra, 54, works as a mechanical systems engineer for a manufacturer of hybrid vehicle technology in Rochester Hills, Michigan. A project engineer, Westra helps implement hydraulic hybrid technology for heavy vehicles. He has been in the automotive industry since 1978 and has worked directly on green automotive applications for the past six years.

Describe your job, including common daily tasks and long-term projects that you have worked on or are working on now. What, specifically, about your job makes it green?

I am a project engineer helping to implement hydraulic hybrid technology for heavy vehicles (trucks and buses). Hybrid technology promises to reduce fuel consumption and thereby reduce emissions of pollutants in vehicles. Hydraulic hybrid

technology is particularly well suited for heavy vehicles as it can store and deliver energy quickly.

My day-to-day activities include the design and procurement of components, coordinating the installation of our system into the vehicles, participating in the development of our system, and assisting in the calibration of the vehicle.

Why/how did you decide to work in a green industry?

I've been in the automotive industry for more than thirty years. While we've been working to improve our efficiencies and reduce our pollutants throughout that time, it's an effort that has gained more momentum recently. So I didn't "go green"; the industry I was already in went "green." But I'm glad we did. I think the time has come.

How did you prepare for your current position?

I obtained a Bachelor of Science degree in industrial engineering from Purdue University. During my time at Purdue, I participated in the cooperative education program that had me alternate semesters on campus with semesters as an intern gaining practical experience. This program also helped me pay for my schooling, which worked out well. After that, I spent a number of years providing computer services for engineering applications, which provided me with exposure to a variety of engineering disciplines.

Which aspect of your education and/or training do you think has been the most helpful and/or useful to you? Why?

Industrial engineering education involves a sampling of the engineering disciplines, and my work in providing computer services for engineers required me to understand their needs. This exposure to a variety of disciplines helps me in my position as project engineer, where I need to understand all of the subsystems that comprise our system.

Do you find that the skills and/or knowledge required for your job continue to evolve? If so, what have you done to keep up-to-date?

We are applying existing technologies to achieve new results, but much of it is new to me. I rely on assistance from my coworkers and my own research for an on-the-job education.

How have continuing education and/or training impacted the way you do your job?

As we move from prototype to production, our internal training is helping me to learn and apply our company's product introduction process and to ensure that we release an effective, reliable product. I should point out that these processes emphasize our environmental responsibility and the importance of minimizing our impact throughout the product life cycle.

What is the most rewarding part of your work, and what do you find to be the most challenging?

Calibrating and testing the vehicles is the most rewarding part of my job. When we load up one of our trucks to 69,000 pounds and take it for a test drive, I'm sure our system is saving energy and thereby reducing pollution. I'm glad to be a part of the effort.

The most challenging part for me is the documentation required. All engineering development efforts must be thoroughly documented. But I'd just rather be doing it than writing about it.

What advice would you give to people interested in pursuing your career?

My position as a project engineer is a perfect example of the importance of variety in education, or what used to be called the "well-rounded education." Make sure you study language(s) so you can communicate effectively. Take some business courses so you can interact with company management—that may help you make your case and obtain the resources you need to complete your task. In engineering, don't be so focused on a single discipline that you can't relate your subsystem to the rest of the product.

Greenest Places to Live and Work in the United States

Every year, a number of magazines and Web sites report on the top 10, 25, or 50 greenest places to live in the United States. The criteria for what makes a city "green" vary somewhat from source to source, but, in general, criteria include factors such as the following:

- Air and water quality
- Amount of mass transit
- Green initiatives
- Level of alternative energy use
- Number of green-certified buildings
- Recycling and waste reduction programs

No two sources assign the same ratings to criteria, but there are similarities in the listings of green cities, as you can see from the following lists of green "big" cities:

From the National Resources Defense Council:

1. Seattle, Washington
2. San Francisco, California
3. Portland, Oregon
4. Oakland, California
5. San Jose, California
6. Austin, Texas
7. Sacramento, California
8. Boston, Massachusetts
9. Denver, Colorado
10. Chicago, Illinois

From *MSN City Guides:*

1. Austin, Texas
2. Berkeley, California
3. Boston, Massachusetts
4. Chicago, Illinois
5. Minneapolis, Minnesota
6. New York City, New York
7. Philadelphia, Pennsylvania
8. Portland, Oregon
9. San Francisco, California
10. Seattle, Washington

The U.S. Green Building Council compiled a list of the top cities with the most LEED-certified buildings:

1. Chicago, Illinois: 88
2. Portland, Oregon: 73
3. Seattle, Washington: 63
4. Washington, D.C.: 57
5. Atlanta, Georgia: 53
6. San Francisco, California: 50
7. New York City, New York: 46
8. Grand Rapids, Michigan: 44
9. Los Angeles, California: 40
10. Boston, Massachusetts: 38

CHAPTER 3

ENERGY-RELATED JOBS IN CONSTRUCTION & BUILDING OPERATIONS

CONSTRUCTION INDUSTRY OVERVIEW

The *Occupational Outlook Handbook* reports that 8.2 million people were employed in the construction trades industry in 2008. This industry was particularly hard hit by the economic downturn that began in 2007. However, the number of jobs is predicted to increase 19 percent through 2018, for a total of 9.9 million workers. Overall, experienced workers should have excellent job opportunities with relatively high wages.

Most of the new jobs are expected for specialty trade workers, including apprentice, journey, and master craft workers. Specialty trades account for about 64 percent of all construction workers and include electricians; carpenters; plumbers; pipe fitters; and heating, air conditioning, and refrigeration installers and mechanics.

Construction workers are divided into structural, finishing, and mechanical workers, though some may do the work of more than one type of worker. Structural workers build the internal and external framework of buildings. Finishing workers give a structure its final appearance. Carpenters, for example, may both frame a structure and put up the drywalls. Mechanical workers install the equipment and materials for basic building operation like the plumbing and electrical system.

About More Jobs in Construction

For a discussion of green jobs in construction, design, and landscaping that include more than energy-related jobs, see *Peterson's Green Careers in Building and Landscaping*.

Heavy construction, including roads, bridges, and tunnels, as well as repairs to existing highways and bridges, is expected to generate most of the demand for construction workers. Major growth in nonresidential green building is expected in the education, office, and health-care sectors, in addition to increased demand in the government, industrial, hospitality, and retail sectors.

However, green nonresidential and residential building should experience an increase in demand, even though construction of new residential and commercial buildings overall has slowed as a result of the recession that lasted from 2007 to 2009. In an April 2009 summary, the U.S. Green Building Council reported that green building is expected to more than double by 2013. Government initiatives, along with increased interest in residential green building, are encouraging energy-efficient, environmentally sustainable green construction. Remodeling of existing structures, especially to retrofit them as green buildings, is expected to generate additional demand for construction workers.

In addition to skilled craft workers, there are job opportunities in construction companies for engineers, especially civil engineers, office managers, accountants and bookkeepers, and clerical workers.

JOBS PROFILED HERE

The following occupations are profiled in this chapter:

- Architect
- Construction Carpenter
- Construction Manager
- Electrician
- Energy Auditor
- Energy Engineer
- Facilities Manager
- Heating, Air Conditioning, and Refrigeration Mechanic and Installer
- Insulation Worker: Floor, Ceiling, and Wall
- Weatherization Installer and Technician

KEY TO UNDERSTANDING THE JOB PROFILES

The job profiles are classified according to one or more of the following categories.

✿ Bright Outlook

🌎 Green Occupation

The classifications "Bright Outlook" and "Green Occupation" are taken from the National Center for O*NET Development's O*NET OnLine job site. O*NET, which is sponsored by the U.S. Department of Labor/Employment and Training Administration (USDOL/ETA), has broken green jobs into three categories

- Green Increased-Demand occupations
  - o These are occupations that are likely to see job growth, but the work and worker requirements are unlikely to experience significant changes.

- Green Enhanced-Skills occupations
  - o These occupations are likely to experience significant changes in work and worker requirements. Workers may find themselves doing new tasks requiring new knowledge, skills, and credentials. Current projections do not project increased demand for workers in these occupations, but O*NET notes that an increase is possible.
- Green New and Emerging occupations
  - o These are new occupations—not growth in existing jobs—that are created as a result of activity and technology in green sectors of the economy.

Video Links

We've provided easy-to-use links that will take you directly to a particular career video from the One-Stop Career System Multimedia Career Video Library at CareerOneStop.org. The links will look like this:

 http://bit.ly/career1

Note that videos are not available for all jobs listed here. The videos come in QuickTime and Mpeg formats, with and without captions; download times may vary. CareerOneStop.org is sponsored by the U.S. Department of Labor/Employment and Training Administration.

Architect 🌎

Alternate Titles and Related Careers

- Architectural Engineer
- Architectural Engineering Consultant
- Architectural and Engineering Manager
- Architectural Project Manager
- Design Architect
- Green Building and Retrofit Architect
- Project Architect

- Project Manager
- Industrial Green Systems and Retrofit Designer

Architect is a "Green Enhanced-Skills" occupation with demand in green construction and also research, design, and consulting services.

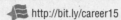 http://bit.ly/career15

Job Trends

The rate of job growth for architects is projected to be faster than average at 14 to 19 percent. In 2008, there were 141,000 architects, and job openings between then and 2018 are estimated to be 46,800. According to the *Occupational Outlook Handbook,* two main forces are driving the need for more architects, namely, population growth and the interest in eco-friendly "green" buildings—residential and commercial. Not only is the size of the population growing, but it is also aging, which results in the need for more healthcare facilities, assisted-living complexes, nursing homes, and retirement communities. Population growth also leads to the need for more schools at all levels, kindergarten through university.

The interest in building or retrofitting existing construction to follow green design principles is also an important source of new jobs for architects. Green design, or sustainable design, emphasizes the efficient use of resources, including energy- and eco-friendly specifications and materials.

Nature of the Work

Architects design houses, schools, hospitals, office buildings, churches, college buildings, urban centers, and industrial parks. In addition to the structure itself, architects also design the electrical system; heating, air conditioning, and ventilation system; plumbing; and communication system. The structures must be safe, functional, and cost-effective. Architects work with many other professionals, such as engineers, landscape architects, interior designers, and urban planners.

In creating their plans, architects must consider federal, state, and local regulations; building codes; zoning laws; and fire codes. Much of their work is done using building information modeling (BIM) and computer-aided design (CAD). Their work also includes preparing reports, cost estimates, environmental impact studies, land-use studies, models and presentations for clients, and plans for regulatory approvals. During construction, architects monitor the work being done by construction contractors.

Green building and sustainable design require the expertise of architects. The U.S. Green Building Council LEED (Leadership in Energy and Environmental Design) building certification program includes credit for energy-efficient systems for heating and cooling, lighting, and water usage and disposal; clean renewable energy use; natural and sustainably produced materials; indoor air quality; innovative design; educating the people who use the building; location to transportation and services; and a sustainable site. This is a great deal of expertise for architects to master.

About Green Building Materials

The Green Guard Institute tests and certifies building products and materials that are low in harmful emissions. You can find listings of these products and materials, a number of which are used in school construction, on the Institute's Web site at www.greenguard.org.

Based on the O*NET database, architects may also perform the following tasks:

- Consult with clients to determine functional and spatial requirements of the construction
- Integrate engineering elements such as the heating and air conditioning and wiring systems into the design
- Prepare scale drawings or direct staff in preparing drawings and specifications
- Plan layout of the project
- Prepare information regarding design, specifications, materials, color, equipment, estimated costs, and construction time

- Represent the client in obtaining bids and awarding contracts
- Prepare and administer contracts for contractors

Career Path

Architecture graduates usually begin a three-year intern program, working under the supervision of a licensed architect. After completing that program, they are eligible to take licensing exams. After passing the exams, they become licensed and gain responsibility for projects. With greater experience, they may become managers or partners in an architecture firm.

About 21 percent of architects are self-employed, and about 68 percent work for architectural, engineering, and related services companies, according to the *Occupational Outlook Handbook*. The remainder work for construction firms and government agencies that deal with housing, community planning, and construction of government buildings.

Earning Potential

Median hourly wage (2009): $34.95

Median annual wage (2009): $72,700

Education/Licensure

A bachelor's degree is the minimum required for architects. Bachelor of Arts or Bachelor of Science in architecture, Bachelor of Environmental Design, and Bachelor of Architectural Studies are considered preprofessional degrees. A preprofessional bachelor's degree may qualify a person for licensure in some states, but in most states, further education is required to get a professional degree. Professional degrees are Bachelor of Architecture (B.Arch.), which usually requires five years; Master of Architecture (M.Arch.); and Doctor of Architecture (D.Arch.) from an architectural program that is accredited by the National Architectural Accrediting Board (NAAB). However, state architectural registration boards set their own standards, so a nonaccredited program may meet the educational requirements in a few states. Most architects, though, earn their professional degree through the five-year bachelor of architecture degree program.

All fifty states and the District of Columbia require architects to be licensed. Licensing normally requires a professional degree from an accredited school, completion of a three-year intern program, and passing a national exam. The National Council of Architectural Registration Boards (NCARB) administers the exam. There are some alternate provisions for those who do not have a professional degree. Only Arizona does not require the three-year intern program. Students who complete part of their internship while in school will have an advantage.

The NCARB offers certification that allows an architect licensed in one state to become licensed in another state through reciprocity.

Most states require continuing education to maintain a license. From 2009 through 2012, The American Institute of Architects (AIA) requires 4 hours of continuing education in sustainable design every year to maintain membership. The Green Building Certification Institute, affiliated with the U.S. Green Building Council, offers LEED (Leadership in Energy and Environmental Design) credentials in green building.

For More Information

American Institute of Architects (AIA)
1735 New York Avenue, NW
Washington, DC 20006
202-626-7300
www.aia.org

Association of Collegiate Schools of Architecture
1735 New York Avenue, NW
Washington, DC 20006
202-785-2324
www.asca-arch.org

National Architectural Accrediting Board (NAAB)
1735 New York Avenue, NW
Washington, DC 20006

202-783-2007

www.naab.org

National Council of Architectural Registration
   Boards
Suite 700K
1801 K Street, NW
Washington, DC 20006
202-783-6500
www.ncarb.org

U.S. Green Building Council (USGBC)
2101 L Street, NW
Suite 500
Washington, DC 20037
800-795-1747 (toll-free)
www.usgbc.org

Construction Carpenter ✿ 🌏

Alternate Titles and Related Careers

- Carpenter Helper ✿ 🌏
- Construction Laborer ✿ 🌏
- Rough Carpenter ✿ 🌏
- Assembler
- Carpenter
- Concrete Carpenter
- Construction Worker
- Custom Stair Builder
- Finish Carpenter
- Installer
- Lead Carpenter
- Trim Carpenter

Construction carpenter is a "Bright Outlook" and a "Green Increased-Demand" occupation. While demand will increase, workers will not need significantly new training. Carpentry crosses a number of industries in addition to building construction, but demand for carpenters will grow in green building construction.

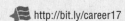 http://bit.ly/career17

Job Trends

Carpentry is the largest building trade occupation. According to the *Occupational Outlook Handbook,* there were about 1.5 million jobs in 2006 and 1.2 million in 2008 after the recession began. However, that number is expected to increase by 2018 at a rate that is average for all occupations—7 to 13 percent. This category includes both construction carpenters and rough carpenters.

The growth rate for jobs for both carpenters' helpers and construction laborers is projected to be 20 percent or higher, much faster than average for all occupations. This translates into 35,300 jobs for carpenters' helpers and 339,400 openings for construction laborers between 2008 and 2018.

The market for home remodeling is currently strong and will be for some time. This is partially driven by economic conditions, but also by environmental concerns. Retrofitting and remodeling homes to improve energy efficiency is increasing. In addition, retrofitting of industrial plants, schools, and government buildings for energy efficiency will also provide job opportunities.

About Calgreen

Calgreen is the name of California's mandatory statewide green building code—the first in the nation. The California Air Resources Board has estimated that 3 million metric tons of emissions will be removed from the air by 2020, which will help Californians meet the state's goal of reducing greenhouse gas emissions by 33 percent by 2020.

Nature of the Work

Carpenters need knowledge of tools, materials, blueprints, sketches, building plans, and basic math as well as safety rules and regulations and local building codes. Those who are self-employed must be able to estimate materials, time, and cost to complete a job. Today, carpenters must also be aware of the latest in energy-efficient doors, windows, and sealants, plus renewable and environmentally friendly wood products.

Specifically, construction carpenters may do any or all of the following tasks as listed by O*NET:

- Measure and mark cutting lines
- Shape or cut materials to specifications
- Assemble and fasten materials
- Remove damaged or defective parts or sections and repair or replace
- Finish surfaces of woodwork or wallboard
- Fill cracks and other defects
- Perform minor plumbing, welding, or concrete mixing
- Verify trueness of the structure using a plumb bob and level
- Build or repair items such as cabinets, doors, frameworks, and floors
- Erect scaffolding and ladders
- Maintain a safe and clean work site

Construction carpenters who are self-employed or become supervisors may also do the following tasks:

- Prepare project layout and determine dimensions and materials that will be needed
- Prepare cost estimate for clients
- Select and order materials
- Arrange for subcontractors for special area such as heating
- Maintain records, document activities, and present written progress reports

Rough carpenters build wooden structures such as scaffolds; tunnel, bridge, and sewer supports; and billboard signs. They measure materials and distances; cut boards and plywood; assemble and fasten materials; and install rough door and window frames, subflooring, or temporary supports in structures that being build or repaired.

Carpenter helpers assist carpenters by doing jobs on a site that require less skill, such as carrying tools to the site, holding tools for carpenters, erecting scaffolding and braces, and cleaning work areas and equipment. They may position and hold lumber and paneling in place so a carpenter can cut it or fasten it, or they may cut and fasten lumber and paneling themselves. Carpenters' helpers may also install hardware.

Career Path

Experienced carpenters may become carpentry supervisors. Because they are involved in all aspects of the construction process, they also have opportunities to advance to general construction supervisor. Some may become building inspectors or sales representatives or purchasing agents for building products. Others become teachers in vocational or technical schools. With additional education and experience, there are opportunities for carpenters in management, including becoming self-employed contractors. Speaking both English and Spanish can be an advantage for those who wish to advance.

Earning Potential

Construction Carpenters and Rough Carpenters

Median hourly wage (2009): $18.98

Median annual wage (2009): $39,470

Helper, Carpenter

Median hourly wage (2009): $12.43

Median annual wage (2009): $25,860

Education/Licensure

Typically, carpentry requires a high school diploma. Carpenters may begin as carpenter's helpers working with experienced carpenters, but they also need some type of formal instruction to become skilled. There are two main options for formal instruction: attending a trade or vocational school or a community college, or enrolling in an apprenticeship program. Apprenticeship programs are offered by some employers and by trade associations, unions, and some trade and vocational schools. These programs may last three to five years and include both classroom and on-the-job training. Upon completing an apprenticeship program, a person becomes a journey worker and, over time, with additional training and experience, a master carpenter.

Some carpenters get certifications in specialized construction techniques such as building scaffolds. These certifications may enable them to earn additional responsibilities and money. The Green Building Certification Institute, affiliated with the U.S. Green Building Council, offers LEED (Leadership in Energy and Environmental Design) credentials in green building.

For More Information

Home Builders Institute
1201 15th Street, NW
Washington, DC 20005
202-266-8927
www.buildingcareers.org

National Association of Home Builders
1201 15th Street, NW
Washington, DC 20005
800-368-5242 (toll-free)
www.nahb.org

United Brotherhood of Carpenters and Joiners of
    America
International Training Center
6801 Placid Street
Las Vegas, Nevada 89119
702-938-1111
www.carpenters.org

U.S. Green Building Council (USGBC)
2101 L Street, NW
Suite 500
Washington, DC 20037
800-795-1747 (toll-free)
www.usgbc.org

Construction Manager ☼⑤

Alternate Titles and Related Careers
- Construction Area Manager
- Construction Foreman
- Construction Superintendent
- General Contractor

- Job Superintendent
- Project Manager
- Project Superintendent

This is a "Bright Outlook" and "Green Enhanced-Skills" occupation that may require new tasks, skills, knowledge, and credentials. In addition to green construction, construction managers also find work in the environmental protection sector of the economy. All kinds of building projects require construction managers.

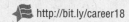 http://bit.ly/career18

Job Trends

According to the Bureau of Labor Statistics, employment growth of 14 to 19 percent is expected for this occupation by 2018. This is faster than the average for all occupations. Job opportunities should be excellent because the need is expected to exceed the number of qualified persons entering this profession.

Demand for construction managers is generated by increasing construction of homes, offices, schools, hospitals, restaurants, and retail spaces as a result of population growth. In addition, the need to replace and repair roads, highways, and bridges will also generate demand. Increasing complexity of projects along with more laws and regulations regarding energy efficiency, environmental protection, worker safety, and environmentally friendly construction processes and materials also contribute to the demand for construction mangers.

Nature of the Work

Construction managers oversee and coordinate the entire construction process from planning and development through the completion of the project. They are responsible for making sure that the work gets done within budget and on schedule. On a very large project, different construction managers may handle different portions of the project.

The majority of construction managers work on residential and nonresidential construction, such as homes, apartment buildings, commercial buildings, schools, and hospitals. However, construction managers also work on large industrial complexes, bridges, highways, and wastewater treatment plants.

O*NET lists the following as among the tasks of construction managers:

- Evaluate construction methods and determine cost-effectiveness of plans and construction for projects
- Select, contract, and oversee general and trades contractors
- Prepare contracts and negotiate changes to contracts with clients, architects, consultants, suppliers, and subcontractors
- Prepare and submit budget estimates and cost and tracking reports
- Schedule projects in logical steps and time periods to meet deadlines
- Obtain necessary permits and licenses
- Interpret and explain plans and contract terms to all necessary parties
- Plan, organize, and direct activities involved in the construction
- Confer with supervisory personnel, owners, contractors, and design professionals to resolve issues related to work process, complaints, and construction problems
- Take actions to deal with the results of delays, bad weather, or emergencies at construction sites
- Inspect and review projects to monitor compliance with all regulations including building and safety codes
- Arrange delivery of materials, tools, and equipment
- Develop and implement quality control programs
- Investigate damage, accidents, and delays at construction sites to ensure proper procedures are being carried out

Career Path

Experienced construction managers in large companies may become high-level managers or administrators. An additional degree in business administration, finance, or accounting may be necessary for the highest positions. Many construction managers are self-employed in their own small construction or consulting companies.

Earning Potential

Median hourly wage (2009): $39.58

Median annual wage (2009): $82,330

Education/Licensure

Traditionally, trades workers such as carpenters, electricians, and plumbers with significant construction experience could advance to construction managers. According to the *Occupational Outlook Handbook,* only about 30 percent of currently employed construction managers have college degrees. However, the trend is for employers to hire people as construction managers with bachelor's degrees or higher in construction management, construction science, or civil engineering. In addition to education, construction industry experience is critical in getting a job. For those in college and university programs, internships are a good way to gain experience.

The American Council for Construction Education (ACCE) provides links to accredited bachelor's and associate-degree programs in construction sciences. The National Center for Construction Education and Research (NCCER) also provides links to accredited programs. In addition, the latter organization sponsors Construction Management Academies that offer professional training and certifications. The American Institute of Constructors (AIC) offers online continuing education courses through www.RedVector.com. Many are green construction courses.

Certification is voluntary for construction managers, but it is a growing trend. Employers value certification because it ensures a certain level of training and experience. The Construction

Management Association of America (CMAA) offers the Construction Manager in Training (CMIT) certification for college juniors, seniors, and recent graduates and the Certified Construction Manager (CCM) for those with experience. The CCM requires a combination of education and experience plus passing an exam. The AIC also offers certification for construction managers. The Green Building Certification Institute provides a credential in LEED construction.

For More Information

American Council for Construction Education (ACCE)
1717 North Loop 1604 E
Suite 320
San Antonio, Texas 78232-1570
210-495-6161
www.acce-hq.org

American Institute of Constructors (AIC)
P.O. Box 26334
Alexandria, Virginia 22314
703-683-4999
www.aicnet.org

Construction Management Association of America (CMAA)
7926 Jones Branch Drive
Suite 800
McLean, Virginia 22102-3303
703-356-2622
www.cmaanet.org

Green Building Certification Institute
2101 L Street, NW
Suite 650
Washington, DC 20037
800-795-1746 (toll-free)
www.gbci.org

National Center for Construction Education and Research (NCCER)
3600 NW 43rd Street
Building G
Gainesville, Florida 32606
888-622-3720 (toll-free)
www.nccer.org

Electrician ✿ 🌐

Alternate Titles and Related Careers
- Commercial Electrician
- Electrical Systems Installer
- Electrician Technician
- Inside Wireman
- Journeyman Electrician
- Journeyman Wireman
- Maintenance Electrician

This is considered a "Bright Outlook" and "Green Increased-Demand" occupation in the green construction sector of the economy.

 http://bit.ly/career19

Job Trends

According to the Bureau of Labor Statistics, there were 695,000 electricians in 2008. Of those, 70 percent were employed in the construction industry. Others work in manufacturing, the motion picture and video industry, and power generation. Approximately 80 percent of electricians working in construction are self-employed.

Employment is expected to increase 7 to 13 percent by 2018, which is about average for all occupations. However, job prospects are very good. By 2018, about 250,900 new jobs are projected. New residential and commercial construction, power plant construction to meet increasing energy demands, computers, telecommunications, and manufacturing automation are all expected to create new jobs during the coming decade. Remodeling homes and retrofitting buildings—public and private—to meet increasing concerns about the environment are also driving demand for construction workers, including electricians.

Nature of the Work

Electricians install, test, maintain, and repair wiring and electrical systems in residential and commercial buildings. Systems may include lighting, security, climate control, communications, or other control systems. Electricians also install electrical equipment and fixtures, like circuit breakers, switches, and fuses. Knowledge of tools, blueprints, materials, and basic mathematics is required. Electricians must also know the National Electrical Code and state and local codes. They must also maintain their electrician's license. If self-employed, they must be able to estimate materials, time, and cost to complete a job.

Some electricians install other types of wiring, such as low-voltage wiring used for voice, data, and video transmission. Others install fiber optic and coaxial cables. In factories, electricians wire and maintain more complex equipment, including generators, transformers, motors, and robots.

O*NET lists the following as among the jobs that electricians perform who work on residential and commercial electrical systems, equipment, and fixtures:

- Connect, repair, or replace wiring, equipment, and fixtures
- Assemble, install, test, and maintain electrical or electronic wiring, equipment, appliances, apparatus, and fixtures
- Inspect electrical and electronic systems to diagnose malfunctions
- Plan layout and installation of electrical wiring, equipment, and fixtures
- Install ground leads and connect power cables
- Fabricate parts
- Place conduit, pipes, or tubing inside partitions, walls, and other concealed areas
- Perform physically demanding tasks such as digging trenches and moving heavy objects

About Air Quality Standards

In 2007, California became the first state to require that the construction industry retrofit heavy equipment to cut down on toxic fumes from diesel engines.

Electricians who go into business for themselves also may do the following:

- Prepare cost estimates
- Prepare sketches and read blueprints
- Direct and train workers
- Maintain records and files, prepare reports, and order supplies and equipment

Career Path

Experienced electricians may become supervisors, and they also have opportunities to advance to construction managers. Many become electrical inspectors, and many start their own businesses as electrical contractors. Speaking both English and Spanish is an advantage for those who wish to advance.

Earning Potential

Median hourly wage (2009): $22.68

Median annual wage (2009): $47,180

Education/Licensure

Most electricians get training and skills through apprenticeship programs that take between four and five years to complete. These programs consist of classroom instruction and supervised training on the job with pay. The Independent Electrical Contractors (IEC) group offers apprenticeship programs, continuing education, and online courses. The National Electrical Contractors Association (NECA) and the International Brotherhood of Electrical Workers (IBEW) jointly sponsor apprenticeship programs. Technical and vocational schools and training academies also offer training programs. All programs require a high school diploma or GED.

Continuing education is important for electricians, so that they can keep up with changes to the National Electrical Code. Many electricians also take courses on contracting and management in preparation for starting their own businesses or for advancing within a company.

Most states require electricians to be licensed. Obtaining a license requires passing an exam about the National Electrical Code, local building and electric codes, and electrical theory. Most states also require electricians who do public work to hold a special license. In some cases, this requires that a person be certified as a master electrician. This process requires seven years or more experience in most states. Some states require a bachelor's degree in electrical engineering.

For More Information

Green Building Certification Institute
2101 L Street, NW
Suite 650
Washington, DC 20037
800-795-1746 (toll-free)
www.gbci.org

Independent Electrical Contractors (IEC)
4401 Ford Avenue
Suite 1100
Alexandria, Virginia 22302
703-549-7351
www.ieci.org

International Brotherhood of Electrical Workers (IBEW)
900 Seventh Street, NW
Washington, DC 20001
202-833-7000
www.ibew.org

National Association of Home Builders (NAHB)
1201 15th Street, NW
Washington, DC 20005
800-368-5242 (toll-free)
www.nahb.org

National Electrical Contractors Association (NECA)
3 Bethesda Metro Center
Suite 1100
Bethesda, Maryland 20814
301-657-3110
www.necanet.org

U.S. Green Building Council (USGBC)
2101 L Street, NW
Suite 500
Washington, DC 20037
800-795-1747 (toll-free)
www.usgbc.org

Energy Auditor ☼ⓢ

Alternate Titles and Related Careers
- Building Performance Consultant
- Energy Consultant
- Energy Rater
- Home Energy Rater
- Home Performance Consultant

This is both a "Bright Outlook" and "Green New and Emerging" occupation. Workers are employed in both the energy efficiency sector and in governmental and regulatory administration.

Job Trends

The Bureau of Labor Statistics considers this occupation part of the "all other business operations specialists" and projects an average growth rate of 7 to 13 percent. However, energy auditor is a "Green New and Emerging" occupation. People's interest in going "green" and saving money on the cost of energy is expected to increase the number of job openings. Energy auditors have a positive impact on the environment because their work directly impacts the amount of energy that their customers consume in their homes or businesses.

Nature of the Work

Energy auditors conduct energy audits of buildings, building systems, and process systems. Among the tools they use are air velocity and temperature monitors, catalytic combustion analyzers, psychrometers, gas monitors, and leak testing equipment. They must be able to use analytical and scientific software, as well as CAD, database, graphics, and spreadsheet software. Knowledge of engineering, energy production, energy use, construction, maintenance, system operation, and process systems can be useful.

Energy auditors may perform any or all of the following tasks according to O*NET:

- Perform tests and collect and analyze field data
- Analyze energy bills including utility rates or tariffs to gather historical energy usage data
- Measure energy usage
- Determine patterns of building use to show annual or monthly needs for heating, cooling, lighting, or other energy needs
- Compare existing energy consumption levels to normative data
- Recommend energy-efficient technologies or alternate energy sources
- Identify opportunities to improve the operation, maintenance, or energy efficiency of building or process systems
- Analyze technical feasibility of energy-saving measures
- Calculate potential energy savings
- Prepare audit reports
- Identify and prioritize energy-saving measures
- Educate customers on energy efficiency strategies
- Prepare job specifications for home energy improvements
- Oversee installation of equipment such as pipe insulation and weatherstripping

Career Path

Because of the newness of the field, it is hard to say how much education will be required, but in general, it appears that many companies are looking for entry-level candidates with a bachelor's degree in engineering. Entry-level employees work under the supervision of an experienced energy auditor. After a certain amount of on-the-job training and experience, support energy auditors are given assignments on their own and over time begin to supervise entry-level workers. Some companies may require that energy auditors earn a business administration degree (MBA) to advance to higher-level management positions. Some may move into sales jobs selling the company's services.

Earning Potential

Median hourly wage (2009): $29.14

Median annual wage (2009): $60,610

Education/Licensure

For entry-level positions, a bachelor's degree in engineering from a college or university program that is accredited by the Accreditation Board for Engineering and Technology (ABET) may be required.

About Energy in Existing Buildings

Reducing energy consumption in the existing building stock in the United States offers the biggest opportunity for reducing our CO_2 emissions, according to the Intergovernmental Panel on Climate Change (IPCC). The U.S. Green Building Council provides a rating system, LEED Existing Building Operations and Maintenance (LEED-EB-O&M), for certifying energy efficiency in existing buildings.

Some colleges and universities offer five-year programs that culminate in a master's degree. Some offer five- or six-year programs that include cooperative experience. Some four-year schools have arrangements with community colleges or liberal arts colleges that allow students to spend two or three years at the initial school and transfer for the last two years to complete their engineering degree.

All fifty states and the District of Columbia require engineers to be licensed as professional engineers (PE) if they serve the public directly. In most states, licensure requires graduation from a four-year engineering program accredited by ABET, four years of experience, and passing the state exam. Many engineers take the Fundamentals of Engineering portion of the exam upon graduation. They are then engineers in training (EIT). After obtaining appropriate work experience, they take the Principles and Practice of Engineering exam to complete their professional license. Most states recognize licenses from other states as long as the requirements are the same or more stringent. Some states have continuing education requirements.

The Association of Energy Engineers (AEE) offers three certificate programs for energy auditors: Certified Energy Auditor (CEA), Certified Energy Auditor in Training (CEAIT), and Certified Residential Energy Auditor. The Building Performance Institute (BPI) offers a certification as building analyst. Some states have their own certification programs. The Residential Energy Services Network (RESNET)* offers programs for Certified In-Home Energy Survey Professional and Diagnostic Home Energy Survey Professional.

For More Information

Accreditation Board for Engineering and
    Technology (ABET)
111 Market Place
Suite 1050
Baltimore, Maryland 21202
410-347-7700
www.abet.org

Association of Energy Engineers (AEE)
4025 Pleasantdale Road
Suite 420
Atlanta, Georgia 30340
770-447-5083
www.aeecenter.org

Building Performance Institute (BPI)
107 Hermes Road
Suite 110
Malta, New York 12020
877-274-1274 (toll-free)
www.bpi.org

California Building Performance Contractors
    Association (CBPCA)
1000 Broadway
Suite 410
Oakland, California 94607
888-352-2272 (toll-free)
www.cbpca.org

Residential Energy Services Network (RESNET)
PO Box 4561
Oceanside, California 92052-4561
760-806-3448
www.resnet.us

U.S. Green Building Council (USGBC)
2101 L Street, NW
Suite 500
Washington, DC 20037
800-795-1747 (toll-free)
www.usgbc.org

About the Next Cool Thing

Dark roofs will be a thing of the past if the scientists at Lawrence Berkeley Laboratory and other researchers have their way. They have been experimenting with light-colored roofs for years. According to various studies, air conditioning use can be reduced by as much as 20 percent with white roofs. Roofs needn't be white to result in energy—and cost—savings, but a lemon-yellow roof won't save as much as a white roof.

RESNET® is an industry not-for-profit corporation that establishes standards for building energy-efficiency rating systems.

Energy Engineer ✿⊛

Alternate Titles and Related Careers

- Distributed Generation Project Manager
- Energy Efficiency Engineer
- Energy Manager
- Environmental Solutions Engineer
- Industrial Energy Engineer
- Measurement and Verification Engineer
- Test and Balance Engineer

This is a "Bright Outlook" and "Green New and Emerging" occupation in the green construction sector of the economy. It is also a "Green New and Emerging" occupation in the energy efficiency and research, design, and consulting services sectors.

Job Trends

The Bureau of Labor Statistics includes this in the engineering category and indicates an average rate of job growth in the 7- to 13-percent range. However, as a "new and emerging" occupation in several green sectors of the economy, it may see a higher growth rate.

Nature of the Work

An energy engineer designs, develops, and evaluates energy-related projects and programs to reduce energy costs or improve energy efficiency during the design, building, or remodeling stages of construction. Energy engineers may specialize in electrical systems; heating, ventilation, and air-conditioning systems; green buildings; lighting; air quality; or energy procurement. They may consult with clients and other engineers on topics such as climate control systems, energy modeling, data logging, energy management control systems, lighting or day-lighting design, sustainable design, energy auditing, LEED principles, and green buildings. In the course of their work, energy engineers ensure acceptability of budgets and time lines, conformance to federal and state laws and regulations, and adherence to approved job specifications.

Among the tasks that energy engineers perform, according to O*NET, are the following:

- Conduct energy audits to evaluate energy use, costs, or conservation measures
- Monitor and analyze energy consumption
- Perform energy modeling, measurement, verification, commissioning, or retro-commissioning
- Oversee design or construction aspects related to energy such as energy engineering, energy management, and sustainable design
- Conduct jobsite observations, field inspections, and sub-metering to collect data for energy conservation analyses
- Review architectural, mechanical, and electrical plans and specifications to evaluate energy efficiency or determine economic, service, or engineering feasibility
- Inspect or monitor energy systems to determine energy use or potential energy savings
- Direct the work of contractors or staff in the implementation of energy management projects
- Prepare project reports and other program or technical documentation
- Analyze, interpret, and create graphical representations of data using engineering software
- Promote awareness or use of alternative and renewable energy sources
- Conduct research or collect data on renewable or alternative energy systems or technologies such as solar thermal energy

If an energy engineer is involved in the procurement of energy sources, the engineer may also

- Make recommendations regarding fuel selection
- Review and negotiate energy purchase agreements

Career Path

Entry-level energy engineers typically begin work under the supervision of experienced engineers. They may also participate in a formal training program if offered by their employer. As they gain knowledge and experience, they are assigned to more complex projects with less supervision. In time, they may become supervisors or team leaders. Some may become engineering managers or choose to enter sales or start their own businesses.

About Cutting the Nation's Energy Use

Two reports released in 2009 estimated that the nation could cut energy use between 15 and 23 percent by 2020 by instituting energy efficiencies such as sealing air ducts and replacing energy inefficient electrical appliances. The study done by the consulting firm McKinsey estimated the cost for a 23 percent decline in energy use at $520 billion. Savings realized in the long term: $1.2 trillion.

Earning Potential

Median hourly wage (2009): $43.06

Median annual wage (2009): $89,560

Education/Licensure

This occupation requires a bachelor's degree in engineering from an institution accredited by the Accreditation Board for Engineering and Technology (ABET). While many colleges and universities offer the major branches of engineering, only a few offer programs in the smaller specialties. However, graduates with a degree in one branch of engineering may qualify for jobs in other branches.

Some colleges and universities offer five-year programs that culminate in a master's degree. Some offer five- or six-year programs that include cooperative experience. Some four-year schools have arrangements with community colleges or liberal arts colleges that allow students to spend two or three years at the initial school and transfer for the last two years to complete their engineering degree.

All fifty states and the District of Columbia require engineers to be licensed as professional engineers (PE) if they serve the public directly. In most states, licensure requires graduation from a four-year engineering program accredited by the Accreditation Board for Engineering and Technology (ABET), four years of experience, and passing the state exam. Many engineers take the Fundamentals of Engineering portion of the exam upon graduation. They are then engineers in training (EIT). After obtaining appropriate work experience, they take the Principles and Practice of Engineering exam to complete their professional license. Most states recognize licenses from other states, as long as the requirements are the same or more stringent. Some states have continuing education requirements.

The Association of Energy Engineers (AEE) offers several certification programs for energy engineers, including Certified Measurement and Verification Professional (CMVP), Certified Lighting Efficiency Professional (CLEP), Certified Building Commissioning Professional (CBCP), and Existing Building Commissioning Professional (EBCP) programs. For those who procure energy, AEE offers the Certified Energy Procurement Professional (CEP) program.

For More Information

Accreditation Board for Engineering and
    Technology (ABET)
111 Market Place
Suite 1050
Baltimore, Maryland 21202
410-347-7700
www.abet.org

Association of Energy Engineers (AEE)
4025 Pleasantdale Road
Suite 420
Atlanta, Georgia 30340
770-447-5083
www.aeecenter.org

U.S. Green Building Council (USGBC)
2101 L Street, NW
Suite 500
Washington, DC 20037
800-795-1747 (toll-free)
www.usgbc.org

Facilities Manager ☼🌎

Alternate Titles and Related Careers
- Administrative Services Manager
- Building Manager
- Building Operations Manager
- Energy Manager
- Maintenance and Operations Manager
- Maintenance Engineer
- Maintenance Manager

Facilities manager belongs to a "Green Increased Demand" category. Rising energy costs to heat and cool buildings is making the job of facilities manager increasingly important.

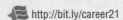 http://bit.ly/career21

Job Trends

According to the *Occupational Outlook Handbook,* administrative managers, the category that includes facilities managers, should rise about as fast as average for all occupations between 2008 and 2018. However, demand for facilities managers is expected to be strong.

Businesses and educational institutions are facing rising energy costs and are concerned about maintaining, securing, and operating their facilities as efficiently as possible. Cost-cutting and streamlining operations will be of increasing importance to organizations and primary goals of their facilities managers.

However, the rebound of the economy from the recession will affect job openings. Companies and organizations will not build new facilities until they feel more confident about the economy.

One trend that is evident in this field is the outsourcing of facilities management and operations to private firms.

About Energy Savings and Profit Margins
Energy savings from buildings is the lowest-cost method of reducing greenhouse gas emissions, according to the consulting firm McKinsey & Company. In addition, greener buildings could save the New York real estate industry alone as much as $230 million a year in operating expenses.

Nature of the Work

Facilities managers "ensure the optimal operation of plants [physical buildings], grounds, and offices," according to the mission statement of the Association of Facilities Engineering. Facilities managers work in manufacturing plants, hospitals, office buildings, apartment buildings, government agencies, and industrial parks. They plan, design, and manage buildings, grounds, equipment, and supplies. Typically, the job involves mechanical, electrical, safety, and building management control systems as well as managing people. Facilities managers' duties increasingly include developing and implementing energy efficiency strategies.

Among the specific tasks of facilities managers are the following:
- Monitor the facility to ensure that it is safe, secure, and well-maintained
- Recommend energy-saving alternatives or production efficiencies
- Coordinate repair activities
- Oversee renovation projects
- Ensure that renovations meet codes and environmental, health, and security standards
- Improve operations including energy efficiency
- Hire and train staff

- Manage staff, including maintenance, grounds, custodial, and office personnel
- Prepare budgets and reports including energy use

Facility managers who work for large companies or for colleges and universities may also be involved in

- Purchase and sale of real estate
- Lease management
- Architectural planning and design

Career Path

Some facilities managers begin by specializing in one area of expertise to gain experience and then move to another field for more experience. In this way, they work their way up within a company or move from company to company gaining more experience, greater responsibilities, and higher pay with each move. Certifications can also help a facilities manager in seeking promotions. Knowledge of business administration, information technology, and architecture, as well as engineering, is useful as facilities managers gain higher-level jobs. Some experienced managers may become consultants, working for themselves or for facilities management and operations consulting firms.

Earning Potential

Mean hourly wage (2009): $36.31

Mean annual wage (2009): $75,520
(Based on "Administrative Services Manager")

Education/Licensure

Facilities managers typically have at least a bachelor's degree in engineering, and some have an undergraduate or graduate degree in engineering, architecture, construction management, business administration, or facility management. A background in real estate, construction, or interior design can also be helpful.

All fifty states as well as the District of Columbia require engineers to be licensed as professional engineers (PE) if they serve the public directly. In most states, licensure requires graduation from a four-year engineering program accredited by the Accreditation Board for Engineering and Technology (ABET), four years of experience, and passing the state exam. Many engineers take the Fundamentals of Engineering portion of the exam upon graduation. They are then engineers in training (EIT). After obtaining appropriate work experience, they take the Principles and Practice of Engineering exam to complete their professional license. Most states recognize licenses from other states as long as the requirements are the same or more stringent. Some states have continuing education requirements.

The International Facility Management Association (IFMA) offers two credentials, the Facility Management Professional (FMP) as the first step and the Certified Facility Manager (CFM) for those with experience in the facility management field. Additional certifications in Facilities Management, Facility Management: Principles, Facility Management: Practices, and Facilities and Environmental Management are available online through IFMA partners.

The Association of Facilities Engineering (AFE) offers three certifications: Certified Plant Engineer (CPE), Certified Plant Maintenance Manager (CPMM), and Certified Plant Supervisor (CPS).

The American Society of Heating, Refrigerating and Air-Conditioning Engineers (ASHRAE) offers professional certificates in Building Energy Modeling, High Performance Building Design, Operations and Performance Management, and Healthcare Facility Design. In addition to general facilities management associations, there are also specific organizations like the Association of Physical Plant Administrators (APPA), which is an organization of managers of educational facilities such as university campuses. It offers two credentials: Educational Facilities Credential (EFC) and the Certified Educational Facilities Professional (CEFP) for experienced managers.

For More Information

Accreditation Board for Engineering and
    Technology (ABET)
111 Market Place
Suite 1050
Baltimore, Maryland 21202
410-347-7700
www.abet.org

American Society of Heating, Refrigerating and
    Air-Conditioning Engineers (ASHRAE)
1791 Tullie Circle NE
Atlanta, Georgia 30329
404-636-8400
www.ashrae.org

Association for Facilities Engineering (AFE)
12801 Worldgate Drive
Suite 500
Herndon, Virginia 20170
571-203-7171
www.afe.org

Association of Physical Plant Administrators
    (APPA)
1643 Prince Street
Alexandria, Virginia 22314
703-684-1446
www.appa.org

International Facility Management Association
    (IFMA)
1 E. Greenway Plaza
Suite 1100
Houston, Texas 77046-0104
713-623-4362
www.ifma.org

National Association of State Facilities
    Administrators (NASFA)
c/o The Council of State Governments
PO Box 11910
Lexington, Kentucky 40578-1910
859-244-8181
www.nasfa.net

Heating, Air Conditioning, and Refrigeration Mechanic and Installer ✿ ⑤

Alternate Titles and Related Careers

- Air Conditioning Technician (AC Tech)
- Commercial Service Technician
- Field Service Technician
- Heating, Air Conditioning, and Refrigeration Mechanic and Installer ✿ ⑤
- HVAC Installer (Heating, Ventilation, and Air Conditioning)
- HVAC Specialist (Heating, Ventilation, and Air Conditioning)
- HVAC Technician (Heating, Ventilation, and Air Conditioning)
- HVAC/R Service Technician (Heating, Ventilation, and Air Conditioning/ Refrigeration)
- Refrigeration Mechanic and Installer ✿ ⑤
- Refrigeration Operator
- Refrigeration Technician
- Service Manager
- Service Technician

This is both a "Bright Outlook" and "Green Enhanced-Skills" occupation. Workers may be required to obtain new skills, knowledge, and credentials to fulfill new job tasks. The two sectors that employ most HVAC/R mechanics and installers are energy efficiency and green construction.

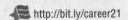 http://bit.ly/career21

Job Trends

According to the Bureau of Labor Statistics, employment for heating, air conditioning, and refrigeration mechanics and installers is expected to increase by 20 percent or more by 2018. This is much faster than average for all occupations. Numerous workers are expected to retire and the number of people entering the occupation is low, so job prospects are expected to be excellent for this trade. By 2018, some 136,200 new employees will be needed.

One area in particular that is driving the demand for HVAC/R mechanics and technicians is home remodeling and retrofitting public and private buildings as the population becomes more energy conscious. The need for people who are able to install new, efficient climate-control systems will increase demand for HVAC/R technicians with knowledge of the latest in HVAC/R technology. New residential and commercial construction also requires skilled HVAC/R technicians and installers.

Retrofitting the HVAC systems in residential, commercial, and industrial buildings can result in significant reduction in energy use. HVAC systems can account for as much as half the energy use in homes and 40 percent of electricity use in commercial buildings. Replacing units that are over ten years old can reduce energy costs between 20 and 50 percent.

Nature of the Work

This job, like a number of construction and building occupations, requires a personable manner in dealing with the public, because much of the job involves face-to-face contact with customers. Heating and air conditioning technicians install and service heating and air conditioning systems in residential and commercial buildings. They test and inspect systems to verify that they comply with specifications and to detect malfunctions if they don't comply. They test all components of a system, including electrical circuits and pressure testing pipes and joints, to ensure that the system meets all standards and that it follows manufacturer's procedures and safety precautions while working.

Refrigeration technicians, another specialty in the category of heating, air conditioning, and refrigeration mechanics and installers, build refrigeration systems that are often used for air conditioning in commercial buildings and are now beginning to be used in residences. They connect pipes, install

the refrigerant, test for leaks, connect the electric power source, and check to ensure that the system meets specifications. Reclaiming and recycling the refrigerant is critical, because it is harmful to the environment.

Among specific tasks, according to O*NET, are the following:

- Test electrical circuits and components, piping, tubing, and connections
- Repair or replace defective equipment, components, and wiring
- Reassemble and test equipment after repairs
- Inspect and test systems to verify system compliance with plans and specifications and to detect and locate malfunctions
- Discuss system malfunctions with users to isolate problems or verify the malfunctions have been corrected
- Recommend, develop, and perform preventive and general maintenance
- Lay out and install wiring and components according to wiring diagrams and blueprints
- Assist with other work in coordination with repair and maintenance teams
- Fabricate, assemble, and install metal work such as ducts
- Comply with all applicable standards, policies, and procedures
- Record the nature of a job, and time and materials used

Career Path

For most HVAC/R technicians, advancement is in the form of higher pay. Some technicians will become supervisors or managers. Others will advance by moving into other positions in the industry, such as sales representative, building supervisor, or contractor.

Earning Potential

Median hourly wage (2009): $19.76

Median annual wage (2009): $41,100

Education/Licensure

Heating, ventilation, air conditioning, and refrigeration technicians may still be able to learn this trade on the job, but those who have completed a formal apprenticeship or postsecondary training program—and may have earned an associate degree—have better opportunities. Community colleges, junior colleges, vocational and trade schools, and the armed forces offer programs, some of which lead to an associate degree. The programs take from six months to two years to complete.

Some states and municipalities require HVAC/R technicians to be licensed. Requirements vary, but all include passing an exam. Some require an apprenticeship, which is another way to be trained. Formal apprenticeship programs last from three to five years. They are often given by local chapters of trade organizations. There are five apprenticeships for heating and air conditioning technicians:

- Air and Hydronic Balancing Technician
- Furnace Installer
- Furnace Installer-and-Repairer, Hot Air
- Heating-and-Air-Conditioning Installer-Servicer
- Oil-Burner-Servicer-and-Installer

There are two apprenticeships for refrigeration technicians:

- Refrigeration Mechanic
- Refrigeration Unit Repairer

Under Section 608 of the Clean Air Act, the U.S. Environmental Protection Agency (EPA) requires anyone who handles ozone-depleting refrigerants to be properly trained. This includes technicians who work on refrigeration systems and stationary air conditioners. The Air-Conditioning Contractors of America offers training.

The North American Technician Excellence (NATE) certification program for HVAC/R technicians is recognized nationwide. HVAC Excellence offers a number of technician certifications at the professional and master levels. The Building Performance Institute offers certifications in Heating and Air Conditioning and Heat Pump. The U.S. Green Building Council offers the LEED (Leadership in Energy and Environmental Design) Associate and LEED AP credentials that may be appropriate for some HVAC/R technicians.

For More Information

Air-Conditioning, Heating and Refrigeration
   Institute
2111 Wilson Blvd.
Suite 500
Arlington, Virginia 22201
703-524-8800
www.ari.org

Building Performance Institute (BPI)
107 Hermes Road
Suite 110
Malta, New York 12020
877-274-1274 (toll-free)
www.bpi.org

HVAC Excellence
1701 Pennsylvania Avenue, NW
Washington, DC 20006
800-394-5268 (toll-free)
www.hvacexcellence.org

North American Technician Excellence
2111 Wilson Blvd. #510
Arlington, Virginia 22201
703-276-7247
www.natex.org

Refrigeration Service Engineers Society
1666 Rand Road
Des Plaines, Illinois 60016
847-759-4051
www.rses.org

Sheet Metal and Air Conditioning Contractors'
   National Association
4201 Lafayette Center Drive
Chantilly, Virginia 20151-1209
703-803-2980
www.smacna.org

U.S. Green Building Council (USGBC)
2101 L Street, NW
Suite 500
Washington, DC 20037
800-795-1747 (toll-free)
www.usgbc.org

The following organizations sponsor
apprenticeships:

Air-Conditioning Contractors of America
2800 Shirlington Road
Suite 300
Arlington, Virginia 22206
703-575-4477
www.acca.org

Associated Builders and Contractors
Workforce Development Department
4250 North Fairfax Drive
9th Floor
Arlington, Virginia 22203
703-812-2000
www.abc.org

Home Builders Institute
National Association of Home Builders
1201 15th Street, NW
6th Floor
Washington, DC 20005
800-795-7955 (toll-free)
www.hbi.org

Mechanical Contractors Association of America
Mechanical Service Contractors of America
1385 Piccard Drive
Rockville, Maryland 20850
301-869-5800
www.mcaa.org
www.mcaa.org/msca

Plumbing-Heating-Cooling Contractors
180 S. Washington Street
P.O. Box 6808
Falls Church, Virginia 22046
703-237-8100
www.phccweb.org

United Association of Journeymen and
Apprentices of the Plumbing and Pipefitting
Industry
United Association Building
Three Park Place
Annapolis, Maryland 21401
410-269-2000
www.ua.org

Insulation Worker: Floor, Ceiling, and Wall ⑤

Alternate Titles and Related Careers
- Insulation Installer
- Installer
- Insulation Estimator
- Retrofit Installer
- Insulation Mechanic
- Insulation Worker, Mechanical

This is a "Green Increased-Demand" occupation found in the energy efficiency and green construction sectors of the economy. While demand may increase because of activities in the green economy and new technologies, there will probably not be significant changes in the work or in the skills and knowledge required of workers.

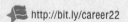 http://bit.ly/career22

Job Trends

The need for insulation workers is expected to grow at the rate of 14 to 19 percent between 2008 and 2018. This translates into 13,200 job openings over the time period. However, as a "Green Increased-Demand" job, growth may be higher. Proper insulation can cut down on energy usage and, therefore, costs for both residential and commercial buildings. Much will depend on the rebound in the housing market—how long it takes and how high it goes—although retrofitting existing buildings also generates business for insulation installers.

Nature of the Work

Insulation workers cover structures with insulating materials to cover flooring, ceilings, and walls. The insulation may be in roll form or blown material—fiberglass, cork, calcium, silicate, foamglass, expanded silicate, and spray insulation—and installers may need to wear protective clothing. Physical abilities such as coordination, strength, and flexibility are important. Depending on their job, insulation workers may need to use analytical or scientific and project management software.

Among the tasks that an insulation installer may perform are the following, according to O*NET:

- Read blueprints and select appropriate insulation based on the space and heat characteristics of insulating materials
- Measure and cut insulation
- Cover and line structures with insulation
- Fit, wrap, staple, or glue insulation
- Distribute blown insulating materials evenly
- Cover, seal, or finish insulated surfaces or access holes
- Prepare surfaces for insulation application
- Remove old insulation

Career Path

Entry-level employees work under the supervision of experienced workers. On-the-job training may take up to four years, depending on whether the company installs insulation in residential or commercial buildings. Over the training period, entry-level workers are given more responsibility with less supervision and earn more money.

Skilled insulation workers may become supervisors, shop superintendents, or estimators working with clients to determine insulation needs. Some experienced insulation workers with continuing education in business organization and finance may start their own businesses. The ability to speak English and Spanish is important for anyone wishing to advance to supervisor in the construction trades.

Earning Potential

Median hourly wage (2009): $15.65

Median annual wage (2009): $32,550

Education/Licensure

Typically, entry-level jobs require a high school diploma or equivalent. "Insulation worker" is an apprenticeship category recognized by the U.S. Department of Labor. Usually, insulation companies that install and maintain mechanical industrial insulation offer apprenticeships, sometimes in conjunction with the local of the International Association of Heat and Frost Insulators and Allied Workers. An apprenticeship usually lasts four or five years and combines classroom instruction with on-the-job training.

The National Insulation Association (NIA) offers an Insulation Energy Appraisal Program that results in a certification as an insulation energy appraiser meant for workers in the industrial insulation sector.

Under the rules of the Environmental Protection Agency (EPA), workers in the asbestos industry must be certified. This includes anyone who removes or handles asbestos; is involved in operations and maintenance, management planning, project design, and project monitoring related to asbestos; and conducts asbestos project air sampling and asbestos inspections. To become certified, workers must complete a training program accredited by their state and pay a license fee.

For More Information

International Association of Heat and Frost Insulators and Allied Workers (AWIU)
9602 Martin Luther King, Jr. Highway
Lanham, Maryland 20706-1839
301-731-9101
www.insulators.org

National Insulation Association (NIA)
12100 Sunset Hills Road
Suite 330
Reston, Virginia 20190-3295
703-464-6422
www.insulation.org

North American Insulation Manufacturers'
    Association (NAIMA)
44 Canal Center Plaza
Suite 310
Alexandria, Virginia 22314-1548
703-684-0084
www.naima.org

Weatherization Installer and Technician ☼ⓢ

Alternate Titles and Related Careers
- Residential Air Sealing Technician
- Weatherization Crew Chief
- Weatherization Field Technician
- Weatherization Operations Manager
- Window/Door Retrofit Technician

This is a "Bright Outlook" and "Green New and Emerging" occupation. This is an example of an occupation that has developed as a result of peoples' concerns about the environment and the high cost of home heating.

Job Trends

The Bureau of Labor Statistics estimated in 2008 that the growth rate for the category would be about average at 7 to 13 percent. However, as a "Green New and Emerging" job, growth may be faster. In promoting his jobs programs, President Barack Obama stressed the importance of weatherization as one way to stimulate job growth during the recession.

One factor driving jobs in this category is the U.S. Department of Energy's (DOE) Weatherization Assistance Program. Although the program has been around since the late 1970s—the last energy crisis—it benefited from the $5 billion allocated to

it in the American Recovery and Reinvestment Act of 2009. The Weatherization Assistance Program provides weatherization services to low-income families. Since its inception, the program has helped more than 6.4 million families save on their energy bills by weatherizing their homes.

The interest in saving energy costs on residential and commercial heating and air conditioning is also a spur to weatherization projects. ENERGY STAR estimates that sealing and insulating homes can save homeowners as much as 20 percent on their heating and air-conditioning bills. Building codes in many municipalities now include energy efficiency requirements.

Nature of the Work

Weatherization installers and technicians weatherize homes to make them more energy-efficient and improve indoor air quality. They may repair windows, insulate heating and air-conditioning ducts, and perform maintenance on the heating, ventilation, and air-conditioning (HVAC) system. They may also perform energy audits and must know applicable energy regulations, codes, policies, and statutes.

O*NET lists the following as among the tasks that a weatherization installer and technician may perform:
- Inspect buildings to identify weatherization strategies such as repair, modification, or replacement
- Test and diagnose air flow systems
- Recommend and explain weatherization and energy conservation measures, policies, procedures, and requirements to clients
- Apply insulation materials
- Install and seal air ducts, combustion air openings, or ventilation openings
- Install storm windows or storm doors and verify proper fit
- Prepare and apply weather-stripping, glazing, caulking, or door sweeps to reduce energy losses

- Wrap air ducts and water lines and water heaters
- Apply spackling, compounding, or other materials to repair holes
- Prepare cost estimates and specifications
- Maintain activity logs and financial records
- Prepare or assist in the preparation of bids, contracts, or written reports.

Career Path

Entry-level employees work under the supervision of experienced workers. Over the training period, entry-level workers are given more responsibility with less supervision and earn more money. With experience, weatherization installers and technicians may become supervisors themselves. With training in business and finance, some may start their own businesses. The ability to speak both English and Spanish is important for anyone wishing to advance to supervisor in the construction trades.

Earning Potential

Median hourly wage (2009): $16.34
Median annual wage (2009): $33,980

Education/Licensure

Typically, employers prefer employees with high school diplomas or the equivalent. Some prior experience in construction, inspection, or energy conservation is useful. States may also have their own training and certification programs for weatherization technicians. Some of these programs may be through community colleges and others through community action associations within states. For example, the Indiana Community Action Association (www.incap.org) has more than a dozen introductory and advanced training classes for weatherization installers and technicians.

The Home Builders Institute of the National Association of Home Builders (NAHB) offers a Green/Weatherizing and ESL certification for native Spanish speakers. The Building Performance Institute (BPI) offers an Envelope Certificate, which includes such topics as stopping air leaks and ensuring the best performance from heating and air-conditioning systems.

For More Information

Building Performance Institute (BPI)
107 Hermes Road
Suite 110
Malta, New York 12020
877-274-1274 (toll-free)
www.bpi.org

National Association of Home Builders (NAHB)
1201 15th Street, NW
Washington, DC 20005
800-368-5242 (toll-free)
www.nahb.org

How Being Green Works for **Larry Gorman, Residential Energy Consultant**

Larry Gorman, 61, is a self-employed residential energy consultant based in Placitas, New Mexico. For the past nine years, Gorman has focused on green industry work and is an example of the many entrepreneurs running one-person service companies to multimillion-dollar energy start-ups that are finding opportunities in the green economy. Here, Gorman conducts a duct leakage test following the installation of ductwork at the completion of rough in, a stage of construction. The test—a part of the HERS rating—is not required at this point. However, Gorman conducts the test because the area has not yet been covered by drywall and is still accessible in the event leakage issues are found. If the ductwork passes the test at this point, it will pass at completion when the official test is made.

Describe your job, including common daily tasks and long-term projects that you have worked on or are working on now. What specifically about your job makes it environmentally green work?

Our services include energy assessments and suggested solutions for existing homes. Daily tasks usually involve infrared analysis, use of a blower door to determine the rate of shell leakage and the identification of the leakage sites, and recommendations for fixing shell leakage issues on existing homes. Also included are recommendations for upgrading the shell (windows, insulation, etc.) and mechanical systems to increase energy efficiency while maintaining indoor air quality. Another concern is heating, ventilation, and air-conditioning (HVAC) duct leakage. However, in New Mexico, most houses have flat roofs and there is no access to fix duct leakage issues.

Most of my business is with new home-builders who want to build above the code minimum and participate in LEED for Homes or the local Build Green New Mexico program. As a Certified Home Energy Rater, or HERS Rater, through the Residential Energy Services Network (RESNET®) (http://www.resnet.us), I provide energy modeling services using REM/Rate™ software and do field verification of the energy features, shell leakage, and duct leakage. I also do verification of the implementation of the Green Building checklist items claimed. In addition, I spend time responding to phone calls and e-mail from both current and potential clients, and, of course, I must complete the paperwork required for the programs, invoicing, etc.

My definition of *green* is reducing energy use while maintaining indoor air quality. There are potential safety issues involved with air tightening of existing homes and even with how new homes are built. These must be addressed.

Why/how did you decide to work in a green industry?

I worked for a large international construction company, which transferred us to the area. [When I left the company, we] wanted to stay. My brother has knowledge of residential building science and performance building, saw great potential for growth, and advised me to investigate. I did. I attended an Affordable Comfort, Inc. (ACI) spring conference (http://www.affordablecomfort.org/), and I was greatly impressed. I decided to go into business here in New Mexico.

How did you prepare for your current position?

Beyond high school, my training was in technical drawing. However, my entire professional career relates to what I am now doing. Also, I have always been looking for ways to reduce that monthly check to the utility company. I spent several years as construction inspector and later as construction engineer with large international construction companies. Most of the work involved large federal projects. None involved residential constructions. However, my experience includes civil, structural, architectural, mechanical, and electrical aspects of these projects.

To become a certified HERS Rater through RESNET®, I completed a 40-hour class. To gain visibility from homebuilders, I became active in the local homebuilders association (HBA) and donated time to the local Habitat for Humanity® organization. I also became active on HBA committees.

Which aspect of your education and/or training do you think has been the most helpful and/or useful to you? Why?

The technical drawing education was very useful as the HERS ratings are usually obtained from plans and specifications. Throughout my career, I was very involved in enforcing specifications. That has also been very useful. My professional experience gave me detailed knowledge of how mechanical systems functioned.

Are you a LEED Accredited Professional? Why or why not?

I work in residential only and am working on my LEED accreditation. However, I also own an interest in another company, which is the LEED for Homes provider here in New Mexico. My responsibilities there include Quality Assurance Designee, or QAD. The QAD responsibilities include technical direction for the residential projects.

Do you find that the skills and/or knowledge required for your job continue to evolve? If so, what have you done to keep up-to-date?

Building codes are evolving, as are requirements to work with the various green building programs and as a HERS Rater. There are continuing education requirements to keep up with.

Attending the annual ACI conference and participating in local training opportunities are necessary. So is being a trainer for local programs. All of the above keep you visible to the local homebuilders and result in new projects and clients.

How have continuing education and/or training impacted the way you do your job?

I always strive to keep up with all the new requirements and think ahead on how these will impact my clients and make sure there are no implementation issues.

What is the most rewarding part of your work, and what do you find to be the most challenging?

I feel that I am making an impact on residential energy use in the community. For the past three years, I have seen that the opportunities were beyond what local resources could provide. So, I have recruited and encouraged my competitors. This has also increased my visibility in the homebuilding community

What advice would you give to people interested in pursuing your career?

Do not expect to just get the minimum training and expect business to come your way. You must get involved in the community of HERS Raters and homebuilders in your area.

How Being Green Works for
Tatyana Shine, Geothermal Designer

Tatyana Shine, 50, is a mechanical engineer and certified geothermal designer. She is also the CEO and COO of a company in Columbia, Maryland, that serves as a distributor of energy-efficient and environmentally friendly mechanical and electrical equipment. Shine has worked within the green industry for the past fifteen years. Here, she is reviewing the energy model for a project she is working on in Baltimore, Maryland. This is one of many steps required before a building can become LEED-certified.

Describe your job, including common daily tasks and long-term projects that you have worked on or are working on now. What, specifically, about your job makes it green?

Our company offers comprehensive engineering consulting services and evaluates the integrated engineering systems to provide the best solutions to building owners and to fulfill the USGBC (U.S. Green Building Council) requirements for LEED (Leadership in Energy and Environmental Design), U.S. Environmental Protection Agency (EPA) ENERGY STAR rating, federal and state incentive program requirements, and utility company rebates and grants requirements. The fact that engineering consulting companies do not sell the equipment and materials often creates problems. Our company evaluates the design documents [from consulting firms] for compliance with all applicable requirements prior to selling the equipment and materials to ensure that both project and owner intentions are met.

Why/how did you decide to work in a green industry?

As a mechanical engineer, I was designing the heating, ventilation, and air-conditioning (HVAC) systems for commercial, institutional, and industrial buildings. I was engineering the mechanical systems that can perform efficiently and operate at the lowest cost. Therefore, coordination with the manufacturers was an important component in creating the right product for our clients. The three "Es"—efficiency, environment, and economics—have become the "center of mass" that the manufacturing industry is revolving around in the process of creating green products. Through close work with industry leaders in green technologies and continuous education, I learned to design high-performance buildings. Green industry is an evolving industry, and we have the best time ahead of us.

How did you prepare for your current position?

I graduated from Kiev Civil Engineering University [in Ukraine] with a master's degree in mechanical engineering. Over the years, I have obtained the following certifications: Professional Engineer, State of Maryland; Certified Energy Manager; Certified Geothermal Designer; LEED

Accredited Professional; and Certified Sustainable Development Professional. I am a member of the Association of Energy Engineers, USGBC, and the International Ground Source Heat Pump Association. I present geothermal system design and economics to builders, architects, and engineers at different conferences and seminars.

Which aspect of your education and/or training do you think has been the most helpful and/or useful to you? Why?

Work on the actual projects allowed me to gain knowledge and experience. I was also involved in troubleshooting "unsuccessful" geothermal installations, which was very challenging, but rewarding. It gave me an opportunity to see the importance of comprehensive knowledge in equipment and control. The mechanical application engineer's job is to design the mechanical systems but not the equipment. However, it is crucial to gain adequate knowledge of the equipment to ensure the quality performance of the mechanical systems.

Why are you a LEED Accredited Professional?

It was a necessary step for me, since I wanted to design mechanical systems for high-performance buildings. The LEED guide was, and still is, the most comprehensive and modern approach to designing energy efficient and sustainable buildings. To be a LEED AP also provides the opportunity to be a part of evolving industries.

Do you find that the skills and/or knowledge required for your job continue to evolve? If so, what have you done to keep up-to-date?

Absolutely! The comprehensive knowledge and understanding of the industry initiatives are mandatory in the design and construction of high-performance buildings. There are many ways of getting information needed in the process of professional growth, such as Web sites, webinars, seminars, conferences, publications, and so on. I try to employ as many options as I can in my spare time.

How have continuing education and/or training impacted the way you do your job?

It helps me to design energy-efficient and environmentally friendly systems. However, the economic aspects, such as available budget, should be considered prior to the start-up of the design. It is very unfortunate that we sometimes need to compromise on the efficiency of the mechanical system to reduce the initial cost at the expense of high energy bills that the owner will pay in future.

What is the most rewarding part of your work, and what do you find to be the most challenging?

The opportunity to work with educated, enthusiastic, and generous people is the most rewarding and challenging part of my work. We all have failures in our business, but we help each other to overcome them. That is how we create and then count our success stories.

What advice would you give to people interested in pursuing your career?

Just do it!

What Is LEED?

LEED stands for Leadership in Energy and Environmental Design and designates the green building certification program of the U.S. Green Building Council (USGBC).

The USGBC is a nonprofit organization with the goal of making green buildings available to all by the next generation. Through its LEED certification program, it offers independent, third-party certification of residential, commercial, and institutional construction as "green." Through the Green Building Certification Institute (GBCI), individuals can become credentialed as green building professionals.

The goal of the LEED program is to integrate sustainable standards of design, construction, and operations into the construction of new buildings and the retrofitting of existing buildings. Several thousand projects worldwide have been LEED-certified. To gain certification, a building must be designed and built keeping the following criteria in mind:

- Sustainable site
- Materials and resources
- Indoor environmental quality
- Water efficiency
- Energy and atmosphere

Using a 100-point scale, green raters assess how well a building matches each criterion. Different scales have been developed for different kinds of buildings: schools, retail stores, health-care facilities, homes, commercial interiors, new construction, and neighborhood development. To become certified, projects must earn a minimum number of points. Four levels of certification exist.

- Platinum 80+ points
- Gold 60+ points
- Silver 50+ points
- Certified 40+ points

In addition, projects may earn up to ten bonus points for innovation and for taking into account regional priorities. Six key environmental concerns have been identified for each region of the country. These have been further refined by ZIP Code to lessen the environmental impact of building as much as possible.

The GBCI oversees the process for credentialing individuals working in the construction field, including interior design. Becoming credentialed requires completing a number of hours of course work, successfully passing examinations, and working on green projects. Classes are taught traditionally or online. In 2010, the Veterans Administration began contributing to the cost of credentialing for veterans through the GI Bill. The three tiers of credential are:

- *LEED Green Associate:* demonstrates basic knowledge and skills of green building; areas of knowledge include design, construction, and operations
- *LEED AP:* in addition demonstrates skill in specialty areas such as building and design, interior design and construction, homes, neighborhood development, and operations and maintenance
- *LEED Fellow:* highest level of experience and contribution to the field of green building

In 2009, the USGBC established the USGBC Students program for college and university groups. The purpose is "to educate students as well as empower them to get engaged in green building and sustainability on their campuses."

CHAPTER 4

ENERGY-RELATED JOBS IN POLICY, ANALYSIS, ADVOCACY, AND REGULATORY AFFAIRS

The area of policy, analysis, advocacy, and regulatory affairs is not an industry in itself but a broad and diverse collection of jobs. The purpose of these jobs is to examine all aspects of the condition of the environment—social, economic, justice, and political—and propose and implement solutions. The people employed in these jobs develop and implement policies, regulations, laws, standards, procedures, and guidelines. They study industries and technology and propose modifications that will be sustainable, create jobs, stimulate the economy, conserve resources, and protect the environment.

Many of the jobs in this area are in federal, state, and local government agencies. Others are in advocacy organizations or special interest groups that influence government and the public. Some jobs are in private companies, consulting firms, and industry groups.

A number of these occupations do not require a background in engineering, science, and/or math. Individuals with majors in English, communications, economics, political science, and similar "soft-side" degrees are good candidates for jobs such as paralegal, policy analyst, and public relations specialist. Job opportunities abound in the green economy for people with diverse interests and backgrounds.

JOBS PROFILED HERE

The following sectors and occupations are profiled in this chapter:

- City and Regional Planning Aide
- Compliance Manager
- Construction and Building Inspector
- Financial Analyst
- Paralegal
- Public Relations Specialist
- Regulatory Affairs Specialist
- Traffic Technician
- Transportation Vehicle, Equipment, or Systems Inspector
- Urban and Regional Planner

KEY TO UNDERSTANDING THE JOB PROFILES

The job profiles are classified according to one or more of the following categories:

✿ Bright Outlook
✪ Green Occupation

The classifications "Bright Outlook" and "Green Occupation" are taken from the National Center for O*NET Development's O*NET OnLine job site. O*NET, which is sponsored by the U.S. Department of Labor/Employment and Training

Administration (USDOL/ETA), has broken green jobs into three categories:

- Green Increased-Demand occupations
  o These are occupations that are likely to see job growth, but the work and worker requirements are unlikely to experience significant changes.
- Green Enhanced-Skills occupations
  o These occupations are likely to experience significant changes in work and worker requirements. Workers may find themselves doing new tasks requiring new knowledge, skills, and credentials. Current projections do not project increased demand for workers in these occupations, but O*NET notes that an increase is possible.
- Green New and Emerging occupations
  o These are new occupations—not growth in existing jobs—that are created as a result of activity and technology in green sectors of the economy.

Video Links

We've provided easy-to-use links that will take you directly to a particular career video from the One-Stop Career System Multimedia Career Video Library at CareerOneStop.org. The links will look like this:

 http://bit.ly/career1

Note that videos are not available for all jobs listed here. The videos come in QuickTime and Mpeg formats, with and without captions; download times may vary. CareerOneStop.org is sponsored by the U.S. Department of Labor/Employment and Training Administration.

City and Regional Planning Aide

Alternate Titles and Related Careers

- Community Planner
- Development Technician
- GIS (Geographic Information Systems) Technician
- Planning Aide
- Planning Assistant
- Planning Technician
- Transportation Planning Assistant
- Zoning Technician

Aides work with urban and regional planners, which is a "Green Enhanced-Skills" occupation, so planning aides/technicians will require up-to-date skills and knowledge.

Job Trends

According to the U.S. Bureau of Labor Statistics, the rate of job growth for the category that includes city and regional planning aides is expected to be 14 to 19 percent, or faster than average for all occupations. Job opportunities will arise from meeting the housing and infrastructure needs of the increasing population, particularly in rapidly expanding communities that need streets and other services.

According to the *Occupational Outlook Handbook,* currently 68 percent of planners are employed in local governments. Only 21 percent are employed in private companies that provide architectural, engineering, and related services. However, employment in the private sector is expected to increase faster than government openings, especially in firms that provide technical services. Planning aides with good computer skills, including competence with geographic information systems (GIS), should have many opportunities.

Nature of the Work

City and regional planning aides assist urban and regional planners by compiling information used to create short- and long-term plans for the use of land and resources. Depending on the job, planning technicians

- Compile data from field investigations, reports, maps, and other sources
- Conduct interviews, site inspections, and surveys to collect data
- Analyze the data and prepare reports that include graphs and charts of statistics on population, zoning, land use, traffic flow, and other factors
- Develop and maintain databases of information, tracking systems, and records
- Review zoning permit applications or building plans
- Investigate violations of regulations

Some technicians specialize. For example, some will be GIS (geographic information system) technicians who provide support to planners by creating specialized maps that could show a variety of features, such as land use, population distribution, location of natural resources, and air pollution sources.

About New Urbanism

A current movement in urban and regional planning is called "New Urbanism." It promotes walkable neighborhoods that include a variety of occupations and different types of housing; for example, single-family homes, duplexes, and garden-style apartments. The emphasis is on reducing the use of cars and energy.

Career Paths

Planning technicians work under the supervision of planners. As they gain experience, they move to positions with greater responsibility and more independence. Some may continue their education to become planners.

Earning Potential

Median hourly wage (2009): $18.03

Median annual wage (2009): $37,500

Education/Licensure

Generally, an associate degree in urban planning, construction management, architecture, or a related field, plus two years of experience in building codes, zoning, or plans review, are required. However, many employers prefer a bachelor's degree, which may be substituted for experience.

A few schools offer a bachelor's degree in urban and regional planning. Graduates of these programs qualify for some entry-level jobs, but they may have limited opportunities for advancement. The Association of Collegiate Schools of Planning Web site (www.acsp.org) provides a list of accredited programs, starting at the bachelor's degree level.

Even though most states do not have requirements for certification, many communities do. The preferred certification is from the American Institute of Certified Planners (AICP), the professional institute of the American Planning Association (www.planning.org/aicp). The AICP certification is based on education, experience, and passing an exam. For those who do not have at least a bachelor's degree, eight years of experience is required. Maintaining certification requires professional development on a two-year cycle.

For More Information

American Planning Association (APA)
1776 Massachusetts Avenue, NW
Suite 400
Washington, DC 20036-1904
202-872-0611
www.planning.org

Association of Collegiate Schools of Planning (ACS)
6311 Mallard Trace
Tallahassee, Florida 32312
850-385-2054
www.acsp.org

Compliance Manager ☼ ⑤

Alternate Titles and Related Careers
- Chief Compliance Officer
- Compliance Administrator
- Compliance Analyst
- Compliance Associate
- Compliance Director
- Compliance Engineer
- Compliance Inspector
- Compliance Officer
- Compliance Program Manager
- Compliance Team Manager
- Regulatory Compliance Manager

This is a "Bright Outlook" and "Green New and Emerging" occupation in government and regulatory affairs. Compliance managers work for public and private organizations in the areas of conservation and pollution control, regulation enforcement, and policy analysis and advocacy.

Job Trends

According to the U.S. Bureau of Labor Statistics, the compliance manager occupation is expected to have a growth rate that is about average of all occupations—7 to 13 percent. Compliance managers are employed in many industries from energy to banking and securities, and a large number of new compliance jobs will be in the financial field as the federal government moves to tighten regulations in this area. However, as state and local governments write new, more stringent energy regulations, and new federal rules and regulations related to energy take effect, parts of the green sector of the economy should see an increase in the need for compliance officers.

Nature of the Work

Compliance managers plan, direct, and coordinate the activities of an organization to ensure compliance with ethical or regulatory standards. They are the point of contact for a company's management, employees, and suppliers for information on government rules and regulations affecting the business. They work with corporate attorneys, internal and external auditors, and regulatory agencies on compliance issues.

Government regulations affect not just the products that a company manufactures, such as gasoline or environmentally friendly sneakers but also how the company operates internally. Compliance officers are needed to assess how well a company abides by government financial reporting regulations such as Sarbanes-Oxley and nondiscrimination laws. This is an occupation for which non-technically trained individuals with an interest in "green employment" can contribute.

According to O*NET, the following are some of the tasks that compliance managers perform:

- Direct the development or implementation of compliance-related policies and procedures
- Disseminate written policies and procedures and provide employee training
- Verify that all company and regulatory policies and procedures have been documented, implemented, and communicated
- Maintain the documentation
- Design or implement improvements in communication, monitoring, or enforcement of compliance standards
- Conduct periodic internal reviews or audits to ensure that compliance procedures are being followed
- Conduct or direct the internal investigation of compliance issues
- File appropriate compliance reports with regulatory agencies
- Prepare management reports regarding compliance operations and progress
- Report violations of compliance or regulatory standards to duly authorized enforcement agencies as appropriate or required
- Keep informed regarding pending industry changes, trends, and best practices and

assess the potential impact of these changes on organizational processes

- Discuss emerging compliance issues and regulations with management or employees

About the Irish Plastic Bag Tax

In 2002, the Irish legislature passed a tax on plastic bags. As a result of the tax, Irish use of plastic bags dropped 94 percent in a few weeks. Now about the only shopping bags you see are cloth, reusable bags. The tax is $0.33 a bag.

Career Path

Typically, an individual interested in a compliance position begins as an associate or assistant working under a compliance manager. Over a period of time, the individual will gain greater responsibilities and take on projects with decreasing supervision. Depending on the area of expertise, a compliance officer may become a consultant, be self-employed, or work for a large company specializing in compliance and risk management issues.

Earning Potential

Median hourly wage (2009): $44.52

Median annual wage (2009): $92,600

Education/Licensure

Entry-level jobs in compliance need at least a bachelor's degree. Typical majors are business administration, human resources, accounting, or finance. In addition to their academic backgrounds, compliance officers must be familiar with applicable rules and regulations and any inspection or testing methods for their particular field. Promotion to a manager's position may require as much as seven years of experience. Additional graduate work or certifications are also useful in advancing to higher positions.

Most states require certification of accountants. The exam is administered under the authority of the American Institute of Certified Public Accountants (AICPA), the National Association of State Boards of Accountancy (NASBA), and the state boards of accountancy.

The Society for Human Resources Management through its Human Resources Certification Institute offers four HR certifications: Professional in Human Resources (PHR®), Senior Professional in Human Resources (SPHR®), Global Professional in Human Resources (GPHR®), and California certification (PHR-CA® and SPHR-CA®).

For More Information

American Institute of Certified Public Accountants (AICPA)
1211 Avenue of the Americas
New York, New York 10036
888-777-7077 (toll-free)
www.aicpa.org

National Association of State Boards of Accountancy (NASBA)
866-696-2722 (toll-free)
www.nasba.org

Society for Human Resources Management
1800 Duke Street
Alexandria, Virginia 22314
800-283-7476 (toll-free)
www.shrm.org

Construction and Building Inspector

Alternate Titles and Related Careers

- Electrical Inspector
- Green Building Inspector
- Home Inspector
- Mechanical Inspector
- Plan Examiner
- Plumbing Inspector
- Public Works Inspector
- Specification Inspector
- Structural Inspector

This is a "Green Enhanced-Skills" occupation found in green construction and governmental and regulatory administration. The job of construction and building inspector, like so many others, is being affected by new technologies. In this case, new modeling technology is increasing the resources available to construction and building inspectors to do their work. Think of construction and building inspectors as ground-level compliance officers.

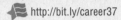 http://bit.ly/career37

Job Trends

The U.S. Bureau of Labor Statistics predicts that employment for construction and building inspectors will grow by 14 to 19 percent by 2018, which is faster than average for all occupations. According to the *Occupational Outlook Handbook*, local governments employed about 44 percent of inspectors in 2008. Architectural and engineering services companies employed another 27 percent who conducted audits for fee, mostly home inspections for potential buyers. Approximately 8 percent of building inspectors were self-employed, many of these as home inspectors.

Concerns for public safety in light of potential disasters arising from natural or human causes and increasing emphasis on high-quality construction are driving the demand for this occupation. Emerging emphasis on sustainable and green building will also stimulate employment opportunities for building inspectors. First, buildings may now be certified as green. The U.S. Green Building Council (USGBC) offers several levels of certification called Leadership in Energy and Environmental Design (LEED). Inspectors who are trained to conduct LEED audits will have new job opportunities. Second, new opportunities exist in local government to develop Green Building Programs and local codes for sustainable building. Once codes are in place, inspecting for compliance will continue to provide jobs.

About Paperless in Hawaii

In 2008, the state senate in Hawaii went paperless—no more stacks of bills on lawmakers' desks, and no more lines of assistants standing at copy machines. By 2010, the senate could boast that it had saved $1.2 million, nearly 8 million sheets of paper, and more than 800 trees.

Home inspection also is an area with potential for good job opportunities. This is partly because of economic conditions but also because of environmental concerns. The market for home remodeling is currently strong, and retrofitting and remodeling work to improve energy efficiency is on the rise. In addition, retrofitting industrial plants, office buildings, government buildings, and schools for energy efficiency will also create job opportunities. New residential construction, commercial construction, and building and repair of bridges and roads all contribute to employment for construction and building inspectors.

Nature of the Work

Building inspectors must know the federal, state, and local codes that regulate construction. The International Code Council (ICC) publishes national construction and building codes, but there are also many local codes. Many localities also have new green building codes that may be voluntary or mandatory. A new specialty called green building inspector evaluates buildings for energy efficiency, indoor air quality, and use of natural materials.

Construction and building inspectors are responsible for monitoring work during all phases of construction. They make necessary measurements and observations to ensure that the work follows plans, meets specifications, and complies with all construction and safety codes. In addition to monitoring new construction, inspectors also oversee repairs, remodeling, and maintenance work.

Career Paths

Certification improves job opportunities and opportunities for advancement. A degree in engineering or architecture may be required in order to advance to a supervisory position.

Earning Potential

Mean hourly wage (2009): $24.77

Mean annual wage (2009): $51,530

Education/Licensure

A high school diploma or GED is generally the minimum educational requirement. Currently, 30 percent of building and construction inspectors have no more than that. About 46 percent have some postsecondary training or an associate degree. Only 23 percent have a bachelor's degree or higher. Substantial construction experience qualifies a person for many jobs in this field. However, employers are increasingly hiring those who have experience and an associate degree from a community college or who have at least studied engineering, architecture, construction technology, building inspection, or home inspection. There are also apprenticeship programs for a variety of inspection specialties.

Many states and municipalities require certification, and individuals who hold certifications have the best job opportunities. Certification generally requires passing an exam, but may also include a specified amount of experience or a minimum level of training and education. There are many ways to become certified. Some states have licensing programs, whereas other states require specialized certification from an association such as the National Fire Protection Association (NFPA). Community colleges often offer certificate programs. The Green Building Certification Institute, affiliated with the U.S. Green Building Council (USGBC), offers green credentials.

The International Code Council (ICC) offers several certifications, including Code Safety Professional; Certified Class A or Class B Underground Storage Tank System to install, retrofit, or decommission petroleum storage tanks; and Code Safety Professional. ICC also provides testing services for a number of state certifications.

Continuing education to stay up-to-date on new materials, construction practices, and techniques, as well as codes, is an important part of an inspector's job.

For More Information

American Society of Home Inspectors (ASHI)
932 Lee Street
Suite 101
Des Plaines, Illinois 60016
800-743-2744 (toll-free)
www.ashi.org

Green Building Certification Institute (GBCI)
2101 L Street, NW
Suite 650
Washington, DC 20037
800-795-1746 (toll-free)
www.gbci.org

International Code Council (ICC)
500 New Jersey Avenue, NW
6th Floor
Washington, DC 20001-2070
888-422-7233 (toll-free)
www.iccsafe.org

National Association of Home Inspectors (NAHI)
4248 Park Glen Road
Minneapolis, Minnesota 55416
800-448-3942 (toll-free)
www.nahi.org

National Fire Protection Association (NFPA)
1 Batterymarch Park
Quincy, Massachusetts 02169-7471
617-770-3000
www.nfpa.org

U.S. Green Building Council (USGBC)
2101 L Street, NW
Suite 500
Washington, DC 20037
800-795-1747 (toll-free)
www.usgbc.org

Financial Analyst ✿⑨

Alternate Titles and Related Careers
- Credit Products Officer
- Equity Research Analyst
- Investment Analyst
- Operational Risk Analyst
- Planning Analyst
- Real Estate Analyst
- Research Analyst
- Securities Analyst

This is a "Bright Outlook" and "Green Enhanced Skills" occupation in energy efficiency, government and regulatory administration, green construction, and research, design, and consulting services.

Job Trends

The Bureau of Labor Statistics projects that the financial analyst occupation will grow at the rate of 20 percent or higher between 2008 and 2018. This is much faster than the average of all occupations. About 47 percent of currently employed financial analysts work in the finance and insurance industries; 11 percent in the management of companies and other enterprises; 11 percent in professional, scientific, and technical services; and the remaining 31 percent across a variety of industries.

The major factors fueling the growth of financial analysts are the increasing number and complexity of government regulations related to businesses, the increasing sophistication and global diversification of investments, and the growth in the overall amount of assets under management. To deal with these issues, companies will need more financial analysts to research and recommend investments.

Nature of the Work

Financial analysts conduct quantitative analyses of information affecting investment programs or public or private institutions. They provide guidance to businesses and individuals making investment decisions. Financial analysts must be able to use a variety of analytical, charting, and database management software as well as spreadsheet and presentation programs.

Financial analysts who work for companies with large amounts of money to invest are buy-side analysts, and their companies are known as institutional investors. Financial analysts who help securities dealers such as banks and corporations sell stocks, bonds, and other types of investments are sell-side analysts. In addition, there are risk analysts who evaluate the risk involved in investment decisions, project potential losses, and determine how to limit such losses. Ratings analysts evaluate the ability of companies or governments to pay their debts.

According to O*NET, among the tasks that financial analysts perform are the following:

- Analyze financial information to produce forecasts of business, industry, and economic conditions for use in making investment decisions
- Interpret data affecting investment programs, such as price, yield, stability, future trends in investment risks, and economic influences
- Monitor fundamental economic, industrial, and corporate developments through the analysis of information obtained from financial publications and services, investment banking firms, government agencies, trade publications, company sources, and personal interviews
- Determine the prices at which securities should be syndicated and offered to the public
- Prepare plans of action for investment based on financial analyses
- Evaluate and compare the relative quality of various securities in a given industry
- Present oral and written reports on general economic trends, individual corporations, and entire industries

- Assemble spreadsheets and draw charts and graphs used to illustrate technical reports
- Contact brokers and purchase investments for companies, according to company policy
- Recommend investments and investment timing to companies, investment firm staff, or the investing public
- Maintain knowledge and stay abreast of developments in the fields of industrial technology, business, finance, and economic theory

Career Path

Entry-level financial analysts begin work under the supervision of experienced managers. Employees advance by moving into positions where they are responsible for larger or more important products. In time, they may supervise teams of financial analysts. With experience and a good track record, a financial analyst may become a portfolio or fund manager and direct the investment of his or her employer or a family of funds.

Earning Potential

Median hourly wage (2009): $35.42

Median annual wage (2009): $73,670

Education/Licensure

Entry-level positions require a bachelor's degree or higher, typically in accounting, statistics, economics, or finance. A master's degree in business administration or finance is desirable, especially for advancement. An understanding of accounting policies and procedures, corporate budgeting, and financial analysis is also important.

Some jobs may also require licenses or certifications. The Financial Industry Regulatory Authority (FINRA) is the main licensing organization for the securities industry. Different licenses are required for different jobs. New employees are not expected to be licensed before they are hired because typically an employer must sponsor its employees for these licenses.

The Chartered Financial Analyst Institute (CFA) offers the Chartered Financial Analyst (CFA) certification for financial analysts who typically work in the areas of institutional money management and stock analysis. They typically are not financial planners. The certification process consists of passing three exams and at least three years' experience in the field. The exams test candidates' knowledge of accounting, economics, portfolio management, securities analysis, and ethical and professional standards.

For More Information

American Academy of Financial Management (AAFM)
200 L&A Road
Suite B
Metairie, Louisiana 70001
www.aafm.us

Chartered Financial Analyst Institute (CFA)
560 Ray C. Hunt Drive
Charlottesville, Virginia 22903
www.cfainstitute.org

Financial Industry Regulatory Authority (FINRA)
1735 K Street NW
Washington, DC 20006
301-590-6500
www.finra.org

Securities Industry and Financial Markets Association (SIFMA)
120 Broadway, 35th Floor
New York, New York 10271
www.sifma.org

Paralegal ☼

Alternate Titles and Related Careers

- Judicial Assistant
- Legal Assistant

If you're interested in environmental issues, but have no inclination for a science career, working as a paralegal in a law firm that litigates on behalf of environmental and related issues is one way to support the movement for a sustainable future. This is a "Bright Outlook" occupation.

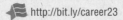 http://bit.ly/career23

Job Trends

The demand for paralegals will increase with the growing population and the issues associated with it—such as health care and elder issues. The Bureau of Labor Statistics predicts that employment for paralegals and legal assistants will increase by 20 percent or more, much faster than the average for all occupations. Competition for jobs is expected because so many people enter this field, but those who have formal training or who specialize will have the best opportunities. Environmental law is one of the areas of specialization where demand for paralegal services is expected to expand.

Law firms employ about 70 percent of paralegals. Government agencies and corporate legal departments employ most of the rest. However, paralegals work in almost any type of organization.

About the EPA

Consider a job with the Environmental Protection Agency. In addition to the federal EPA, states have similar agencies charged with the same mission. The federal EPA site has the following description of jobs with its Office of Enforcement and Compliance Assurance: the office "maximizes compliance with the nation's environmental laws and reduces threats to public health and the environment through an integrated approach of compliance assistance, compliance incentives, and innovative civil and criminal enforcement."

Nature of the Work

Paralegals are also called legal assistants. In a law firm or a corporate legal department, including nonprofit corporations, their duties may include the following:

- Preparing the background documentation that lawyers need for a case by researching facts and legal precedents, like relevant laws, court decisions, and legal articles
- Searching legal databases to find the information they need
- Preparing summaries and briefs for lawyers
- Organizing documentation for a case

Paralegals are allowed to prepare some types of documents, such as wills, estate plans, contracts, and real estate closings.

In corporate law departments, paralegals monitor environmental laws, regulations, and statutes that may be relevant to the business of the corporation and review health and safety regulations. They must be aware of existing requirements and any new requirements to make sure that the corporation is in compliance.

Paralegals who work for government agencies may prepare materials that explain the agency's policies, laws, and regulations. These materials inform the public about the requirements of laws and regulations.

Career Paths

At the beginning of their careers, paralegals handle routine tasks. After gaining some experience, they also gain responsibility. Paralegals may supervise other employees or lead project teams. Some paralegals go on to law school to become lawyers themselves.

Earning Potential

Median hourly wage (2009): $22.58

Median annual wage (2009): $46,980

Education/Licensure

There are a variety of ways to become a paralegal. The most common way is to earn an associate degree in paralegal studies from a community college. A person with a bachelor's degree can complete a paralegal certificate program. A few colleges offer a bachelor's degree in paralegal studies. Other ways include apprenticeships and employer on-the-job training. Some college and community college programs include an internship, which also is an advantage in getting a job.

Many colleges, universities, and law schools offer formal programs to train paralegals. About 260 of these are approved by the American Bar Association (ABA). A list of and links to those programs are available on the ABA's Web site, www.abanet.org. While it is not necessary to be trained in an ABA-approved program, it may improve job opportunities. About 350 members of the American Association for Paralegal Education (AAPE) also provide paralegal training programs, and these are listed on the association's Web site at www/aafpc.org.

Certification is voluntary, but it is an advantage in getting a job. The National Association of Legal Assistants offers the Certified Legal Assistant/ Certified Paralegal (CLA/CP) credential. Requirements include education, experience, and passing an exam. The Advanced Paralegal Certification (APC) is for experienced paralegals. The American Alliance of Paralegals offers the American Alliance Certified Paralegal (AACP) certification, which is based on experience and education. The National Federation of Paralegal Associations offers the Paralegal Advanced Competency Exam (PACE) Registered Paralegal certification based on experience, education, and passing the exam. NALS offers the Professional Paralegal (PP) certification based on experience and passing an exam.

For More Information

American Alliance of Paralegals, Inc. (AAPI)
4001 Kennett Pike
Suite 134-146
Wilmington, Delaware 19807
www.aapipara.org

American Association for Paralegal Education (AAPE)
19 Mantua Road
Mt. Royal, New Jersey 08061
856-423-2829
www.aafpe.org

American Bar Association (ABA)
Standing Committee on Paralegals
321 North Clark Street
Chicago, Illinois 60610
312-988-5000
www.abanet.org/legalservices/paralegals

National Association of Legal Assistants, Inc. (NALA)
1516 South Boston Street
Suite 200
Tulsa, Oklahoma 74119
918-587-6828
www.nala.org

National Federation of Paralegal Associations (NFPA)
P.O. Box 2016
Edmonds, Washington 98020
425-967-0045
www.paralegals.org

About Making Sense of "Green" Labels

See www.greenerchoices.org/eco-labels/eco-home.cfm to find out whether some of those supposedly "green" labels are really green. The site is sponsored by Consumers Union, an independent, nonprofit testing and information organization that was founded in 1936 and publishes *Consumer Reports®*.

Public Relations Specialist ☼🌐

Alternate Titles and Related Careers

- Public Affairs Specialist
- Public Information Officer
- Public Information Specialist
- Communications Director
- Communications Specialist
- Public Relations Coordinator
- Press Officer

This is both a "Bright Outlook" and "Green Enhanced-Skills" occupation. Like paralegal, public relations specialist is a good occupation for individuals without a science or math background who would like to further environmental causes, including energy efficiency.

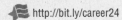 http://bit.ly/career24

Job Trends

This category is projected by the Bureau of Labor Statistics to grow much faster than average, about 24 percent between 2008 and 2018. This translates into 131,300 job openings between 2008 and 2018 across all the types of businesses and organizations that employ public relations specialists. In addition to business organizations, nonprofits use public relations specialists to get the organization's message out to the public.

One force that will drive the increase is social media. Organizations will be looking for individuals who understand how to use this media to reach the increasing number of people comfortable with it. Those organizations are as likely to be environmental groups looking to build support for their activities as businesses looking for sales.

Nature of the Work

Public relations professionals work for Fortune 500 corporations, colleges and universities, government agencies, and nonprofit foundations. They can be found in the offices of the Sierra Club, Exxon Mobil, and the American Petroleum Institute.

Public relations specialists need to be articulate and communicate clearly both in person and through written communications. They also need to be personable and quick thinking, and have good judgment. Their job involves establishing and maintaining interpersonal relationships with fellow employees, the public, and media representatives.

According to O*NET, among the tasks that public relations specialists may perform are the following:

- Develop public relations strategies to influence the public to see the organization favorably
- Plan and direct the development and communication of informational programs about the organization
- Work with vendors to develop promotional campaigns, ads, and promotional pieces for a variety of media
- Set up public appearances, lectures, contests, or exhibits
- Purchase ad space and time in media
- Respond to requests for information from the media
- Plan and conduct market and public opinion research

Career Path

Entry-level employees handle routine work under the supervision of an experienced manager. They may maintain files, clip articles about the organization from newspapers and magazines or search the Web for articles, prepare invitation lists for events, and escort visitors. With more experience, they will write press releases and speeches and plan and execute events. Employees in smaller companies and nonprofits typically have more responsibility and gain experience in a greater variety of tasks, whereas those in large organizations may specialize. Over time, public relations specialists who show initiative and the ability to handle more demanding assignments advance to supervisory positions. Some may decide to start their own businesses.

Earning Potential

Median hourly wage (2009): $24.98

Median annual wage (2009): $51,960

Education/Licensure

Typically, entry-level positions require a bachelor's degree, often in public relations, journalism, communications, or advertising. Internships can be an advantage in looking for a job and so can work experience in one's particular field of interest or in some aspect of print or electronic journalism.

The Web site for the Public Relations Society of America, Inc. (PRSA), www.prsa.org, includes a list of schools offering degrees in public relations. PRSA also administers the Universal Accreditation Board's Accredited Public Relations program. Business communicators can earn the designation of Accredited Business Communicator (ABC) through the International Association of Business Communicators' (IABC) professional credential program, which recognizes those who have attained a globally accepted standard of knowledge and proficiency in their chosen field. While certification is not necessary in this field, it can help in gaining advancement.

For More Information

International Association of Business
    Communicators (IABC)
601 Montgomery Street
Suite 1900
San Francisco, California 94111
www.iabc.com

Public Relations Society of America, Inc. (PRSA)
33 Maiden Lane
11th Floor
New York, New York 10038-5150
www.prsa.org

Regulatory Affairs Specialist ✿🌎

Alternate Titles and Related Careers

- Compliance Manager
- Compliance Officer

This is a "Bright Outlook" and "Green New and Emerging" occupation in government and regulatory administration. Regulatory affairs specialists work for public and private organizations in the areas of conservation and pollution control, regulation enforcement, and policy analysis and advocacy.

Job Trends

The Bureau of Labor Statistics projects that the category of compliance officer, which includes regulatory affairs specialist, will grow at a rate of more than 20 percent between 2008 and 2018. This is much faster than average for all occupations.

About 64 percent of regulatory affairs specialists are employed in the government sector working with private industry on compliance with government regulations. About 11 percent work in the finance and insurance industries, and the remaining 25 percent are employed in other industries, such as energy and pharmaceuticals.

The trend toward additional government regulations in a variety of fields from banking and the financial industry to greater fuel efficiency for motor vehicles and better monitoring of agricultural products will result in the need for more regulatory affairs specialists to work with organizations to see that they know and comply with the regulations.

Nature of the Work

Regulatory affairs specialists coordinate and document regulatory processes within organizations. These include internal audits of practices, government inspections, and license renewals and registrations. Regulatory affairs specialists may compile and prepare materials for submission to regulatory agencies. This is an occupation for which individuals who may not have technical training but do have an interest in "green employment" can contribute.

According to O*NET, among the tasks that regulatory affairs specialists perform are the following:

- Coordinate, prepare, or review regulatory submissions for domestic or international projects
- Provide technical review of data or reports that will be incorporated into regulatory submissions to assure scientific rigor, accuracy, and clarity of presentation
- Review product promotional materials, labeling, batch records, specification sheets, or test methods for compliance with applicable regulations and policies
- Interpret regulatory rules or rule changes and ensure that they are communicated through corporate policies and procedures
- Determine the types of regulatory submissions or internal documentation that are required in situations such as proposed device changes and labeling changes
- Advise project teams on subjects such as premarket regulatory requirements, export and labeling requirements, and clinical study compliance issues
- Prepare or maintain technical files as necessary to obtain and sustain product approval
- Coordinate efforts associated with the preparation of regulatory documents or submissions
- Prepare or direct the preparation of additional information or responses as requested by regulatory agencies
- Analyze product complaints and make recommendations regarding their reportability
- Escort government inspectors during inspections and provide post-inspection follow-up information as requested
- Participate in internal or external audits
- Communicate with regulatory agencies regarding presubmission strategies, potential regulatory pathways, compliance test requirements, or clarification and follow-up of submissions under review
- Identify relevant guidance documents, international standards, or consensus standards and provide interpretive assistance
- Review protocols to ensure collection of data needed for regulatory submissions
- Compile and maintain regulatory documentation databases and systems
- Prepare responses to customer requests for information such as product data, written regulatory affairs statements, surveys, and questionnaires
- Coordinate recall or market withdrawal activities as necessary
- Direct the collection and preparation of laboratory samples as requested by regulatory agencies
- Develop and track quality metrics
- Maintain current knowledge base of existing and emerging regulations, standards, or guidance documents
- Recommend changes to company procedures in response to changes in regulations or standards
- Obtain and distribute updated information regarding domestic or international laws, guidelines, or standards
- Write or update standard operating procedures, work instructions, or policies
- Develop or conduct employee regulatory training

Regulatory affairs specialists who work in federal, state, and municipal government agencies see the regulatory process from the other side of the desk, reviewing regulatory filings by private industry, inspecting facilities, and investigating complaints and problems.

Career Path

Entry-level regulatory affairs specialists begin under experienced regulatory affairs specialists or compliance officers. Over time, new hires gain greater responsibility and take on projects with decreasing supervision. After a number of years, a regulatory affairs specialist may advance to become a compliance officer in charge of a regulatory affairs or compliance department.

Regulatory affairs specialists employed by a government agency must pass a civil service exam. Advancement is based on moving up the grades.

Earning Potential

Median hourly wage (2009): $23.92

Median annual wage (2009): $49,750

(Earnings based on figures for Compliance Officers)

Education/Licensure

Typically, entry-level employees require a bachelor's degree. Typical majors are business administration, human resources, accounting, and finance. Regulatory affairs specialists must also be familiar with all applicable rules and regulations for their particular field and any inspection or testing methods. Specialists must also keep up-to-date on regulatory trends. Additional graduate work or certifications, depending on the field, are useful in advancing to higher positions.

Most states require certification of accountants. The exam is administered under the authority of the American Institute of Certified Public Accountants (AICPA), the National Association of State Boards of Accountancy (NASBA), and the state boards of accountancy.

The Society for Human Resources Management through its Human Resources Certificate Institute offers four certifications: Professional in Human Resources (PHR), Senior Professional in Human Resources (SPHR), Global Professional in Human Resources (GPHM), and a California certificate for those working in California.

For More Information

American Institute of Certified Public Accountants (AICPA)
1211 Avenue of the Americas
New York, New York 10036
888-777-7077 (toll-free)
www.aicpa.org

National Association of State Boards of Accountancy (NASBA)
866-696-2722 (toll-free)
www.nasba.org

Society for Human Resources Management
1800 Duke Street
Alexandria, Virginia 22314
800-283-7476 (toll-free)
www.shrm.org

Traffic Technician

Alternate Titles and Related Careers

- Engineering Technician, Traffic
- Field Traffic Investigator
- Traffic Analyst
- Traffic Control Technician
- Traffic Engineering Technician
- Traffic Investigator
- Traffic Signal Technician (TST)
- Transportation Planning Technician
- Transportation Technician

This occupation has a role in urban and regional planning.

Job Trends

The Bureau of Labor Statistics projects that the occupation of traffic technician will experience an average growth rate of 7 to 13 percent between 2008 and 2018. This translates into 3,400 job openings. About 86 percent of traffic technicians are employed by government agencies, typically a state highway department or a local municipality's streets department.

The continuing increase in the nation's population and its spread beyond traditional metropolitan centers are two factors spurring the building of new roads and highways. As existing roads and highways age, they require repairs and improvements. Both result in the need for traffic technicians to determine traffic patterns and the best use of resources to link highways and roads in efficient networks.

Nature of the Work

Traffic technicians work under the supervision of traffic engineers and conduct field studies to determine traffic volume, vehicular speed, the effectiveness of traffic signals, the adequacy of lighting, and other factors influencing traffic conditions. This information can be used to alter traffic patterns to be more efficient. The ability to use software, especially database and spreadsheet programs and computer-aided drafting (CAD) programs, is important.

According to O*NET, among the tasks that traffic technicians perform are the following:

- Interact with the public to answer traffic-related questions, respond to complaints and requests, or discuss traffic control ordinances, plans, policies, and procedures
- Analyze data related to traffic flow, accident rate, and proposed development to determine the most efficient methods to expedite traffic flow
- Study factors affecting traffic conditions, such as lighting and sign and marking visibility, to assess their effectiveness
- Gather and compile data from hand count sheets, machine count tapes, and radar speed checks; code data for computer input
- Operate counters and record data to assess the volume, type, and movement of vehicular and pedestrian traffic at specified times
- Compute time settings for traffic signals and speed restrictions, using standard formulas
- Prepare drawings of proposed signal installations or other control devices
- Plan, design, and improve components of traffic control systems to accommodate current and projected traffic and to increase usability and efficiency
- Prepare work orders for repair, maintenance, and changes in traffic systems
- Lay out pavement markings for striping crews
- Monitor street and utility projects for compliance to traffic control permit conditions
- Review traffic control or barricade plans to issue permits for parades and other special events and for construction work that affects rights of way, providing assistance with plan preparation or revision as necessary
- Establish procedures for street closures and for repair or construction projects
- Visit development and work sites to determine projects' effect on traffic and the adequacy of traffic control and safety plans or to suggest traffic control measures
- Provide technical supervision regarding traffic control devices to other traffic technicians and laborers
- Place and secure automatic counters and retrieve counters after counting periods end
- Measure and record the speed of vehicular traffic, using electrical timing devices or radar equipment
- Prepare graphs, charts, diagrams, and other aids to illustrate observations and conclusions
- Study traffic delays by noting times of delays, the numbers of vehicles affected, and vehicle speed through the delay area
- Time stoplights or other delays using stopwatches
- Maintain and make minor adjustments and field repairs to equipment used in surveys

- Interview motorists about specific intersections or highways to gather road-condition information for use in planning
- Develop plans and long-range strategies for providing adequate parking space

Career Path

Entry-level employees typically undergo a short training program that combines classroom instruction and on-the-job training. They work under the direction of experienced traffic technicians or traffic engineers. Over time and with experience, traffic technicians may become supervisors and manage less experienced technicians. With additional coursework and a bachelor's degree at the minimum, a technician may become a traffic or transportation engineer.

Earning Potential

Median hourly wage (2009): $19.87

Median annual wage (2009): $41,330

Education/Licensure

About half of all currently employed traffic technicians have a high school diploma or equivalent. About 43 percent have some college, typically a two year degree, which for many employers is becoming the minimum requirement. About 7 percent of current traffic technicians have a bachelor's degree. Associate and bachelor's degrees are typically in an engineering discipline, particularly civil engineering. City planning, CAD, physics, and statistics are useful courses for future traffic technicians.

Students need to make sure that their college's engineering program is accredited by the Accreditation Board for Engineering and Technology (ABET). This is true for both two-year and four-year college programs.

Through the Transportation Professional Certification Board, Inc. (TPCB), the Institute of Transportation Engineers (ITE) offers the Traffic Operations Practitioner Specialist certification for "practitioners without professional licensure" and also the Traffic Signal Operations Specialist for technicians.

The National Institute for Certification in Engineering Technology (NICET) also offers certifications appropriate for traffic technicians. These include certifications in Highway Design, Highway Surveys, and Highway Traffic Operations.

Because most traffic technician jobs are with government agencies, they are typically civil service jobs that require that candidates take and pass civil service exams. Advancement is based on moving up the grades.

For More Information

Accreditation Board for Engineering and
    Technology (ABET)
111 Market Place, Suite 1050
Baltimore, Maryland 21202
410-347-7700
www.abet.org

American Society of Civil Engineers
Transportation and Development Institute
1801 Alexander Bell Drive
Reston, Virginia 20191-4400
800-548-2723 (toll-free)
www.asce.org

Institute of Transportation Engineers
1099 14th Street NW, Suite 300 West
Washington, D.C. 20005-3438
202-289-0222
www.ite.org

National Institute for Certification in Engineering
    Technologies (NICET)
1420 King Street
Alexandria, Virginia 22314
888-476-4238 (toll-free)
www.nicet.org

National Society of Professional Engineers
   (NSPE)
1420 King Street
Alexandria, Virginia 22314
703-684-2800
www.nspe.org

Transportation Vehicle, Equipment, or Systems Inspector 🕏

Alternate Titles and Related Careers
- Chief Mechanical Officer (CMO)
- Diesel Engine Inspector
- Emission Inspector Technician
- Motor Carrier Inspector
- Quality Assurance Inspector
- Rail Technician
- Smog Check Technician
- Smog Technician
- Transit Vehicle Inspector

This is a "Green Enhanced-Skill" occupation in energy efficiency, government and regulatory administration, and transportation. This occupation is related to pollution prevention and the enforcement of regulations by reducing the environmental impact of various modes of transportation.

Job Trends

The overall category of transportation inspector is expected to grow faster than average at a rate of 14 to 19 percent between 2008 and 2018. This translates into 11,300 job openings. About 45 percent of the 27,000 transportation inspectors were employed by various levels of government in 2008. Another 37 percent were employed in transportation and warehousing, and the rest were employed across a variety of industries. The category includes freight inspectors, car inspectors, and rail inspectors but not aircraft inspectors.

As part of the American Recovery and Reinvestment Act, the federal government provided $8 billion in 2010 to thirty-one states to increase the amount of high-speed rail service in the United States. This will add thirteen high-speed passenger rail corridors to the nation's rail system and provide jobs for construction workers, and it will also increase the need for inspectors for all phases of railroad operations.

Nature of the Work

Transportation inspectors inspect and monitor transportation equipment such as railroad engines; vehicles such as cars, buses, and trucks; or systems such as roadbeds and tracks to ensure compliance with rules, regulations, and safety standards at the federal, state, and local levels. Inspectors look for evidence of abuse, damage, or mechanical malfunction. Motor vehicle inspectors also test for compliance with air pollution standards. Transportation inspectors may also investigate accidents and equipment failures. Depending on the field, a transportation inspector may need to be able to use certain types of diagnostic equipment and read and interpret basic mechanical drawings.

According to O*NET, among the tasks that transportation inspectors perform are the following tasks:
- Examine transportation vehicles, equipment, or systems to detect damage, wear, or malfunction
- Conduct vehicle or transportation equipment tests, using diagnostic equipment
- Inspect repairs to transportation vehicles and equipment to ensure that repair work was performed properly
- Prepare reports on investigations or inspections and actions taken
- Issue notices and recommend corrective actions when infractions or problems are found
- Investigate complaints regarding safety violations
- Examine carrier operating rules, employee qualification guidelines, and carrier training

and testing programs for compliance with regulations or safety standards

- Investigate and make recommendations on carrier requests for waiver of federal standards
- Review commercial vehicle logs, shipping papers, and driver and equipment records to detect any problems and to ensure compliance with regulations
- Investigate incidents or violations, such as delays, accidents, and equipment failures
- Negotiate with authorities, such as local government officials, to eliminate hazards along transportation routes
- Evaluate new methods of packaging, testing, shipping, and transporting hazardous materials to ensure adequate public safety protection

Career Path

Entry-level jobs typically require knowledge of the overall transportation industry and the characteristics of the particular field in which the employee will be working, such as railroads or commercial vehicles. This includes knowledge of health and safety principles and practices. New hires typically work under the supervision of experienced inspectors and over time may become supervisors themselves.

Earning Potential

Median hourly wage (2009): $27.06

Median annual wage (2009): $56,290

Education/Licensure

Entry-level positions typically require a high school diploma or equivalent. Some employers may prefer candidates with associate degrees or even bachelor's degrees, for example, the federal government. The most significant source of post-secondary education or training is typically work experience in a related occupation, for example, automotive engineering technician.

Inspector, motor vehicles is the only recognized apprentice specialty associated with the occupation of transportation inspector.

Depending on the field, the states and the federal government may require certain training and/or certification. For example, the Federal Railroad Administration (FRA) requires that railroads hire track inspectors who are qualified to inspect tracks as outlined under its Track Safety Standards. The FRA does not certify track inspectors, however. Nor does the federal government certify motor carrier inspectors; it does require that they successfully complete a state or federal training program or either a truck manufacturer-sponsored training program or a commercial training program and have a certain number of years of experience as a mechanic or inspector in a maintenance occupation. It is up to the employer to see that the qualifications are met by inspector-employees and that their documentation is kept on file.

For More Information

Federal Motor Carrier Safety Administration
1200 New Jersey Avenue SE
Washington, D.C. 20590
800-832-5660 (toll-free)
www.fmcsa.dot.gov

Urban and Regional Planner 🌐

Alternate Titles and Related Careers

- Airport Planner
- Building, Planning, and Zoning Director
- City Planner
- Community Development Planner
- Community Development Director
- Community Planning and Development Representative
- Neighborhood Planner
- Planning Director
- Regional Planner

This is considered a "Green Enhanced-Skill" occupation.

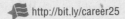 http://bit.ly/career25

Job Trends

The Bureau of Labor Statistics projects that between 2008 and 2018 the need for urban and regional planners will grow at a rate of 14 to 19 percent, which is faster than average for all occupations. This translates into 14,700 new job openings.

Nature of the Work

Urban and regional planners develop long- and short-term plans for land use and the growth and revitalization of urban, suburban, and rural communities and the regions in which they are located. These plans include transportation systems, conservation policies, utilities, and commercial, industrial, residential, and recreational use of land, facilities, and infrastructure. Urban and regional planners recommend locations for roads, schools, and other infrastructure and suggest zoning regulations. They promote the best use of land and resources. Their recommendations about such elements as transportation networks and public utilities, and noting residential and commercial areas in relation to mass transit and highways may indeed affect an area's energy use.

As part of their job, urban and regional planners project the future population needs of the location. In the course of their work, urban and regional planners hold public meetings, so all the stakeholders—the public, government officials, social scientists, lawyers, land developers, and special interest groups—can address the issues, for example, infrastructure involved in developing land use or community plans.

Among the duties that urban and regional planners may perform are the following, according to O*NET:

- Conduct field investigations, surveys, impact studies, and other research to compile and analyze data on economic, social, regulatory, and physical factors affecting land use

- Design, promote, and administer government plans and policies affecting land use, zoning, public utilities, community facilities, housing, and transportation

- Create, prepare, or requisition graphic or narrative reports on land use data, including land area maps

- Review and evaluate environmental impact reports pertaining to private and public planning projects and programs

- Recommend approval, denial, or conditional approval of planning proposals, identifying necessary changes

- Coordinate work with economic consultants and architects during the formulation of plans and designs of large pieces of infrastructure

- Keep informed about economic and legal issues involved in zoning codes, building codes, and environmental regulations

- Determine the effects of regulatory limitations on projects

- Advise planning officials on project feasibility, cost-effectiveness, regulatory conformance, and possible alternatives

- Mediate community disputes and assist in developing alternative plans and recommendations for programs or projects

Career Path

As planners gain experience, they advance to more independent assignments and gain greater responsibility in areas such as policy and budgeting. They may become senior planners or community-planning directors and meet with officials and supervise a staff. Often, advancement is to a larger jurisdiction with greater responsibilities and more difficult problems. In larger jurisdictions, an urban and regional planner may advance to community development director. About two thirds of all planners work for local governments. Students who have experience with planning software, especially GIS software, will have an advantage in the job market.

> ### About Smart Growth
>
> Learn more about how the smart growth movement is working to counteract sprawl at www.epa.gov/smartgrowth and www.smartgrowth.org.

Earning Potential

Median hourly wage (2009): $29.72

Median annual wage (2009): $61,820

Education/Licensure

Generally, a master's degree in urban and regional planning from an accredited program is required. The Planning Accreditation Board accredits college and university programs. Its Web site (www.planningaccreditationboard.org) includes links to schools with accredited planning programs. Master's degrees in related fields, such as geography, urban design, urban studies, economics, or business, may be acceptable for many planning jobs. Most planning departments offer specializations in areas such as urban design, environmental and natural resources planning, land-use or code enforcement, and urban design.

There were fifteen schools that offered a bachelor's degree in urban and regional planning in 2009. Graduates of these programs qualify for some entry-level jobs, but they may have limited opportunities for advancement.

Even though most states do not have requirements for certification, many communities do. The preferred certification is from the American Institute of Certified Planners (AICP), the professional institute of the American Planning Association (www.planning.org/aicp). The AICP-certified planner designation is based on education, experience, and passing an exam. Maintaining certification requires professional development on a two-year cycle.

Only two states currently have requirements for licensing planners. New Jersey requires that planners pass two exams to qualify for a license. One exam tests general planning knowledge, and the other tests knowledge of New Jersey laws. Michigan requires community planners to register in order to use that designation, and the registration is based on passing state and national exams and on professional experience.

For More Information

American Planning Association
1776 Massachusetts Avenue, NW
Suite 400
Washington, DC 20036-1904
202-872-0611
www.planning.org

Association of Collegiate Schools of Planning
6311 Mallard Trace
Tallahassee, Florida 32312
850-385-2054
www.acsp.org

How Being Green Works for **Loyola French**

Loyola French works as a paralegal at the Connecticut Clean Energy Fund (CCEF) in Rocky Hill, Connecticut. CCEF, a nonprofit agency created by the Connecticut legislature in 2000, is charged with developing, investing in, and promoting clean, sustainable energy sources within the state. French has held this position since 2007. Here, French (left) reviews contracts with CCEF Associate Counsel Matt Stone and CCEF President Lise Dondy. Monitoring contracts is an important part of French's job as a paralegal.

Describe your job, including common daily tasks and long-term projects that you have worked on or are working on now. What, specifically, about your job makes it green?

I draft contracts between the Fund and entities obtaining state grants for the procurement and installation of renewable energy. I am responsible for monitoring these contracts from legal review and negotiation through final execution. I also file documents with various state agencies. Examples include filing Uniform Commercial Code (UCC) financing statements with the Connecticut Office of the Secretary of the State, as well as various filings with our state Department of Public Utility Control.

Why/how did you decide to work in a green industry?

Having lived in a solar home for the past twenty-three years, I have a personal interest in renewable energy. I find the work the CCEF does to be rewarding, and I get personal satisfaction out of knowing that I am, in my own small way, helping to secure a more sustainable environment in our state.

How did you prepare for your current position?

I obtained a paralegal associate degree from a local community college, graduating Phi Theta Kappa. I now take continuing education courses offered through various paralegal associations and the Institute for Paralegal Education™. These include courses in contract law, legal writing, legal research, and technology. I am a member of the National Federation of Paralegal Associations® (NFPA®) and the Central Connecticut Paralegal Association, Inc.

Which aspect of your education and/or training do you think has been the most helpful and/or useful to you? Why?

As the bulk of my responsibilities fall under the heading of contract and regulatory law, those courses, both in my initial paralegal education and in my continuing education, have proven most valuable for me. Also, keeping current on legal research and technology skills is imperative.

Do you find that the skills and/or knowledge required for your job continue to evolve? If so, what have you done to keep up-to-date?

I strive to keep my skill set current by taking courses offered through the NFPA® and the Central Connecticut Paralegal Association, Inc.

How have continuing education and/or training impacted the way you do your job?

The renewable energy environment necessitates keeping up-to-date on the new laws and regulations that impact the industry. Learning the most expedient methods of legal research is key to being successful.

What is the most rewarding part of your work, and what do you find to be the most challenging?

I find it most rewarding to be an integral part of a very dedicated team whose goal is to bring renewable energy to our state. The teamwork and camaraderie exhibited by my coworkers makes the CCEF a very enjoyable work environment. Dealing with state and federal bureaucracies tends to be very challenging!

What advice would you give to people interested in pursuing your career?

I encourage anyone who is interested in the legal aspects of green jobs to consider pursuing a paralegal program at an accredited two- or four-year college. I find that having good, solid paralegal training makes one a viable candidate for a multitude of opportunities—be it in law firms or state agencies—to work in the green energy field.

How Being Green Works for
Mahfam Malek,
Program Manager

Mahfam Malek, 29, is a program manager for Green For All, a national organization located in Oakland, California, that works to bring opportunities from the green economy to disadvantaged communities. It supports a clean energy economy as a way to "improve the health of families and neighborhoods" and create "millions of quality jobs and careers." Malek is in charge of the Green For All Academy, which was established in partnership with Al Gore's We Campaign. The Green For All Academy is a fellowship program for emerging leaders from low-income communities and communities of color to spread the word about the benefits of the clean energy economy. Malek has worked in the environmental movement for six years. Here, Malek uses her background in environmental education and activism to teach a workshop on the relevance of environmentalism to low-income communities and communities of color.

Describe your job, including common daily tasks and long-term projects that you have worked on or are working on now. What, specifically, about your job makes it environmentally green?

My job includes everything from coordinating logistics for an Academy meeting and facilitating training to supporting Academy graduates, or Fellows, during their year-long fellowships. I do this by connecting them with resources or giving them advice. Daily tasks might include e-mail/phone communication with current Fellows, alumni, and/or folks interested in the program; culling resources, such as job/scholarship/fellowship opportunities or conference/training/workshop opportunities; doing outreach; and involving our Fellows in campaigns at Green For All. An example of a long-term project I worked on last year was co-writing a curriculum that Fellows and other interested folks could take back to their communities and use as an educational and organizing tool.

My job is about supporting those who are working to bring true sustainability to the communities that, for too long, have been left out of the environmental movement.

Why/how did you decide to work in a green industry?

I began working in the environmental movement due to a series of personal revelations about, and shifts in attitude toward, being considerate of the effects humans have on the environment. I saw how the effects of how we treat our planet cycle back to impact humans. Through professional and personal growth, I began to see my vision through a social/racial justice lens. This ultimately led to my interest in working for an organization that is for both people and our planet.

How did you prepare for your current position?

Though I have a B.A. in film studies from the University of California at Santa Barbara (UCSB), I prepared for my current position mostly through on-the-job training. I initially developed the basis of my environmental understanding through personal study, which was implemented in an environmental education curriculum that I co-developed and co-taught to children in elementary schools. It was further developed through working for the environmental organization Circle of Life[1]. Since I began working for Green For All, I have received training on facilitation. I have facilitated staff meetings and sometimes co-facilitated retreats. I have participated in leadership development and facilitation training such as Rockwood Leadership Institute's[2] "Art of Leadership," Training for Change's[3] "Training for Social Action Trainers," and the Engage Network's[4] "What's Your Tree?" I also participated in the Green For All Academy training before beginning to manage the program.

Which aspect of your education and/or training do you think has been the most helpful and/or useful to you? Why?

The training I previously mentioned was helpful, as well as on-the-job facilitation practice. The training was important because it offered a holistic approach to leadership development and training. This is invaluable, and many people do not have access to this. This is why I love my job! We can provide access to high-quality training for folks who may not otherwise have it! On-the-job facilitation practice, such as leading weekly staff meetings, has also been helpful, because consistent practice is what it takes to get comfortable speaking to a group of people.

Do you find that the skills and/or knowledge required for your job continue to evolve? If so, what have you done to keep up-to-date?

Certainly, but they probably do not evolve as rapidly as they do for folks who work in the field. Professional development through training and personal development through workshops [. . .] seem to keep me on my toes.

How have continuing education and/or training impacted the way you do your job?

Facilitation training sessions always give me good ideas for future workshops. I try to integrate these ideas into things like the educational curriculum I worked on last year. In addition, every training opportunity I have been a part of has provided me with immeasurable tools in communication and relationship management. This affects everything—from how I speak in front of a group to how I interact with people one-on-one.

What is the most rewarding part of your work, and what do you find to be the most challenging?

The most rewarding part of my job is definitely the relationships that I get to build with Fellows. Hearing about their successes brings the biggest smile to my face, and few things can make me happier than when a Fellow asks for my advice on something. Knowing that we have built that kind of trust is irreplaceable. The most challenging thing is that resources are scarce. I want to be able to provide more tangible resources to our Fellows, such as funding. We are working on ways to be able to do that, but I always wish that we could do more. It's hard to see someone with a great idea and the capacity to implement it, but without the resources to do so.

What advice would you give to people interested in pursuing your career?

Follow your heart. Take advantage of every opportunity to get trained, whether it's basic environmental/sustainability education, professional development, or personal development.

[1]Circle of Life was an environmental organization that promoted sustainable and eco-friendly living practices. Its successor is the Engage Network.

[2]The Rockwood Leadership Institute, based in Berkeley, California, provides training in leadership and collaboration.

[3]Training for Change, based in Philadelphia, Pennsylvania, provides training for activists who are working for social change.

[4]The Engage Network is a nonprofit social venture based in Albany, California, that focuses on community organizing and civic engagement. It is a successor to the Circle of Life.

10 Tips for Reducing Your Carbon Travel Footprint

Concerned about the carbon emissions you'll be responsible for on vacation? Here are some tips to help you minimize your environmental impact while having a good time.

1. **Calculate the energy you expect to use for travel.** You can calculate travel by car, plane, motorbike, train, or bus at www.carbonfootprint.com.

2. **Then consider purchasing carbon offsets, or carbon credits, for your trip.** Offsets help neutralize carbon emissions by funding projects such as wind farm development that create an emissions reduction equal to your use. Each carbon offset unit represents the reduction of 1 metric ton of CO_2 or its equivalent in other greenhouse gases. To find high-quality providers of carbon offsets, visit www.carboncatalog.org.

3. **Minimize air travel, usually the most energy-consuming aspect of a trip.** Stay longer in a single destination rather than making several trips from place to place. Likewise, pack only what you need. This also helps reduce your luggage weight, which has an impact on greenhouse gas emissions.

4. **Select hotels, tour operators, and other travel service providers based on sustainability practices.** Check whether the company has environmental initiatives or strategies for saving energy and reducing waste; ask whether it belongs to a sustainable tourism program.

5. **Before you leave home, turn off lights and unplug unnecessary appliances.** Do the same at your hotel, and turn off the air conditioner/heater in your room each time you go out.

6. **Use as little water as possible when showering, bathing, shaving, and washing up.** Stay at a hotel that participates in a linen and towel reuse program.

7. **Use public transportation.** Most cities have buses, trains, or trolleys to help you get around. Consider walking or renting a bicycle for short trips.

8. **Use rechargeable batteries whenever possible for cameras and other electronic devices.**

9. **Eat locally.** While exploring, visit a farmers' market or a locally owned grocery store for the freshest food options. Take a picnic along for lunch. If you are choosing a restaurant, eat in a local one, not an outlet of a U.S. chain. Part of sustainability is keeping money in the local economy.

10. **Buy locally.** Buy goods made by local artisans, but never buy crafts, apparel, household goods, or other products derived from protected or endangered plants or animals.

PART II

COLLEGES AND UNION ORGANIZATIONS WITH GREAT GREEN PROGRAMS

CHAPTER 5

25 FOUR-YEAR SCHOOLS WITH GREAT GREEN PROGRAMS

The twenty-five colleges and universities profiled in this chapter support innovative programs in energy studies and related subjects, such as automotive engineering, materials science, and urban and regional planning that impact energy use. These institutions also have vibrant on-campus sustainability programs and organizations. Each school listed here includes inventive programs in its curricula, and all have made a commitment to making their campus communities sustainable.

Many of the undergraduate programs listed here are interdisciplinary and draw on the strengths of the faculty in many areas. Many of the programs include research opportunities or internships for undergraduates. Most of the universities on this list also have graduate programs that lead to advanced degrees or certificates in disciplines related to sustainable or alternative energy, including engineering, business, policy, planning, and public administration. Some of these schools offer online degrees and courses, and some have centers or institutes that specialize in some aspect of energy research. The information presented here has been culled not only from college Web sites, but also from *Peterson's Survey of Sustainability Efforts in Higher Education,* sent to two-year and four-year schools in the United States and Canada and completed by representatives of the schools themselves.

In addition to strong academics, each college or university on this list has a strong commitment to sustainability. Approximately 40 percent have signed the American College & University Presidents Climate Commitment, pledging to eliminate global-warming emissions through policy and curriculum. Four are signatories to the Talloires Declaration, an internationally recognized commitment among college administrators to incorporate sustainability in curriculum and operations. These schools have sustainability policy committees and active student groups promoting the environment through advocacy, action, awareness, and activities. Some offer green residence halls and are either building or have already built buildings certified by LEED (Leadership in Energy and Environmental Design).

The colleges and universities in this chapter represent a broad cross-section of schools in the United States: public and private institutions, large and small schools, schools in urban and rural settings, state universities, liberal arts colleges, and schools specializing in a single discipline.

Keep in mind that this is a list of highlights: Many other colleges and universities not listed here also offer energy studies programs. Check out *Peterson's Four-Year Colleges* and look for any of the majors listed in the "Majors" index to find other schools offering similar programs.

ABOUT THE LISTINGS

Here's what you need to know to navigate this chapter.

Contact Info

The school profile lists the school name, address, phone number, e-mail address, and Web site.

College Videos

Virtual college tours are available for many of the colleges and universities listed here on YOUniversityTV.com. You'll find easy-to-use links to campus videos that look like this:

 http://bit.ly/collvid1

YOUniversityTV.com assists students with the college-selection process by providing access to videos and educational resources for colleges across the United States. YOUniversityTV.com is free-of-charge and does not receive compensation from any of the universities it features.

Undergraduate Degrees

This section includes majors and minors in energy-related subjects and other degree programs that have an energy-related focus. Inclusion of majors depends on how the college or university describes its program—so a certain program, for example, chemistry, may be included for one school, but not for another, even if the second school also offers the degree.

Many schools offer a number of options, concentrations, or specializations within a degree program. Information relevant to energy has been included to show the wide variety of possible study areas.

Undergraduate Distance Learning

A number of schools offer courses online, some of which may meet requirements of the degrees listed in this guide. Some schools offer online degrees, but few are at the undergraduate level. They are more often at the master's level. However, many offer certificates online at both the undergraduate and graduate levels.

Undergraduate Costs

The information on the costs for an undergraduate is the latest available at the time that this publication went to press.

Undergraduate Financial Aid

Scholarships are generally based on merit rather than need. Only scholarship information that is useful to undergraduates majoring in energy-related fields is included here. For most schools, these scholarships are awarded through the individual academic departments, so you are advised to visit departmental Web sites for details. If this information is accessible through the college Undergraduate Financial Aid Web page, that information is provided here.

Undergraduate Admissions Requirements

General admissions requirements to undergraduate programs are listed in this section. Where appropriate, any special prerequisites for science majors are listed.

Undergraduate Application Information

This section includes the type of application that is required by each school, application fees, and deadlines for applying and for notification.

Green Campus Organizations and Projects

This section gives a sampling of green extracurricular activities—not limited to those with an energy focus—that students may participate in. The colleges and universities included in this guide have substantial sustainability efforts and thus offer a variety of ways in which students may become involved and take leadership roles.

Fast Facts

The section "Fast Facts" provides insight into a school's commitment to sustainability and the environment.

Graduate Degrees

This guide focuses on undergraduate programs, but graduate programs are listed here for several reasons. First, graduate programs combined with the undergraduate degree offerings show the depth and breadth of the energy and energy-related programs available at these colleges and universities.

Second, many of the schools included in this guide encourage or require undergraduates to participate in research projects or internships during their upper-class years. By listing the graduate programs, you can get an idea of the possibilities for junior or senior research projects. Even though as a prospective freshman you may not be thinking about graduate school, these programs show you possibilities and give you additional information to consider as you choose your school and major, and map your education.

Third, if you already hold a bachelor's degree, you may be interested in becoming "green" by pursuing an advanced degree, certificate, or training. The graduate programs and certificates listed in this guide show you the myriad possibilities.

Graduate Distance Learning

A number of schools offer courses online, some of which may meet requirements of the degrees listed in this guide at the master's level. Some distance learning programs are geared toward certificate programs at the graduate level.

Schools Profiled Here

The following four-year colleges and universities are profiled in this chapter:

- Arizona State University
- California Institute of Technology
- California Polytechnic State University, San Luis Obispo
- Carnegie Mellon University
- Colorado School of Mines
- Drexel University
- Ferris State University
- Idaho State University
- Massachusetts Institute of Technology
- Oregon Institute of Technology
- Pennsylvania State University
- Portland State University
- Purdue University
- Rutgers, The State University of New Jersey
- Stanford University
- Syracuse University
- Texas A&M University
- University of Alaska, Fairbanks
- University of California, Berkeley
- University of Michigan
- University of Tennessee
- University of Tulsa
- University of Washington
- Washington State University
- West Virginia University

ARIZONA STATE UNIVERSITY (ASU)

University Drive and Mill Avenue
Tempe, Arizona 85287
480-965-9011
E-mail: campus.asu.edu/tempe
www.asu.edu

 http://bit.ly/collvid1

About ASU's Conservation Initiatives

Check out the Campus Metabolism site at http://cm.asu.edu. It shows in real time the campus's energy use. You can download a variety of information about ASU's energy conservation initiatives at http://sustainability.asu.edu/campus/energy.php.

Undergraduate Degrees

All degrees are offered at the Tempe campus unless otherwise noted.

Bioengineering
Business (Sustainability), Tempe and West
    campuses
Environmental Chemistry
Civil Engineering (Construction Engineering,
    Environmental Engineering)
Electrical Engineering (Electric Power and
    Energy Systems)
Electronics Engineering Technology (Alternative
    Energy Technologies), Polytechnic campus
Electronics and Energy Systems, Polytechnic
    campus
Environmental Technology Management,
    Polytechnic campus
Industrial Design
Mechanical Engineering (Electric Power and
    Energy Systems, Energy and Environment),
    Polytechnic campus
Mechanical Engineering Technology
    (Automotive, Aeronautical), Polytechnic
    campus
Sustainability
Urban Planning

Undergraduate Certificates

Automotive Entrepreneurs and Leaders
Technology Entrepreneurship

Undergraduate Costs

Academic year 2010–11 (estimate): $7793 resident, $20,257 nonresident (tuition); $10,996 books, room and board

Undergraduate Financial Aid

FAFSA required.

Undergraduate Admissions Requirements

Required: High school diploma or GED. One of the following: 3.0 GPA in competency courses, top 25 percent of class, ACT 22 (24 nonresidents) or SAT 1040 (1110 nonresidents). Competency requirement: 4 years English, 4 years math, 3 years laboratory science, 2 years social science, 2 years same foreign language, 1 year fine arts. Some exceptions may be considered, and some programs have higher requirements.

Undergraduate Application Information

Option: Online application

Application fee: $25 (residents), $55 (nonresidents)

Required: Application, high school transcript

Application deadlines: March 1 (freshmen), June 1 (fall transfers), December 26 (winter transfers), December 1 (spring transfers)

Notification: Continuous

Green Campus Organizations

Society of Automotive Engineers (SAE): Student chapter of this international organization; works on projects related to automotive and aerospace technology, including Mini Baja car competition.

Recycling Club of ASU: Promotes recycling on and off campus by collecting and disposing of recyclable items and holding activities to raise awareness.

Sustainability Jedi: Enhances students' educational experience through involvement in real-world sustainability projects that improve rural and underprivileged communities worldwide.

ASU Emerging Green Builders (EGB): For students interested in the green building movement. Offers opportunities for involvement with the U.S. Green Building Council (USGBC) and similar organizations to create a network of green building leaders.

EcoAid on Campus: Provides scholarship and internship opportunities, mentoring, and training to students in green industries.

Students of Arizona Network for Sustainability: A network of student organizations and community groups dedicated to promoting sustainability in Arizona. Activities include education, outreach, and action. Web site: http://azsans.com/.

Fast Facts

ASU's Center for Nanotechnology in Society researches the social aspects of nanotechnology, its goals and implications, and partners with other nanoscale science and engineering labs in projects.

The Global Institute of Sustainability, which includes the School of Sustainability, conducts research, problem solving, and education with an emphasis on urban sustainability. The institute grew out of the Arizona State University Center for Environmental Studies that conducted research for more than 30 years. Phoenix, because it is among the fastest growing urban areas in the country, is a prime laboratory for the institute's studies. For more information, visit sustainability.asu.edu.

ASU's School of Sustainability is the first such school in the nation.

ASU's W.P. Carey School of Business began offering a BA in sustainability in 2008. Students can combine their traditional course work with specializations in sustainability, urban policy, communication, or tourism management.

Graduate Degrees

Alternative Energy Technologies (MSTech), Polytechnic campus
Biochemistry (MS, PhD)
Chemical Engineering (MS, MSE, PhD)
Civil/Environmental Engineering (MS, MSE, PhD)
Electronic Systems Engineering Technology (MSTech), Polytechnic campus
Environmental Design/Planning (PhD)
Environmental Technology Management (MSTech), Polytechnic campus
Integrated Electronics Systems (MSTech), Polytechnic campus
Mechanical Engineering Technology (MSTech), Polytechnic campus
Professional Science Masters in Nanoscience (PSM)
Science and Technology Policy (MS)
Sustainability (MA, MS, PhD)
Urban and Environmental Planning (MUEP)
Urban Design (MUD)

Graduate Certificates

Nuclear Power Generation
Transportation Systems

Graduate Distance Learning

Electrical Engineering (MSE)
Electrical Engineering (MBA/MSE)

Industrial Engineering (MBA/MSE)
Materials Science and Engineering (MSE)

Graduate Distance Learning Certificates

Nuclear Power Generation
Supply Chain Management

CALIFORNIA INSTITUTE OF TECHNOLOGY (CALTECH)

1200 East California Boulevard
Pasadena, California 91125
626-395-6811
E-mail: www.caltech.edu/contacts
www.caltech.edu

 http://bit.ly/collvid2

About the Caltech/MIT Enterprise Forum

The forum is a joint venture of Caltech's Industrial Relations Center, Caltech's Office of Technology Transfer, the Caltech Alumni Association, and the MIT Alumni Association. Its mission is "to encourage the growth of technology-based entrepreneurial ventures in Southern California." In addition to advances in the life sciences, medical technologies, and software, the organization provides assistance in growing energy ventures.

Undergraduate Degrees

Chemistry
Chemical Engineering
Civil Engineering
Computer Science (Control and Dynamical
    Systems option)
Electrical Engineering
Materials Science (Energy Science and
    Technology option)
Mechanical Engineering (Energy Science and
    Technology option)

Undergraduate Costs

Academic year 2009–10 (estimated): $49,968 (tuition, fees, room and board)

Undergraduate Financial Aid

CSS PROFILE® and FAFSA required.

Undergraduate Admissions Requirements

Required: SAT or ACT (ACT Writing Test is optional); SAT Subject Tests: Mathematics Level 2 and one science.

High school preparation: 4 years of math (including calculus), 1 year physics, 1 year chemistry, 3 years English (4 years recommended), 1 year U.S. history/government (waived for international students).

Note: No credit given for AP, IB, or college courses taken prior to enrollment.

Undergraduate Application Information

Options: Online application, early admission, early action, deferred entrance

Application fee: $60

Required: Common Application and Caltech Supplemental Application, high school transcript, two teacher recommendations, school report, mid-year report, essay or personal statement

Application deadline: January 1 (freshmen), November 1 (Early Action), February 15 (transfers)

Notification: Mid-March (freshmen), December 15 (Early Action), June 1 (transfers)

Green Campus Organizations

The Caltech Electric Vehicle Club (CEVC): Educates the Caltech community about electric vehicles through first-hand experiences and presents information about the design, construction, and politics of electric vehicles.

Caltech Student Solar Initiative: Fosters culture of sustainability on campus through sustainability-oriented projects; provides experiences for the campus community that promote demand for cleaner, cheaper, globally accessible energy; adds to the 1.2-megawatt solar power generation at Caltech.

Caltech Environmental Task Force: Promotes environmental responsibility on campus and in southern California.

Engineers for a Sustainable World @ Caltech: Caltech chapter of the national organization; aims to raise awareness of social responsibility for scientists and engineers; coordinates forums, workshops, and research opportunities.

The Caltech Community Garden Project: Students committed to sustainable lifestyles who work to increase the number of vegetable, flower, and fruit gardens that are accessible to the Caltech community.

Fast Facts

The mission of Caltech Center for Sustainable Energy Research is "to transform the industrialized world from one powered by fossil fuels to one that is powered by sunlight." The center currently conducts research on solar electric generation, solar-driven fuel synthesis, and fuel cell development. Caltech's Power, Environmental, and Energy Research Center focuses on fundamental research in the science and engineering technologies that underlie energy and environmental technologies. The Caltech Undergraduate Sustainability Project (CUSP) fosters sustainability projects, financing, and research in conjunction with the school's core curriculum. A current CUSP project aims to produce ethanol using cellulose-based agriwaste produced during the normal operations of the campus.

Caltech's Materials and Process Simulation Center has a variety of fuel cell research projects underway "from low-temperature polymer electrolyte membrane fuel cells to high-temperature solid oxide fuel cells." For more information on their fuel cell projects, visit http://wag.celtech.edu/fuelcells/.

Graduate Degrees

Chemistry (PhD)
Chemical Engineering (PhD)
Electrical Engineering (MSEE, PhD)
Materials Science (PhD)
Mechanical Engineering (ME, PhD)

CALIFORNIA POLYTECHNIC STATE UNIVERSITY (CAL POLY), SAN LUIS OBISPO

San Luis Obispo, California 93407
805-756-1111
www.calpoly.edu

About Green Certificate Programs Online

Cal Poly's Continuing Education and University Outreach program offers six-month online courses for certificates for HVAC, Modern Automotive Service Technician, Oil Refinery Operations, and Power Plant Operations as well as Entrepreneurship, Principles of Designing Green Buildings, Performing Comprehensive Building Assessments, and Green Supply Chain Certification Training.

Undergraduate Degrees

Aerospace Engineering
Architecture and Environmental Design
City and Regional Planning (major or minor)
Civil Engineering
Electrical Engineering (Power concentration)
Environmental Engineering
Industrial EngineeringIndustrial Technology
    (major or minor)

Materials Engineering

Manufacturing Engineering

Mechanical Engineering (Mechatronics concentration)

Real Property Development (minor)

Undergraduate Costs

Academic year 2010–11: $16,569 resident (tuition, room and board); nonresident, the same plus an additional $248 per unit

Undergraduate Financial Aid

FAFSA required.

Departmental scholarships: www.ess.calpoly .edu/_finaid/types_aid/scholarships.htm.

Undergraduate Admissions Requirements

General admissions requirements for the California State University System follow; check the Cal Poly site admissions site for individual Cal Poly college requirements.

Required: SAT or ACT (Writing Test not included).

High school preparation: 4 years English, 3 years math (algebra I and II, geometry), 2 years history and social science (including 1 year U.S. History or U.S. History/Government), 2 years science with lab (one biological and one physical), 2 years of the same foreign language, 1 year of visual and performing arts (single year-long course), and 1 year of a college-prep elective, all with C grade or higher.

Undergraduate Application Information

Options: Online application preferred; Early Assessment Program for California residents who attend or attended public high schools

Application fee: $55

Required: CSU application, SAT or ACT scores, official high school transcript

Application deadline: November 30 (freshmen and transfers)

Green Campus Organizations

Green Campus Program: Part of the Alliance to Save Energy's Green Campus Program; participants on thirteen University of California, California State University, and private campuses in the state; campaigns and competitions to improve campuswide energy efficiency.

Hydrogen Energy Club: Student group to learn about and explore the field of hydrogen energy production and use.

Electric Vehicle Club: Students interested in learning about, developing, and promoting technologies that will sustain alternative energies.

Society of Automotive Engineers: Student teams build and race formula and formula hybrid cars in national competitions with other schools.

Power and Energy Society: Promotes and networks for career opportunities in the power engineering industry.

Engineers Without Borders: Cal Poly chapter of the international nonprofit organization that partners with communities to improve their quality of life through environmentally and economically sustainable engineering projects.

Fast Facts

In 2009, Cal Poly expanded its student learning objectives to include four related to sustainability. According to the institute, "graduating seniors should be able to define and apply sustainability principles within their academic programs; explain how natural, economic, and social systems interact to foster or prevent sustainability; analyze and explain local, national, and global sustainability using a multidisciplinary approach; and consider sustainability principles while developing personal and professional values."

Cal Poly's Controlled Environment Agriculture and Energy Working Group brings together faculty from different colleges and departments to develop controlled environment agriculture as a sustainable biomass/bioenergy production option. Activities are related to energy conservation, biofuels, cogeneration systems, and heat storage systems. Faculty specialties include simulation and transport processes, biofuels and fermentation engineering, algae physiology, and agribusiness.

One goal of Cal Poly's Center for Sustainability in Engineering is to incorporate environmental and social considerations into engineering design and management. The center conducts research on topics like campus mobility and transportation and hydrogen fuel cell materials performance. The Electric Power Institute is a center for research related to the use of electric power and houses the Power Quality Technology Center.

The Renewable Energy Institute promotes research and development of solar and renewable energy technologies and sustainable community infrastructure.

In 2005, Cal Poly participated in the U.S. Department of Energy's Solar Decathlon and took first place in the lighting and appliances category. The competition occurs every two years and schools are selected to participate by the DOE on the strength of their applications.

Graduate Degrees

City and Regional Planning (MCRP)
Civil and Environmental Engineering (MS)
Civil and Environmental Engineering with a
  Specialization in Transportation Planning
  (MCRP, MS)
Electrical Engineering (Power concentration)
  (MS)
Industrial Engineering (MS)
Mechanical Engineering (MS)
Polymers and Coatings (MS)

CARNEGIE MELLON UNIVERSITY (CMU)

5000 Forbes Avenue
Pittsburgh, Pennsylvania 15213
412-268–2000
E-mail: www.cmu.edu/contact/index.shtml
www.cmu.edu

About CMU and Green Power

In 2010, the U.S. Environmental Protection Agency named CMU number 41 of the top 50 purchasers of green power. CMU was purchasing nearly 87 million kilowatt-hours of wind-generated power annually, which met 75 percent of CMU's electric power needs. CMU also ranks number 2 in the EPA's top 20 colleges and universities purchasing green power.

Undergraduate Degrees

Architecture (Urbanism)
Chemical Engineering
Chemistry (Environmental Chemistry, Polymer
  Science, Materials Chemistry)
Civil and Environmental Engineering
Engineering and Public Policy
Engineering, Automation and Control (minor)
Engineering, Environmental Engineering and
  Sustainability (minor)
Environmental Policy (open to all students as an
  additional major)
Materials Science and Engineering
Mechanical Engineering with minor in
  Environmental Engineering

Undergraduate Costs

Academic year 2010–11: $52,886 resident, $42,136 nonresident (tuition, fees, room and board)

Undergraduate Financial Aid

FAFSA required.

See www.cmu.edu/fso/index.html for scholarships. There are also internships available in various departments.

Undergraduate Admissions Requirements

Required: SAT or ACT with Writing, 2 SAT Subject Tests.

High school preparation: 4 years of English, 4 years of math, 1 year chemistry, 1 year physics, 1 year biology, 2 years foreign language, 3 electives.

Undergraduate Application Information

Options: Online application, early admission, early decision

Application fee: $70

Required: Common application and Carnegie Mellon supplement, high school transcript, teacher and guidance counselor recommendations, essay, personal statement

Recommended: Interview, campus visit

Application deadline: January 1 (freshmen), November 1 (Early Decision I), December 1 (Early Decision II), October 15 (transfers for spring), March 1 (transfers for fall)

Notification: December 15 (Early Decision I), January 15 (Early Decision II), March 15 to April 15 (freshmen), December 15 (transfers for spring), June 30 (transfers for fall)

Green Campus Organizations

Engineers for a Sustainable World: CMU chapter of this national network of engineering students, faculty, and professionals.

Eco-Reps: Students who promote environmental awareness among their peers in their housing units.

Solar Splash: Sponsored by the IEEE Power Electronics Society; invites participating schools to compete in the World Championship of Intercollegiate Solar Boating, in which each school designs and builds a solar-powered boat to compete in three events. The goal is to showcase the interdisciplinary work of undergraduate and graduate students in electrical and mechanical engineering in a sustainable way.

Sustainable Earth: Student-run environmental organization dedicated to peaceful and collaborative efforts to improve the environment.

Fast Facts

The Steinbrenner Institute for Environmental Education and Research, established in 2004, promotes research and education opportunities for CMU's faculty and students across all schools and majors. Among the twenty-one centers that it supports are Advanced Energy Solutions, Building Performance and Diagnostics, Electricity Industry, International Corporate Responsibility, Remaking Cities Institute, and Study and Improvement of Regulation.

The Green Design Institute, one of the Steinbrenner research centers, is an interdisciplinary effort to improve product and environmental quality and enhance economic development through partnerships with companies, foundations, and government agencies. Among its research projects are investigating the infrastructure requirements of alternative fuels and the environmental impacts of electricity production.

The Laboratory for Carbon Footprinting of the Green Design Institute studies and models the impacts of products and processes on the environment. Among their partners are FedEx, IBM, Consol Energy, and SAP.

The Center for Sustainable Engineering, also a Steinbrenner Institute research center, is a partnership between CMU, the University of Texas at Austin, and Arizona State University and is supported by the National Science Foundation and the U.S. Environmental Protection Agency. Its mission is "to help future engineers better manage increased stress on the world's limited resources."

The Center for the Environmental Implications of Nanotechnology (CEINT) undertakes inter-disciplinary research in the environmental and health risks involved in nanomaterials and prop-erties. CEINT draws on expertise in the depart-ments of Civil and Environmental Engineering, Engineering and Public Policy, and Materials Science and Engineering among others.

Graduate Degrees

Chemical Engineering (MChE, MS, PhD)
Civil and Environmental Engineering/Green Design (MS, PhD)
Civil and Environmental Engineering/ Engineering and Public Policy (PhD)
Engineering and Technology Innovation Management (MS)
Energy Science, Technology, and Policy (MS)
Mechanical Engineering (MS, PhD)
Mechanics, Materials, and Computers (MS, PhD)
Material Science and Engineering (MS, PhD)
Public Policy and Management (MSPPM)

COLORADO SCHOOL OF MINES (CSM)

1600 Maple Street
Golden, Colorado 80401
E-mail: admit.mines.edu
www.mines.edu

Undergraduate Degrees

Chemical Engineering
Chemical and Biochemical Engineering
Civil Engineering
Electrical Engineering (Energy Systems and Power Electronics specialty)
Engineering Physics—Applied Physics
Engineering Physics—Nuclear Engineering
Petroleum Engineering
Energy (minor)

Undergraduate Costs

Academic year 2009–10: $23,464 resident (esti-mated; includes tuition, fees, room and board, books, supplies, and miscellaneous expenses); $37,624 nonresident (estimated; includes tuition, fees, room and board, books, supplies, and mis-cellaneous expenses). The tuition for in-state residents includes the Colorado Opportunity Fund allowance.

Undergraduate Financial Aid

FAFSA required.

Grants, scholarships, loans, and campus employment are available. Visit http://finaid .mines.edu/Financial _Aid.

Undergraduate Admissions Requirements

Required: High school diploma or GED. Rank in upper third of class with average GPA of 3.7/4.0; SAT 1260 (critical reading and math) or ACT 28. 4 units of English; 2 units of algebra, 1 unit of geometry, 1 unit of trigonometry; 3 units of history or social studies; 3 units of lab science including chemistry or physics; 2 units of academic electives.

Undergraduate Application Information

Options: Colorado Uniform Application: online or paper mailed in

Application fee: $45 if paper application submitted

Required: Application, high school transcript or GED; all college or university transcripts, SAT or ACT scores (writing test not required)

Application deadline: April 1 for fall; November 1 for spring

About Green Chemistry

In 2009, Colorado School of Mines (CSM) hosted the American Chemical Society's Annual Summer School for Green Chemistry and Sustainable Energy for graduate and post-doctoral students. Topics included "Greening the Supply Chain" and "Green Nanoscience." CSM was chosen as the site for its leading role in sustainability and alternative fuels research.

Green Campus Organizations

Sustainability Committee: Promotes sustainability practices on campus.

Blue Key International Honor Society: Group raised money and replaced the 1,653 incandescent light bulbs in CSM's landmark logo "M" for LEDs, saving the school about $1700 a year in the cost to light the landmark.

Engineers Without Borders, Society of Petroleum Engineers, American Association of Petroleum Engineers: Student chapters of national professional organizations; promote applications of learning and networking.

Fast Facts

The goal of the Colorado Fuel Cell Center is to conduct fuel cell research, development, and commercialization, especially as it leads to business opportunities in the state. Among the research projects that are being carried on are solid-oxide fuel cell development and testing, modeling and simulation, and advanced materials processing and evaluation.

Renewable Energy Materials Science and Engineering Center (REMSEC) is supported by the National Science Foundation (NSF) and works in conjunction with the federal National Renewable Energy Laboratory (NREL) to develop renewable energy resources.

Among the topics that are the subject of research at the Center for Solar and Electronic Materials are photovoltaics, polymer science, and electronic materials processing.

The mission of the Center for Revolutionary Solar Photoconversion (CRSP) is to convert sunshine into clean, low-cost electricity and fuels. CRSP is an outgrowth of a partnership among CSM, the state of Colorado, NREL, and several other Colorado universities, as well as a variety of companies with operations or headquarters in the state.

CSM offers a unique opportunity with its Humanitarian Engineering program. Students may enroll in program as an Area of Special Interest or work toward a minor in Humanitarian Studies and Technology or a minor in Humanitarian Engineering. Courses include "Cultural Dynamics of Global Development," "African Crisis," "Energy Economics," and "Environmental Politics and Policy."

Graduate Degrees

Applied Physics (Nuclear Physics, Electronic Materials, Nanoscale Materials (MS, PhD)
Chemical Engineering (MS, PhD)
Chemical and Biochemical Engineering (MS)
Civil Engineering (MS, PhD)
Engineering—Systems (Energy Systems and Power Electronics, Fluid Mechanics and Thermal Sciences (MS, PhD)
Nuclear Engineering (MS, PhD)
Petroleum Engineering (ME, MS, PhD)
Petroleum Reservoir Systems (PM)

DREXEL UNIVERSITY

3141 Chestnut Street
Philadelphia, Pennsylvania 19104
215-895-2000
E-mail: www.drexel.edu/about/contact/general
  .aspx
www.drexel.edu

 http://bit.ly/collvid3

Undergraduate Degrees

Architectural Engineering
Chemical Engineering
Civil Engineering
Computer Engineering (major or minor)
Construction Management (major or minor)
Industrial Engineering
Materials Engineering (Nanoscale Materials and
  Nanotechnology, Soft Materials and Polymers)
Mechanical Engineering and Mechanics
Urban Environmental Studies (major or minor)

Architectural Engineering (minor)
Entrepreneurship (minor)
Materials Engineering (minor)
Paralegal Studies (minor)

Undergraduate Certificate

Construction Management

Undergraduate Costs

Academic year 2010–11 (estimate): Four-year plan (one or no co-ops): $53,730 (tuition, fees, room and board); Five-year plan (three co-ops): $46,519 (tuition, fees, room and board). Travel tuition reduction program: Travel expenses up to $500 deducted from first tuition bill for full-time freshman or transfer student visiting campus from a distance of 150 miles or greater after enrollment confirmation. NOTE: Total cost varies depending on a student's course of study and whether a student chooses a co-op program or not.

Undergraduate Financial Aid

FAFSA required.

Scholarship information may be found on the scholarship Web site: www.drexel.edu/financialaid/sg_ug.asp.

Undergraduate Admissions Requirements

Required: 2.0 GPA. SAT or ACT. Admission prerequisites vary with majors; see: www.drexel.edu/em/undergrad/apply/admissions-policies.aspx

Undergraduate Application Information

Options: Online application, VIP application, deferred entrance

Application fee: $75 (waived for online or on-campus application)

Required: Drexel's Online Application, The Common Application (online), Universal College Application (online), or Drexel's Undergraduate Admission Application (paper); high school transcripts, two letters of recommendation (one by high school counselor), 1- to 2-page essay online (not accepted on paper)

Recommended: Two letters of recommendation, interview

Application deadline: March 1 (freshmen), August 15 (fall transfers), February 15 (spring transfers)

Notification: Continuous

Green Campus Organizations

Drexel Green: An initiative begun in 2008 by students, faculty, and staff dedicated to transforming Drexel's campus into a sustainability leader. The initiative covers all aspects of operations, buildings, academic initiatives, and student life and is responsible for the strategic plan to further campus sustainable practices and policies.

Drexel Smart House: A student-led, multidisciplinary project to design an urban home that serves as a "living laboratory" for exploring cutting-edge design and technology. Participants conduct research and develop designs for the environment, energy, interaction, health, and lifestyle of potential users, with the ultimate goal of improving the quality of life in an urban residential setting.

Drexel Student Sustainability Committee (DSSC): A subgroup of the Undergraduate Student Government Association and Drexel Green program; goal is to reduce campus energy waste and pollution.

Energy Club: For students interested in energy conservation technologies on campus and in the community; goals are to promote environmental and societal awareness and to support professional development of members.

Engineers Without Borders: Drexel chapter of EWB-USA; works on sustainable development projects worldwide.

Fast Facts

Drexel uses biodiesel fuel in its eleven shuttle buses, has six hybrid vehicles in its fleet, and uses bicycles and battery-powered vehicles for patrolling the campus. Its biodiesel fuel uses a 20-percent soy blend.

Among the first universities to purchase wind-generated energy, Drexel now derives 30 percent of its total annual electric use from wind energy. Computer control systems turn off lighting after hours or when unnecessary, and stand-alone occupancy sensors are being used in newer construction and in renovations to conserve lighting.

Drexel University's first green dorm features concrete walls that do not need to be painted; windows that reflect heat, but allow light to enter; and a lobby floor made of recycled tires.

In 2009, *Sierra* magazine, a publication of the Sierra Club, named Drexel one of its "Cool Schools" for its "eco-enlightened" policies.

Graduate Degrees

Chemical Engineering (MS, PhD)
Civil Engineering (Building/Energy Engineering) (MS, PhD)
Computer Engineering (MS, PhD)
Engineering Technology (MS)
Environmental Engineering (MS, PhD)
Materials Science and Engineering (MS, PhD)

Graduate Distance Learning

Engineering Technology (MS)

Graduate Certificates

Power Engineering Management
Sustainability and Green Construction

FERRIS STATE UNIVERSITY

1201 S. State Street
Big Rapids, Michigan 49307
231-591-2000
www.ferris.edu

About Associate Degrees at Ferris State University

In addition to bachelor's and master's degrees related to energy, Ferris offers associate degrees in the following subjects related to energy: Building Construction Technology (AAS); Civil Engineering Technology (AAS): Heavy Equipment Technology (AAS); Heating, Ventilation, Air Conditioning, and Refrigeration (HVACR) Technology (AAS); Industrial Chemistry Technology (AAS); Industrial Electronics Technology (AAS); and Mechanical Engineering Technology (AAS).

Undergraduate Degrees

Automotive Engineering Technology
Automotive Management
Construction Management (Commercial/
    Industrial Building concentration)
Electrical/Electronics Engineering Technology
Facility Management
Facility Operations Management (minor)
Facility Planning Management (minor)
Heavy Equipment Service Engineering
    Technology
HVACR Engineering Technology
Industrial Control Systems (minor)
Mechanical Engineering Technology
Operations and Supply Management (major and
    minor)

Undergraduate Certificates

Advanced Construction Management
Customer Energy Specialist
Electrical Power Generation
Facility Management

Undergraduate Distance Learning

HVACR Engineering Technology (BS)

Undergraduate Costs

Academic year 2009–10: $18,582 resident (tuition, fees, room and board), $23,337 nonresident (tuition, fees, room and board)

Undergraduate Financial Aid

FAFSA required.

Scholarships: Great Lakes Scholarship (allows eligible out-of-state students pay lower in-state tuition for up to 15 credit hours/semester); freshmen resident and nonresident scholarships; one-year departmental scholarships awarded annually. Go to www.ferris.edu/admissions/financialaid/scholarships.html for more information.

Undergraduate Admissions Requirements

Required: ACT/SAT scores.

High school preparation: Strong college preparatory curriculum in high school is encouraged. Specific requirements vary by program.

Undergraduate Application Information

Options: Online application; rolling admission

Application fee: $30 (no charge for online application)

Required: Online application, official high school transcript; ACT/SAT scores; guidance counselor form

Application deadline: Fall semester: freshmen, August 1/transfer, July 1; spring semester: freshmen, December 15/transfer, December 1; summer semester: freshmen, April 15/Transfer April 1

Notification: Two to four weeks after receiving application

Green Campus Organizations

American Society of Heating, Refrigerating, and Air-Conditioning Engineers: Promotes advances in HVACR that "serve humanity and promote a sustainable world."

Ferris Recyclers: Efforts to improve the campus and create a more eco-friendly environment through a campuswide recycling program.

Human-Powered Vehicle Competition: Students from a variety of majors working together to compete in an annual competition featuring vehicles developed for sustainable transportation.

Fast Facts

FSU sponsors the annual Michigan Energy Conference, which is "dedicated to affecting positive advancement and opportunity associated with energy, energy efficiency, and sustainability."

For more information, visit http://www.ferris.edu/energy/index.htm.

According to the American Society for Engineering Education, FSU's College of Engineering Technology has had more full- and part-time engineering technology students seeking bachelor's degrees over the past three years than any other school in the nation. The College ranks first in most bachelor's degrees awarded and third for the most women graduating with a bachelor's degree.

Graduate Degrees

Business Administration/Design and Innovation Management concentration (MBA)

Graduate Certificates

Design Innovation Management (Offered at Kendall College of Art and Design in Grand Rapids, Michigan)

IDAHO STATE UNIVERSITY (ISU)

921 S. 8th Avenue
Pocatello, Idaho 83209
208-282-0211
www.isu.edu

 http://bit.ly/collvid4

Undergraduate Degrees

Aircraft Maintenance Technology
Automotive Technology
Chemistry
Civil Engineering (Engineering Geology emphasis)
Civil Engineering Technology
Diesel/On-site Power Generation Technology
Earth and Environmental Systems (Environmental Policy and Management, Global Environmental Change, or Environmental Geochemistry track)
Electrical Engineering
Electrical Technician
Electromechanical Technology
Energy Systems Electrical Engineering Technology
Energy Systems Instrumentation and Controls Engineering Technology
Geology (Engineering Geology emphasis)
Mechanical Engineering
Nuclear Engineering

Undergraduate Certificates

Automotive Technology
Civil Engineering Technology
Diesel/On-site Power Generation Technology
Electrical Technician
Electromechanical Technology
Global Environmental Change
Power Plant

Undergraduate Costs

Academic year 2009–10: $4968 resident, $14,770 nonresident (full-time tuition); room and board costs vary. Residence Hall (charged by semester): $1175 to $1675. On-campus apartments (charged by month): $240 to $590. Some restrictions apply to on-campus apartments.

Undergraduate Financial Aid

FAFSA required.

Scholarships: Eastern Idaho Council on Industry and Energy scholarship awarded to juniors and seniors from Southeastern Idaho who are enrolled in an energy-related engineering program; John R. Horan Memorial awarded annually to a full-time student majoring in nuclear engineering with at least a 3.0 cumulative GPA; up to 12 Electrical Generating Systems Association/Coran, David I. Memorial scholarships of $2500 each awarded to full-time students majoring in on-site power generation industry (including diesel technician); the U.S. Department of Energy Nuclear Energy University Programs (NEUP) scholarships beginning at $5,000 to students studying nuclear science or engineering or a related field.

Undergraduate Admissions Requirements

Required (for assured admission): Cumulative GPA of 2.5 or better; math score of at least 18 on ACT or 490 on SAT; English score of at least 18 on ACT or 500 on SAT writing exam.

High school preparation: 8 semesters English (composition, literature); 6 semesters math (at least 4 semesters must be taken during grades 10 through 12); 6 semesters natural science (at least 2 semesters must include a laboratory experience); 5 semesters social science; 2 semesters humanities/foreign language; 3 semesters other college prep (up to 2 semesters of approved vocational courses may apply).

Undergraduate Application Information

Options: Online application

Application fee: $40

Required: Application; official ACT or SAT scores (students 21 or older are exempt); official high school transcript (sent by school in sealed envelope)

Application deadline: Freshmen and transfer applicants: August 1 (fall semester), December 1 (spring semester), open (summer semester); International Applicants: June 1 (fall semester), October 1 (spring semester), applications not accepted for summer semester

Notification: Typically within 10 days of receiving completed application

Green Campus Organizations

Student Action Volunteers for the Environment (SAVE): Student group that sponsors, enacts, and encourages environmental action and awareness both on campus and in the larger community.

Community Environmental Fair: Annual event held in honor of Earth Day. The goal of the fair is to promote constructive and sustainable environmental values, actions, and solutions. For more information, go to http://www.envirofair.org/about.html.

Fast Facts

The Idaho Accelerator Center has laboratories in three different locations and provides both university and private sector scientists and engineers a unique facility in which to conduct research and development in nuclear physics applications in materials science, biology, and national security.

The Institute of Nuclear Science and Engineering is a collaborative entity among ISU, University of Idaho, and Boise State University. Under this umbrella, the three universities offer a unique focus on nuclear science and engineering education at the Idaho Falls campus.

The Measurement and Control Engineering Research Center (MCERC), located in ISU's College of Engineering, focuses on advancing state-of-the-art MCE technology. Areas of research include thermal, nuclear, and aerospace engineering.

Graduate Programs

Chemistry (MS)
Civil Engineering (MS)
Engineering and Applied Science (PhD)
Environmental Engineering (MS)
Environmental Science and Management (MS)
Geology (Environmental Geoscience emphasis) (MS)
Hydrology (MS)
Measurement and Control Engineering (MS)
Mechanical Engineering (MS)
Nuclear Science and Engineering (MS, PhD)

Graduate Certificates

Applied Nuclear Energy

MASSACHUSETTS INSTITUTE OF TECHNOLOGY (MIT)

77 Massachusetts Avenue
Cambridge, Massachusetts 02139-4307
617-253-1000
web.mit.edu

About the EPA's P3 Program

The Environmental Protection Agency sponsors six grants for college students under its People, Prosperity, and the Planet Program. The goal is to develop programs that use technology to "tackle global environmental challenges." For more information, check out http://epa.gov/ncer/p3.

Undergraduate Degrees

Aerospace Engineering
Architecture
Art and Design (Building Technology Stream)
Chemical Engineering
Civil Engineering
Civil and Environmental Engineering

Electrical Engineering and Computer Science
Electrical Science and Engineering
Materials Science and Engineering
Mechanical Engineering
Nuclear Science and Engineering
Planning
Urban Studies and Planning (minor)

Undergraduate Costs

Academic year 2010–11: $38,940 (tuition and fees), $5820–$7906 (housing)

Undergraduate Financial Aid

CSS PROFILE® and FAFSA required.

Scholarships: Public Service Center Fellowships: Living expenses and stipend for one semester for students working on independent sustainable community projects; Morris K. Udall Scholarship; Department of Defense Science, Mathematics and Research for Transformation (SMART) Scholarship for Service Program. For more information, go to: http://www.asee.org/fellowships/smart/.

Undergraduate Admissions Requirements

Required: SAT Reasoning Test with writing component or ACT with the writing test; SAT Math Subject Test (Level 1 or 2); one SAT Science Subject Test (physics, chemistry, or biology).

High school preparation: 1 year physics; 1 year chemistry; 1 year biology; math, through calculus; 2 years foreign language; 4 years English; 2 years history and/or social sciences.

Undergraduate Application Information

Options: Online application

Application fee: $75

Required: Biographical information form; essays, activities, and tests form; self-reported course work form; ACT/SAT scores; two teacher evaluation forms; secondary school report form; high school transcript; mid-year report; financial aid materials

Recommended: Interview

Application deadline: November 1 (early action); January 1 (regular action)

Notification: mid-December (early action); mid-to late March (regular action)

Green Campus Organizations

MIT Electric Vehicle Team: Students from various disciplines who research, design, build, and test electric vehicles.

MIT Energy Club: Student and faculty group dedicated to all issues related to energy; hosts a lecture series that features prominent guest speakers in the energy world; sponsors classes, seminars, and tours of energy-related facilities.

Solar Electric Vehicle Team: Student group that designs, builds, and races solar electric vehicles; participates in environmental and ecological events where they promote vehicles powered by alternative energy.

Fast Facts

The MIT Energy Initiative's interdisciplinary research program engages MIT students who are interested in energy and related disciplines through classroom education and campus-oriented activities. Research focus areas include biofuels, buildings/urban design, industrial processes, markets and policy, oil and gas, solar, geothermal, storage, systems/power, and vehicles/transportation systems.

MIT's Department of Nuclear Science and Engineering conducts research in three categories of nuclear science including fission engineering and nuclear energy. MIT has its own 5-megawatt reactor. The Center for Advanced Nuclear Energy Systems conducts research in the areas of advanced reactor technology, advanced fuel cycle technology and economics, enhanced performance

of nuclear power plants, and nuclear energy and sustainability.

The Department of Civil and Environmental Engineering undertakes research projects on such diverse topics as smart grids, next-generation utility systems, tunnel design and construction, enhanced oil recovery, energy flows between natural and built environments, and transforming Chicago's transit system.

Graduate Degrees

Aeronautics and Astronautics (EAA, MS, PhD, ScD)
Architecture Studies (MSArchS)
Building Technology (MSBT, PhD)
Chemical Engineering (MS, PhD)
City Planning (M)
Civil and Environmental Engineering (CE, MS, MEng, PhD, ScD)
Electrical Engineering and Computer Science (EE, MS, MEng, PhD, ScD)
Engineering Systems (MS, PhD)
Materials Science Engineering (MatE, MS, MEng, PhD, ScD)
Mechanical Engineering (MechE, MS, MEng, PhD, ScD)
Nuclear Science and Engineering (NuclE, MS, PhD)
Technology and Policy (MS)
Transportation (MS)
Urban Studies and Planning (PhD)

About the Morris K. Udall Scholarship

In 1992, Congress established the Udall Foundation in honor of Morris K. Udall, who served in the U.S. House of Representatives from Arizona for 32 years and an early champion of environmentalism. The foundation awards undergraduate scholarships annually to sophomores and juniors "who have demonstrated commitment to careers related to the environment." For more information, check out www.udall.gov/OurPrograms/MKU Scholarship/MKUScholarship.aspx.

OREGON INSTITUTE OF TECHNOLOGY (OIT)

3201 Campus Drive
Klamath Falls, Oregon 97601
800-422-2017 Ext. 1 (toll-free)
www.oit.edu

Undergraduate Degrees

Most programs are given at the Klamath Falls campus.

Civil Engineering
Electrical Engineering
Electronics Engineering
Embedded Systems Engineering Technology
Environmental Sciences (Sustainable
    Technologies emphasis)
Manufacturing Engineering Technology (also
    offered at The Boeing Company)
Mechanical Engineering Technology
Renewable Energy Engineering

Undergraduate Costs

Academic year 2009–10: resident $3216 for 24 credit hours tuition and fees; WUE (Western Undergraduates) $4584 for 24 credit hours tuition and fees; nonresident $9360 for 24 credit hours

Undergraduate Financial Aid

FAFSA required.

Expanding Participation in Computing (EPIC) scholarship program for low-income and academically talented students (women, members of minority populations, students with disabilities, first-generation college students, and students from rural communities) wishing to major in embedded systems engineering technology, computer engineering technology, software, and information technology; check www.oit.edu/programs/epic.

For information on scholarships, see www.oit.edu/financial-matters.

Undergraduate Admissions Requirements

Required: 4 years of English, 3 years of math, 3 years of social studies, 2 years of science, 2 years of the same foreign language.

Undergraduate Application Information

Option: Online application, or mail-in paper application

Application fee: $50

Required: Application, official high school transcript or GED diploma, ACT or SAT scores including writing sections; GPA 3.00; scores required on the ACT or SAT are determined by the GPA

Application deadlines: February 1 (fall, freshmen priority and financial aid), Sept. 6 (fall), May 31 (summer), March 8 (spring)

Notification: Rolling

Green Campus Organizations

Sustainability Club: Promotes eco-friendly practices on campuses; in 2008–09, worked to replace Styrofoam takeout containers with disposable, compostable containers made from 100 percent renewable resources.

OIT Sustainability Office: Coordinates Recycle Mania and Earth Day activities.

Sustainability Internship Program: Involves students in sustainability activities on campus, such as conducting energy audits, conducting greenhouse gas inventories, and assesses campus's program on OIT's Sustainability Plan.

Fast Facts

When OIT introduced its bachelor of science degree in Renewable Energy Systems (now Renewable Energy Engineering) in 2005, it was the first such degree program in North America.

In April 2010, OIT dedicated a geothermal electric power plant, the first geothermal combined heat and power plant in Oregon, and the only geothermal electric plant in operation with a maximum capacity output of 280 kilowatts. The plant uses existing wells on campus.

OIT offers Boeing Company employees the opportunity to earn certifications as Certified Manufacturing Technologist and Certified Manufacturing Engineer through a program in Seattle, Washington.

Graduate Degrees

Civil Engineering
Manufacturing Engineering Technology

PENNSYLVANIA STATE UNIVERSITY

201 Old Main
University Park, Pennsylvania 16802
814-865-4700
E-mail: ask.psu.edu/psu.html
www.psu.edu

 http://bit.ly/collvid5

Undergraduate Degrees

Some degrees are completed at other campuses in the Penn State system.

Aerospace Engineering
Automotive Technology Management
Aviation Maintenance Technology
Chemical Engineering (Energy and Fuels option)
Civil Engineering

Community, Environment and Development
Energy, Business and Finance
Energy Engineering (major or minor)
Geosciences
Materials Science and Engineering
Mining Engineering
Nuclear Engineering
Petroleum and Natural Gas Engineering
Plastics Engineering Technology
Public Policy
Structural Design and Construction Engineering
    Technology
Supply Chain and Information Systems

Energy, Environmental, and Mineral Economics
    (minor)
Energy and Fuels Engineering (minor)
Global Business Strategies for the Earth, Energy,
    and Material Industries (minor)
Information Sciences and Technology for Earth
    and Mineral Sciences (minor)
Nanotechnology (minor)
Supply Chain and Information Sciences and
    Technology (minor)

Undergraduate Distance Learning

Automotive Technology Management (BAU)

Undergraduate Costs

Academic year 2009–10 (estimate): $23,236 residents, $34,766 nonresidents (tuition, room and board). Tuition rates vary by campus, student level, program, and residency.

Undergraduate Financial Aid

FAFSA required.

Scholarships, grants, loans, and work study available. See www.psu.edu/studentaid.

Undergraduate Admissions Requirements

Required: SAT or ACT.

High school preparation: 4 years English, 3 years mathematics, 3 years science, 5 years total foreign language, social studies, art, and humanities.

Recommended high school preparation: 2 years same foreign language. Some programs have additional math and science requirements.

Undergraduate Application Information

Options: Online application

Application fee: $50

Required: Application, high school transcript, counselor form. Letters of recommendation and/or interview required for some programs.

Application deadline: November 30 (fall freshmen), November 1 (spring freshmen), December 31 (fall transfers for Architecture and Landscape Architecture), February 1 (fall transfers), October 15 (spring transfers)

Notification: January 31 (fall freshmen), December 15 (spring freshmen, transfers), April 1 (fall transfers)

Green Campus Organizations

Mechanical Contractors Association of America, Penn State Student Chapter: Hosts an annual fall project in which participants create a proposal for the mechanical contract of a construction project aimed at acquiring a LEED rating; top 4 contestants present their proposal at the MCAA National Convention.

National Electrical Contracting Association (NECA) and ELECTRI International (EI) Student Chapter Competition: Competition in which student teams identify a community building needing energy-efficiency improvements, conduct an energy audit, and create a preliminary design for an energy retrofit for power and/or lighting systems.

American Indian Housing Initiative: A collaborative effort to adapt and deploy sustainable building technologies on American Indian reservations.

Students Taking Action to Encourage Recycling (Staters): Promotes campus recycling.

Sustainability Coalition: Coordinates relationships among students, staff members, faculty members, clubs, and the community to provide outreach, education, and support regarding sustainability issues.

3E-COE (Environment, Ecology, Education in the College of Education): Student organization in the College of Education, which initiated the project of installing refill stations that easily accommodate reusable drinking cups and large containers in buildings across the campus. The unit features a touchless dispenser with an automatic shutoff timer, diminishing the use of imperishable, one-time-use plastic water bottles that are taking over landfills and littering roadways. (See essay by Peter Buckland, 3E-COE president and graduate student in the Educational Theory and Policy program.)

Fast Facts

On April 22, 2009, Penn State became the first member of the Environmental Protection Agency's Sustainability Partnership Program (SPP) for the Mid-Atlantic region. The SPP, a pilot project of the EPA, enlists large organizations like Penn State to reduce energy and water use, waste generation, and climate impact.

In 2009, the Penn State Solar Decathlon Team participated in the competition sponsored by the U.S. Department of Energy to design, build, and operate an entirely solar-powered home. Penn State's team of more than 900 faculty members and students designed and built the MorningStar Solar Home; the project stimulated sustainability-related curriculum.

In 2010, the U.S. Environmental Protection Agency named Penn State number 43 of the top 50 purchasers of green power. It was purchasing 83 million kilowatt-hours of green power annually, which met 20 percent of the university's electric power needs. Biomass, small hydro, and wind were the alternate sources of energy that the university used. Penn State also ranks number 3 in the EPA's ranking of the top 20 colleges and universities using green power.

The mission of Penn State Institutes of Energy and the Environment is "to expand Penn State's capacity to pursue the newest frontiers in energy and environmental research by encouraging cooperation across disciplines and the participation of local, state, federal, and international stakeholders." The Penn State Institutes of Energy and the Environment is one member of larger consortia of institutes at Penn State that conduct research in the social sciences and arts and humanities as well as the hard sciences.

The Penn State Center for Nanotechnology Education and Utilization offers one-day and three-day Nanotechnology Camps for Pennsylvania high school students to acquaint them with nanotechnology and nanotechnology processing and applications.

The Ecological Systems Laboratory is a student-run DEP-funded project consisting of a natural wastewater treatment facility that mimics natural processes in wetlands and marshes. The ESL Center features a grid-tied Solar Array and Tracker that provides power for the bio-filter wastewater treatment facility.

Penn State received $5 million in funding under the American Recovery and Reinvestment Act (ARRA) in 2010 for the GridSTAR Center (Smart Grid Training Application Resource Center). The university will contribute another $5 million to the center that will provide a system-based continuing education and train-the-trainer program in advanced power systems design, energy economics, cyber security, distributed energy generation, and building-vehicle-grid systems.

Graduate Degrees

Biogeochemistry (PhD as part of a dual degree)
Chemical Engineering (MS, PhD)
Civil Engineering (MS, MEng, PhD)
Energy and Geo-Environmental Engineering (MS, PhD)
Energy and Mineral Engineering (MS, PhD)
Geosciences (MS, PhD)
Landscape Architecture (Community and Urban Design option) (MLA)
Mineral Processing (MS, PhD)
Mining Engineering (MS, MEng, PhD)
Nuclear Engineering (MS, MEng, PhD)
Oil and Gas Engineering Management (MEng)
Petroleum and Mineral Engineering (MS, PhD)
Petroleum and Natural Gas Engineering (MS, PhD)

Certificates

Community and Economic Development
Policy Analysis and Evaluation
Supply Chain Management

Distance Learning Certificate

Supply Chain Management

PORTLAND STATE UNIVERSITY

PO Box 751
Portland, Oregon 97207-0751
800-547-8887 Ext. 5-53511 (toll-free)
www.pdx.edu

 http://bit.ly/collvid6

About Portland State's Green Programs

Check out Portland State's EcoWiki for all things green on campus. The site lists information about upcoming sustainability events, green jobs, fellowships, grants, scholarships, courses, and campus projects: www.ecowiki.pdx.edu.

Undergraduate Degrees

Architecture
Chemistry
Civil Engineering
Electrical Engineering
Environmental Engineering (major or minor)
Geology (major or minor)
Mechanical Engineering
Supply and Logistics Management

Environmental Geology (minor)
Sustainable Urban Development (minor)

Undergraduate Costs

Academic year 2009–10 (estimate): $15,474 (residents), $27,021 (nonresidents) (tuition, fees, room and board based on three semesters—fall/winter/spring)

Undergraduate Financial Aid

FAFSA required.

Enterprise Community Investment Fellowship: Undergraduate/graduate students in Urban Studies and Community Development; Mechanical and Materials Engineering Industry Advisory Board Scholarship; Rolf and Blanka Schaumann Scholarship: Full-time upper division student studying electrical and computer engineering; Vatheuer Family Foundation Scholarships: $150/month, civil engineering students who are minorities or recent immigrants.

Undergraduate Admissions Requirements

Required: High school graduation or GED; 3.0 GPA; ACT or SAT.

High school preparation: 14 units of college prep coursework with grades of C or better, or meet Oregon Proficiency-based Standards System in the following areas: 4 units English; 3 units math (including Algebra II); 2 units science (1 year laboratory science recommended); 3 units social studies; 2 units of same foreign language.

Undergraduate Application Information

Option: Online application, rolling basis

Application fee: $50

Required: Application, official high school transcript, ACT or SAT scores

Application deadlines: June 1 (fall freshmen, transfers), October 1 (winter freshmen, transfers), February 1 (spring freshmen, transfers), May 1, (summer freshmen, transfers)

Notification: continuous, allow four to six weeks

Green Campus Organizations

Environmental Club: Students interested in environmental issues; connects within the university and with the wider community.

Food for Thought Organization: Promotes and offers food choices that support sustainability in its environmental, cultural, and economic aspects, including composting and recycling.

PSU Recycles: Team committed to recycling and reducing waste; welcomes student participation.

Sustainability Group: Volunteer and intern opportunities for students.

Fast Facts

The Oregon Transportation Research and Education Consortium conducts multidisciplinary research on innovations in "sustainable transportation through advanced technology, integration of land use and transportation, and healthy communities."

In its commitment to sustainability, Portland State has six green buildings, which have been either designed or retrofitted according to green building guidelines. Three of them meet the U.S. Green Building Council's Silver or Gold LEED certification criteria. In addition, the campus has several buildings that are constructed with renewable natural materials.

PSU and Portland General Electric (PGE) have a partnership to promote the Portland region as a leader in developing and implementing urban sustainability. The two organizations focus their work on urban mobility and the integration of energy and sustainable design. The Center for Sustainable Processes and Practices supports multidisciplinary research for the development of sustainable solutions and strategies that work in the real-world. One of its focuses is on creating sustainable urban communities.

Graduate Degrees

Architecture (MRCH)
Chemistry (Environmental Chemistry, Materials Chemistry) (MS, MA, PhD)
Civil and Environmental Engineering (MS, MEng, PhD) (Transportation Specialization)
Civil and Environmental Engineering Management (MEng, PhD) (Transportation Specialization)
Electrical Engineering (MS, MEng, PhD)

Electrical and Computer Engineering (MS, MEng, PhD)
Systems Engineering (MEng)
Urban and Regional Planning (MURP) (Transportation Specialization)

Graduate Certificates

Engineering Geology
Integrated Circuit Test, Verification, and Validation
Micro and Nano Electronics
Transportation
Systems Engineering

PURDUE UNIVERSITY

West Lafayette, Indiana 47907
765-494-4600
www.purdue.edu

 http://bit.ly/collvid7

> ### About the Donald Danforth Plant Science Center
>
> Purdue is one of six partners supporting the Donald Danforth Plant Science Center, which is located in St. Louis, Missouri. Researchers at the Center are attempting to alleviate world hunger and preserve the environment by creating a sustainable food supply through research on ways to enhance the nutritional content in plants and reduce the use of pesticides. They are also working on the development of new and sustainable biofuels.

Undergraduate Degrees

Aeronautical and Astronautical Engineering
Aeronautical Engineering Technology
Chemistry (Materials Chemistry specialization)
Civil Engineering
Construction Engineering

Electrical and Computer Engineering Technology
Electrical Engineering
Industrial Engineering
Materials Engineering
Mechanical Engineering
Mechanical Engineering Technology
Nuclear Engineering
Physics

Undergraduate Costs

Academic year 2010–11: Resident $18,190; non-resident $35,742 (tuition, fees, room and board). Some programs have additional fees: Technology ($526), Engineering ($1050), Management ($1338)

Undergraduate Financial Aid

FAFSA required.

Undergraduate Admissions Requirements

Required: High school transcript; SAT or ACT (with writing test).

High school preparation: 8 years English; 4 years math; 2 or 3 years laboratory science (depends on program; 3 years social studies; 2 years foreign language.

Undergraduate Application Information

Option: Online application, early admission, deferred entrance

Application fee: $50

Required: Application, ACT or SAT scores (including writing); official high school transcript

Application deadlines: November 15 (freshmen seeking scholarship consideration); March 1 (freshmen); July 1 (fall transfers); November 1 (spring transfers)

Notification: Continuous beginning early December (freshmen)

Green Campus Organizations

Boiler Green Initiative: Multidisciplinary student organization that raises awareness of sustainability issues at Purdue and in the community; particular focus on green building. The organization is leading the way in installing the first green roof on campus.

Carbon Neutrality at Purdue University: Student organization whose goals are to reduce energy consumption on campus and raise awareness of carbon neutrality in the community; part of Boiler Green Initiative.

GreenBuild: A student/faculty/staff organization promoting green building practices; provides students with green career opportunities through industry partners and sponsors.

Purdue Green Week: A week of campus activities to bring awareness to sustainability issues.

Purdue Sustainability Council: Members from various departments and offices identifies issues and options, educates the campus community, and makes recommendations for sustainability improvements.

Fast Facts

In 2004, the Indiana legislature created the Center for Coal Technology Research. The goal of the Center is to find environmentally responsible ways to use Indiana coal.

Purdue's Energy Center aims to "facilitate high-impact, multidisciplinary projects in support of Purdue's vision to be one of the global leaders in energy." A number of the Center's research projects focus on advanced ground vehicle power; batteries and advanced electrochemical system; bioenergy; clean coal; green building; hydrogen; nuclear energy; social, economic, and political aspects of energy use and policy; solar energy; water; and wind energy.

Purdue University held the inaugural Electric Vehicle Grand Prix in April 2010. The event is part of a program designed to attract the next generation of workers who will design, build, and service electric vehicles.

Purdue was chosen by the U.S. Department of Energy to participate in the 2011 Solar Decathlon. Teams from twenty colleges in the United States, Canada, Belgium, New Zealand, and China were chosen on the basis of competitive applications to create solar homes.

Purdue Climate Change Research Center, a multidisciplinary research center, was chartered in 2004 to study all aspects of climate change. Course offerings include Engineering Environmental Sustainability, Environmental and Natural Resource Economics, Organizational Leadership and Supervision, and Environmental Data Handling, among others. Graduate fellowships and PhD program are also offered.

Graduate Degrees

Aeronautics and Astronautics (MSAAE, MSE, MS, PhD)
Chemical Engineering (MS, NT-MS, PhD)
Chemistry (MS, PhD)
Civil Engineering (MS, PhD)
Ecological Sciences and Engineering (MS, NT-MS, PhD)
Electrical and Computer Engineering (MSECE, MSE, MS, PhD)
Industrial Engineering (MSIE, PhD)
Materials Engineering (MS, PhD)
Mechanical Engineering (MSME, PhD)
Nuclear Engineering (MS, PhD)

Graduate Certificates

Applied Heat Transfer
Materials Engineering

Graduate Distance Learning

Aeronautics and Astronautics (NT-MSAAE)
Electrical and Computer Engineering (MSECE)
Industrial Engineering (MSIE)
Mechanical Engineering (MSME)

RUTGERS, THE STATE UNIVERSITY OF NEW JERSEY

New Brunswick, New Jersey 08901
732-445-4636
www.rutgers.edu

http://bit.ly/collvid8

About Rutgers and the Environmental Community

The Rutgers Environmental Stewards Program was created in 2008 to educate the public about the importance of preserving the environment in New Jersey. It is a cooperative effort between the Rutgers Cooperative Extension and Duke Farms. The program is open to all New Jersey residents who earn an Environmental Stewardship Certificate after 60 hours of classwork and 60 hours of service in a volunteer internship. Details can be found at www.envirostewards.rutgers.edu.

Undergraduate Costs

Academic year 2010–11: $22,262 resident, $33,172 nonresident. The cost includes tuition, fees, and room and board.

Additional tuition for students in Environmental and Biological Sciences: $1054 resident, $2246 nonresidents.

Part-time tuition: $307 per credit hour for residents, $664 per credit hour for nonresidents.

Undergraduate Financial Aid

FAFSA required.

Undergraduate Admissions Requirements

Required: High school graduation (with at least 16 academic credits) or GED. SAT or ACT.

High school preparation: Varies according to program; check the admissions Web site for details: admissions.rutgers.edu/021202B.asp#3

Undergraduate Application Information

Options: Online application

Application fee: $65

Required: Application, interim high school transcript (only if Self-Reported Academic Record is not completed), high school transcript required for enrollment, personal statement (only for honors programs or merit award consideration)

Recommended: Self-Reported Academic Record (SARA)

Application deadline: December 1 (fall freshmen), January 15 (fall transfers), October 15 (spring freshmen, transfers)

Notification: February 28 (fall freshmen), April 15 (fall transfers), December 12 (spring freshmen, transfers)

Undergraduate Degrees

Most urban planning degrees are offered at the New Brunswick campus.

Biotechnology (Bioscience Policy and
   Management)
Chemical Engineering
Chemistry (Environmental Option)
Civil and Environmental Engineering
Electrical Engineering
Environmental Planning and Design
   (Environmental Planning Option)
Environmental Policy, Institutions and Behavior
   (International Environmental and Resource
   Policy Option, U.S. Environmental and
   Resource Policy Option)
Environmental Policy, Institutions and Behavior
   (minor)
Geology
Geoscience Engineering
Mechanical Engineering
Planning and Public Policy (major or minor)
Urban Studies and Metropolitan Planning,
   Camden
Public Administration, Newark (BA or BS/MAP
   five-year program)

Undergraduate Certificates

Environmental Planning
Community Development
Urban Planning

Undergraduate Distance Learning

Selected courses for the majors listed above are available online each term. See the Rutgers Online Course Schedule: soc.ess.rutgers.edu/soc. For direct access to School of Environmental and Biological Sciences, go to http://sebs.rutgers.edu/distance.

Green Campus Organizations

Energy Innovation: Sponsored by The Rutgers Energy Institute to engage students in developing innovative solutions to reducing energy waste at Rutgers.

Ecological Change Coalition: Works with other campus organizations to inform the university community about issue concerning global warming.

Outdoors Club: Promotes responsible conservation in addition to sponsoring outdoor activities.

Students for Environmental Awareness: Organized to educate students and encourage environmental change on campus.

Fast Facts

The Edward J. Bloustein School of Planning and Public Policy is a major center for the theory and practice of planning and public policy scholarship and analysis. Among its programs are the Center for Energy, Economic, and Environmental Policy; The Center for Planning Practice; The Center for Urban Policy Research; Initiative for Regional and Community Transformation; National Center for Neighborhoods and Brownfields Redevelopment; National Transit Institute; Rutgers Center for Green Building; and Alan M. Voorhees Transportation Center.

The Center for Energy, Economic, and Environmental Policy is part of the Edward J. Bloustein School of Planning and Public Policy. Established in 2003, the Center conducts applied research to evaluate and help develop policy at the state, regional, national, and international levels on the interrelation of energy, economic, and environmental policy issues.

The New Jersey Public Policy Research Institute, part of the Edward J. Bloustein School of Planning and Public Policy, conducts and disseminates research related to public policy affecting African American communities in New Jersey and the region.

The Center for Urban Policy Research of the Bloustein School is nationally and internationally recognized for its work on land use policy, environmental impact analysis, land development practice, infrastructure assessment, the costs of sprawl, transportation information systems, and community economic development.

The Center for Advanced Infrastructure and Transportation (CAIT) in the Department of Civil and Environmental Engineering conducts research and supports educational efforts in transportation and infrastructure. Topics include mobility, congestion, asset management, and environmental impact.

In 2009, Rutgers opened a seven-acre solar energy facility on its Livingston campus. It is one of the largest renewable energy systems on a single campus in the nation and generates approximately 11 percent of the campus's demand for electric power. It reduces the university's carbon dioxide emissions by more than 1,300 tons a year and will save Rutgers several hundred thousand dollars a year.

Rutgers was chosen by the U.S. Department of Energy to participate in the 2011 Solar Decathlon. Teams from twenty colleges in the United States, Canada, Belgium, New Zealand, and China were chosen on the basis of competitive applications to create solar homes.

Graduate Degrees

City and Regional Planning (Environmental and Physical Planning, International Development and Regional Planning, Transportation Policy and Planning, Urban and Community Development) (MCRP)

City and Regional Planning and Business Administration (MCRP/MBA)

City and Regional Studies (Environmental and Physical Planning, International Development and Regional Planning, Transportation Policy and Planning, Urban and Community Development) (MCRS)

Civil and Environmental Engineering (MS, PhD)

Construction and Regional Planning and Business Administration (MCRP/MBA)

Planning and Public Policy (PhD)

Public Policy (MPP)

Public Policy/Business Administration (MPP/MBA)

Public Policy/City and Regional Planning (MPP/MCRP)

Transportation

Urban Systems (PhD)

Graduate Certificates

Human Dimensions of Environmental Change
Public Policy
Transportation Studies

STANFORD UNIVERSITY

450 Serra Mall
Stanford, California 94305
650-723-2300
www.stanford.edu

 http://bit.ly/collvid9

About the Global Climate and Energy Project

Energy experts from private industry and research institutions are working at Stanford University's Global Climate and Energy Project (GCEP) on ways to supply energy that will meet the world's growing population demands, but, at the same time, will protect the environment by lowering greenhouse gas emissions. The scientists, who believe that the answer isn't likely to lie in any single source, are conducting experiments on a variety of low-emission, high-efficiency energy technologies.

Undergraduate Degrees

Chemical Engineering (major or minor)
Chemistry
Civil and Environmental Engineering
Electrical Engineering (major or minor)
Energy Resources Engineering (major or minor)
Engineering (Aeronautics and Astronautics interdisciplinary program)
Engineering (Atmosphere and Energy interdisciplinary program)
General Engineering (Interdisciplinary Major in Aeronautics and Astronautics)

Geological and Environmental Sciences (major or minor)
Geophysics (major or minor)
Materials Science and Engineering (major or minor)
Mechanical Engineering (major or minor)
Public Policy (Urban and Regional Policy concentration)

Aeronautics and Astronautics (minor)
Civil Engineering (minor)

Undergraduate Certificates

Architecture and Engineering
Engineering Physics
Geological Engineering
Materials Science and Engineering

Undergraduate Costs

Academic year 2010–11: $50,576 (tuition, fees, room and board)

Undergraduate Financial Aid

CSS PROFILE® and FAFSA required.

Undergraduate Admissions Requirements

Required: ACT with writing test or SAT (critical reading, math, and writing)

Recommended: 4 years English; 4 years math; 3 or more years history/social studies; 3 or more years laboratory science; 3 or more years of same foreign language.

Undergraduate Application Information

Option: Early action; online Common Application with Stanford Supplement (paper application available if approved by Director of Admission)

Application fee: $90

Required: Application with Stanford Supplement; mid-year school report; official high school transcript; secondary school report; two teacher evaluations; essays

Application deadlines: November 1 (Early Action); January 1 (freshmen); March 15 (transfers)

Notification: December 15 (Early Action); April 1 (freshmen); May 15 (transfers)

Green Campus Organizations

Energy Crossroads: Coalition for clean and secure energy future.

Engineers for a Sustainable World, Stanford Chapter: Engineering students and students from other majors working to provide sustainable solutions to developing communities in the United States and abroad by networking within Stanford and with outside organizations.

Green Living Council: Students teaching others ways to incorporate sustainability into their everyday lives.

The Stanford Nanoscience and Nanotechnology Society: Collaboration of students from the five nanoscience and technology sub-fields: provides a forum for students to exchange ideas. The group also promotes interaction between industrial and academic institutes.

Students for a Sustainable Stanford: Undergraduate and graduate students seeking to raise campus awareness about sustainability issues, including environmental practices and green building, economics, and business.

Fast Facts

The Energy Modeling Forum is an international forum for experts on energy policy and global climate issues. A single energy/environment problem is selected as the topic for each forum. The goal of each forum is to improve understanding of the issue, explore alternative approaches to the problem, and identify high-priority research directions for the future.

At Stanford's Precourt Institute for Energy, scientists engage in a broad-ranging, interdisciplinary program of research and education on energy. Their research addresses the problems of "supplying energy in environmentally and economically acceptable ways, using it efficiently, and facing the behavioral, social, and policy challenges of creating new energy systems for the U.S. and the world." Major research is carried out through the Global Climate and Energy Project and the Precourt Energy Efficiency Center.

Graduate Degrees

Aeronautics and Astronautics (MS, Eng, PhD)
Chemical Engineering (MS, PhD)
Civil and Environmental Engineering (Atmosphere/Energy designation) (MS, PhD)
Civil and Environmental Engineering (Sustainable Design and Construction) (MS, Eng, PhD)
Earth, Energy, and Environmental Sciences (MS, PhD)
Electrical Engineering (MS, Eng, PhD)
Energy Resources Engineering (Dual major BS/MS, Eng, MS, PhD)
Environmental Earth Systems Science (MS, PhD)
Environmental Engineering and Science (MS, Eng, PhD)
Geological and Environmental Sciences (MS, Eng, PhD, PhD minor)
Geophysics (MS, PhD)
Materials Science and Engineering (MS, PhD)
Mechanical Engineering (MS, Eng, PhD)
Petroleum Engineering (MS, PhD, PhD minor)
Public Policy (MPP, MA, MBA/MPP, JD/MPP)

Graduate Certificates

Dynamics and Simulation
Electronic Circuits
Micro/Nano Systems and Technology

Nanoscale Materials Science
Sustainable Energy Conversion and Storage

Graduate Distance Learning

Master's degrees offered completely or partially online:

Aeronautics and Astronautics
Civil and Environmental Engineering
Electrical Engineering
Materials Science and Engineering
Mechanical Engineering

SYRACUSE UNIVERSITY (SU)

Syracuse, New York 13244-5040
315-443-1870
www.syr.edu

 http://bit.ly/collvid10

About Syracuse and Green Power

In 2010, the U.S. Environmental Protection Agency ranked Syracuse number 15 out of the top 20 colleges and universities that purchase green power. The university gets 20 percent of its electricity, almost 23 million kilowatt hours, from small hydro power.

Undergraduate Degrees

Aerospace Engineering
Architecture
Chemical Engineering
Civil engineering
Computer Engineering (major or minor)
Electrical Engineering (major or minor)
Environmental Engineering
Geology
Mechanical Engineering
Physics (major or minor)

Earth Sciences (minor)
Energy Systems Engineering (minor)

Undergraduate Costs

Academic year 2010–11: $49,152 (tuition, fees, average room and board)

Undergraduate Financial Aid

CSS PROFILE® and FAFSA required.

The Office of Financial Aid and Scholarship Programs can provide detailed information on a variety of SU and external scholarship sources. Go to: http://financialaid.syr.edu/scholarships.htm.

Undergraduate Admissions Requirements

Required: High school graduation; SAT or ACT with writing test. Some colleges have specific high school preparation requirements.

General preparation: 4 years English; 4 years science; 4 years social studies; 4 years mathematics (through geometry and intermediate algebra); at least 3 years foreign language.

Undergraduate Application Information

Option: Online application; early decision; early admission; deferred entrance

Application fee: $70

Required: Common Application with Syracuse University Supplement or Syracuse University Application for Admission; high school transcript; senior year grade report; SAT or ACT (with writing test) scores; secondary school counselor evaluation; two academic recommendations

Recommended: Interview

Application deadlines: November 15 (early decision); January 1 (fall freshmen)

Notification: Mid-December (early decision); mid-March (fall freshmen)

Green Campus Organizations

Campus Sustainability Committee: Students, staff, and faculty committee; develops policies and guidelines for the university sustainability program.

Irish Today, Green Forever: Joint project between the Residence Hall Association, the university residence hall office, and the university sustainability program to increase recycling in residence halls and decrease consumption of bottled water.

SU Sustainability Showcase: Annual event held in conjunction with Earth Day that features student sustainable design projects.

University Sustainability Action Coalition: Committed to improving sustainability, energy use, and recycling on campus; sponsors campus events to educate and raise awareness.

Fast Facts

In September 2009, the Syracuse Center on Excellence in Environmental and Energy Innovations (SyracuseCoE) opened its new headquarters, a LEED Platinum-certified building—the highest LEED rating given by the U.S. Green Building Council. The building has many energy-conserving and environmental features and houses research space for SyracuseCoE's three focus areas: clean and renewable energy, indoor environmental quality, and water resources.

Syracuse University has teamed up with IBM and New York State to build and operate a new computer data center on campus. By incorporating an advanced infrastructure and smarter computing technologies, designers expect to cut energy usage by 50 percent, making this one of the greenest computer centers in existence.

The H. H. Franklin Center for Supply Chain Management conducts research and provides opportunities for students to interact with alumni and practitioners in the field.

The Department of Entrepreneurship and Emerging Enterprises (EEE) is one of the few formal academic departments in the nation devoted to entrepreneurship.

In 2010, the U.S. Environmental Protection Agency named Syracuse University number 15 of the top 20 college and university purchasers of green power. It was purchasing almost 23 million kilowatt-hours of green power annually, which met 20 percent of the university's electric power needs. Small hydro was the alternate source of energy that the university used.

In 2010, the university received $2.5 million under the American Recovery and Reinvestment Act to partially fund a Strategic Training and Education in Power Systems (STEPS) program. It is a multi-institutional program to develop and deliver degree and certificate curricula to create the new smart-grid workforce. STEPS is an academic and industry partnership across New York State.

Graduate Degrees

Architecture (MArch I, MArch II)
Civil Engineering (MS, PhD)
Computer Engineering (MS)
Electrical Engineering (MS)
Electrical and Computer Engineering (PhD)
Environmental Engineering (MS)
Environmental Engineering Science (MS)
Environmental Engineering with a specialization in Public Administration (MS)
Geology (MS, PhD)
Mechanical and Aerospace Engineering (MS, PhD)
Physics (MS, PhD)

TEXAS A&M UNIVERSITY

College Station, Texas 77843
979-845-3211
E-mail: services.tamu.edu/directory-search
www.tamu.edu

 http://bit.ly/collvid12

Undergraduate Degrees

Aerospace Engineering
Architecture (Home Architecture Track)
Chemical Engineering
Civil Engineering
Environmental Design (Architecture)
Geology (Petroleum Geology Track)
Geotechnical Engineering
General Civil Engineering
Materials Engineering
Mechanical Engineering
Nuclear Engineering
Petroleum Engineering
Transportation Engineering
Urban and Regional Sciences

Aerospace Engineering (minor)
Geoinformatics (minor)
Nuclear Engineering (minor)
Petroleum Engineering (minor)
Urban Planning (minor)

Undergraduate Certificate

Energy Engineering
Polymer Specialty

Undergraduate Distance Learning

Many courses are available online, through the TTVN interactive videoconferencing system or a combination of formats. Some meet requirements of the degrees listed above. For a complete listing of all e-learning courses, degrees, certificates, and programs, check out http://distance.tamu.edu/futureaggies/distance-degrees.

Undergraduate Costs

Academic year 2010–11: $16,375 (residents), $30,925 (nonresidents) (tuition, fees, room and board)

Undergraduate Financial Aid

FAFSA, or TASFA for students ineligible for federal aid.

Scholarships, grants, and internships and co-ops are available. See http://financialaid.tamu.edu.

Undergraduate Admissions Requirements

Required: SAT or ACT with Writing Test.

High school preparation: 4 years English, 3.5 years mathematics (including algebra I and II, geometry, ½ year advanced math), 3 years science (2 years must be biology, chemistry, or physics). For Engineering: minimum math score 550 SAT or 24 ACT.

Recommended high school preparation: 2 years same foreign language. Meet the Texas State Distinguished Achievement Program requirements.

Undergraduate Application Information

Options: Online application

Application fee: $60

Required: Apply Texas Application, high school transcript, Essays A and B

Recommended: Essay C, interview, campus visit, or any Academic Association activity.

Application deadline: January 21 (fall, summer freshmen), October 1 (spring freshmen), March 15 (fall, summer transfers), October 15 (spring transfers)

Notification: Continuous (by early April for fall and summer, by early December for spring)

Green Campus Organizations

Aggies Cleaning the Environment: Promotes leadership and service regarding environmental issues.

Emerging Green Builders: Student chapter of the U.S. Green Building Council; for students and others getting started in the green building industry.

Environmental Issues Committee: Committee of the Student Government Association providing environmental awareness and education and promoting environmental legislation.

Texas Environmental Action Coalition: Students and community members work to improve the environment and increase awareness of environmental issues.

Environmental Programs Involvement Committee: Promotes awareness of environmental departmental programs and encourages involvement in dealing with issues impacting the environment

Fast Facts

The Residence Hall Association ran a Compact Florescent Light (CFL) Program to replace all incandescent light bulbs in the thirty residence halls with CFLs.

The Crisman Center for Petroleum Research houses four research institutes that work to solve a variety of problems related to technology development for petroleum resources. The institutes include the Halliburton Center of Unconventional Resources, the Chevron Center of Well Construction and Production, the Schlumberger Center for Reservoir Description and Dynamics, and the Center for Energy, Environment, and Transportation Innovation.

The Center for Housing and Urban Development confers the Sustainable Urbanism Certificate. The program addresses the integration and interdependence of the various aspects of the urban environment including energy, infrastructure, and transportation networks, and land use and urban design.

A team from the College of Architecture designed and built a solar-powered home for the 2007 U.S. Department of Energy's Solar Decathlon. Twenty teams from across the United States and Europe competed. The Aggie's Gro-Home took first place from the American Institute of Architecture Students and the American Institutes of Architects' Committee on the Environment.

In 2010, the U.S. Environmental Protection Agency named the Texas A&M system number 7 of the top 20 college and university purchasers of green power. The system was purchasing 43 million kilowatt-hours of green power annually, which met 15 percent of the university's electric power needs. Wind power was the alternate source of energy that the university uses.

Graduate Degrees

Architecture (MS, MArch, 4+2 BArch/MArch, PhD)
Chemical Engineering (MS, MEng, PhD, DEng)
Chemistry (PhD)
Geotechnical Engineering (MS, MEng, PhD)
Mechanical Engineering (MS, MEng, PhD, DEng)
Public Service Administration (Public Management Track, Public Policy Track) (MPSA)
Transportation Engineering (MS, MEng, PhD)
Urban and Regional Science (PhD)
Urban Planning (MUP)
Urban Planning and Land Development (MUP/MSLD)

Graduate Certificates

Community Development
Petroleum Geosciences
Sustainable Urbanism
Transportation Planning

Graduate Distance Learning

Petroleum Engineering (MEng)

UNIVERSITY OF ALASKA, FAIRBANKS

505 South Chandalar Drive
P.O. Box 757500
Fairbanks, Alaska 99775
907-474-7211
www.uaf.edu

About the International Polar Year

The University of Alaska, Fairbanks, has been participating in the International Polar Year (IPY) since its inception in 2007 along with more than 300 institutions around the world. Researchers at the university have taken leading roles in the many research and educational projects in polar science.

Undergraduate Degrees

Applied Physics
Civil Engineering
Computer Engineering
Electrical Engineering
Geological Engineering
Geology (major or minor)
Mechanical Engineering
Mining Engineering
Petroleum Engineering
Physics (major or minor)

Undergraduate Certificates

Airframe and Powerplant
Automotive Technology
Diesel/Heavy Engine
Mining Applications and Technologies
Power Generation
Powerplant

Undergraduate Costs

Academic year 2010–11: $12,318 residents; $23,188 nonresidents; $14,568 Western Undergraduate Exchange (undergraduates living in western states); (tuition for 30 credits of 100- and 200-level courses, fees, double room, and 19 meals/week)

Undergraduate Financial Aid

FAFSA required.

Alaska Space Grant Scholarships: Awarded to undergraduate students for participation in aerospace-related research projects.

The College of Engineering and Mines offers a large variety of privately funded scholarships. For information, go to: http://www.alaska.edu/uaf/cem/students/scholarships.xml.

Other privately funded scholarships are available. See department Web sites and Undergraduate Financial Aid Scholarship Web site: http://www.alaska.edu/uaf/cem/students/scholarships.xml.

Undergraduate Admissions Requirements

Required: High school diploma; ACT with writing test (preferred) or SAT; 2.5 GPA on 16-credit high school core curriculum; 3.0 GPA overall or 2.5 GPA with ACT score of at least 18 or SAT sore of at least 1290 (including writing skills section).

High school preparation: 4 years English, 3 years college preparatory math; 3 years social sciences; 3 years natural/physical sciences (including 1 year laboratory science). For additional requirements from specific colleges, go to: http://www.uaf.edu/catalog/catalog_09-10/admissions/baccalaureate.html.

Undergraduate Application Information

Option: Online application, early admission, deferred entrance

Application fee: $50

Required: Application, high school transcript

Application deadlines: July 1 (fall freshmen, transfers), November 1 (spring freshmen, transfers)

Notification: Continuous until space is filled

Green Campus Organizations

Alternative Spring Break: Volunteers for a variety of community organizations and agencies that address issues in Alaska such as sustainable living and conservation.

SpringFest Service: Volunteers for community projects, including conservation and community clean-up.

Sustainable Campus Task Force (SCTF): Students working for a sustainable campus and community while also considering global implications.

Fast Facts

Scientists at the International Arctic Research Center are trying to understand the Arctic as a system in order to get a clear understanding of its role in climate change. Current research includes everything from a study of the destabilization and venting of arctic seabed methane stores to the monitoring of CO_2 emissions in boreal forests.

The Institute of Northern Engineering specializes in research and engineering solutions in cold regions of the world. Among its research topics are Arctic energy technology development and system testing for alternative energy prototypes; mineral extraction; petroleum development including methane, gas hydrates, and gas-to-liquids conversion, and drilling and production.

Graduate Degrees

Arctic Engineering (MS)
Civil Engineering (MCE, MS)
Electrical Engineering (MEE, MS)

Engineering (Arctic, Civil, Computer, Electrical, Geological, Mechanical, Mining, and Petroleum concentrations) (PhD)
Geological Engineering (MS)
Geology (MS, PhD)
Mechanical Engineering (MS)
Mineral Preparation Engineering (MS)
Mining Engineering (MS)
Petroleum Engineering (MS)
Physics, (MS, MAT, PhD)

Graduate Distance Learning

Arctic Engineering (MS)
Global Supply Chain Management (certificate)

UNIVERSITY OF CALIFORNIA, BERKELEY (UC BERKELEY)

Berkeley, California 94720
510-642-6000
www.berkeley.cdu

 http://bit.ly/collvid13

About Reducing Greenhouse Gas Emissions

UC Berkeley has pledged to reduce its greenhouse gas emissions to 1990 levels by 2014 (six years earlier than the rest of California) through more than 200 energy-efficiency projects. Through various energy-saving projects, Berkeley campus students have reduced the school's energy consumption by more than 8.5 million kWh and its water usage by 3 million gallons.

Undergraduate Degrees

Architecture (major or minor)
Chemical Engineering
Chemistry
Earth and Planetary Science (Geology) (major or minor)

Engineering
   Civil Engineering
   Electrical and Computer Engineering
   Electrical Engineering and Computer Sciences
   (major or minor)
   Engineering Physics
   Environmental Engineering Science
Industrial Engineering and Operations Research
   Manufacturing Engineering
Materials Science and Engineering
   Mechanical Engineering
Nuclear Engineering

City and Regional Planning (minor)
Energy and Resources (minor)
Environmental Engineering (minor)
Geoengineering (minor)
Public Policy (minor)
Structural Engineering (minor)
Sustainable Design (minor)

Undergraduate Certificates

Civil and Environmental Engineering

Undergraduate Distance Learning (Professional Certificates)

Construction Management
HVAC
Integrated Circuit Design and Techniques

Undergraduate Distance Learning (Specialized Programs of Study)

Facilities Management
Leadership in Sustainability and Environmental
   Management
Solar Energy and Green Building
Sustainability and Energy
Sustainability and Transportation
Sustainable Design

Undergraduate Costs

Academic year 2010–11: $30,972 resident; $53,851 nonresident (housing and utilities, food, books and supplies, personal, transportation, fees)

Undergraduate Financial Aid

FAFSA required.

Scholarships: Berkeley Undergraduate Scholarship; Regents' and Chancellor's Scholarship (invitation only); and California Alumni Association Scholarships. Visit Berkeley's Scholarship Connection Web site at http://scholarships.berkeley.edu/ for information on scholarships funded by sources outside of the university.

Undergraduate Admissions Requirements

Required: Two SAT Subject Tests (optional beginning with fall 2012 admissions) and either the ACT (Writing Test required) or SAT Reasoning Test. Minimum GPA is 3.0 for California residents, 3.4 for nonresidents.

High school preparation: 2 years history/social science, 4 years English, 3 years math (4 years recommended), 2 years laboratory science (3 years recommended), 2 years the same foreign language (3 years recommended), 1 year visual and performing arts, 1 year college-prep electives in engineering technology, visual and performing arts (nonintroductory level courses), history, social science, English, advanced mathematics, laboratory science, or a language other than English.

Undergraduate Application Information

Option: Online or paper Common Application, early admission

Application fee: $60

Required: Common Application; personal statement; official ACT and/or SAT scores

Application deadlines: November 30 (fall freshmen, transfers); July 31 (spring freshmen, transfers)

Notification: March 25 (freshmen); April 30 (transfers)

Green Campus Organizations

Bay-Area Environmentally Aware Consulting Network (BEACN): Nonprofit student organization specializing in sustainable business consulting in the San Francisco Bay Area. BEACN is sponsored by the Walter A. Haas School of Business.

BicyCal: Student group that teaches local youth about the historical and environmental connections between energy and transportation. Participants receive the tools and resources necessary to build their own free bicycle.

Boalt Environmental Law Society: An organization of student activists at Boalt Hall School of Law dedicated to environmental protection, education, and social justice. ELS provides opportunities for Boalt law students to gain hands-on legal experience with established environmental organizations in the community, to discuss local, national, and international issues with prominent environmental attorneys; and to learn to appreciate and protect nature.

Greening at Berkeley: Student group facilitating environmental education and awareness through hands-on public service activities.

Students for Energy and Environmental Development (SEED): Student volunteers who teach K–12 curriculum about traditional and alternative energy sources, efficiency, and conservation.

Fast Facts

The Berkeley Institute of the Environment is a campuswide initiative aimed at conducting multidisciplinary research and teaching and dedicated to addressing the most critical environmental problems.

The Green Initiative Fund (TGIF) is a grant-making fund for sustainability projects on UC Berkeley's campus. About $250,000 is available each year for grants; students as well as members of the faculty and staff are eligible to submit project proposals.

Graduate Degrees

Architecture (MS, MArch, PhD)
Chemical Engineering (MS, PhD)
Chemistry (PhD)
City and Regional Planning (MCP, PhD)
Civil and Environmental Engineering (Engineering and Project Management, Geoengineering, Transportation Engineering) (MS, MSEng, MS/PhD, PhD)
Earth and Planetary Science (MA, MS, MS/PhD, PhD)
Electrical Engineering and Computer Sciences (MS, MS/PhD, PhD)
Energy Resources (MA, MS, PhD)
Industrial Engineering and Operations Research (MS, MS/PhD, PhD)
Materials Science and Engineering (MS, MEng, MS/PhD, PhD)
Mechanical Engineering (MS, Deng, MEng, MS/PhD, PhD)
Nuclear Engineering (MS, MEng, MS/PhD, MEng/PhD, PhD)
Public Policy (MPP, PhD)
Urban Design (MUD)

Graduate Degrees: Concurrent

Architecture (MArch)/City and Regional Planning (MCP)
City and Regional Planning (MCP)/Civil and Environmental Engineering (MS)
City and Regional Planning (MCP)/Law (JD)
Public Policy (MPP)/Civil and Environmental Engineering (MS)
Public Policy (MPP)/Electrical Engineering and Computer Sciences (MS)

Public Policy (MPP)/Industrial Engineering and Operations Research (MS)

Public Policy (MPP)/Materials Science and Engineering (MS)

Public Policy (MPP)/Mechanical Engineering (MS)

Public Policy (MPP)/Nuclear Engineering (MS)

Graduate Certificates

Engineering for Business and Sustainability
Management of Technology

UNIVERSITY OF MICHIGAN

Ann Arbor, Michigan 48109
734-764-1817
www.umich.edu

 http://bit.ly/collvid14

Undergraduate Degrees

Aerospace Engineering
Architecture
Chemical Engineering
Chemistry
Civil Engineering (major or minor)
Computer Engineering
Earth Sciences (Geological Sciences or Environmental Geosciences concentrations)
Electrical Engineering (major or minor)
Engineering Physics
Materials Science and Engineering
Mechanical Engineering (Energy concentration)
Nuclear Engineering and Radiological Sciences
Public Policy

Environmental Geology (minor)
Geochemistry (minor)

Undergraduate Costs

Academic year 2010–11: $20,583 (residents), $43,861 (nonresidents (tuition, fees, room, board)

Undergraduate Financial Aid

FAFSA and CSS PROFILE® required.

Scholarships: University of Michigan Alumni Clubs throughout the country provide scholarships and awards for students from their communities (amounts vary), based on academic achievement, financial need, and community service; State of Michigan scholarships include Michigan Competitive Scholarship and Robert C. Byrd Honors Scholarship. School, college, and department scholarships are also available: Information at www.finaid.umich.edu/Types_of_Financial_Aid/Scholarships/scholar.asp. For information specific to scholarships for the College of Engineering, go to: http://www.engin.umich.edu/students/scholarships/.

Undergraduate Admissions Requirements

Required: SAT or ACT (with writing)

High school preparation: 4 years English; 3 years mathematics (4 years for engineering); 3 years science (4 years for engineering, including chemistry and physics); 3 years social studies; 2 years same foreign language.

Recommended: 4 years foreign language; 2 years laboratory science; AP, International Baccalaureate, and honors courses.

Undergraduate Application Information

Option: Online application; Early Response; Deferred Entrance

Application fee: $40

Required: Application, high school transcript; high school counselor recommendation; teacher recommendation; two short-answer essay questions; one extended-essay question. Supplemental application required for architecture.

Application deadlines: February 1 (freshmen, transfers); November 1 (Early Response)

Notification: Continuous until April 30 (freshmen, transfers); December 24 (Early Response)

Green Campus Organizations

BLUElab: Student group focusing on engineering solutions to sustainability issues.

Environment Action (EnAct): Student group that organizes the annual Earth Week events, lobbies for environmental responsibility, and provides educational outreach to the campus and community.

Environmental Issues Commission: Commission of the Michigan Student Assembly.

Michigan Students Advocating Recycling: Student group that promotes recycling by utilizing resources on and off campus.

Fast Facts

Nine different University of Michigan schools and colleges work together through the Graham Environmental Sustainability Institute. The Institute is the university's focal point for research, education, and outreach efforts related to environmental sustainability issues.

Researchers at the university's Center for Solar and Thermal Energy Conversion in Complex Materials study complex structure on the nanoscale. Their goal is to "identify key features for their potential use to convert solar energy and heat to electricity."

National energy independence is the ultimate goal of scientists at the Transportation Energy Center. Researchers there are studying everything from synthetic fuels to energy conversion systems.

The Nuclear Engineering and Radiological Sciences Department was ranked number 1 in the country by *U.S. News and World Report* in 2010. The department conducts research in a variety of topics including advanced nuclear power plants, advanced fuel cycles, and nuclear safety applications.

Graduate Degrees

Aerospace Engineering (MSE, MEng, PhD)
Architecture (MArch, MSc, PhD)
Chemical Engineering (MSE, PhD)
Chemistry (PhD)
Civil Engineering (MSE, PhD) (Environmental Sustainability concentration)
Computer Science and Engineering (MS, MSE, PhD)
Construction Engineering and Management (MSE, MEng)
Construction Engineering and Management/ Master of Architecture (dual MSE, dual MEng)
Construction Engineering/Master of Business Administration (dual MSE, dual MEng)
Electrical Engineering (MS, MSE, PhD)
Electrical Engineering: Systems (MS, MSE, PhD)
Engineering Physics (MS, PhD)
Environmental Engineering (MSE, PhD) (Environmental Sustainability concentration)
Geochemistry (MS, PhD)
Geology (MS, PhD)
Materials Science and Engineering (MSE, PhD)
Mechanical Engineering (MSE, PhD)
Nuclear Engineering and Radiological Sciences (MS, PhD)
Public Policy (MPP, MPA, PhD)
Robotics and Autonomous Vehicles (MEng)
Structural Engineering (MEng)
Urban Planning (MUP, PhD)

Graduate Distance Learning

Automotive Engineering (MEng)
Energy Systems Engineering (MEng) (Civil Power, Transportation Power, and Microelectric and Portable Power concentrations)
Emerging Automotive Communications and Control for Leaders (certificate)
Emerging Automotive Technologies Leaders (certificate)

Professional Education Programs

Design and Control of Hybrid Vehicles
EMC Shielding on Hybrid and Electric Vehicles

THE UNIVERSITY OF TENNESSEE (UT KNOXVILLE)

Knoxville, Tennessee 37996
865-974-1000
www.utk.edu

 http://bit.ly/collvid15

About Renewable, Biobased Energy and Fuel Products

The University of Tennessee is one of five land-grant universities selected to join the Sun Grant Initiative, a federally funded program that conducts research on bioenergy and biofuels production. The goal of the program is to reduce the nation's reliance on imported fossil fuels and petroleum-based products. Researchers hope to achieve this by producing feedstock for a bio-based shift in the production of items ranging from fuels and electrical power to cosmetics and pharmaceuticals.

Undergraduate Degrees

Aerospace Engineering (major or minor)
Architecture
Chemical Engineering
Chemistry (major or minor)
Civil Engineering
Computer Engineering
Electrical Engineering
Engineering Physics
Geology (major or minor)
Materials Science and Engineering (major or minor)
Mechanical Engineering (major or minor)
Nuclear Engineering

Plant Sciences (Bioenergy concentration) (major or minor)
Environmental Engineering (minor)
Reliability and Maintainability Engineering (minor)

Undergraduate Costs

Academic year 2010–11: Resident $14,946; nonresident $29,432 (tuition, fees, room and board)

Undergraduate Financial Aid

FAFSA required.

Scholarships: Entering freshmen must complete the Entering Freshman Academic Scholarship Application, which serves as an application for all General University, Honors, Alumni, and Academic College four-year merit/academic scholarships prior to November 1 (priority applicants) or December 1 (regular deadline). Other students must complete the Continuing and Transfer Student Undergraduate Scholarship Application by February 1 (returning students) or April 1 (transfers). For complete information, go to http://finaid.utk.edu/.

Undergraduate Admissions Requirements

Required: ACT or SAT scores.

High school preparation: 4 units English; 2 units algebra; 1 unit geometry, trigonometry, advanced math, or calculus; 2 units natural science, including at least 1 unit of biology, chemistry, or physics; 1 unit American history; 1 unit European history, world history, or world geography; 2 units of the same foreign language; 1 unit of visual or performing arts.

Other relevant factors: Personal statement; extracurricular or leadership activities; special talents or skills; rigor of applicant's curriculum; difficulty of senior-level coursework; recommendations from teachers and counselors (optional).

Undergraduate Application Information

Option: Online (recommended)

Application fee: $30

Required: Application; official high school transcript; official ACT or SAT scores

Application deadlines: December 1 (fall freshmen); June 1 (fall transfers); November 1 (spring freshmen and transfers)

Notification: End of February for students who met December 1 application deadline

Green Campus Organizations

Committee on the Campus Environment: Committee of students, faculty, and staff appointed by the UT Knoxville Chancellor "to advise the administration on institutional policies and behaviors that promote environmental stewardship at the university."

Society of Automotive Engineers UT Biodiesel Project: Student-run pilot plant that creates biodiesel from waste cooking oil collected from campus dining services. Energy created from this model for recycling helps supplement campus energy use.

Students Promoting Environmental Action in Knoxville (SPEAK): Student eco-activists who work to promote sustainable living at UT and in the region, including UT's Clean Energy Initiative, which uses student fees to do everything from the purchase of green power and hybrid cars to increase energy efficiency in campus buildings. Because of SPEAK's efforts, the university is now one of the Southeast's leading purchasers of green energy.

Fast Facts

The UT Knoxville campus has been widely recognized for its efforts toward "green" campus operations. In 2009, the university received the Energy Efficiency Leadership Award at the first annual Summit for Campus Sustainability.

The Make Green Orange campaign is a comprehensive program that promotes and coordinates environmental stewardship activities at the University of Tennessee.

The University of Tennessee's Institute for a Secure and Sustainable Environment (ISSE) is a multidisciplinary foundation that promotes the development of policies, technologies, and educational programs that address pressing environmental issues. For example, in 2009, the ISEE's Center for Clean Products was asked to take the lead in a national green product standard for toys through the Ecologo program.

UT Knoxville was chosen by the U.S. Department of Energy to participate in the 2011 Solar Decathlon. Teams from twenty colleges in the United States, Canada, Belgium, New Zealand, and China were chosen on the basis of competitive applications to create solar homes.

Graduate Degrees

Aerospace Engineering (MS, MS/MBA, PhD)
Architecture (MArch)
Chemical Engineering (MS, PhD)
Chemistry (MS, PhD)
Civil Engineering (MS, MS/MBA, PhD)
Computer Engineering (MS, MS/MBA, PhD)
Electrical Engineering (MS, MS/MBA, PhD)
Engineering Science (MS, MS/MBA, PhD)
Geology (MS, PhD)
Materials Science and Engineering (MS, PhD)
Mechanical Engineering (MS, MS/MBA, PhD)
Nuclear Engineering (MS, MS/MBA, PhD)
Plant Sciences (Bioenergy) (MS, PhD)
Reliability and Maintainability Engineering (MS)

Graduate Certificates

Mechanical Engineering
Nuclear Engineering

Reliability and Maintainability Engineering (also available online)

Graduate Distance Learning

Reliability and Maintainability Engineering (MS)
Nuclear Engineering (MS)

UNIVERSITY OF TULSA (TU)

800 South Tucker Drive
Tulsa, Oklahoma 74104-9700
918-631-2000
www.utulsa.edu/

About North Campus at TU

There is no other research facility in the United States like University of Tulsa's North Campus facility. North Campus contains field-scale petroleum facilities that give students, researchers, private industry, and governments an accurate environment in which to perform experiments and practice new technologies. To learn more, go to http://www.utulsa.edu/research/Centers-Institutes-and-Facilities/North-Campus.aspx.

Undergraduate Degrees

BiogeosciencesBusiness Administration (Energy Management option)
Chemistry
Chemical Engineering (Environmental Engineering, Petroleum Refining options)
Electrical Engineering
Engineering Physics
Environmental Policy
Geology
Geosciences (Geology, Geophysics, Environmental Science options)
Mechanical Engineering
Petroleum Engineering (Chemical Engineering, Geosciences, and Mechanical Engineering options)

Undergraduate Costs

Academic year 2010–11: $37,803 (tuition, fees, room and board)

Undergraduate Financial Aid

FAFSA required.

Undergraduate Admissions Requirements

Required: High school diploma or GED; ACT or SAT scores (writing components are not required) for students aged 25 or younger; high school guidance counselor evaluation form.

High school preparation: 4 units English; 3 units math; 3 units science; 3 units social science; 2 units foreign language; 1 unit computer science.

Recommended: Essay and personal interview highly recommended, as interview is considered in the scholarship evaluation process.

Undergraduate Application Information

Options: Online application; common application accepted

Application fee: $35

Required: Application; high school transcript or GED; SAT or ACT scores

Application deadlines: February 15 (freshmen); semester prior to enrollment (transfers)

Notification: Rolling basis beginning in October

Green Campus Organizations

Challenge X/Hurricane Motor Works: A team of university students competes in the annual Challenge X engineering competition, which is sponsored by General Motors and the U.S. Department of Energy. The goal is to "re-engineer a GM crossover sport utility vehicle to minimize energy consumption, emissions, and greenhouse gases while maintaining or exceeding the vehicle's utility performance." The team is supported by Hurricane Motor Works, the university's hybrid electric vehicle project.

Earth Matters: Students work to foster environmental activism on campus.

Engineers Without Borders: Nonprofit humanitarian organization; partners with developing communities worldwide to implement sustainable engineering projects.

Food Garden: Provides land, tools, and instructions, so students can learn about and grow their own food. The underlying purpose is to spread organic gardening practices and create a more sustainable environment.

Tulsa Energy Management Student Association: Provides opportunities to students in the Energy Management program to learn about the responsibilities of citizenship and service in a changing world.

Fast Facts

University of Tulsa's professors and students have developed a patented process for batteries. The batteries are so small that 240 of them can fit across a human hair. The tiny batteries could increase battery capacity for everything from cell phones to fuel cells used to generate electricity in remote places.

TU produces *Petroleum Abstracts,* the world's leading source of information about published knowledge related to oil and gas exploration, production, transportation, and storage.

The Tulsa Alternative Energy Institute is a multidisciplinary research group established by the Research Office to promote next-generation energy researchers. The Institute is currently divided into two main areas: fuels and biofuels, and devices and fuel cells.

The Integrated Petroleum Environmental Consortium (IPEC) is a joint effort of four major research universities: The University of Tulsa, the University of Oklahoma, Oklahoma State University, and the University of Arkansas. IPEC's mission is to increase the competitiveness of the domestic petroleum industry through a reduction in the costs of compliance with U.S. environmental regulations.

Graduate Degrees

Biochemistry (MS)
Business Administration (JD/MSBA)
Chemical Engineering (ME, MSE, PhD)
Chemistry (MS, PhD)
Electrical Engineering (ME, MSE)
Engineering Physics (MS)
Geosciences (MS, PhD, JD/MS)
Mechanical Engineering (ME, MSE, PhD)
Petroleum Engineering (ME, MSE, PhD

Graduate Certificates

Resources, Energy, and Environmental Law

UNIVERSITY OF WASHINGTON (UW)

Seattle, Washington 98195
206-543-2100
E-mail: www.washington.edu/home/siteinfo/form
www.washington.edu

Undergraduate Degrees

Aeronautics and Astronautics
Architecture
Chemical Engineering
Construction Management
Electrical Engineering
Industrial and Systems Engineering
Materials Science and Engineering
Urban Design and Planning

Undergraduate Costs

Academic year 2009–10: Residents $17,676; Nonresidents $34,351 (tuition, fees, room and board)

Undergraduate Financial Aid

FAFSA required.

Scholarships: UW Undergraduate Academic Excellence Awards (4-year tuition waiver awards of $3,000 per year) for 50 incoming freshmen who are state residents and demonstrate financial need. Each school or department also maintains its own scholarship list; check www.washington.edu/students/osfa/ugaid/scholarship.html.

Undergraduate Admissions Requirements

Required: SAT or ACT with Writing Test.

High school preparation: 4 years English, 3 years mathematics (including algebra I and II and geometry), 3 years social sciences, 2 years same foreign language, 2 years science (at least one full year of biology, chemistry, or physics), 0.5 year arts, 0.5 year electives.

Undergraduate Application Information

Options: Online application, early admission

Application fee: $50

Required: Application, personal statement, and short-response essays. High school transcripts are only required for application in special situations outlined on the admissions Web site (admit.washington.edu/Apply/Freshman/Transcripts)

Optional: Additional comments regarding information not covered in the application

Application deadline: January 15 (fall freshmen), Sept. 15 (winter freshmen and transfers), December 15 (spring freshmen and transfers), February 15 (fall transfers)

Notification: December 1 to April 15 (fall freshmen), November to December (winter freshmen and transfers), February to March (spring freshmen and transfers), June to July (fall transfers)

Green Campus Organizations

Earth Club, UW Chapter: Sponsors projects that promote environmental stewardship on campus and in the community.

Go Green: Educates the Greek community on environmental sustainability and focuses on water and energy conservation.

Green Coalition: Aims to increase environmental stewardship on campus by effecting collaboration among campus organizations committed to protecting the environment.

GreenLaw: UW's environmental law society is devoted to education, advocacy, community outreach, outdoor recreation, and other programming related to environmental law.

Students Expressing Environmental Dedication (SEED): Encourages environmentally sound practices in residence halls and raises awareness of environmental issues affecting campus residents.

Urban Farmers UW Chapter: Promotes sustainability on campus and supports urban agriculture.

Fast Facts

The University of Washington is a signatory of the American College & University Presidents' Climate Commitment; as part of this commitment, all new campus buildings must meet at least the LEED Silver standard.

The school is a founding member of the Seattle Climate Partnership, which requires that it purchase 100 percent renewable power and enact extensive energy-conservation measures. It was named Number 2 (with an A+ grade) in *Sierra*

Magazine's third annual "Cool Schools" list for 2009.

Undergraduates in the Departments of Chemical Engineering, Electrical Engineering, and Mechanical Engineering are conducting research on proton exchange membrane (PEM) fuel cells.

The University of Washington's Center for Biofuels is conducting research on ways to convert the state's mixed biomass sources into transportation fuels and is seeking federal support to enlarge its efforts.

UW's Center for Innovation and Entrepreneurship sponsored an Environmental Innovation Challenge in 2010 that engaged nineteen teams from seven Washington State universities in a competition to find solutions to our current energy problems. The solutions had to be eco-friendly. The prototypes and business plans were judged by 130 representatives of local green-interested companies.

Graduate Degrees

Aeronautics and Astronautics Engineering (MS)
Architecture (MArch, MS)
Built Environments (Sustainable Systems and
     Prototypes) (PhD)
Civil Engineering (Transportation Engineering)
     (MS, MSCE, MSE, PhD)
Construction Management (MS)
Electrical Engineering (PMP)
Materials Science and Engineering (five-year BS/
     MS, MS, PhD)
Mechanical Engineering (MSE, MSME, PhD)
Urban Design and Planning (PhD)
Urban Planning (MUP)

Graduate Certificates (classroom)

Low-Impact Development
Paralegal Studies
Smart Grid Technologies

Graduate Distance Learning

Construction Management (MS)
Industrial and Systems Engineering (PMP-ISE)
Mechanical Engineering (MSME)

Graduate Distance Learning Certificates

Construction Management
Paralegal Studies
Public Relations
Sustainable Transportation
Urban Green Infrastructure

WASHINGTON STATE UNIVERSITY (WSU)

Pullman, Washington 99164
509-335-3564
E-mail: about.wsu.edu/contact
www.wsu.edu

http://bit.ly/collvid16

Undergraduate Degrees

Architecture
Chemical Engineering (Fuel Processing)
Chemistry (Environmental Chemistry) (major or
     minor)
Civil Engineering (Geotechnical and
     Transportation Engineering, Infrastructure
     Engineering)
Electrical Engineering
Materials Science and Engineering (major or
     minor)
Mechanical Engineering (major or minor)
Nanotechnology (minor)

Undergraduate Distance Learning

A variety of courses that apply to the degrees listed above are offered online. See the Center for

Distance and Professional Education Web page: online.wsu.edu/future_students.

Undergraduate Costs

Academic year 2010–11: $19,154 residents, $30,196 nonresidents (tuition, fees, double room, and board dining level 1).

Undergraduate Financial Aid

FAFSA required.

Scholarship opportunities include University Achievement Award, Cougar Academic Award/ Western Undergraduate Exchange (WUE), Washington State University Alumni Association Scholarships. Each college, department, and academic program also maintains its own scholarship list. See the scholarship Web page for information: futurestudents.wsu.edu/scholarships/process.aspx.

Undergraduate Admissions Requirements

Required: SAT or ACT.

High school preparation: 4 years English, 3 years mathematics (1 year each algebra I and II and geometry), 2 years science (including 1 year biology, chemistry, or physics), 2 years same foreign language, 3 years social studies, 1 year arts. Beginning in 2010, 2 years algebra-based biology, chemistry, or physics will be required.

Undergraduate Application Information

Options: Online application

Application fee: $50

Required: Application, high school transcript, personal statement

Optional: Letters of recommendation

Application deadline: January 31 (priority application date)

Notification: Continuous

Green Campus Organizations

Environmental Science Club: Supports university sustainability program and promotes environmental education and awareness.

Environmental Task Force: Supports the university sustainability programs and sponsors environmental awareness activities and education.

"Green Living Guide": Created by students to help fellow students be green; covers recycling on and off campus, where to find green spaces in Pullman, and tips for saving water, electricity, and other energy resources.

The One Thing Challenge: Invites students to make a personal commitment to change one aspect of their normal routines to become more environmentally friendly. Competes for highest number of campus participants against the University of Washington in five categories (transportation, recycling/composting, sustainability, daily life, consumption); winner receives One Thing Cup made of recycled material.

Solar Splash at WSU: Sponsored by the IEEE Power Electronics Society, Solar Splash invites participating schools to compete in the World Championship of Intercollegiate Solar Boating, in which each school designs and builds a solar-powered boat to compete in three events. The goal is to showcase the interdisciplinary work of undergraduate and graduate students in electrical and mechanical engineering in a sustainable way.

Sustainable Agriculture Club: Works to improve sustainability of the university and community through interdisciplinary interactions, educational opportunities, and activities.

Fast Facts

The newest residence hall on campus, which was opened in 2009 and houses 230 students, was designed to meet LEED Silver rating requirements. Its green features include natural lighting, geothermal cooling and heating, and certified wood and recycled or regional construction materials.

The WSU Energy Program is a department within the university's Extension Service that provides energy services, products, education, and information to a wide range of consumers. Its projects have included working with the Washington State legislature to put together a package of solar, wind, and economic incentives for businesses and working with the U.S. Department of Energy's Building America Program to design or evaluate hundreds of energy-efficient home constructions in the region. It also manages the Northwest Combined Heat and Power (CHP) Application Center to assist district energy projects to be more efficient.

The Washington State Transportation Research Center is a collaborative effort among WSU, the University of Washington, and the state Department of Transportation to conduct research on transportation issues like vehicle design and operation, transportation planning, and freight travel.

The Power Systems Engineering Research Center conducts studies on the "future electric energy system." Current projects include research on power system model estimation and verification, advanced computer applications for the power systems, and power system operation and control.

In 2010, Washington State received $2.5 million from the American Recovery and Reinvestment Act funding to develop a comprehensive undergraduate and graduate program for degrees and certificates in clean energy and smart-grid engineering. The courses are a prototype for online delivery of the information. WSU will provide the other half of the funding for the program.

Graduate Degrees

Architecture (MS)
Chemical Engineering (MS, PhD)
Civil Engineering (Geotechnical and
    Transportation Engineering) (MS, PhD)
Electrical Engineering (Electric Power Systems)
    (MS, PhD)
Environmental Science (Planning and
    Environmental Policy, Land-Use Planning)
    (MS, PhD)
Mechanical Engineering (MS, PhD)

Graduate Certificates

Engineering Nanotechnology

WEST VIRGINIA UNIVERSITY (WVU)

P.O. Box 6009
Morgantown, West Virginia 26506-6009
304-293-2121
E-mail: go2wvu.@mail.wvu.edu
www.wvu.edu

 http://bit.ly/collvid17

About NAFTC

West Virginia University hosts the National Alternative Fuels Training Consortium (NAFTC), which is the only nationwide alternative-fuel vehicle and advanced-technology vehicle training organization. It promotes programs and activities to reduce the nation's use of petroleum and to create energy independence and the greater use of cleaner transportation. The consortium includes a variety of partners, including colleges and universities, fuel providers, equipment and parts manufacturers, federal and state agencies, and professional, educational, and training associations. The partners operate a network of training centers across the country that has trained technicians from hundreds of companies, academic institutions, and government agencies in the use, maintenance, and service of alternative fuel vehicles.

Undergraduate Degrees

Aerospace Engineering
Civil Engineering (Structural Engineering, Transportation Systems)
Electrical Engineering (Power Systems)
Geology
Industrial and Management Systems Engineering
Mechanical Engineering
Mining Engineering
Petroleum and Natural Gas Engineering

Geology (minor)
Public Relations (minor)

Undergraduate Distance Learning

Public Relations

Undergraduate Costs

Academic year 2009–10 (estimate): In-state $15,792 resident, out-of-state $26,890 nonresident (tuition, fees, room and board, books, supplies, and miscellaneous expenses)

Undergraduate Financial Aid

FAFSA required.

Grants, scholarships, loans, and campus employment are available. Visit www.finaid.wvu.edu.

Undergraduate Admissions Requirements

Required: High school diploma or GED. GPA of 2.0 (nonresidents 2.5); SAT 960 (critical reading and math) or ACT 19 (nonresidents SAT 990 or ACT 21).

High school preparation: 4 units of English; 4 units of math including algebra I and II and plane geometry; 3 units of social studies including U.S. history; 3 units of lab science; 2 units of same foreign language; 1 unit of fine are. There are additional requirements for specific schools, colleges, or programs. See http://wvu.edu/freshman/university_admissions_requirements.

Undergraduate Application Information

Options: Online or paper mailed in

Application fee: $25 resident; $45 nonresident

Required: Application, high school transcript or GED standard score 45 or above; any college or university transcripts, SAT or ACT scores (writing test not required)

Application deadline: January 1 for fall

Notification: Rolling beginning September 15

Green Campus Organizations

Sustainability Committee: Collaboration of faculty, students, and administration to develop sustainability policies for the university including construction and renovation of buildings.

WECAN (WVU Environmental Conservation Awareness Now): Subcommittee of the Sustainability Committee. Poster competition for middle and high school students on sustainability.

Transportation and Parking Advisory Committee: Recommends policy administration; launched WE GO! campaign to encourage car- and vanpooling, walking, and bicycle programs.

Mountaineers Recycle: Student recycling program, including textbooks and clothing.

Fast Facts

Among the research foci of the Advanced Power and Electricity Research Center is investigating controls to ensure reliability and availability for large-scale systems such as the transmission grid.

The Center of Alternative Fuels, Engines, and Emissions in the Department of Mechanical and Aerospace Engineering conducts research on reducing exhaust emissions and the consumption of petroleum-based fuels. The program focuses on heavy-duty trucks, buses, locomotives, and ships because improvements to these vehicles have been slower to come to market.

The Coal and Energy Research Bureau investigates ways to develop new, safer, and more economical ways to mine, transport, and use coal in light of the environmental issues that coal mining can create. The bureau also researches other energy fuels and allied minerals.

The multidisciplinary and multidepartmental National Institute of Fuel-Cell Technology (NIFT) works cooperatively with the U.S. Department of Energy, including its National Energy Technology Laboratory. The NIFT conducts research on how fuel cells can become an affordable, efficient, clean source of energy. The center's researchers use nanotechnology to develop and fabricate materials for advanced coal-based fuel cells among other advanced technologies and research projects.

WVU's sustainability efforts include converting all dining halls to trayless facilities and using plates made from potatoes, hot cups made from paper and sugarcane, and cold cups made from plant resins.

Graduate Degrees

Civil Engineering (MSCE, PhD)
Geology (MS, PhD)
Industrial and Management Systems Engineering (MS), PhD)
Mechanical and Aerospace Engineering (MAE, PhD)
Mechanical Engineering (MSME, PhD)
Mining Engineering (MS, PhD)
Petroleum and Natural Gas Engineering (MS, PhD)

About Your Old Tech Equipment

Check your campus for a recycling drop-off location. Many local communities also run drop-off locations for recycling used computers, printers, DVD players, and similar equipment. Staples and Best Buy will take most electronics for free, but charge $10 for computers. For information on why responsible recycling of toxic wastes is important, check www.ban.org.

RecycleMania

RecycleMania began in 2001 with a competition between Miami University of Ohio and Ohio University to see which school could recycle the most campus waste. By 2010, the ten-week competition had grown to 607 schools, more than 5 million students and 1.3 million staff and faculty members, and eight categories of awards. Participating colleges and universities in 49 states, the District of Columbia, Canada, and Qatar recycled or composted 84 million pounds of waste in 2010. RecycleMania is a joint project of the RecycleMania Steering Committee of the College and University Recycling Coalition, Keep America Beautiful, and the U.S. Environmental Protection Agency's WasteWise program.

The following list names the 2010 participating schools profiled in this chapter:

Arizona State University
Carnegie Mellon University
Clemson University
Drexel University
Ferris State University
Massachusetts Institute of Technology
Oregon Institute of Technology
Portland State University
Purdue University
Rutgers, The State University of New Jersey*
Stanford University**
Texas A&M University
University of California, Berkeley
University of Michigan***
University of Tennessee
University of Tulsa
Washington State University

Won the "Gorilla Prize" in four consecutive years (2007–2010) for the greatest overall tonnage recycled; third place in Targeted Material—Corrugated Cardboard; fifth place in Targeted Materials—Bottles and Cans

**Second place in Gorilla Prize*

***Fifth place in Gorilla Prize*

Top 10 Green Tips for Campus Life

1. **Don't buy anything in polystyrene.** This includes coffee and take-out food. Americans fuel their caffeine habits with 25 million polystyrene cups a year, and almost all of them end up in landfills, where they will sit for centuries without decomposing. Buy a metal mug that can be reused.

2. **Skip soda in cans and fancy water in plastic bottles.** First, buy a couple of refillable plastic-free bottles. Then mix 2 parts tap water to 1 part juice for flavored water, or 2 parts mineral water to 1 part juice as a replacement for soda.

3. **Recycle pizza boxes.** You can't recycle the bottom of boxes if they are greasy or food stained, but you can recycle the tops and sides if they haven't come in contact with the pizza. So tear off the bottom, toss it in the trash, and recycle the rest.

4. **Shut down your electronic equipment.** You probably already turn off the lights when you leave a room, but you can do more to save energy. Don't turn on the screen saver on your computer; put your computer in sleep mode when you are going to be gone for a while. Screen savers use more energy. Unplug your cell phone charger and your MP3 player when you're not using them. Anything that charges batteries or has an LCD light uses power even when it's not "on."

5. **Cut down on paper use.** Read your e-mails online and file them online or on your computer. When you need to print a document, use both sides of the paper. If you receive documents that are printed on one side only, use the blank side for scratch paper. If only half of a sheet is blank, fold the page in half, and use the blank part for scratch paper.

6. **Rethink your snacks.** Skip the chips and buy organically produced, locally grown fruits and vegetables. When you have ice cream to go, ask for a cone, not a plastic spoon and a cup—polystyrene or paper.

7. **Buy recycled products.** All kinds of things like toilet paper, umbrellas, and plates are now made from post-consumer waste. Look for labels that indicate recycled materials.

8. **Buy Fair Trade tea and coffee.** Look for the U.S. Fair Trade label on packages of coffee and tea. Ask where you buy cups of coffee or tea if it's Fair Trade. If it's not, lobby to get Fair Trade beverages.

9. **Join a green organization.** Join one of your campus's green organizations and support its efforts to make your campus sustainable. Join a national or international organization and spread the word to the larger community.

10. **RECYCLE. REUSE. REDUCE. RETHINK.**
    - Separate your trash. Toss recyclables into recycle bins on campus.
    - Buy ceramic mugs and dishes, glass drinking glasses, and metal cutlery for in-room eating.
    - Reduce the amount of plastic you use by taking your own reusable cloth bags when you shop. Look for dorm room furniture like a chair or a lamp at used-furniture stores.

CHAPTER 6

25 TWO-YEAR SCHOOLS WITH GREAT GREEN PROGRAMS

The twenty-five community colleges in this chapter were chosen to represent a cross-section of types of programs, areas of the country, settings, and innovative curricula. All of the colleges have their own campus sustainability programs, and many have green student organizations that sponsor a variety of educational and community service projects. Some of the colleges offer online courses, and some also have research facilities or energy demonstration projects that involve students as part of their course work.

If you are interested in retraining for the new economy, degree and certificate programs at local community colleges are a good way to learn new skills. Community colleges welcome older students and career-changers.

Keep in mind that this is a list of highlights; other community and junior colleges not listed here also offer programs related to careers in energy-related fields. Check out *Peterson's Two-Year Colleges* and check the "Majors" index to find other schools offering any of the majors listed in this chapter.

ABOUT THE LISTINGS

Here's what you need to know to navigate the two-year college profiles.

Contact Information

The first paragraph of each school profile lists the school name, address, phone number, e-mail address, and Web site.

Degrees and Certificates

This section includes associate degrees as well as certificates and diplomas offered in programs that are related to energy, such as Fuel Cell Technician. Some degrees allow a student to concentrate in a particular aspect of a science, such as a Photovoltaic Technology concentration in the Environmental Technology associate degree at Cape Cod Community College.

Costs

Costs are quoted for the most recent period available. In most cases, both full-time and credit hour costs are given, as are in-state and out-of-state residency costs.

Financial Aid

All schools offering financial aid require that FAFSA forms be filled out. Usually, these forms can be found online. Any other requirements or special financial aid are detailed.

Admission Requirements

Most schools require a high school diploma or GED. Any specific testing and/or requirements are detailed.

Application Information

Most schools have online applications for admission. Fees for applications are noted.

Distance Learning

A number of two-year schools offer courses online, some of which may meet requirements of the degrees listed in this guide.

Green Campus Organizations

This section gives a sampling of green activities that students may participate in. The schools included in this guide have a variety of sustainability efforts and, thus, a variety of ways students may become involved and take leadership roles. This section also lists campus groups focused on energy issues and projects and students' future career fields.

Fast Facts

The Fast Facts section gives an insight into the school's commitment to sustainability and the environment.

Schools Profiled Here

The following two-year colleges are profiled in this chapter:
- Cape Cod Community College
- Crowder College
- Edmonds Community College
- Great Basin College
- Greenfield Community College
- Houston Community College
- Hudson Valley Community College

- Iowa Lakes Community College
- Kalamazoo Valley Community College
- Kankakee Community College
- Lakeshore Technical College
- Lanc Community College
- Lansing Community College
- Long Beach City College
- Los Angeles Trade-Technical College
- Macomb Community College
- Mercer County Community College
- Mesalands Community College
- Midlands Technical College
- Mount Wachusett Community College
- Red Rocks Community College
- Santa Fe Community College
- St. Petersburg College
- Tulsa Community College
- Wake Technical Community College

CAPE COD COMMUNITY COLLEGE (CCCC)

2240 Iyannough Road
West Barnstable, Massachusetts 02668
877-846-3672 (toll-free)
E-mail: info@capecod.edu
www.capecod.edu

Degrees and Certificates

Associate Degrees:
Environmental Studies (A.A.)
Environmental Technology (A.S.)

Certificates:

The Environmental Technology certificates are a collaborative partnership among CCCC, Massachusetts Maritime Academy, and University of Massachusetts Dartmouth. Students may need to travel to each of the institutions in order to complete all the courses in any of the following certificate programs:

Environmental Site Assessment
Geographic Information Systems
Photovoltaic Technology
Small Wind Technology
Solar Thermal Technology

Costs

(Academic year 2009–10) Full-time tuition and fees per year: $4320 for Massachusetts residents; $10,500 for nonresidents.Part-time tuition and fees: $144 per credit hour for Massachusetts residents; $350 for nonresidents.

Financial Aid

Financial aid consists of scholarships, grants, loans, and employment opportunities to help students who lack sufficient financial resources to attend college. This aid is considered as a supplement to the contributions made by the student and family. Any student receiving financial aid must abide by the Satisfactory Academic Progress Policy as defined by College policy and stated in the Student Handbook.

Admissions Requirements

A high school diploma, GED, or passing grade on an "Ability to Benefit" test is required of applicants regardless of age or previous college experience. Students who graduated from a Massachusetts public high school after 2003 must have successfully completed all MCAS requirements.

Application Information

Options: Online application form or request for application via e-mail or phone; completed applications must be returned via fax or mail.

Application fee: None

Required: Transcript of any prior postsecondary course work; high school transcript or GED certificate required, if either have not yet been attained at time of application.

Application deadline: Applications reviewed on a rolling admissions basis until seats are filled; priority to candidates who apply by August 15 for fall semester and January 10 for spring semester.

Distance Learning

Some courses are available as e-courses. Class lectures are accessed via the Web; assignments are submitted by fax, mail, or over the Internet; and testing is scheduled on a flexible basis. Some materials for online courses or online components may be available from the Web via the college's Learning Management System. For more information, contact the Office of Distance Learning at 508-362-2131 Ext. 4040.

Green Campus Organizations

CCCC is a signatory of the American College & University Presidents' Climate Commitment (ACUPCC) and is actively planning ways to reduce the campus's carbon footprint under this initiative.

Students for Sustainability: Promotes awareness among students, faculty and staff members, and the Cape Cod community about sustainability issues; it encourages community involvement.

Fast Facts

The Lorusso Applied Technology Center, completed in 2006, was the first state-owned building in Massachusetts to receive Gold LEED certification. This "green" building uses alternative energy sources, such as solar panels; was built with recycled materials; was designed for water conservation; and has low-impact and environmentally appropriate landscaping.

Cape Cod Community College's Wilkens Library is powered by a 200-kilowatt fuel cell.

About Being Car-Less

Need a car for a couple of hours? Try Zipcar, the car-sharing company. More than 100 campuses now have Zipcars. You can rent a car for a couple of hours or a day. Check out www.zipcar.com.

CROWDER COLLEGE

601 Laclede
Neosho, Missouri 64850
417-451-3223
E-mail: admissions@crowder.edu
www.crowder.edu

Degrees and Certificates

Associate Degrees:
Alternative Energy: Biofuels (A.A. and A.A.S.)
Alternative Energy: Solar (A.A. and A.A.S.)
Alternative Energy: Wind (A.A. and A.A.S.)
Environmental Science (A.A.)
Pre-Engineering, Alternative Energy Option
   (A.S.)

Certificates:
Active Solar Technician
Biodiesel Technician
Bioethanol Fuel Technician
Biofuels Technician
Biogas Technician
Wind Energy Technician

Costs

(Academic year 2009–10) In-district resident: $68 per credit hour; in-state resident: $95 per credit hour; nonstate resident: $123 per credit hour.

Technology/facility use fee: $12 per credit hour; distance learning fee: $7 per credit hour.

Financial Aid

FAFSA required (www.fafsa.gov). Students are eligible for federal financial aid programs, work-study grants, and various scholarship programs. If a student has been designated an A+ student by his/her high school, the state of Missouri will pay tuition and common student fees at Crowder.

Crowder Connection Scholarship: Qualifying students who are residents of Kansas, Oklahoma, and Arkansas are granted the privilege of enrolling at in-state tuition rates. Initially, the total number of grantees is limited to 100.

Admission Requirements

Required: High school diploma or GED

Application Information

Options: Online application

Application fee: $25

Required: High school transcript or GED scores, placement exam (ACT or COMPASS)

Notification: Continuous

Distance Learning

Courses available online are indicated in the course catalog. Online courses are available through the Blackboard e-education platform.

Green Campus Organization

Solar Vehicle Club: Annual Solar Challenge solar car and bike races.

Fast Facts

In 1984, Crowder students designed and built the first solar-powered vehicle to successfully complete a coast-to-coast journey across the United States. They continue to organize the biannual

North American Solar Challenge solar car race and bike race.

Crowder's Solar House entry in the Solar Decathlon in Washington, D.C., in 2009 was selected as the "People's Choice" and placed sixth overall in the competition. Students used their solar trailer to power the tools used during the build process on the Mall.

Since 2006, Crowder has been the host of the annual E-conference that features local, regional, and national experts in the fields of energy, efficiency, and the environment. The mission of the E-conference is to provide a forum for discussing new energy sources, energy efficiency, and environmentally sound practices to create economic opportunity and a sustainable future for the region.

The Missouri Alternative and Renewable Energy Technology Center (MARET) was established at Crowder in 1992 by the Missouri state legislature. The mission of the MARET Center is to expand renewable energy throughout the state with education, applied research, and economic development.

Crowder's soccer field has been equipped with solar power to run the scoreboard and sprinkler system.

About Electricity Usage

The U.S. Department of Energy (DOE) estimates that buildings use nearly three-fourths of the electricity generated annually in the nation. Efficient design, energy-saving appliances, and clean, renewable energy sources are strategies that can help reduce this figure.

EDMONDS COMMUNITY COLLEGE

20000 68th Ave West
Lynnwood, Washington 98036
425-640-1459
E-mail: info@edcc.edu
www.edcc.edu

Degrees and Certificates

Associate Degrees:
Environmental Science (A.S.)
Energy Management (A.T.A.)
Materials Science Technology (A.A.S.-T)
Paralegal (A.T.A.)

Certificates:
Advanced Paralegal
Building Inspection Certificate
Civil Construction Management and Inspection
Commercial Lighting Auditor
Energy Accounting Specialist
Energy Efficiency Technician
Material Science Technology
Residential Energy Auditor

Costs

(Academic year 2009–10) State residents: $80.60 per credit hour; nonresidents: $252.60 per credit hour. Eligible veterans, National Guard, and dependents: $50.45 per credit hour.

Financial Aid

FAFSA required. Award offers attempt to meet financial need with 45 percent "gift" aid (grants, waivers, scholarships), and 55 percent "self-help" aid (work/study and loans). Funds are limited and awarded to eligible students based on date financial aid paperwork is completed. May 1 for early priority consideration for all terms and August 15 for secondary consideration for fall quarter.

Admission Requirements

Required: High school diploma, GED certificate, or qualifying under "ability to benefit"

Application Information

Options: Online application

Application fee: $28.00

Required: ACCUPLACER assessment test (can be taken online); meeting with academic adviser

Application deadline: Rolling

Notification: Continuous

Distance Learning

A number of courses and even complete degree and certificate programs are offered either online or as a hybrid, that is, part on campus and part online. Contact the Distance Learning Office by e-mail at its@edcc.edu or by phone at 425-640-1098.

Green Campus Organizations

The Energy Management Group: Enhances the energy management program by expanding available resources through mentorships, tutoring, networking, and extracurricular activities.

The Learn-and-Serve Environmental Anthropology Field (LEAF) School: Provides an opportunity for students to earn academic credit and an AmeriCorps scholarship while working collaboratively with local tribes, governments, nonprofits, and businesses to help make fishing, farming, and forestry more sustainable. Financial aid for this program is available through AmeriCorps awards (www. americorps.org) or from the Edmonds Community College Foundation (http://foundation.edcc.edu).

Peace and Justice Club: Raises awareness and promotes dialogue around issues of sustainability.

S.A.V.E. the Earth Club (Student Association for a Viable Environment): Participates in community and save-the-earth projects.

Sustainability Council: Composed of faculty members, administrators, staff members, and students. It is a major component of the college's sustainability initiative.

Recycling Program: Headed by grounds department with student assistance.

Fast Facts

Edmonds Community College is a participant in a grant to help train workers as part of a new State Energy Sector Partnership and Training grant. Through the project, more than 4,700 Washington State workers will be trained for jobs in the growing clean energy economy.

The Campus Tree Walk was developed with a Community Forestry Assistance Grant provided by the Washington State Department of Natural Resources, with support from the U.S. Department of Agriculture Forest Service. Over seventy species of trees have been identified on the College's 50-acre campus, and the horticulture department has developed a map to help students and community members learn about and understand how trees benefit the environment and improve the quality of life.

GREAT BASIN COLLEGE (GBC)

1500 College Parkway
Elko, Nevada 89801
775-738-8493
www.gbcnv.edu

Degrees and Certificates

Associate Degrees:
Electrical Systems Technology (A.A.S.)
Diesel Technology (A.A.S.)
Industrial Energy Efficiency (A.A.S.—available
    through distance learning)
Industrial Millwright Technology (A.A.S.)
Welding Technology (A.A.S.)

Bachelor's Degrees:

GBC also grants a limited number of Bachelor of Applied Science (B.A.S.) degrees. Those degree programs related to "green industries" include a B.A.S. in Land Surveying/Geomatics. In addition, a Bachelor of Arts in Integrative Studies (B.A.I.S.) degree in social science and resource management is also offered.

Certificates:
Diesel Technology
Electrical Systems Technology
Industrial Millwright Technology
Instrumentation Technology
Welding Technology

Costs

(Spring 2010) Nevada residents: $63 per lower-division credit; Western Undergraduate Exchange (WUE) residents: $93 per lower-division credit; Good Neighbor residents: $99 per lower-division credit; nonresidents: $129.00 per lower-division credit.

Financial Aid

FAFSA required (www.fafsa.gov).

Graduating Nevada high school students may be eligible for a Millennium Scholarship. Students in career/technical education (CTE) programs may be eligible for an MTC Scholarship. Many other scholarships and other forms of financial aid are available.

Admission Requirements

Required: Qualifying scores on the ACT or SAT, or qualifying scores on a GBC-administered Accuplacer test, or successful completion of developmental courses; student orientation course.

Application Information

Options: Online application

Application fee: $10.00

Required: Placement testing, student orientation course

Application deadline: Rolling

Notification: Continuous

Distance Learning

Great Basin College offers many "distance" education courses for those who are unable to enroll in traditional face-to-face classes. Some are offered as Internet courses on the college's WebCampus; some are Internet "enhanced," with the Internet used to exchange or submit assignments, take tests, or communicate with the instructor or other students; some are offered as LiveNet classes, a special type of Internet class that meets online at specific times; and there are the Interactive Video Courses that originate in one facility and are broadcast to one or more other locations simultaneously.

Green Campus Organization

Electrical Systems Technology Program: Constructed an electric car that is solar-power rechargeable. (http://www2.gbcnv.edu/programs/AAS-EL.html)

Fast Facts

The new A.A.S. degree program in Industrial Energy Efficiency is a distance learning program and combines courses from existing HVAC, construction technology, electrical systems, and millwright technology programs.

GREENFIELD COMMUNITY COLLEGE (GCC)

One College Drive
Greenfield, Massachusetts 01301-9739
413-775-1000
E-mail: admission@gcc.mass.edu
www.gcc.mass.edu

Degrees and Certificates

Associate Degree:
Renewable Energy/Energy Efficiency (A.A.)

Certificate:
Renewable Energy/Energy Efficiency

Costs

(Spring 2010) In-state: $26 per credit hour; out-of-state $281 per credit hour plus a college service fee of $130.50 per credit hour. Students from other New England states who qualify for the Regional Student Program of the New England Board of Higher Education (NEHBE) currently pay 150 percent of the Massachusetts resident tuition, $39 per credit hour.

Financial Aid

FAFSA is required. The Financial Aid Office has an online site with links to all types of financial aid available, as well as a link to complete the FAFSA online, www.gcc.mass.edu/financial_aid/.

Admission Requirements

Greenfield Community College maintains a policy of open admission for all but a few of its degree and certificate programs. Under this policy, students who have earned a high school diploma or its equivalent, or earned a General Education Diploma (GED), or scored satisfactorily on a federally approved Ability-to-Benefit test, or completed an approved home-schooling plan may matriculate into a degree or certificate program.

Application Information

Option: Online application

Fee: $10 for Massachusetts residents, $35 for others

Required: Immunization documentation

Distance Learning

GCC offers both fully online and hybrid courses. A fully online course generally offers 80 to 100 percent of its instruction online. A hybrid course generally offers 50 to 79 percent of its instruction online, reducing, but not eliminating, some of the face-to-face classroom time. Online courses are offered through the Blackboard system.

Green Campus Organization

Green Campus Committee: Advises and establishes policy on issues related to the investigation and advocacy for and implementation of a green GCC campus. Monthly Green Tips are published online to help make the campus more environmentally friendly.

Fast Facts

GCC has two sets of solar panels on campus that make up their solar array. Panel 1 is fixed, and Panel 2 is a tracking panel that rotates to follow the movement of the sun.

Greenfield is part of the American College & University President's Climate Commitment.

Greenfield is under contract with the U.S. Fish and Wildlife Service and the owners of the Holyoke Dam, the Turner Falls Dam, and Cabot Station Hydroelectric Facility to mark, trap, and count anadromous and catadromous fish on the Connecticut River. The studies and work is essential to ensuring the success of migratory fish passage and the revival of populations on the Connecticut River. For GCC students, the project represents an opportunity for hands-on and paid work experience in an exciting environmental program.

Management of the GCC College Store committed to the campuswide effort to reduce, reuse, and conserve natural resources by buying locally or purchasing from earth-friendly manufacturers whenever possible. In 2009, the store's buyers informed manufacturers and their sales representatives that the store would only consider new merchandise if it contained some recycled content or if the company had made other eco-friendly choices. As a result, most of the items for sale now contain recycled content.

HOUSTON COMMUNITY COLLEGE (HCC)

3100 Main Street
Houston, Texas 77002
713-718-2000
E-mail: admissions@hccs.edu
http://www.hccs.edu/portal/site/hccs

Degrees and Certificates

Associate Degrees:
Biotechnology (A.A.S.)
Chemical Engineering Technology (A.A.S.)
Chemical Laboratory Technology (A.A.S.)
Drafting and Design Engineering Technology (A.A.S.)
Instrumentation and Controls Engineering Technology with Fuel Cells Specialization (A.A.S.)
Manufacturing Engineering Technology (A.A.S.)
Petroleum Engineering Technology (A.A.S.)
Process Technology (A.A.S.)

Certificates:
Biotechnology
Chemical Laboratory Technology
Heating, Air Conditioning and Refrigeration Mechanic
Heating, Air Conditioning and Refrigeration Commercial Technician: Commercial Air Conditioning
Heating, Air Conditioning and Refrigeration Technician/Installer: Residential Air Conditioning Systems Design
Manufacturing Engineering Technology
Manufacturing Processes
Petroleum Engineering Technology
Process Technology–Process Operator

Costs

(Academic year 2009–10) In-district, full-time: $645; out-of-district full-time: $1293; in-district $87.50 per semester hour; out-of-district $141.50 per semester hour; out-of-state $300.50 per semester hour.

Financial Aid

FAFSA is required (www.fafsa.gov). Various scholarships, loans, work-study and other financial assistance options are available. Contact the Financial Aid Office, www.hccs.edu/hccs/future-students, or eServices, www.hccs.edy/hccs/future-students/financial-aid-eservices/loans-by-web for information.

Admission Requirements

HCC has an open-door admissions policy for individuals meeting at least one of the following qualifications: diploma from accredited high school;

GED certificate; college-level hours earned at other accredited colleges; international students who meet college and state requirements.

Application Information

Options: Online or at an Admissions Center; or the Texas Common Application for two-year schools at: www.applytexas.org. Those using this option should allow extra processing time before registering.

Required: Transcripts to determine placement

Application deadline: Rolling

Notification: Continuous

Distance Learning

Distance Education credit courses are semester-long courses in the following lengths:

16-week regular term
12-week second-start during the fall and spring
    semesters
10-week summer
8-week fall, spring and summer
5-week summer I & II

These courses are equivalent to on-campus courses and typically earn 3 semester hours of credit. No distinction between distance education and on-campus courses is made on the college transcript. Students should consult an HCC counselor for more details on transferability of courses.

Green Campus Organizations

The Energy Institute at HCC–Northeast: Offers students with education, training, seminars, forums, and workshops dedicated to the understanding, promotion, development, and application of a wide variety of green energy generating technologies and practices. (http://www.treec.org/consort_hccs.php. Also, see video at http://vimeo.com/5825013)

The Houston Community College System participated in the 2009 RecycleMania in the Benchmark Division focusing on waste minimization and targeted materials categories.

Fast Facts

Dr. Mary Spangler, the Chancellor of Houston Community College, is Executive Committee Co-Chair of the American College and University Presidents Climate Commitment (ACUPCC).

The Chancellor holds an annual symposium series that brings together high school and HCC students for a full day of information about educational and career paths in a variety of fields. The 2009 Symposium was on Energy Solutions.

HUDSON VALLEY COMMUNITY COLLEGE (HVCC)

80 Vandenburgh Avenue
Troy, New York 12180
518-629-HVCC
877-325-HVCC (toll-free)
E-mail: admissions@hvcc.edu
www.hvcc.edu

Degrees and Certificates

Associate Degrees:
Automotive Technical Services (A.O.S.*)
Automotive Technical Services–Chrysler
    (A.O.S.)
Automotive Technical Services–General Motors
    (A.O.S.)
Civil Engineering Technology (A.A.S.)
Engineering Science (A.S.)
Environmental Science (A.S.)
Heating/Air Conditioning/Refrigeration Technical
    Services (A.O.S.)
Plant Utilities Technology (A.A.S.)

Associate in Occupational Studies (A.O.S.)

Certificates:
Alternative Fuels
Heating Systems
Overhead Electric Line Worker
Photovoltaic Installation
Refrigeration and Air Conditioning

Costs

(Academic year 2009–10) Residents of New York State: Full-time: $1550; part-time: $129 per credit hour. Nonresidents: Full-time: $4650; part-time: $387 per credit hour.

Financial Aid

FAFSA required (www.fafsa.gov).

Nonresidents of New York State who are enrolled exclusively in distance learning will receive a scholarship in the amount of the nonresident tuition charge, effectively reducing tuition to that of a New York State resident.

New York State residents may be eligible for a variety of Tuition Assistance Programs (TAP). The Express TAP Application (ETA) must be completed to apply for all TAP awards. There are also Tuition Awards for Gulf War and Vietnam Veterans who are New York State residents.

Other financial aid is available to qualified students in the form of Federal Aid or scholarships.

About NASCAR's Going Green

In 2008, NASCAR announced plans for a green initiative to reduce energy use at its stockcar racing venues and to encourage sponsors to develop their own initiatives related to the sport. It's even exploring replacing carburetors with fuel injection and possibly introducing alternative fuels.

Admission Requirements

Required: High school diploma or GED. Most fields of study also require a high school average of 70 or above. The Educational Opportunity Program (EOP) is provided for New York State residents meeting the requirements of the state-supported program.

Application Information

Options: Online application

Application fee: $30

Required: High school transcript or copy of GED score report

Application deadline: Rolling

Notification: Continuous

Distance Learning

A number of courses and some degree programs offer fully online programs through Blackboard or Hybrid, which is a combination of online and on-campus meetings. An online self-evaluation exercise is available to help determine if distance learning is a good option for you.

Green Campus Organizations

A-Tech (Automotive Technicians Club): Club for any student with an interest in automotives.

Air Conditioning Club: Student branch of the American Society of Heating, Refrigeration and Air Conditioning Engineers (ASHRAE).

American Society of Civil Engineers Student Club (ASCE): Promotes understanding of the work of civil engineers; holds steel bridge competition.

Associated General Contractors of America (AGGC) Student Chapter: Promotes interest in and understanding of the construction industry.

Environmental Club: Promotes and practices responsible use of the Earth's natural resources on campus and in the community; educates and encourages participation in conserving, improving, and enjoying the natural world.

Hudson Valley Community College Builders Club: Student chapter of the National Association of Home Builders (NAHB).

Society of Refrigeration (Mechanics) Technicians: Students interested in the application of commercial refrigeration and air conditioning.

Fast Facts

Hudson Valley Community College's Workforce Development Institute was one of the hosts and led the educational sessions for the first Northeast Green Building Conference, the leading green building educational event in upstate New York. New York State is the first state to register for LEED certification for the governor's residence as part of the "Greening the Executive Mansion" initiative.

HVCC's Workforce Development Institute includes the Center for Energy Efficiency & Building Science, which provides ongoing training on incorporating energy efficiency methods into the building trades. Check out https://www.hvcc.edu/ceebs/index.html.

HVCC's newest facility, TEC-SMART (Training and Education Center for Semiconductor Manufacturing and Alternative and Renewable Technologies), opened January 25, 2010. It features more than a dozen state-of-the-art classrooms and laboratories that will be used to train the workforce in green technologies, including semiconductor manufacturing, photovoltaic, home energy efficiency, geothermal, alternative fuels, and wind energy. See https://www.hvcc.edu/tecsmart/.

IOWA LAKES COMMUNITY COLLEGE (ILCC)

3200 College Drive
Emmetsburg, Iowa 50536
712-362-2604
800-521-5054 (toll-free)
E-mail: info@iowalakes.edu
www.iowalakes.edu

Degrees and Certificates

Associate Degrees:
Automotive Technology (A.A.S.)
Biorenewable Fuels Technology (A.A.S.)
Farm Equipment and Diesel Technology (A.A.S.)
Sustainable Energy Resource Management (A.S.)
Wind Energy and Turbine Technology (A.A.S.)

Certificates:
Biorenewable Fuels Technology
Sustainable Energy Resource Management
Welding Technology

Diplomas:
Welding Technology
Wind Energy and Turbine Technology

Costs

(Academic year 2009–10) Resident tuition: $128 per credit; nonresident tuition: $130 per credit. Minnesota residents receive waiver of nonresident tuition through a reciprocity agreement.

Financial Aid

FAFSA required (www.fafsa.gov). Online scholarship applications; scholarship deadlines vary, but April 1 is a typical deadline for full scholarships and October 1 for spring term scholarships. In addition to scholarships, various loans, grants, and work-study opportunities exist.

Admission Requirements

Required: High school diploma or GED

Recommended: ACT scores

Application Information

Options: Online application

Application fee: None

Required: High school transcript or GED certification

Application deadline: Rolling

Notification: Continuous

Distance Learning

Iowa Lakes offers a number of distance learning formats that include online Internet courses, alternative delivery formats, and TV formats. Iowa Lakes is part of the Iowa Community College Online Consortium (ICCOC), which consists of seven Iowa community colleges. For more information on taking online credit courses or obtaining an online degree from ILCC, visit the consortium Web site at www.iowacconline.org.

Green Campus Organizations

Wind Energy Club: Promotes and educates public about wind energy and the ILCC program.

Conservation Club: Projects include an extensive prairie restoration project at Fort Defiance State Park, participation in the Iowa Adopt-A-Highway program, tree-planting project for the Estherville city park system, and various projects for local county conservation boards and the Iowa Department of Natural Resources.

Landscape and Turfgrass Club: Community projects to promote and educate; money-making projects such as aerating yards, laying sod, and landscaping.

Fast Facts

The Wind Energy and Turbine Technology program is the first in Iowa and has been in existence since 2004. The college owns and operates a V-82 turbine located about a half-mile south of the campus in Estherville. Power generated there is sold to the city of Estherville with proceeds used to offset the energy consumed by the college. Students learn maintenance activities as well as equipment operation and safety practices. (See http://www.iowalakes.edu/programs_study/industrial/wind_energy_turbine/index.htm.)

KALAMAZOO VALLEY COMMUNITY COLLEGE (KVCC)

6767 West O Avenue
P.O. Box 4070
Kalamazoo, Michigan 49003-4070
269-488-4400
www.kvcc.edu

Degrees and Certificates

Associate Degrees:
Automotive Technology (A.A.S.)
Electrical Technology (A.A.S.)
Engineering Technology (A.A.S.)
Maintenance Mechanic–Facility (A.A.S.)
Maintenance Mechanic–Industrial (A.A.S.)

Certificates:
Advanced Electric Vehicle Control System
Auto-Hybrid and Advanced Technology Vehicles
Automotive General Service Technician
Carpentry
Electrical Construction
Electrical Control
Heating, Ventilation, and Air Conditioning
Machinist
Maintenance Mechanic–Facility
Maintenance Mechanic–Industrial
Welding Technologies
Wind Energy Technology

Costs

(2010 Winter and Summer) Tuition*: $71 per credit hour for in-district students; $113 per credit hour for Michigan out-of-district students; $152 per credit hour for out-of-state students. The Wind Turbine Technician Academy (26 weeks) has a fixed fee of $12,000. (*Fees are charged for specific courses and are listed with the individual course listing.)

Financial Aid

FAFSA is required (www.fafsa.gov). Numerous options exist for qualified students, including grants, scholarships, work opportunities, and loans. The Financial Aid Office can be reached at www.financialaid@kvcc.edu.

Admission Requirements

Students should be over age 16. High school students can apply, as can high school graduates or nongraduates. Home-schooled students must have the signature of their home school representative or parent on their application form.

Admission to the Wind Turbine Technician Academy is currently limited to 16 seats, and specific skills are tested prior to acceptance. The skills are listed on the Web site of the Academy: mtec.kvcc.edu/windtechacademy.html.

Application Information

Option: Online

Fee: None

Required: Placement test for skill-level evaluation

Distance Learning

KVCC offers a number of courses online. Moodle is the Learning Management System used. (http://moodle.org)

Green Campus Organizations

Automotive Technology Club: Provides social, recreational, and vocational learning opportunities for automotive technology students.

Recycle Now!: Group in charge of recycling receptacles.

Fast Facts

The first class at KVCC's Wind Turbine Technician Academy graduated in April 2010. The second class began its 26-week intensive training in June 2010, and among the 16 students was a woman from New York. The third class is scheduled to begin in January 2011. The Academy is an educational cooperative between KVCC, Fuhrlaender North America, Inc., and Fuhrlaender AG of Germany. The program is certified by Bildungszentrum fur Erneuerbare Energien (BZEE), the Renewable Energy Education Center based in Husum, Germany. BZEE was created and supported by major wind-turbine manufacturers, component makers, and enterprises that provide operation and maintenance services. Additional program support came from a collaboration with the Michigan firm of Crystal Flash Renewable Energy LLC. Crystal Flash will provide learning opportunities for students at KVCC. A $550,000 appropriation in the federal budget for 2010 allows the Academy to purchase laboratory equipment, including a 90-foot tower and turbine-unit platform. (See essay by James DeHaven, VP of Economic & Business Development, KVCC)

KANKAKEE COMMUNITY COLLEGE (KCC)

100 College Drive
Kankakee, Illinois 60901
815-802-8100
E-mail: www.kcc.edu/Pages/ContactUs.aspx
www.kcc.edu

Degrees and Certificates

Associate Degrees:

Air Conditioning and Refrigeration (A.A.S.)
Automotive Technology (A.A.S.)
Electrical Technology (A.A.S.), with specialization in Renewable Energy Technology
Welding (A.A.S.)

Certificates:

Air Conditioning and Refrigeration
Automotive Technology
Global Supply Side Management
Paralegal/Legal Assistant Studies
Supply Chain Management
Welding Technology

Costs

(Academic year 2009–10) District residents: $84 per credit hour; out-of-district state residents: $172.26 per semester hour; out-of-state residents: $387.69 per semester hour.

Students from certain counties in Indiana are charged the Illinois out-of-district tuition and fees rather than the out-of-state rates. There is a charge-back program and a cooperative agreement with some other districts in Illinois.

Financial Aid

FAFSA required (www.fafsa.gov). Scholarships are awarded annually by the KCC Foundation to over 350 students. There are a number of other sources of federal and state aid, including loans, grants, and work-study programs.

About Recycling Clothes

In 2005, Patagonia launched Common Threads Garment Recycling for its used Capilene® Performance Baselayers, Patagonia® fleece clothing, Polartec® fleece clothing, Patagonia cotton T-shirts, and other Patagonia clothing with the Common Threads tag. The goal is to reduce the use of new polyester fabrics and, thus, use less petroleum each year. To learn more, check out www.patagonia.com.

Admission Requirements

Required: High school diploma or GED.

Application Information

Options: An online application form is available and can be electronically submitted or printed and mailed to the Office of Admissions.

Application fee: None

Required: High school or GED and prior college transcript, assessment testing for some programs and courses, academic advisement appointment, orientation session

Application deadline: Rolling

Notification: Continuous

Distance Learning

Some courses are offered online through the college's ANGEL system. A self-assessment to determine if this type of learning will be beneficial to you is available at www.kcc.edu/students/onlinelearning/pages/isonlineforme.aspx.

Green Campus Organization

Campus Sustainability Committee: Projects include campus recycling, auditing energy consumption, curriculum and course development, annual Sustainability Week events, and dissemination of information about sustainability issues.

Fast Facts

The 2009 Sustainability Week featured the Solar Globe Art Project. The globe uses light and dark orange to depict energy use throughout the world. Solar panels mounted on the globe collect solar energy, which is stored and used at night to power the lights that represent the energy use of major cities.

The KCC Sustainability Center opened in January 2009. It is a one-stop-shop for information about energy incentives and grant opportunities, energy efficiency and conservation, renewable energy, career development, and employment referral.

As a result of the Kankakee Community College's Community Sustainability Initiative, community leaders in Kankakee created the Council for Community Sustainability with the goal of promoting sustainability in the Kankakee River Valley. Their four-pronged approach is based on developing a green community, green jobs and businesses, sustainable agriculture and local food, and energy efficiency.

LAKESHORE TECHNICAL COLLEGE (LTC)

1290 North Avenue
Cleveland, Wisconsin 53015
920-693-1000
888-468-6582 (toll-free)
E-mail: www.gotoltc.com/contactus/index.php
www.gotoltc.com

Degrees and Certificates

Associate Degrees:
Electro-Mechanical Technology (A.A.S.)
Nuclear Technology (A.A.S.)

Nuclear Technology with Radiation Safety
  Concentration (A.A.S.)
Paralegal (A.A.S.)
Supply Management (A.A.S.)
Wind Energy Technology (A.A.S.)

Certificates:
Paralegal Post Baccalaureate
Radiation Safety Technician, Basic, Intermediate,
  Advanced
Supply Chain Management
Transportation, Distribution and Logistics
Welder Training Short Term

Diplomas:
Automotive Maintenance Technician Welding,
  Maintenance, and Fabrication

Costs

(Academic year 2009–10) Wisconsin residents: $101.40 per credit; nonresidents: $606.85 per credit.

Financial Aid

FAFSA required (www.fafsa.gov). State and Federal grants, loans, and work-study options are available. The LTC Foundation awards approximately $70,000 in scholarships each year. Scholarships are need-based as well as merit-based and cover all divisions and disciplines.

Deadlines: November 15 (spring scholarships); April 15 (fall scholarships).

Admission Requirements

Required: High school diploma or GED or HSED.

Application Information

Options: Online application

Application fee: $30

Required: High school transcript, GED, or HSED; entrance assessment (ACT, Accuplacer, or Compass)

Application deadline: Rolling

Notification: Continuous

Distance Learning

A number of courses are offered either online, over ITV, or blended.

Green Campus Organizations

Auto Tech Club: For students in the Automotive Maintenance Technician program.

Welding Club: For students enrolled in the Welding program.

Fast Facts

LTC constructed a grid-tied small commercial wind turbine on campus in 2004. It takes advantage of the campus's location along the windy shoreline of Lake Michigan and supplies nearly 3 percent of the campus's electrical energy. The turbine is also used for technical training, workshops, seminars, and courses on renewable energy resources. LTC received a grant from Focus on Energy to help construct the wind turbine.

LTC received the 2005 Innovation Award from the Interstate Renewable Energy Council for its Wind Energy Demonstration Site.

Keep America Beautiful: Great American Cleanup™

In addition to RecycleMania, students can join the Keep America Beautiful: Great American Cleanup™ every year from March 1 through May 31. More than 3 million people from nearly 1,000 organizations participate each year. In 2009, Americans gave more than 5.2 million hours in 32,000 communities to work on 30,000 specific events. Communities in all fifty states took part.

Projects ranged from cleaning up parks, playgrounds, and recreation centers to conducting educational workshops and hosting community beautification events. Participants removed litter from waterways, beaches, and nature trails; planted trees and flowers, and removed graffiti to enhance urban areas; and collected clothing, paper, batteries, and electronics for reuse and recycling.

National sponsors, including The Dow Chemical Company, The Glad Products Company, Pepsi-Cola Company, The Scotts Miracle-Gro Company, Solo Cup Company, and Waste Management, Inc., provided a variety of support, including in-kind donations for local initiatives and employee volunteers.

To see how you can become involved, visit www.kab.org.

LANE COMMUNITY COLLEGE

4000 East 30th Avenue
Eugene, Oregon 97405
541-463-3100
E-mail: enrollmentadvisors@lanecc.edu
www.lanecc.edu

Degrees and Certificates

Associate Degrees:
Auto Body and Fender Technology (A.A.S.)
Automotive Technology (A.A.S.)
Aviation Maintenance Technician (A.A.S.)
Diesel Technology (A.A.S.)
Energy Management Technician (A.A.S.)
Fabrication/Welding Technology (A.A.S.)
Legal Assistant and Paralegal Studies (A.A.S.)
Renewable Energy Technology (A.A.S.)
Sustainability Coordinator (A.A.S.)

Certificates:
Auto Body and Fender Technology
Automotive Technology
Aviation Maintenance Technician
Diesel Technology
Fabrication/Welding Technology
Legal Assistant and Paralegal Studies
Professional Truck Driver
Welding Processes

Costs

(Academic year 2009–10) Residents: $81 per credit; nonresidents: $213 per credit. Residents of Idaho, Nevada, and Washington pay the Oregon in-state tuition rate.

Financial Aid

FAFSA must be filed as early as possible after January 1 for any need-based aid (www.fafsa.gov). Grants, work-study, and loans as well as a number of scholarships are available to eligible students. Visit the Financial Aid Web page for more information at www.lanecc.edu/finaid/index.htm.

Admission Requirements

Required: 18 years of age or older; high school diploma, or GED

Application Information

Options: Online application

Application fee: None

Required: Placement testing

Application deadline: None

Notification: Continuous

Distance Learning

Lane offers a variety of options for some courses. These include live interactive courses either via cable TV or IP video to off-campus locations; online courses via Moodle, the online course management system; or as telecourses.

Green Campus Organizations

Green Chemistry Club: Currently building a biodiesel processor that will be used to turn waste grease from the campus kitchen into fuel for campus boilers and vehicles.

Oregon Student Public Interest Research Group (OSPIRG): Chapter of the national organization.

Learning Garden Club: Oversees all aspects of Lane's organic learning garden; provides practical hands-on experience in sustainable local food production. Bulk of harvest goes to Culinary Arts Department as part of the national Farm to Cafeteria Program.

Sustainability Group: Committee of Lane staff and student volunteers who work together on sustainability issues; initiatives include recycling, reuse, composting, using organic and local foods, energy conservation, and water conservation.

Fast Facts

Lane received a $100,000 grant from the Eugene Water & Electric Board (EWEB) to build a solar-powered electric vehicle charging station for use by students and community. Slated for completion by students in summer 2010, the site uses solar panels that also act as covered parking with thirty-six charging stations for electric vehicles.

In 2008, Lane hosted the first Conference on Sustainability for Community Colleges. Forty-seven colleges and organizations from sixteen states attended.

Lane is a signatory college of the American College & University Presidents' Climate Commitment (ACUPCC).

Lane has set a goal of becoming carbon-neutral by 2050 and has established benchmarks and mechanisms for tracking progress and impact of efforts.

The Northwest Energy Education Institute is located at Lane and provides energy and building-related continuing education across the United States. Visit www.nweei.org for more information.

With a grant from the American Recovery and Reinvestment Act (ARRA), Worksource Lane/The Workforce Network offered a number of no-cost training classes, including Weatherization Auditor and Technician, Sustainable Building Practices, and Basic Manufacturing Certificate with Solar Emphasis. See www.laneworkforce.org/LINKS/WFnetwork.html for more information.

LANSING COMMUNITY COLLEGE (LCC)

P.O. Box 40010
Lansing, Michigan 48901-7210
517-483-1957
800-644-4522 (toll-free)
E-mail: wilso23@lcc.edu
www.lcc.edu

Degrees and Certificates

Associate Degrees:
Advanced Technology Vehicles (A.A.S.)
Alternative Energy Technology (A.A.S.)
Automotive Air Conditioning/Electrical
    Accessories (A.A.S.)
Automotive Technology (A.A.S.)
Civil Technology (A.A.S.)
Customer Energy Specialist (A.A.S.)
Energy Management Technology (A.A.S.)
Environmental Technology (A.A.S.)
Geographic Information Systems and Geospatial
    Technology (A.A.S.)
Heating and Air Conditioning (A.A.S.)
High Performance Automotive (A.A.S.)
HVAC/R-Energy Management Engineering
    Technology (A.A.S.)
Powerplant Maintenance Technology (A.A.S.)
Welding Technology (A.A.S.)

Bachelor's Degree:
Paralegal studies (A.B.)

Certificates:
Advanced Technology Vehicles
Alternative Energy Engineering Technology
Automotive Drive Lines
Automotive Technology
Building Maintenance
Customer Energy Specialist
Electrical Utility/Lineworker
Energy Efficiency Technician
Geographic Information Systems
Geothermal Technician
Heating and Air Conditioning

High Performance Engine Machinist
High Performance Engine Specialist
Paralegal Post-Bachelor
Powerplant Maintenance Technology
Solar Energy Technician
Truck Driver Training
Welding Technology
Wind Turbine Technician

Costs

(Academic year 2009–10) District residents: $73 per billing hour*; nondistrict residents: $134 per billing hour; nonresidents: $201 per billing hour.

(*Note: A billing hour is not the same as a credit hour. A billing hour represents an amount of time that a student spends in direct contact with an instructor or with laboratory equipment.)

Financial Aid

FAFSA required (www.fafsa.gov). Students wishing to receive financial aid must submit a FAFSA prior to March 1 for priority consideration, or six weeks prior to payment due date for other aid programs. This aid can be in the form of loans, grants, scholarships, or work-study. For more information, visit www.lcc.edu/finaid.

Various awards and scholarships are available to qualified students. Applications must be submitted at the appropriate deadline date, generally before the end of January. The LCC Foundation provides more than $780,000 in scholarships annually.

Admission Requirements

Required: Students must be 18 years of age or older, or they must have graduated from high school.

Application Information

Options: Online application, print and mail application, apply in person

Application fee: $25

Required: Many courses have minimum skill level requirements that must be met before enrollment. Skill prerequisites can be met either by taking a placement test or passing specific courses at LCC. Assessment testing should be completed prior to orientation. Academic advisers and counselors are available to provide information.

Application deadline: Rolling

Notification: Continuous

Distance Learning

Some courses are available online via the ANGEL Computer Management System, which is administered by LCC's eLearning Department.

Green Campus Organizations

Sustainability Advisory Committee: Made up of students and faculty members; supports sustainability initiatives on campus and with the wider community.

Annual "Spring Fling Goes Green": Sponsors a Dumpster-diving competition.

Fast Facts

LCC is one of the nation's first colleges to incorporate alternative energy into its curricula and its sustainable practices on campus.

LCC's West Campus is heated and cooled by a geothermal system, which is seeking LEED certification. The college also has a small solar array and wind turbine on campus.

Automotive technology students work on hybrid vehicles and are building an internal combustion engine powered by a fuel cell.

LONG BEACH CITY COLLEGE (LBCC)

4901 East Carson Street
Long Beach, California 90808-1706
562-938-4353
www.lbcc.edu

Degrees and Certificates

Associate Degrees:
Advanced Transportation Technology, Alternate Fuels (A.S.)
Advanced Transportation Technology, Electric Vehicles (A.S.)
Auto Mechanics (A.S.)
Air Conditioning /Refrigeration-Carpentry Tech/ Trade Home Remodel and Repair
Diesel Mechanics (A.S.)
Welding Technology (Prep)

Certificates:
Advanced Transportation Technology, Light-Medium Duty Alternate Fuels
Advanced Transportation Technology, Electric Vehicles
Advanced Transportation Technology, Heavy Duty Alternate Fuels
Arc Welding and Fabrication
Carpenter Trainee
Home Remodeling and Repair Technician

Costs

(Academic year 2009–10) Residents: $26 per unit (subject to change by the California state legislature); nonresidents: $210 per unit.

Financial Aid

FAFSA required (www.fafsa.gov). Through Long Beach Community College Foundations, the college awards hundreds of scholarships each year. In addition, graduating high school seniors who meet certain requirements are eligible for CAL Grants.

Admission Requirements

Required: High school graduate, GED, or 18 years of age

Application Information

Options: Online application

Application fee: None for residents

Required: Orientation, academic counseling, and assessment

Recommended: Campus visit

Application deadline: Continuous

Notification: Rolling

Distance Learning

LBCC offers online, hybrid, and some Web-enhanced courses.

Green Campus Organizations

Eco-Terra: Promotes environmental issues, participates in political action campaigns, and runs outdoor field trips.

LBCC participated in RecycleMania 2010 in the Benchmark Division.

Fast Facts

In 2010, LBCC was awarded $2.3 million in grants to support workforce training programs. These grants were part of the $27 million in grants recently announced by the California Recovery Taskforce, in collaboration with the Green Collar Jobs Council, the California Energy Commission, the Employment Training Panel, and the California Workforce Investment Board. LBCC won three grants in two major areas, the California Clean Energy Workforce Training Program and the Renewable Fuel and Vehicle Technologies Workforce Development and Training Program.

LBCC was the only community college in California to receive more than one grant.

LBCC's Advanced Transportation Technology Center provides courses in alternate fuels, such as compressed natural gas, liquefied natural gas, and propane, and in automotive technologies, such as hydrogen fuel cells, hybrids, and electric vehicles.

LOS ANGELES TRADE-TECHNICAL COLLEGE (LATTC)

400 West Washington Boulevard
Los Angeles, California 90015
213-763-7000
E-mail: McintoMF@lattc.edu
http://college.lattc.edu

Degrees and Certificates

Associate Degrees:
Automotive and Related Technology, with concentrations in Engine Performance Technology, Transmission Repair Technology, Mechanical Repair Technology
Chemical Technology (A.S.)
Community Planning and Economic Development (A.A.)
Construction Technologies, with concentration in Refrigeration and Air Conditioning Mechanics
Diesel and Related Technology (A.S.)
Refrigeration and Air Conditioning Mechanics (A.S.)
Welding (A.S.)

Certificates:
Chemical Technology
Community Planning and Economic Development
Construction Technologies, with concentration in Refrigeration and Air Conditioning Mechanics
Diesel and Related Technology
Electrical Utility Line Worker
Refrigeration and Air Conditioning Mechanics

Solar Energy Systems, Installation, and Maintenance
Weatherization and Energy Efficiency
Welding

Costs

(Academic year 2009–10) Residents: $26 per unit (subject to change by the California state legislature); nonresidents: $213 per unit.

Financial Aid

FAFSA required (www.fafsa.gov). Scholarships are available, as well as Board of Governors fee waivers. Graduating high school seniors may also be eligible for CAL Grants. For full financial aid information, go online to http://college.lattc.edu/financialaid/financial-aid/.

Admission Requirements

Required: Must be a high school graduate or at least 18 years old and able to benefit from instruction.

Application Information

Options: Online application or paper application mailed or delivered to Admissions Office

Application fee: None

Required: High School diploma or assessment test, orientation, academic counseling

Application deadline: Continuous

Notification: Continuous

Distance Learning

LATTC is moving to offer all courses online. Monitor progress at http://college.lattc.edu/online/

Green Campus Organizations

Culinary Arts Department: Recycling of used vegetable oil for biodiesel fuel.

Electronics Department: Computer recycling program.

Building Green/Building Healthy: As part of the commitment to sustainable principles, four major building initiatives that are underway are seeking LEED certification.

LATTC participated in the 2010 RecycleMania in the Benchmark Division.

Fast Facts

The Utilities and Construction Prep Program (UCPP) at LATTC prepares low-skilled youth and adults for entrance into utilities or the construction trades. UCPP is based on strong partnerships with the Los Angeles Department of Water and Power, the Southern California Gas Company, locals for the International Brotherhood of Electrical Workers (IBEW), and the UAW Labor Employment and Training Corp, among others. For more information, go online to http://www .lattc.edu/dept/lattc/WED/UtilityPrep.html

The White House Office of Urban Affairs brought U.S. Secretary of Labor Hilda Solis to the LATTC campus in 2009 for an overview of the biofuel, weatherization, photovoltaic, and green construction programs that are a keystone of the education-industry-labor partnership at the College.

In May 2008, the College established the Sustainable Energy Center, a dedicated lab for courses, activities, and programs related to renewable energy and energy efficiency technologies. The Green College Initiative now offers numerous courses, degrees, and certificates in a variety of green disciplines. See http://www.lattc .edu/dept/lattc/WED/GCIPrograms.html for more information.

In 2010, the students and instructor in the Alternative Fuels course were featured in the ABC News feature story "Going Green to Make Green," which aired on the show *Focus Earth* with Bob Woodward.

The Natural Resources Defense Council (NRDC) recently released a video featuring students and faculty members in LATTC's Solar, Energy Efficiency (Weatherization), and Diesel-Technology Alternative Fuels courses. The video highlights companies and training and education programs that support California's clean energy sector, which is rapidly growing as a result of AB 32, the state's landmark global warming law. You can watch the video at http://college.lattc.edu/ wed/2010/05/28/trade-tech-green-education-and-training-programs-featured-in-natural-resources-defense-council-video/.

LATTC is the only community college with a community development program.

Green Business Certification Project: LATTC is developing a green business certification program that consists of changing departments to operate within the standards of a green certified business. The Automotive and Diesel Technology programs are developing a pilot program to offer green business certification education modules.

MACOMB COMMUNITY COLLEGE

14500 E. 12 Mile Road
Warren, Michigan 48088
586-445-7999
866-Macomb1 (toll free)
E-mail: answer@macomb.edu
www.macomb.edu

Degrees and Certificates

Associate Degrees:
Automated Systems Technology, Mechatronics
   (A.A.S.)

Automotive Technology, Comprehensive
Automotive Training (A.A.S.)
Automotive Program, Automotive Service
Education Program (A.A.S.)
Climate Control Technology (A.A.S.)
Civil Construction (A.A.S.)
Climate Control Technology (A.A.S.)
Customer Energy Specialist (A.A.S.)
Legal assistant (A.A.S.)

Certificates:
Architectural Technology, Civil Construction
Automotive Technology, Comprehensive
Automotive Training
Customer Energy Specialist
Land Surveying
Land Surveying, Field Technician
Land Surveying, Office Technician
Millwright
Refrigeration Operator
Renewable Energy Technology
Sheet Metal Fabricating
Welding, Manufacturing and Maintenance

Costs

(Academic year 2009–10) In-district: $72 per
credit hour; out-of-district: $110 per credit hour;
out-of-state/international: $143 per credit hour;
affiliate: $91 per credit hour.

Financial Aid

FAFSA required (www.fafsa.gov). Macomb
participates in a variety of financial aid programs, including scholarships, grants, loans, and
employment opportunities.

Admission Requirements

Admission is open to any citizen or permanent
resident of the United States whose high school
class has graduated or is at least 18 years of age.

Application Information

Option: Apply online or submit a completed
application to the Enrollment Office

Application fee: None, but there is a $40 regis-
tration fee

Distance Learning

More than 250 online and hybrid course sections
are available each semester in virtual classrooms
supported by ANGEL Learning software.

Green Campus Organizations

Macomb Community College has two nature areas
preserved for the study of the environment, both of
which are open to the public.

Go Green Eco-Olympics: Series of monthly events
designed to reduce the campus's carbon footprint
with a reward system; for examples, turn in five
incandescent bulbs to Student Activities and get
an energy-saving CFL bulb; turn in twenty-five
plastic bags and get a reusable tote bag.

Fast Fact

Macomb's renewable energy technology certificate program debuted in fall 2009 and focuses
on five different emerging technologies: wind,
solar, biomass, geo-thermal, and hydrogen fuel
cell. The Renewable Energy Technology certificate is designed to complement several
existing program paths, including, but not limited
to, associate degree programs in Automated
Systems Technology, Mechatronics; Maintenance
Technology; Manufacturing Technology; Building
Construction Technology; Electronic Engineering
Technology; Architectural Technology; Business;
Environmental Science; and others.

MERCER COUNTY COMMUNITY COLLEGE (MCCC)

1200 Old Trenton Road
West Windsor, New Jersey 08550
609-586-4800
E-mail: admiss@mccc.edu
www.mccc.edu

Degrees and Certificates

Associate Degrees:
Architectural and Building Construction
  Technology (A.A.S.)
Automotive Technology (A.A.S.)
Civil Engineering Technology (A.A.S.)
Electronic Engineering (A.A.S.)
Energy Utility Technology (A.A.S.)
Heating, Refrigeration and Air Conditioning
  (A.A.S.)
Paralegal (A.A.S.)

Certificates:
Architectural and Building Construction
  Technology
Heating, Refrigeration and Air Conditioning
Solar/Energy Technology

Costs

(Summer and Fall 2010) County resident: $127 per credit hour; noncounty resident $169.50 per credit hour; out-of-state or international student: $254.50 per credit hour.

About IKEA

Looking for a job with an environmentally responsible company? Check out IKEA. It buys wood products only from responsibly managed forests and bans harmful substances from its merchandise. Beginning in 2009, IKEA sells only solar-powered outdoor electric lights.

Financial Aid

To be considered for all federal, state, and MCCC financial aid, students must complete the FAFSA. Deadlines are May 1 for the full academic year or fall semester, and October 1 for spring semester. A range of financial aid opportunities exist. Details can be found on the college Web site.

Admission Requirements

Admission is open to all people who will benefit from a postsecondary education.

Application Information

Option: Application can be completed online or mailed in

Required: High school transcripts or GED scores; immunization records for full-time students; college transcripts. The results of standardized tests are not required, but SAT scores may be used for placement and should be sent.

Distance Learning

MCCC offers The Virtual College. For full information, see http://mccc.edu/programs_tvc.shtml.

Green Campus Organization

Horticulture Club: Projects include planning and planting gardens on campus, participating in Earth Day celebrations, helping schools in the area build terrariums and start gardening projects on their own, participating in planting and clean-up projects for local organizations.

Fast Facts

The A.A.S. in Technical Studies program provides a means for students to earn an applied science degree based partly on credits received through technical training within their employing organization. The opportunity to earn college credit based on a certified apprenticeship in the construction and building trades is provided in cooperation with New Jersey PLACE and the U.S. Department of Labor.

MCCC offers a 70-hour Green Future Management Certificate Program for professionals in architecture, engineering, real estate, government, nonprofits, and sales who want information on the latest in sustainable practices and projects. Much of the content relates to LEED.

MESALANDS COMMUNITY COLLEGE

911 South Tenth Street
Tucumcari, New Mexico 88401
575-461-4413
E-mail: jarredp@mesalands.edu
www.mesalands.edu

Degrees and Certificates

Associate Degrees:
Automotive Technology (A.A.S.)
Building Trades (A.A.S.)
Diesel Technology (A.A.S.)
Wind Energy Technology (A.A.S.)

Certificates:
Advanced Carpentry
Wind Energy Technology

Costs

(Academic year 2009–10) Resident: $40.45 per credit hour; nonresident: $75 per credit hour.

Financial Aid

FAFSA required (www.fafsa.gov). In addition to federal and state aid programs, including grants, loans, work-study, and scholarships, there are institutional, Mesalands Community College Foundation, community-based, and private scholarships available.

Admission Requirements

Required: High school diploma or GED

Application Information

Options: Students may apply online for a $5 fee, or they may print the application and mail in free of charge.

Application fee: A $200 nonrefundable deposit is required for the Wind Energy program.

Required: High school transcript or GED score; Success/Assessment Placement Test; meeting with adviser. A physical exam is required for entry into the Wind Energy program.

Application deadline: Rolling, but positions in the Wind Energy program are limited.

Notification: Continuous

Distance Learning

Mesalands offers a variety of courses through several different media including Moodle, podcasting, and digital interactive video.

Fast Facts

Mesalands is home to the North American Wind Research and Training Center. The approximately 30,000-square-foot building is used for training technicians for the wind energy generation industry.

Mesalands installed a GE 1.5-megawatt wind turbine in 2008. It is the latest cutting-edge ESS model.

MIDLANDS TECHNICAL COLLEGE (MTC)

P.O. Box 2408
Columbia, South Carolina 29202
803-738-8324
800-922-8038 (toll free)
www.midlandstech.edu

Degrees and Certificates

Associate Degrees:
Automotive Technology (AIT)
Civil Engineering Technology (AET)
Building Construction Technology (AIT)
Heating, Ventilation, Air Conditioning
    Technology (AIT)
Mechanical Technology, with specialization in
    Nuclear Systems (AOT)
Paralegal (APS)

Certificates:
Architectural Systems and CodesAutomotive:
    Drive Train Repair, Electrical System Repair,
    Engine Performance, Engine Repair
Building Systems
Environmental and Economic Design
Geographic Information Systems Technology
Geomatics
Heating/Ventilation/Air Conditioning/
    Refrigeration
Low-Impact Land Development
Mechanical Systems Technician
Paralegal
Power Generation and Delivery (including fuel
    cells)
Structural Technology
Welding Technologies

Diplomas:
Air Conditioning/Refrigeration Mechanics

Costs

(Spring 2010) Richland and Lexington County
residents: $131 per credit hour; Fairfield County
residents $131 per credit hour (tuition varies
depending on county funding); residents of other
South Carolina counties: $164 per credit hour;
out-of-state students: $393 per credit hour.

Financial Aid

FAFSA required (www.fafsa.gov). Types of aid
available include lottery-funded tuition assis-
tance, Federal Pell Grants, Academic Competitive
Grant, Federal Work Study, Stafford Loans, SC
Needs-Based Grants, LIFE Scholarships, MTC
Foundation Scholarships, and Department of
Energy Student Fellowship.

Admission Requirements

All applicants must possess a high school diploma
or its equivalent or must be at least 18 years old

Application Information

Option: Online

Fee: None

Required: High school transcript or proof of GED
completion

Deadline: Three weeks prior to published application deadline

Notification: Continuous

Distance Learning

Midlands offers a variety of distance-based
courses. Computer-based courses use instructional CDs and a computer to view lectures.
Broadcast classes are transmitted from a studio
to other classroom locations where students view
the lecture on television. Internet courses are also
offered.

Fast Fact

Midlands's fuel cell laboratory opened in 2006 to offer basic fuel cell training. Two additional labs—a fuel cell subsystems lab and a commercial-variety analytical testing lab—are also on campus.

MOUNT WACHUSETT COMMUNITY COLLEGE (MWCC)

444 Green Street
Gardner, Massachusetts 01440
978-632-6600
E-mail: admissions@mwcc.mass.edu
www.mwcc.edu

Degrees and Certificates

Associate Degrees:
Automotive Technology (ATD)
Energy Management (EGD)
Natural Resources Degree (NRD)
Paralegal (PLD)

Certificates:
Automotive Technology
Energy ManagementParalegal

Costs

(Academic year 2009–10) Residents: $165 per credit hour; New England Regional Student Program: $177.50 per credit hour; nonresidents: $370 per credit hour.

Financial Aid

FAFSA required (www.fafsa.gov). The MWCC scholarship application deadline is March 10 for the fall semester. An essay and two letters of recommendation must be submitted with the application. Final deadline for the MASSGrant program is May 1.

Admission Requirements

Required: High school diploma or GED preferred; otherwise, a placement test or waiver is required. Certain courses of study require a high school diploma.

Application Information

Options: Online application

Application fee: $10

Required: High school transcript or GED suggested; otherwise a placement test or waiver is required. Certain courses of study require a high school transcript.

Application deadline: Rolling

Notification: Continuous

Distance Learning

MWCC offers many courses online through Blackboard. See www.mwcc.edu/distance/default.html.

Green Campus Organizations

Auto Club: Students maintain vehicles of fellow students as well as faculty and staff members, putting into practice what they learn in the automotive program.

Green Society: Promotes awareness and interest in the campus greenhouse and the Natural Resource program.

Other green activities: Community Garden, Farmers Market, and a composting program that recycles food waste from the cafeteria and kitchen for use in an organic garden that produces food for the kitchen.

Fast Facts

Mount Wachusett converted its all-electric main campus to a biomass heating system, using wood chips as fuel. The system saves the college an estimated $300,000 a year. It was partially funded by a $1 million grant from the U.S. Department of Energy.

In 2008, Mount Wachusett Community College was named the winner of the National Wildlife Federation's Campus Ecology Chill-Out Contest. The competition recognizes institutions of higher education that are implementing innovative programs to reduce the impacts of global warming. The award was made based on the biomass heating system and solar and wind technology that reduce the college's dependence on fossil fuels and reduce greenhouse gas emissions.

In January 2010, MWCC released its Climate Action Plan that details the college's commitment to achieve carbon neutrality by 2020.

MWCC offers the perfect setting for its natural resources program with its hundreds of acres of undeveloped plant communities and forested areas, two pond ecosystems, and a life studies center consisting of a greenhouse, potting area, and lecture facility.

About Your Old Athletic Shoes

Don't trash your old athletic shoes. Recycle them for reuse. Check out these Web sites:

- www.oneworldrunning.com—sends wearable shoes to athletes in Africa, Latin America, and Haiti
- www.nikereuseashoe.com—recycles old shoes into playground and athletic flooring

RED ROCKS COMMUNITY COLLEGE (RRCC)

13300 West Sixth Avenue
Lakewood, Colorado 80228
303-914-6600
E-mail: admissions@rrcc.edu
www.rrcc.edu

Degrees and Certificates

Associate Degrees:
Electro-Mechanical Industrial Maintenance (A.A.S.)
Environmental Technology (A.A.S.)
Industrial Maintenance Technology, Electrical (A.A.S.)
Industrial Maintenance Technology, Mechanical (A.A.S.)
Process Technology, Energy Operations (A.A.S.)
Renewable Energy Technology: Solar Photovoltaic Specialty (A.A.S.)
Renewable Energy Technology: Solar PV Business Owner Specialty (A.A.S.)
Renewable Energy Technology: Solar Thermal Business Owner Specialty (A.A.S.)
Renewable Energy Technology: Solar Thermal Specialty (A.A.S.)
Wind Energy Technology (A.A.S.)

Certificates:
Advanced PV Installation
Codes and Standards
Electro-Mechanical Technician
Energy Efficiency Weatherization
Energy Auditing
Environmental Compliance Operations
Environmental Pre-Engineering
Environmental Safety Systems
Grid Tie, Entry Level
Industrial Electrical Technician
Industrial Maintenance Technology
Introduction to Air Compliance
Introduction to Process Equipment
Introduction to Process Plant Instrumentation

Introduction to Process Plant Operations
Introduction to Process Plant Quality
  Management
Introduction to Process Plant Safety
Introduction to Wind Energy Technology
Low-Voltage Technician
Post EIC Degree Solar Photovoltaic
Post HVA Degree Solar Thermal
Solar PV Designer
Solar Thermal Designer
Solar Thermal Entry Level
Solar Thermal Installer
Wind Energy, Advanced Electrical
Wind Energy, Advanced Mechanical
Wind Energy, Basic Electro-Mechanical
Wind Energy Safety

Costs

(Academic year 2009–10) Residents: $156.30 per credit hour; nonresident: $393.90 per credit hour. Colorado residents can apply for a College Opportunity Fund tuition rebate, which entitles them to a credit of $68 per credit hour on their tuition bill.

Financial Aid

FAFSA required (www.fafsa.gov). Types of aid available include grants, loans, and work study. A number of scholarships are also available. RRCC Foundation provides over $200,000 annually in scholarships. Contact www.finaid@rrcc.edu.

Admission Requirements

Required: High school graduate; nongraduate: must be 17 years or older.

Application Information

Options: Online application

Application fee: None

Required: Skills testing (exemption proof via ACT/SAT scores or previous college degree), must meet with adviser

Application deadline: Rolling

Notification: Continuous

Distance Learning

Many courses are available online and as hybrid/flex courses. Students may also take courses from other Colorado community colleges through the CCC Online network.

Green Campus Organization

Campus Green Initiative: Engages students, faculty and staff members, and community members in efforts to promote sustainable technologies and behaviors related to conserving energy; includes businesspeople as advisers for course additions.

Fast Facts

RRCC was honored with the 2008 Governor's Excellence in Renewable Energy Award. RRCC's Energy Technology Program grew from 10 students in fall 2007 to 231 students by spring 2009.

The Environmental Training Center at RRCC is one of only twelve centers in the country where students can acquire the knowledge and skills needed to develop a career in environmental technology. The center is also the home of the only Water Quality Management Technology degree program in Colorado. For more information, see http://www.rrcc.edu/rmec/cetc.html.

In 2009, RRCC became one of the first community colleges in Colorado to offer the state's new Green Advantage certification program. The program teaches the latest in green construction practices and technologies. For more information, go online to http://www.greenadvantage.org/greengov.php.

SANTA FE COMMUNITY COLLEGE (SFCC)

6401 Richards Avenue
Santa Fe, New Mexico 87508-4887
505-428-1000
E-mail: info@sfccnm.edu
www.sfccnm.edu

Degrees and Certificates

Associate Degrees:
Environmental Technologies (A.A.S.)
Paralegal Studies (A.A.S.)

Certificates:
Biofuels (focus on biodiesel and algae)
Environmental Technology
Facility Technologies
Green Building Construction Skills
Green Building Systems
Paralegal Studies
Solar Energy

Costs

(Spring 2010) In-state/in-district: $34 per credit hour, Early Bird* $30 per credit hour; in-state/out-of-district: $45 per credit hour, Early Bird $41 per credit hour; nonresident: $88 per credit hour, Early Bird $73 per credit hour.

*Dates for Early Bird registration vary, but generally end about a month prior to start of class.

About Your Unused Cell Phone

Donate old cell phones, batteries, chargers, and PDAs to help

- Protect victims of domestic violence: www.nnedv.org
- Soldiers call home: www.cellphonesforsoldiers.com
- Charities nationwide: www.collectivegood.com.

Financial Aid

Scholarships, loans, grants, and work study are available. Most require FAFSA. Scholarships have deadlines and require a separate application; see www.sfcnm.edu/financial_aid.

Admission Requirements

Required: High school diploma or GED

Application Information

Options: Online application

Application fee: None

Required: Placement testing (ACT/SAT scores or prior college transcripts can be used to determine appropriate placement), adviser/counselor session, orientation

Application deadline: Rolling

Notification: Continuous

Green Campus Organization

Green Task Force: Composed of faculty and staff members, students, and members of the community to promote sustainability initiatives.

Fast Facts

The SFCC Sustainable Technologies Center (STC) incorporates 21st-century trades with advanced technologies and "green" curricula to promote a sustainable economy. The new facility, completed in 2010, provides space for credit and noncredit courses, as well as for workforce development programs. For more information, visit www.sfccnm .edu/sustainable_technologies_center.

New campus buildings such as STC and the Health and Science building are being constructed with a view to obtaining LEED green building certification at the highest levels.

Campus electricity is generated by a grid-tied solar photovoltaic system. Solar thermal collectors heat the campus swimming pool.

Students in the Principles of Accounting classes completed a campuswide survey and calculations for a profile of campus energy usage and carbon footprint as benchmarks for efforts at energy efficiency and reduction of carbon emissions.

SFCC is a signatory to the American College & University Presidents' Climate Commitment (ACUPCC).

SFCC was awarded over $500,000 in grant money for the 2009–10 academic year for its green initiatives. The money was targeted to scholarships, curriculum development, a biofuels program, and training at-risk youth in green technologies.

ST. PETERSBURG COLLEGE (SPC)

P.O. Box 13489
St. Petersburg, Florida 33733-3489
727-341-4772
E-mail: information@spcollege.edu
www.spcollege.edu

Degrees and Certificates

Associate Degrees:
Environmental Science Technology (A.S.)
Environmental Science Technology, Environmental Resources/Energy Management (A.S.)
Environmental Science Technology, Sustainability (A.S.)

Certificates:
Building Construction Technology
Paralegal Studies

Costs

(Academic year 2009–10) In-state residents: $87.12 per credit hour; out-of-state residents: $316.35 per credit hour.

Financial Aid

FAFSA required (www.fafsa.gov). Federal and state grants, loans, and work study, as well as various scholarships, are available. See the financial aid Web site at www.spcollege.edu/central/SSFA/HomePage/prooff.htm.

Admission Requirements

Required: High school diploma or GED

Application Information

Options: Online application or by mail or in person

Application fee: $40

Required: High school transcript or GED scores; orientation; Computerized Placement Test (CPT) or ACT/SAT substituted; meet with academic adviser

Application deadline: Rolling

Notification: Continuous

Distance Learning

St. Petersburg's eCampus offers hundreds of accredited online college courses in dozens of majors, plus online student support services. A sample online course is available at www.spcollege.edu/ecampus to help students evaluate how online learning works.

Green Campus Organizations

Club Green: Based on the Clearwater Campus, initiatives include Earth Day participation, volunteer support for Pinellas Living Green Expo, coastal cleanups, native tree planting, and invasive species removal.

Emerging Green Builders: Based at the Clearwater Campus, initiatives include volunteer support for the local chapter of the U.S. Green Building Council at the Pinellas Living Green Expo, bus tour of LEED-certified buildings in St. Petersburg, presentation of a "Green Lecture Series" focusing on sustainability as related to architecture, solar installation, and building construction.

Environmental Science Club: Based on the Seminole Campus, initiatives include participating in community clean-ups, volunteering for environmental organizations, sponsoring "Green Day" with the student government.

Friends of Florida Environmental Club: Based on the Gibbs Campus, initiatives include participating in annual Earth Day activities; volunteering at the Pinellas Living Green Expo; and participating in coastal cleanups, native tree planting and invasive species removal, and environmental lecture series.

Sustainability Club: Based on the Tarpon Springs Campus. Coordinates the recycling program and participates in community events; plans and coordinates educational environmental activities on campus.

Fast Facts

SPC installed its first photovoltaic system on the roof of its LEED-Gold Natural Science, Mathematics, and College of Education building, one of Tampa's most environmentally friendly buildings. The 3.5-kilowatt thin-film solar blanket is the first commercial installation of the new generation of solar collection systems installed in the area. The system was chosen partly because of its tolerance to hurricane force winds and harsh environments.

SPC participated in the World Wildlife Fund's Annual Earth Hour Initiative, turning off all non-essential lighting to demonstrate its concern for climate change.

SPC is developing a Natural Habitat Park and Environmental Center on the Seminole Campus to serve as an educational, environmental, and passive recreational "green zone" for use by SPC students, faculty and staff members, and the larger community. All invasive species growing in the area were cleared and 1,000 native slash pines were planted around the perimeter of the wetlands. This planting was accomplished by students and other volunteers in a single day.

The Natural Science Department planted a Botanical Garden at the Clearwater Campus, which will be used as a teaching tool for upper and lower biology classes. The gardens consist of only native Florida plants.

TULSA COMMUNITY COLLEGE

6111 East Skelly Drive
Tulsa, Oklahoma 74135
918-595-7000
www.tulsacc.edu

Degrees and Certificates

Associate Degrees:
Civil Engineering/Surveying Technology (A.A.S.)
Civil Engineering/Surveying Technology–Construction Option (A.A.S.)
Electronics Technology–Alternative Energy Option (A.A.S.)
Electronics Technology–Nanotechnology Option (A.A.S.)
Environmental Science and Natural Resources (A.S.)

Geography (A.S.)
Geology (A.S.)
Paralegal (AA, A.A.S.)

Certificates:
Civil Engineering/Surveying Technology
Electronics Technology–Alternative Energy
Electronics Technology–Nanotechnology Option

Costs

(Academic year 2009–10) In-state residents $62.20 per credit hour; nonresidents $217.75 per credit hour.

Financial Aid

Financial aid is available through grants, scholarships, loans, and part-time employment from federal, state, institutional, and private sources. The types and amounts of aid awarded are determined by financial need, availability of funds, student classification, and academic performance.

Among the requirements for financial aid, students must maintain a minimum cumulative 1.70 grade point average (GPA) for the first 30 credit hours attempted; and a minimum cumulative 2.0 GPA for all hours attempted thereafter.

Admission Requirements

The admission criteria set forth at Tulsa Community College are the minimum standards established by the Oklahoma State Regents for Higher Education. Although they provide for "open door" admission to the College, certain programs require additional standards to be met before a student is admitted. Selected workforce development programs require that a separate program application for admission be submitted prior to entry into specific courses.

Application Information

To apply for admissions at Tulsa Community College, contact the Enrollment Services Office located on each campus. The phone number for all campuses is 918-595-2010. An online application is also available, as well as a PDF version that can be mailed or faxed.

Application fee: $20

Required: Students seeking a degree or those seeking financial aid or veterans' benefits must provide official transcripts and test scores from ACT, SAT, or the TCC College Placement Test if age 20 years or younger.

Application deadline: Applications and transcripts should be submitted a minimum of ten working days in advance of registration for classes.

Notification: Continuous

Distance Learning

Internet courses offered through Blackboard include a variety of disciplines and may require some on-campus orientations or exams. Many other Internet courses are offered completely online and have no on-campus requirements.

Green Campus Organization

EcoFest: Event to cultivate "Practical, Sustainable, Green Living."

Fast Facts

Oklahoma is ranked eighth in the United States for windmill utility operation, and solar production is growing with the reduced cost of manufacturing solar cells. The Alternative Energy students measure and analyze wind and solar power systems, as well as biofuels and hydrogen power conversion systems.

Tulsa Community College hosted a green living festival to celebrate the College's eco-friendly initiatives and promote a new farmers market that opened in North Tulsa in spring 2010.

WAKE TECHNICAL COMMUNITY COLLEGE

9101 Fayetteville Road
Raleigh, North Carolina 27603
919-866-5500
www.waketech.edu

Degrees and Certificates

Associate Degrees:
Associate in Science College Transfer Degree (A.S.)
Associate in Science Pre-Engineering College Transfer Degree (A.S.)
Automotive Systems Technology (A.A.S.)
Civil Engineering Technology (A.A.S.)
Environmental Science Technology (A.A.S.)
Electrical/Electronics Technology (A.A.S.)
Heavy Equipment and Transport Technology (A.A.S.)

Certificates:
Electrical/Electronics Technology Commercial/ Residential WiringAnalyst for Home Safety and Energy Saving

Costs

(Academic year 2009–10) Residents: $50 per credit hour; nonresidents: $241.30 per credit hour.

Financial Aid

FAFSA required (www.fafsa.gov). Scholarships, loans, grants, and work-study are available.

Admission Requirements

Required: High school diploma or GED.

Application Information

Options: Online application

Application fee: None

Required: High school transcript or GED scores; COMPASS placement test in reading, writing and math; ACT/SAT scores can result in exemption from testing

Application deadline: Rolling

Notification: Continuous

Distance Learning

Wake Tech uses both Blackboard and Moodle as online course delivery tools for credit and non-credit courses.

Green Campus Organizations

Architecture Club: Promotes real-world exploration of the field of architecture.

Students for Environmental Education Club: Focus on energy issues.

Fast Facts

Wake Tech's Northern Wake Campus, opened in 2007, is the first campus in North Carolina and one of the first in the nation to be completely LEED-certified.

The Energy Conservation and Awareness Committee was established in July 2006 to address the impact of rising energy costs and to develop a coordinated effort for an aggressive energy conservation program for Wake Tech. The Committee's focus is on awareness, sustainability, and continued improvements in energy conservation.

Are You Being Fashionably Green?

You can be fashionable and still be environmentally responsible. Here are a few ideas to get you started.

1. **Shop at second-hand stores and vintage clothing stores.** Remember that shirt your aunt gave you and you hated, but your friend loved? Your castoffs can be someone else's find, and vice versa. Also check out eBay for previously owned clothing and accessories.

2. **If you want new, look for items that are made from post-consumer waste materials.** The label or packaging will tell you. Bagallini® handbags, wallets, backpacks, and luggage are made from recycled plastic bottles. You can find them at www.travelsmith.com.

3. **If you want new clothes, look for items made from natural fibers.** But be a careful consumer. Look for items made with organic cotton like those from www.underthecanopy.com and www.truly-organic .com. Cotton uses 18–25 percent of the world's pesticides, depending on which expert you read, so be sure it's organic cotton. Other natural fibers to look for are hemp and bamboo. Bamboo makes really soft fabric.

4. **See how far your dollars can go.** Buy the Sak™ Shopper Tote made of bamboo and recycled cotton from www.travelsmith.com and your money will benefit the Nature Conservancy's Plant a Billion Trees Campaign. Other retailers are also supporting this project that was certified in 2010 for fighting climate change. Check out www.plantabillion.org.

5. **Eco-friendly is high style.** Banana Republic launched its Heritage Collection of organic cotton and soy silk clothing in 2009. Check out http://bananarepublic.gap.com/. On its Corporate Responsibility page, H&M lists the sustainable materials that its manufacturers use for H&M clothing: organic wool, organic linen, recycled cotton, recycled polyester (from recycled plastic bottles and textile waste), recycled polyamide (from fishing nets and textile waste), recycled wool, and tencel.

6. **Even your shoes can be eco-friendly.** The Simple® shoe company makes sneakers from organic cotton, hemp, and recycled car tires. Other eco-friendly shoe brands are Acorn, El Naturalista, Greenbees, Merrell, Nava, Patagonia, Terrasoles, Teva, and Timberland.

7. **Dry your hair and save energy at the same time.** Rusk manufactures the Go Green Blow Dryer. It uses 23 percent less energy than similar dryers. It is packaged in recycled corrugated with soy ink printing.

8. **Make your hair environmentally friendly.** A variety of hair-care products now boast natural ingredients, recycled packaging, and a commitment to preserving the environment. Check out www.paul-mitchell.com, http://telabeautyorganics.com/science, and www.pureology.com.

9. **Think globally and shop globally.** Shop for interesting and unusual clothing, accessories, and furniture at stores like Ten Thousand Villages (www.tenthousandvillages.com) and online at http://worldofgood .ebay.com/. You can help the environment by buying goods made from natural materials and at the same time help poor workers in this country and in developing nations support themselves and their families.

10. **Find repurposed garments to wear.** A repurposed garment was at one point another, or many other, articles of clothing. Fashion designers have become more and more involved in repurposed fashion. You may find a unique look by breathing new life into older fabric.

CHAPTER 7

UNION TRAINING PROGRAMS FOR GREEN JOBS

This chapter contains profiles of labor unions that offer apprenticeship and training programs to upgrade members' skills for the new green energy economy. It also profiles the National Labor College that grants undergraduate degrees and certificates to AFL-CIO members.

Because of the move away from manufacturing to new green industries and the greening of older industries, unions are working aggressively to train current members and recruit new members for jobs in these industries. The goal is not only to provide a well-trained union membership to fill these "green jobs," but to gain new members for the labor movement and to ensure that all members have access to "family-sustaining careers" in the words of John Sweeney, former president of the AFL-CIO.

APPRENTICESHIPS

Apprenticeship programs are available through union locals. To join a union, a person has to contact the local and see if there are any openings for apprentices. Unions try not to hire more apprentices than they think they will need in the foreseeable future, so there may be a wait, especially if the work is seasonal like construction. A potential union member must meet certain requirements and often has to pass an interview with a committee of the local. Training costs are negotiated as part of contracts with employers, and, as

a result, apprenticeships are earn-while-you-learn programs.

Local One-Stop Career Centers and state apprenticeship programs can also help with finding apprenticeship programs. Check out www.doleta .gov/OA/stateoffices.cfm and www.careeronestop .org for more information.

ABOUT THE UNION PROGRAM LISTINGS

Here's what you need to know to navigate the union training and apprentice program profiles.

Contact Info

The first paragraph of each union profile lists the union's name, address, phone number, e-mail address, and Web site information.

About the Union

This section details important information about the union. It may include union goals or the history of the organization, as well as any relevant data about available apprenticeships.

Programs and Training

The final paragraph of the profile includes a description of the program or apprenticeship. In some cases, more than one may be listed. This section will also explain the training process and the necessary program skills and requirements.

Unions and Union Activities Profiled Here

The following unions and union activities are profiled in this chapter:

- National Labor College
- International Association of Bridge, Structural, Ornamental and Reinforcing Iron Workers (Iron Workers)
- International Association of Heat and Frost Insulators and Allied Workers (AWIU)
- International Brotherhood of Electrical Workers (IBEW)
- International Union of Operating Engineers (IUOE)
- Laborers' International Union of North America (LIUNA)
- Service Employees International Union (SEIU)
- United Association of Journeymen and Apprentices of the Plumbing and Pipefitting Industry of the United States and Canada (UA)
- United Brotherhood of Carpenters and Joiners (UBC)
- United Steel, Paper and Forestry, Rubber, Manufacturing, Energy, Allied Industrial & Service Workers International Union (USW) (Steelworkers)

About the Center for Green Jobs

In February 2009, the AFL-CIO created the Center for Green Jobs to partner with affiliated unions to, according to AFL-CIO President John Sweeney, "make progressive energy and climate change a first order priority" and ". . . to help our labor unions implement real green jobs initiatives—initiatives that retain and create good union jobs, provide pathways to those jobs, and assist with the design and implementation of training programs to prepare incumbent workers as well as job seekers for these family-sustaining careers."

NATIONAL LABOR COLLEGE (NLC)

10000 New Hampshire Avenue
Silver Spring, Maryland 20903
301-431-6400
800-462-4237 (toll-free)
www.nlc.edu

About the College

The National Labor College was originally founded in 1969 by the AFL-CIO as a labor studies center. In 1974, the center moved to its present site and began offering undergraduate degrees through a partnership with Antioch College. In 1997, the center was granted the authority to confer undergraduate degrees and was renamed the National Labor College. It offers certificate and degree programs and is "the nation's only accredited higher education institution devoted exclusively to educating union leaders, members, and activists."

Programs and Training

The NLC offers a Green Workplace Representative Certificate program, which is part of the AFL-CIO's Center for Green Jobs (CGJ) initiative.

Offered for the first time in spring 2010 in response to innovative work on sustainability and climate change by unions in the United States and Great Britain, this program provides union members and working people with the theoretical knowledge and practical training they need to conduct workplace sustainability audits. "This certificate program will provide education that empowers workers to become change agents, working to advance sustainability values and practices that meet the mutual interests of worker and managers, as well as enhance the competitiveness of American firms in the global economy," said Tom Kriger, NLC provost, when the program was announced.

The NLC offers degree and certificate programs online using the Blackboard online management system. In 2010, the AFL-CIO joined the National Labor College and the Princeton Review to create an online college for the Federation's 11.5 million members and their families. The purpose is to provide education and retraining for members in an affordable and accessible way. The new program builds on the NLC's existing distance learning curricula. One of the new degree programs under consideration is in the field of sustainability and green jobs.

About Green Initiatives

The Iron Workers are an affiliate of the Building and Construction Trades Department (BCTD) of the AFL-CIO. The BCTD is partnering with the Green Jobs Center of the AFL-CIO to help the more than 1,100 affiliate training programs incorporate the skills needed for the new green economy.

INTERNATIONAL ASSOCIATION OF BRIDGE, STRUCTURAL, ORNAMENTAL AND REINFORCING IRON WORKERS (IRON WORKERS)

1750 New York Avenue, NW
Suite 400
Washington, DC 20006
202-383-480
E-mail: iwmagazine@iwintl.org
www.ironworkers.org

About the Union

The union's Department of Apprenticeship and Training and the National Training Fund oversee, coordinate, and manage the education and training programs that range from the basic to the very advanced. The goal is to ensure that members receive comprehensive and effective education and training that will enable them to carry out their work safely and efficiently and with the highest standards of quality.

Programs and Training

Apprenticeship Programs

Apprentices are required to sign an indenture agreement with their Joint Apprenticeship Committee/Trade Improvement Committee that spells out the requirements and expectations of an apprentice ironworker. Most ironworker apprenticeships are three or four years in length, depending on the requirements of the local union. An ideal schedule provides equal training in structural, reinforcing, ornamental, welding, and rigging. The actual length of training for each subject may vary depending on the predominant type of work available in the local area.

Apprentices are required to receive at least 204 hours of classroom and shop instruction during each year of training. The subjects taken in the shop and classroom components complement the hands-on training received in the field. Subjects include blueprint reading, care and safe use of tools, mathematics, safety issues, welding, and oxy-acetylene flame cutting.

Apprentices receive an evaluation about every six months to determine if they are learning the craft. If the on-the-job or school work is not satisfactory, they may be dropped from the program or sent back to repeat that segment. If, however, their work is satisfactory, they will receive a pay raise.

Additional Training Options

Beyond the apprenticeship program, additional training options exist. Apprenticeship training in the ironworking trade can be applied toward college credit. A worker can earn as many as 65 credits toward a college degree. An associate degree can be completed online through Ivy Tech Community College of Indiana. A bachelor's degree can be completed online through the National Labor College.

Journeyman upgrade classes (available through the local union and contractors) provide opportunities to continually increase skills and keep up with the new technologies being introduced into the industry.

INTERNATIONAL ASSOCIATION OF HEAT AND FROST INSULATORS AND ALLIED WORKERS (AWIU)

9602 M.L. King Jr. Highway
Lanham, Maryland 20706
301-731-9101
http://www.insulators.org/pages/index.asp

About the Union

The insulation industry, which insulates mechanical systems and equipment, is a specialized craft within the framework of the building and construction trades. The Heat and Frost Insulators and Allied Workers Union is committed to providing an adequate supply of trained insulation mechanics with the competitive skills necessary to meet industry needs now and in the future.

Because proper insulation can result in a significant drop in energy use, the AWIU in partnership with National Insulation Association (NIA) compiled data for commercial buildings documenting the jobs potential of energy conservation and emission reductions through the use of mechanical insulation. According to the results, 89,000 new jobs would be generated if mechanical insulation is repaired and replaced on piping and duct work in industrial facilities and on HVAC equipment in commercial buildings.

As a result, the AWIU updated its apprenticeship program and added a course to train members to use the *3EPlus* computer program to analyze the effectiveness of insulation in reducing energy use and costs.

Programs and Training

Apprenticeship Programs

The goal of the apprentice program is to provide the highest level of training to apprentices, so they may assume positions as fully qualified journeymen ready to meet the professional challenges of the insulation industry. The program is structured for entry-level workers, as well as for insulation workers already employed within the industry who wish to upgrade their skills and to advance to journeyman status.

The apprenticeship program takes five years and integrates on-the-job training with classroom instruction to give participants a thorough knowledge of the trade. Apprentices are assigned to work for an insulation contractor, which enables the apprentice to work side by side with experienced journeymen who understand both the practical application and the theory. As apprentices progress through each year of the program, the tasks they are assigned become more complicated and the amount of supervision decreases. In addition, earnings are adjusted upward each year to reflect advancing skills and increasing knowledge of the trade. The average starting wage for first-year apprentices is 50 percent of the mechanics wage rate plus fringe benefits.During the five-year program, apprentices take about 160 hours of related classroom instruction each year, and the apprentice is indentured to the Joint Apprenticeship Committee of the Local Union.

To qualify to become an apprentice, a candidate must be at least 18 years of age, have a high school education or the equivalent, and be in good physical condition. To be admitted, the Joint Apprenticeship Committee requires completion of an application with picture; submission of a birth or baptismal certificate, high school diploma or GED scores, high school transcripts, and two letters of reference; and attaining a qualifying score on an aptitude test.

Additional Training Option

Insulators may also be certified for an asbestos abatement program that is approved by the Environmental Protection Agency (EPA). Certified insulators remove asbestos from schools, hospitals, power plants, and chemical and industrial facilities.

INTERNATIONAL BROTHERHOOD OF ELECTRICAL WORKERS (IBEW)

900 Seventh Street, NW
Washington, DC 20001
202-833-7000
www.ibew.org

About the Union

The National Joint Apprenticeship and Training Committee (NJATC) of the National Electrical Contractors Association (NECA) and the International Brotherhood of Electrical Workers (IBEW) operate programs for apprentice and journeyman electricians. The programs are privately funded, and most apprenticeship programs last five years. The NJATC developed uniform standards that have been adopted and used nationwide to select and train thousands of qualified men and women annually.

About the IBEW's Commitment to Going Green

In May 2009, the IBEW's apprenticeship and training committee launched a new green jobs training curriculum. According to the IBEW, the program is being "woven into the . . . apprenticeship training and will serve as a resource of journeymen looking to upgrade their skills in the growing green market." The seventy-five program lessons include topics such as green building fundamentals and automated building operation.

Programs and Training

Through the NJATC, the IBEW and NECA sponsor hundreds of local programs offering apprenticeship and training in the following areas:

Residential Wireman: Specializes in installing the electrical systems in single-family and multi family homes.

Outside Lineman: Installs the distribution and transmission lines that move power from power plants to buildings and homes.

Inside Wireman: Installs the power, lighting, controls, and other electrical equipment in commercial and industrial buildings.

Telecommunication VDV Installer-Technician: Installs circuits and equipment for telephones, computer networks, video distribution systems, security and access control systems, and other low-voltage systems.

Journeyman Tree Trimmer: Works outdoors year-round clearing trees from around powerlines.

INTERNATIONAL UNION OF OPERATING ENGINEERS (IUOE)

1125 17th Street, NW
Washington, DC 20036
202-429-9100
www.iuoe.org

About the Union

The union consists of two broad job classifications: operating engineers and stationary engineers. Operating engineers do the heavy lifting and are often referred to as hoisting and portable engineers, because the equipment they control lifts and/or moves. Stationary engineers operate, maintain, renovate, and repair mechanical systems in a facility. For example, in the wind-turbine industry, operating engineers run the cranes that put the turbines and towers in place. Stationary engineers are in charge of continuing operations, maintenance, and repair.

About Green Jobs for Operating Engineers

Operating Engineers are essential in the construction of wind farms. This is a major growth initiative, especially in the corridor of the Texas/Oklahoma Panhandle, western Oklahoma, and along the corridor north to the Canadian border.

Programs and Training

Operating Engineer

IUOE locals provide training programs nationwide, and most are registered with a state or federal apprenticeship agency. Apprentices are paid while they work and learn. Apprentices work with skilled journey-level operators on actual job sites as well as attend related classroom instruction and field training. The average length of an operating engineer apprenticeship is three to four years.

After completing an apprenticeship, many journey workers take additional classes offered by their locals. Continued training upgrades skills, making union members more employable, and also helps them move into management and supervisory jobs. Certification is conducted by outside groups. For example, crane operators are tested by the National Commission for the Certification of Crane Operators (NCCCO).

Stationary Engineer

IUOE stationary local unions provide skill-development training programs for apprentices and journey-level engineers. The programs are jointly sponsored by IUOE local unions and the employers who hire stationary engineers.

The average length of an apprenticeship is four years. During this period, apprentices learn their craft by working with skilled stationary engineers at an actual workplace and also attend related classroom instruction. Apprentice training may also be supplemented by course work at trade or technical schools. Training is critical for preparing apprentices to take the test for the stationary engineer license, which is required by most states.

Employers often encourage journey-level stationary engineers to continue their education. Many IUOE locals offer free training to members to help them broaden and update their skills and improve their employability. Because of the increasing complexity of the equipment, many stationary engineers also take college courses.

LABORERS' INTERNATIONAL UNION OF NORTH AMERICA (LIUNA)

905 16th Street, NW
Washington, DC 20006
202-737-8320
www.liuna.org

About the Union

LIUNA members build and repair roads, highways, bridges, and tunnels; construct residential and commercial buildings; clean up hazardous waste sites; drill and blast sites; build scaffolds; prepare and clean up job sites; lay pipe underground; pour concrete; flag and control traffic on highways; and remove asbestos and lead from buildings.

Programs and Training

LIUNA training is available in every state in the United States and every province in Canada. Among the fifty courses that are offered are hazardous materials remediation, remote tunneling, concrete work, and a variety of building construction skills. Apprenticeship training consists of a minimum of 288 hours of classroom training. These skills are practiced with a skilled journey worker for 4,000 hours of on-the-job training.

About a Green Jobs Pilot and LIUNA

A green-collar job initiative between LIUNA and the state of New Jersey was launched in January 2009. Its first training class of 22 graduated in April 2009 in Newark. They had previously been unemployed or underemployed. The program trained them to work in green construction and in retrofitting existing buildings. A similar program was launched in June 2009 in Trenton.

SERVICE EMPLOYEES INTERNATIONAL UNION (SEIU)

1800 Massachusetts Ave, NW
Washington, DC 20036
202-730-7000
800-424-8592 (toll-free)
www.seiu.org

About the Union

The Service Employees International Union is the largest and the fastest-growing union in the nation, reflecting the changing nature of the U.S. economy from manufacturing to service. The union represents workers in three key service sectors: health care, public service, and property services. Health-care union members include registered nurses, licensed practical nurses, doctors, lab technicians, nursing home workers, and home health care workers. Union members in the public service sector include local and state government workers, public school employees, bus drivers, and childcare providers. Workers who protect and clean commercial and residential office buildings, private security officers, and public safety personnel make up the membership of the property services sector. Membership depends on whether a jobsite is organized.

Programs and Training

Environmental Labor-Management Committees are involved in many green initiatives. Green initiatives, which are part of contract negotiations, include the use of green cleaning products, healthier health-care practices, and recycling.

SEIU Green Training Initiative

The following summary is provided by James Barry, Manager of Program Development, Building Service 32BJ, Thomas Shortman Training Program (TSTP): SEIU Local 32BJ in New York City is the largest building service workers union in the country, representing more than 100,000 cleaners, doormen, porters, maintenance workers, superintendents, resident managers, window cleaners, and security guards. TSTP, founded in 1971, is a nonprofit education fund supported primarily by contributions from participating employers. Every year, the program provides industry, academic, and computer courses to thousands of Local 32BJ building service workers at over twenty locations in New York, New Jersey, Connecticut, Pennsylvania, the District of Columbia, and Maryland.

Since 2005, the Thomas Shortman Training Program has worked with the New York State Energy Research and Development Authority (NYSERDA) and other partners to offer a wide range of training focusing on existing buildings. The major program is an eleven-session green building review that includes basic instruction on green building concepts, energy and water efficiency, building controls, and green cleaning supplies, as well as two building tours: an energy audit of a typical residential building and a tour of a LEED-certified green building.

The Shortman program has also launched a lighting retrofitting workshop, provided a recycling seminar, hosted a LEED-Existing Building (EB) Technical Review and worked with The Center for Sustainable Energy to prepare several 32BJ instructors for the Building Performance Institute's (BPI) Building Analyst Certification.

Starting in 2009, the 32BJ expanded its training to give workers a deeper understanding of the connection between their jobs and the environment. The local offered a second green building course and a series of new trades-oriented U.S. Green Building Council certifications such as "Green Buildings Operations and Maintenance," "Green Buildings: Building Operator Certification," and "Green Buildings: New Technologies and Materials." The certification program offers an educational track for those who wish to work in green buildings or make improvements in the buildings where they currently work. Workers learn how to run a building efficiently, use cleaning supplies and materials that have a low impact on indoor air quality, reduce waste, and recycle effectively in their buildings.

"One Year, One Thousand Green Supers Program," which is approved by the U.S. Green Building Council and the Building Performance Institute, is part of the Thomas Shortman Training Fund. The program enrolls building service workers in 40 hours of classwork in which they will learn the latest, state-of-the-art practices in energy-efficient operations. The curriculum trains workers to identify and address wasted energy, create a green operating plan, and perform cost-benefit analysis for building owners and managers. The program, launched in late 2009, is a labor-management partnership.

In January 2010, the U.S. Department of Labor granted the 32BJ Thomas Shortman Training Fund nearly $3 million to expand green buildings training in New York City as part of the American Recovery and Reinvestment Act. This is expected to increase the number of trained workers by 2,000. This grant also provides training for 200 Local 32BJ workers to attend specialized building training through the City University of New York.

UNITED ASSOCIATION OF JOURNEYMEN AND APPRENTICES OF THE PLUMBING AND PIPEFITTING INDUSTRY OF THE UNITED STATES AND CANADA (UA)

Three Park Place
Annapolis, Maryland 21401
410-269-2000
E-mail: http://www.ua.org/contact.asp
www.ua.org

About the Union

The UA has a variety of apprenticeship and training programs, as well as delivery methods, which are coordinated through its Sustainable Technologies Department. This department is responsible for all the activities, training, and outreach for sustainable technologies in the plumbing and pipefitting industry.

Programs and Training

5-Star Service Training Program

This apprenticeship program teaches the core skills of plumbing, pipefitting, sprinkler fitting, or HVAC/R services, along with basic mathematics, safety, and customer service skills. On-the-job training is combined with classroom training in this five-year program. Apprentices earn while learning.

At the completion of the program, the apprentice has 32 college credits towards an Associate in Applied Science (AAS) degree and is a UA STAR certified technician. The college credits can be transferred to a local community college or the UA's College On Demand degree program in partnership with Washtenaw Community College in Ann Arbor, Michigan. College On Demand is a distance-learning program that delivers text, Web-based materials, and classroom lectures on DVD for self-paced study. Graduates earn an AAS degree in Sustainable Technology, with a choice of majoring in HVAC/R, plumbing, sprinkler fitting, or construction supervision.

Green Systems Awareness Certificate

The UA offers a Green Systems Awareness Certificate. It requires a 16- to 20-hour course and a written exam, administered by a third-party certification group. The U.S. Green Building Council recognizes the UA as a certified training provider.

Partnership in Environmental Leadership

The Partnership in Environmental Leadership provides less formal training in sustainable mechanical service and construction, and "new building system technologies that promote greater energy efficiency, use fewer natural resources, have minimal impact on the environment, and use materials that can be reused or recycled." The program is a collaboration of the UA, Mechanical Contractors Association of America (MCAA), Mechanical Service Contractors of America (MSCA), Plumbing Contractors of America (PCA), U.S. Green Building Council (USGBC), and Green Mechanical Council.

Training is delivered through the Green Trailer and the Sustainable Technology Demonstration Trailer. Both are mobile units that travel from local to local. The Green Trailer provides trainers and simulators. The trailer drives to a site, the sides go up, the chairs come out, and the training begins. Topics include the latest environmental systems: fuel cell technologies, wind power generation, solar heating system, solar photovoltaic system, gray water toilet flushing system, anaerobic treatment process, infiltration demonstrator, geothermal system trainer, gas-fired warm air heating demonstrator, 1/8 GPF urinal, high-efficiency toilet, and water-saving toilet.

The Sustainable Technology Demonstration Trailer is the newest mobile unit used for outreach and training. While the Green Trailer provides simulators, the Sustainable Technology Demonstration Trailer contains working systems in the latest green technologies, including, among other items, a geothermal heat pump that feeds the radiant heating and cooling systems used in the trailer.

UNITED BROTHERHOOD OF CARPENTERS AND JOINERS (UBC)

101 Constitution Ave, NW
Washington, DC 20001
202-589-0520
http://carpenters.org/Home.aspx

When the stimulus package was signed in 2009, the Brotherhood members from the Carpenters District Council of Kansas City and Vicinity were the first in the country to start a funded project: They broke ground on a new bridge over the Osage River in Tuscombia, Missouri, to replace the Depression-era span that was crumbling with age. It is one of about 20 stimulus-funded projects in Missouri that will put UBC members to work driving piles, setting forms, completing interior systems, constructing concrete forms, laying floors, and doing finish work at worksites such as bridges, schools, hospitals, and every kind of infrastructure improvement.

About the Union

The skilled members of the United Brotherhood of Carpenters touch every aspect of a construction project. The union represents one trade with many crafts, including carpenters, cabinetmakers and millworkers, floor coverers, framers, interior systems carpenters, lathers, millwrights, and pile drivers. At the UBC's International Millwright Leadership Conference in 2010, a major topic was the union's role in the green economy. Speakers spoke of a future in which the power-generation business will be greener and command a greater share of construction dollars, creating opportunities for UBC millwrights and carpenters. Speakers noted that over the next twenty years, the demand for more efficient, environmentally sound, renewable energy sources is going to drive the demand for skilled workers who know how to build and service power plants. Bill Irwin, Executive Director of the Carpenters International Training Fund, which develops UBC training, said all instructional materials from now on will incorporate green elements.

Programs and Training

With a $175 million annual budget, 2,000 full-time instructors, and 250 centers across North America, the UBC's affiliated training programs offer a variety of skills-development courses in the construction industry. Apprenticeship programs are typically four-year programs, but can vary depending on the skill area.

The state-of-the-art Carpenters International Training Center (ITC) serves as a hub in a system that can rapidly get in-demand skills into the field. At the 12-acre campus in Las Vegas, new craft-skill training is developed for UBC members in areas like commercial door and hardware, concrete formwork, and gas- and steam-turbine installation and maintenance. The ITC's Curriculum Development Project has published nearly 50 training manuals.

About Manufacturing for the Green Economy

Spain's Gamesa Corporation located its first U.S. manufacturing plant for wind turbines in Pennsylvania. Gamesa is one of the largest makers of wind turbines in the world and is the only major wind turbine manufacturer that produces its blades, nacelles, and towers in the United States. Tax incentives, the adoption of a Renewable Portfolio Standard (RPS), and coordinated efforts by the governor, the state's environmental secretary, the state legislature, the Apollo Alliance, and the USW made Gamesa's investment in new manufacturing jobs in Pennsylvania possible.

UNITED STEEL, PAPER AND FORESTRY, RUBBER, MANUFACTURING, ENERGY, ALLIED INDUSTRIAL & SERVICE WORKERS INTERNATIONAL UNION (USW) (STEELWORKERS)

Five Gateway Center
Pittsburgh, Pennsylvania 15222
412-562-2400
www.usw.org

About the Union

The Institute for Career Development (ICD), head-quartered in Merrillville, Indiana, develops and offers workforce training programs for the United Steelworkers Union. The ICD was created in 1989 as a result of contract negotiations between the USW and major steel companies. Since then, ICD has expanded to include training programs for the employees of rubber companies.

Programs and Training

ICD is a joint initiative between labor and man-agement. The emphasis is on teaching "portable" skills that workers can use in their current careers or take with them to new careers. Most classes are taught in learning centers in or near the plants or in the union halls and are offered before and after shift changes.

Union members may also take other courses, such as those offered by community colleges, through a tuition assistance program. Each worker may receive up to $1800 annually for tuition, books, and fees at accredited institutions. The program is paid for by a fund created as a result of con-tract negotiations in 1989 between the USW and participating companies. Companies pay a certain amount into the fund for each hour worked by a steelworker.

Partnerships for Green Jobs

In addition to providing training and apprenticeship programs, labor unions have been active in lobbying for and supporting the growth of green jobs. Their influence was evident in passage of the economic stimulus package in 2009. While working to help their members adapt to the changing economy, union leaders also recognize their responsibility to the environment. The following two alliances, which bring together union leaders with environmentalists and business leaders, are examples on the national level of these partnerships.

Apollo Alliance

The slogan of the Apollo Association is "Clean Energy, Good Jobs." According to its mission statement, the Apollo Alliance is "a coalition of labor, business, environmental, and community leaders working to catalyze a clean energy revolution that will put millions of Americans to work in a new generation of high-quality, green-collar jobs. Inspired by the Apollo space program, we promote investments in energy efficiency, clean power, mass transit, next-generation vehicles, and emerging technology, as well as in education and training. Working together, we will reduce carbon emissions and oil imports, spur domestic job growth, and position America to thrive in the twenty-first–century economy."

The Board of Apollo Alliance includes the president of United Steelworkers Union, the executive vice president of Service Employees International Union, the general president of Laborers International Union of North America, and business, environmental, and community leaders. Among union supporters are the national AFL-CIO and various state affiliates. The Alliance has published numerous reports and research on environmental issues and is active in lobbying efforts to promote increasing the number of well-paying, career-track, green-collar jobs.

For more information, check the Web site http://apolloalliance.org.

Blue Green Alliance

The Blue Green Alliance is a national partnership of labor unions (blue) and environmental organizations (green) dedicated to expanding the number and quality of jobs in the green economy. The alliance, now numbering more than 6 million people, was launched in 2006 by the Sierra Club and United Steelworkers. Today, it includes the Communications Workers of America (CWA), National Resource Defense Council (NRDC), Laborers' International Union of North America (LIUNA), and Service Employees International Union (SEIU).

Among its goals, the Blue Green Alliance seeks to educate the public about solutions that "reduce global warming in the timeframe necessary to avoid the effects of climate change" and "curb the use of toxic chemicals in order to enhance public health and promote safer alternatives." The Alliance also advocates for fair "labor, environmental, and human rights standards in trade policies."

To achieve these goals, the Alliance works in partnership with the Good Jobs, Green Jobs National Conference; the Green Jobs for America campaign, including additional partners such as Working America, the community affiliate of the AFL-CIO; Green for All; the Center for American Progress; and the Labor-Climate Project, a partnership with Al Gore's Alliance for Climate Protection. The Blue Green Alliance also publishes groundbreaking research reports focused on renewable energy and green chemistry.

For more information, check the Web site: www.bluegreenalliance.org.

PART III

WORKFORCE
TRAINING

CHAPTER 8

STATE AND FEDERAL WORKFORCE TRAINING

The Web site for the state of Arkansas defines "workforce development" as follows:

[E]ducation and/or training beyond high school which leads to a GED, certificate, two- to four-year degree; and/or other short-term, customized training designed to meet the needs of employers to upgrade the skills of existing, emerging, transitional, and entrepreneurial workforces.

The other forty-nine states and the District of Columbia view workforce development similarly. In every case, the emphasis is on *employer* needs and attracting new employers to the state. Training and apprenticeship programs are also geared to a state's major employers, who often receive tax incentives and access to free services for hiring employees or for implementing existing training resources. What does this mean for you, the job seeker? Workforce development emphasizes the provision of resources for finding jobs, writing resumes, and developing interview skills to satisfy the employment needs of a state's employers.

USING THE INTERNET

Every state has an Internet portal through which job seekers can post resumes, search for job openings, or apply for unemployment benefits—and where state employers can post job openings and review resumes of prospective employees. The quality and thoroughness of these portals vary by state:

Some are more user-friendly than others; some are more comprehensive than others. To access these resources, one usually needs to establish an online user ID and password, so you'll have at least a minimum level of security for the information you post.

FINDING A ONE-STOP CAREER CENTER

The Workforce Investment Act (WIA) of 1998, which took effect in 2000, was enacted to replace the Job Training Partnership Act and other federal job-training laws. The WIA aims to encourage businesses to participate in local Workforce Development Services through Workforce Investment Boards. These boards are chaired by community members in the private sector. The WIA established a national workforce preparation and employment system—called America's Workforce Network—to meet the needs of businesses and workers who are interested in furthering their careers.

A main feature of Title I of the WIA is the creation of the One-Stop Career Center system through which job seekers can access a broad range of employment-related and training services from a single point of entry. Each year, nearly 16 million Americans find job placement assistance through One-Stop Career Centers. The following programs are required by federal law to deliver their services through this system:

- Title I of WIA (adults, youth, and dislocated workers)
- Job Corps
- Native American Job Programs
- Wagner-Peyser (employment service)
- Unemployment Insurance
- Trade Adjustment Assistance
- North American Free Trade Association (NAFTA) Transitional Adjustment Assistance
- Welfare-to-Work
- Senior Community Service Employment
- Veterans Employment and Training
- Vocational Rehabilitation
- Adult Education
- Postsecondary Vocational Education
- Community Services Block Grant
- Employment and Training Activities
- Housing and Urban Development
- Migrant and Seasonal Farm Worker Programs

You'll find One-Stop Career Centers in every state and the District of Columbia. All are funded with federal money, and users are not charged for services. The number, locations, and types of resources in One-Stop Centers vary by state and are largely based on population density (for example, rural states will have fewer resources in outlying areas). One-Stop Centers play several roles: They operate as career centers, workforce centers, job centers, unemployment benefit centers, and state or regional government services centers all at once. The following is a list of general services that you may find at your local One-Stop Center:

- Assistance with filing for unemployment benefits
- Assessment of career goals, skills, interests, and abilities
- Information and guidance on choosing education and training programs
- Assistance with basic skills and GED preparation
- Assistance in developing and revising resumes
- Assistance with preparing for job interviews
- Information on the local labor market
- Job search and placement counseling
- Internet access for job searches
- Information on and referrals for childcare, transportation, and other supportive services

In many states, Workforce Development is a separate department or agency within the state government. In other states, it is part of the Departments of Labor, Commerce, or Employment. Each state is required to have a specific entity to administer the services required under WIA, to certify providers of services, and to report regularly to the federal government. The list in this chapter provides main contact information for One-Stop Centers in all fifty states and the District of Columbia, as well as a general description of the individual programs and other relevant workforce development information provided in each center. Use your state's workforce home page to find the location of the center nearest to you and the services that it offers. Not all centers or states have green training or retraining programs, but this is the place to start your search.

VETERANS' SERVICES

Services for veterans are provided through One-Stop Career Centers. For example, Helmets to Hardhats is a national program that connects National Guard, Reserve, and transitioning active-duty military members with career training and employment opportunities in the construction industry. The program is administered by the Center for Military Recruitment, Assessment, and Veterans Employment and is headquartered in Washington, DC.

Go online to www.careeronestop.org/military-transition/ and click on "Find State Resources for Veterans" under "Hot Topics." Here you can search by state for veteran-specific job and educational resources. Some are provided by the One-Stop Centers, and others by other agencies and institutions.

REGISTERED APPRENTICESHIP PROGRAMS

Your state may also participate in the Registered Apprenticeship Program supported by the Department of Labor's Employment and Training Administration Office of Apprenticeship (OA). There are close to 1,000 apprenticeship titles recognized by the OA. An apprenticeship program is a partnership of employers, labor management organizations, state and local workforce development agencies and programs, two- and four-year colleges, and economic development organizations to provide on-the-job training and classroom instruction to entry-level workers for certain skills or trades. It's a way to earn and learn at the same time.

Many of the apprenticeship programs partner with colleges, so enrollees can earn college credit, as well as experience and a paycheck. Some programs also lead to nationally recognized certification. Examples of registered apprenticeships are carpenter, construction laborer, electrician, and over-the-road truck driver. Not all apprenticeships are available in all states. It depends on the needs, interests, and capacity of sponsoring organizations.

Check www.doleta.gov/OA/stateoffices.cfm for your state's contact information for apprenticeship programs. Your One-Stop Center can help you find out what apprenticeships are available in your area, or go online to http://oa.doleta.gov/bat/cfm for apprenticeship sponsors and lists of apprenticeships.

ARRA GREEN JOB TRAINING GRANTS

Note that the American Recovery and Reinvestment Act (ARRA), which was signed into law in 2009 to stimulate the economy, included $4 billion for workforce investment initiatives in retraining and education. Your state, in partnership with local colleges and training providers, may have applied for some of this money to increase its workforce training programs. Nearly $100 million in green job training grants was dedicated to programs to help dislocated workers and others, including women, African Americans, and Latinos, find jobs in expanding green industries and related occupations. Funding also went to projects in communities impacted by auto industry restructuring. Nearly $190 million was provided to thirty-four states through the State Energy Sector Partnership and Training Grants to train workers in emerging industries including energy efficiency and renewable energy. Most of these initiatives are available through the appropriate Workforce Investment Boards.

About ARRA Programs and Grants

Check your state's Web site to see if your state won federal money for green industries and green training programs. Also look for information for programs your own state is supporting.

The following are a few examples of ARRA grants:

- *California:* Funding to train unemployed workers or upgrade skills of employed workers for jobs that reduce energy or water use in the building trades or for jobs that produce or transmit renewable energy.
- *Maryland:* Funding to prepare 1,500 veterans, reservists, low-wage workers, and ex-offenders as the first wave of a goal of 100,000 workers in new green jobs in the state by 2015.

- *Michigan:* Funding to create ia pipeline of skilled workers for alternative energy opportunities' by training workers displaced by the loss of jobs in the auto industry.
- *International Training Institute for Sheet Metal and Air Conditioning:* Funding to prepare 240 sheet metal workers in *Michigan* for careers in energy-efficient building construction, retrofitting, and manufacturing.
- *New Mexico:* Funding to prepare workers for careers in biofuels, solar energy, wind energy, and green building/energy efficiency.

STATES' ONE-STOP CAREER CENTERS

About Resource Areas in One-Stop Career Centers

Many One-Stop Career Centers have resource rooms or separate areas where job seekers can access the Internet and use the printers, phones, copiers, and fax machines in their job searches. Employment professionals in these resource rooms are there to help job seekers find what they need. Some centers may have childcare areas as well, but call your local center to be sure.

ALABAMA
Office of Workforce Development
PO Box 302130
Montgomery, Alabama 36130-2130
334-293-4700
https://joblink.alabama.gov/ada

Alabama Joblink is a portal to services offered through the Alabama Career Center system, which administers the state's One-Stop Centers. CareerLink centers are located in each county and are administered by three regional centers:

Central Alabama Skills Center at Southern Union State Community College, North Alabama Skills Center, and South Alabama Skills Center.

ALASKA
Alaska Workforce Investment Board
1016 West 6th Avenue
Suite 105
Anchorage, Alaska 99501
907-269-7485
www.jobs.state.ak.us/offices

Job-related training services are available to eligible youth, adults, and dislocated workers through the Alaska Job Center Network (AJCN) and select training providers and partners across the state. Funding for these training services is available primarily through WIA, the State Training Employment Program (STEP), the Trade Assistance Act (TAA), and the High Growth Job Training Initiative (HGJTI). These funds may be leveraged with federal Pell grants and/or the Alaska State Student Loan program. For Alaska Native Americans, other funding for training is available through recognized tribal organizations throughout the state. Job training resources are available for a limited number of residents of select rural locations through the Denali Training Fund via the Denali Commission.

ARIZONA
Department of Commerce: Workforce
  Development
1700 W. Washington
Suite 600
Phoenix, Arizona 85007
602-771-1100
www.azworkforceconnection.com

Arizona Workforce Connection is a statewide system of workforce development partners that provide free services to employers seeking access to skilled new hires or to existing worker training resources. Through a network of One-Stop Centers and online services, Arizona Workforce Connection provides access to employee recruitment, labor market information, job training and hiring tax credits, customized training and skills upgrading, and pre-layoff assistance.

Note that as of January 1, 2010, the state of Arizona has a new tool in advancing its solar platform and capacity in renewable energy, that is, the Arizona Renewable Energy Tax Incentive Program. The program is designed to stimulate new investments in manufacturing and in headquarter operations of renewable energy companies, including solar, wind, geothermal, and other renewable technologies. It is administered by the Department of Commerce.

ARKANSAS
Arkansas Workforce Centers
Department of Workforce Services
Two Capitol Mall
Little Rock, Arkansas 72201
501-371-1020
E-mail: arkansaswib@arkansas.gov
www.arworks.org/index.html

Arkansas Workforce Centers provide locally developed and operated services, including training and linking employers and job seekers through a statewide delivery system. Convenient One-Stop Centers are designed to eliminate the need to visit different locations. The centers integrate multiple workforce development programs into a single system, making the resources more accessible and user-friendly to job seekers and expanding services to employers.

CALIFORNIA
Employment Development Department
800 Capitol Mall, MIC 83
Sacramento, California 95814
916-654-7799
www.edd.ca.gov/Jobs_and_Training

California's Employment Development Department (EDD) provides a comprehensive range of employment and training services in partnership with state and local agencies and organizations. These services are provided statewide through the state's One-Stop Career Center system, or EDD Workforce Services Offices. Each county has at least one One-Stop Career Center.

On January 11, 2010, Southern California Edison (SCE) announced a $1 million gift to California's community colleges to launch the iGreen Jobs Education Initiative.î This program will provide scholarship support for students with financial need who are enrolled in green job workforce preparation or training programs.

COLORADO
Department of Labor and Employment
633 17th Street
Suite 700
Denver, Colorado 80202
303-318-8000
www.colorado.gov/cs/Satellite/
    CDLE-EmployTrain/CDLE/1248095319014

In nearly all of Colorado's nine federally recognized workforce regions, program administration and service delivery of WIA and Wagner-Peyser Act programs are consolidated, providing local businesses and job seekers with easy access to a broader range of workforce center services. The centers provide an array of employment and training services at no charge to employers or job seekers.

CONNECTICUT
Department of Labor
200 Folly Brook Boulevard
Wethersfield, Connecticut 06109
860-263-6000
www.ctdol.state.ct.us/ContactInfo

The One-Stop Career Center system in Connecticut is called CTWorks. The system helps more than 80,000 state residents annually with resume writing, interviewing skills, job training, and much more. Most training results in certification and job placement.

About Funding for Training or Retraining

If you need financial help, ask your local One-Stop employment professionals about the possibility of funding while training. Some states and programs may also provide supportive funding.

DELAWARE

Department of Labor: Workforce Investment
   Board (WIB)
4425 N. Market Street
Fox Valley
Wilmington, Delaware 19802
302-761-8160
www.delawareworks.com/wib

The WIB oversees Delaware's One-Stop Centers to ensure that the state's citizens are provided with occupational training and employment service opportunities to help them gain employment that will sustain them and their families. One-Stop Centers are located within each of Delaware's Department of Labor locations: Wilmington, Newark, Dover, and Georgetown.

DISTRICT OF COLUMBIA

Department of Employment Services (DOES)
Government of the District of Columbia
64 New York Avenue NE
Suite 3000
Washington, DC 20002
202-724-7000
E-mail: does@dc.gov
http://does.dc.gov/does/site/default.asp

The Department of Employment Services administers One-Stop Career Centers in the District of Columbia. Each DOES center provides a range of services, including career counseling, career planning, resume assistance, direct job placement, classroom and on-the-job training, online and phone access to America's Job Bank, information about local and national labor markets, and unemployment compensation. In addition to the traditional One-Stop Centers, DC's Department of Employment Services has pioneered an advanced Web-based workforce development system to better serve the citizens and employers of the District. Virtual One-Stop offers job seekers, employers, training providers, benefit applicants, students, youth, and other One-Stop customers a comprehensive array of services via the Internet.

FLORIDA

Agency for Workforce Innovation
107 East Madison Street
Caldwell Building
Tallahassee, Florida 32399-4120
866-352-2345
www.floridajobs.org/onestop/onestopdir

Florida's Office of Workforce Services (WFS) provides One-Stop program support services to the twenty-four Regional Workforce Boards that administer the One-Stop Centers.

Employ Florida Marketplace (www.employ-florida.com) is Florida's official online portal to virtual job-matching services and many other workforce resources. The site offers assistance in selecting a new career, finding a new job, or locating suitable education or training.

GEORGIA

Department of Labor
404-232-3540
www.dol.state.ga.us/find_one_stop_centers.htm

Most of the direct services of Georgia's Department of Labor are provided through the Internet or by staff in fifty-three local Career Centers, more than fifty local Vocational Rehabilitation Offices, and twenty Workforce Areas, offering a wide range of services to both job seekers and employers. Each county has multiple One-Stop Centers that provide individuals who seek employment with the most up-to-date tools to find and keep jobs, including resource areas, education and training services, local and national job listings, and job search and financial management workshops.

HAWAII

Department of Labor and Industrial Relations:
    Workforce Development Division
830 Punchbowl Street #329
Honolulu, Hawaii 96813
808-586-8877
http://dlir.workforce.develop@hawaii.gov
http://hawaii.gov/labor/wdd/onestops

Hawaii's One-Stop Centers provide free services to job seekers and employers, including job-search assistance; personal career-planning services; training opportunities; support for HireNet Hawaii, the online employment site; and a resource area. Centers are located on Oahu, Maui, Hila, Kona, and Kauai.

IDAHO

Department of Labor
317 W. Main Street
Boise, Idaho 83735
208-332-3570
http://labor.idaho.gov/dnn/StateCouncil/
    CareerCenters/tabid/2042/Default.aspx

The IdahoWorks Career Center is the primary point of access to a full range of labor market and education services. More than seventeen programs have been assembled under the One-Stop system to meet the needs of workers, students, and businesses. Six centers throughout the state offer a variety of self-service options, a comprehensive resource center, and highly trained staff. For those seeking employment or education, the Career Centers provide one-stop access to national, state, and local job listings; career guidance; specialized workshops; and education and training services and resources in the community. IdahoWorks also provides online access to finding jobs and applying for various services from your own computer at http://labor.idaho.gov/iw/.

The Workforce Development Training Fund helps eligible Idaho companies with up to $2000 per employee for job skills training. The fund underwrites training for new employees of companies expanding in Idaho and skills upgrade training to prevent layoffs of current workers. The application process is designed for quick response and turnaround with minimal paperwork.

ILLINOIS

Illinois Department of Employment Security
    (IDES)
33 South State Street
Chicago, Illinois 60603
www.ides.state.il.us/

IDES provides employment services and guidance to workers, job seekers, and employers through a statewide network of IDES offices and Illinois workNet local centers. The agency combines federally funded job training programs in Illinois into a "workforce development" system where individuals can find a job or train for a new career. With nearly sixty locations throughout the state, local IDES offices and Illinois workNet Centers are the primary one-stop sources for the state's workforce development services. IDES also provides an online resource to help workers and job seekers find job listings, job training information, and help with creating resumes through the Illinois workNet Web site.

INDIANA

Department of Workforce Development
Indiana Government Center South
10 North Senate Avenue
Indianapolis, Indiana 46204
800-891-6499 (toll-free)
www.in.gov/dwd/WorkOne/

Indiana's WorkOne portal provides valuable information about WorkOne and its programs. The WorkOne Center is the heart of Indiana's workforce development system and helps people find a new or better job, choose a career, find a good employee, or find training. Indiana has eleven WorkOne Regions, with centers located throughout the state. IndianaCAREERconnect.com is the state's new innovative online job-matching system.

IOWA

Iowa Workforce Development
1000 East Grand Avenue
Des Moines, Iowa 50319-0209
515-281-5387
800-JOB-IOWA (toll-free)
www.iowaworkforce.org/centers/regionalsites
.htm

Fifteen regions make up the Iowa Workforce Development network. The network provides complete one-stop services for job search, unemployment information, career guidance, and training.

KANSAS

Department of Commerce
Workforce Services Division
1000 S.W. Jackson Street
Suite 100
Topeka, Kansas 66612-1354
785-296-0607
E-mail: workforcesvcs@kansasworks.com
www.kansascommerce.com/WorkforceCenters/
tabid/160/Default.aspx

The Kansas Department of Commerce administers the KansasWorks workforce system that links businesses, job seekers, and educational institutions to ensure that the state's employers can find skilled workers. The system operates workforce centers throughout the state to help connect Kansas businesses with skilled job seekers in their area. Its online portal is https://www.kansasworks .com/ada.

KENTUCKY

Office of Employment and Training
275 East Main Street
2nd Floor
Frankfort, Kentucky 40601
502-564-7456
http://workforce.ky.gov/

The Kentucky Office of Employment and Training (OET) is part of the Department for Workforce Investment. OET staff members provide job services, unemployment insurance services, labor market information, and training opportunities. Kentucky One-Stop Career Centers, which are located throughout the state, are designed to give job seekers and employers quick, easy access to necessary services.

LOUISIANA

Louisiana Workforce Commission
1001 N. 23rd Street
Baton Rouge, Louisiana 70802
225-342-3111
https://www.voshost.com/default.asp

The Louisiana Workforce Commission, under the LaWorks network, provides an online portal to services like resume posting, career options, education, and training. It also provides access to information on youth services and administers One-Stop Career Centers throughout the state.

MAINE

Department of Labor
54 State House Station
Augusta, Maine 04333
207-623-7981
E-mail: mdol@maine.gov
www.mainecareercenter.com/

Maine's CareerCenter, the state's online workforce portal, offers a variety of job-related information, including links to One-Stop Centers located throughout the state.

MARYLAND

Department of Labor, Licensing and Regulation
Division of Workforce Development and Adult
Learning
1100 North Eutaw Street
Baltimore, Maryland 21201
410-230-6001
E-mail: det@dllr.state.md.us
https://mwe.dllr.state.md.us

Workforce Exchange is a virtual one-stop network aimed at improving access to information about jobs, training, and workforce support throughout Maryland. The exchange connects agencies, programs, and services electronically to assist employers and individuals in making the right career decisions. The heart of Maryland's workforce system is its more than forty workforce service centers, which provide locally designed and operated services to meet local labor market needs.

MASSACHUSETTS

Labor and Workforce Development, Division of Career Services
Charles F. Hurley Building
19 Staniford Street
Boston, Massachusetts 02114
617-626-5300
E-mail: DCSCustomerfeedback@detma.org
https://web.detma.org/JobQuest/Default.aspx

The state's online portal, JobQuest, provides access to job-search and training programs available online. Thirty-seven One-Stop Career Centers form the foundation of the state's delivery system for employment and training services.

MICHIGAN

Department of Energy, Labor and Economic Growth
201 N. Washington Square
Victor Office Center
5th Floor
Lansing, Michigan 48913
888-253-6855 (toll-free)
E-mail: careerhelp@michigan.gov
www.michiganworks.org

Michigan's Employment Service program provides services to job seekers online through the Michigan Talent Bank portal and more than 100 Michigan Works! Service Centers statewide. Local Michigan Works! agencies oversee a wide variety of programs designed to help employers find skilled workers and help job seekers find satisfying careers. The programs are also designed to prepare youth and unskilled adults for entry into the labor force and to aid individuals who face serious barriers to employment to obtain the assistance necessary to get and keep a job.

MINNESOTA

Department of Employment and Economic Development (DEED)
1st National Bank Building
332 Minnesota Street
Suite E-200
Saint Paul, Minnesota 55101-1351
651-259-7114
http://www.positivelyminnesota.com/

There are nearly fifty WorkForce Centers throughout the state where people looking for jobs can find employment and career assistance. An online job bank "MinnesotaWorks.net" connects job seekers and employers.

MISSISSIPPI

Department of Employment Security
Office of the Governor
1235 Echelon Parkway
PO Box 1699
Jackson, Mississippi 39215-1699
601-321-6000
www.mdes.ms.gov/wps/portal

Workforce Investment Network (WIN) Job Centers, located throughout Mississippi, provide convenient, one-stop employment and training services to employers and job seekers. Online services are provided through the AccessMississippi portal.

MISSOURI

Department of Economic Development
Division of Workforce Development
421 East Dunklin Street
PO Box 1087
Jefferson City, Missouri 65102-1087
573 751-3349
888-728-JOBS (toll-free)
E-mail: wfd@ded.mo.gov
www.missouricareersource.com/mcs/mcs/default.seek

MissouriCareerSource.com is the portal to Internet resources available to job seekers and employers in Missouri. Missouri Career Centers provide training development services to workers and employers through the coordination of a variety of partner agencies. Career Centers are located throughout the state. A wealth of information and resources about workforce services can be found on WorkSmart Missouri, a Web site of the Division of Workforce Development.

MONTANA

Department of Labor: Workforce Services
  Division
PO Box 1728
Helena, Montana 59624-1728
406-444-4100
http://wsd.dli.mt.gov/service/officelist.asp

Montana's Workforce Services Division (WSD) is a gateway to government services in employment and training. The WSD consists of twenty-three Job Service Workforce Center sites located throughout Montana along with a team of experts who are located in a central support office. The focus is on developing and maintaining a high-quality workforce in the state. The online portal to jobs and job information is https://jobs.mt.gov.

NEBRASKA

Department of Labor: Nebraska Workforce
  Development
550 South 16th Street
Lincoln, Nebraska 68508
402-471-9000
http://nejoblink.nebraska.gov/

Joblink is Nebraska's Internet portal providing job searches, resume services, and assistance to job seekers. Seventeen Workforce Development Career Centers are located statewide, offering comprehensive services, including training programs, to job seekers.

NEVADA

Department of Employment, Training and
  Rehabilitation
500 East Third Street
Carson City, Nevada 89713-0021
E-mail: detrinfo@nvdetr.org
www.nevadajobconnect.org/

Nevada's JobConnect Career Centers provide businesses and job seekers with personalized attention and a variety of services, including access to job listings and placement; work registration; labor market information; career information, guidance, and assessment; information about education and training opportunities; unemployment insurance information; resume preparation; referrals to other partner agency services; and more.

NEW HAMPSHIRE

Department of Employment Security (NHES)
32 South Main Street
Concord, New Hampshire 03301
603-224-3311
800-852-3400 (toll-free)
www.nhworks.org

New Hampshire's Department of Employment Security offers free services, resources, and tools to help the job seeker with the entire job-search process. NH WORKS Resource Centers, located within each of the thirteen local offices, provide services, information, resources, and tools for job seekers in a one-stop setting. The NH WORKS system is a partnership of a number of government agencies and community organizations to provide services, resources, and information to job seekers and employers. NH WORKS is an online portal offering comprehensive services to job seekers and employers alike.

About the Energy Star Program

For information on the Energy Star program of the U.S. Department of Energy, go to www.energystar.gov or call 888-782-7937 (toll-free). For information on available Energy Star tax credits for energy-efficient home improvements, check out www.energystar.gov/taxcredits.

NEW JERSEY

Department of Labor and Workforce
 Development
1 John Fitch Way
PO Box 110
Trenton, New Jersey 08625-0110
http://lwd.dol.state.nj.us/labor/wnjpin/findjob/
 onestop/services.html

Located county-wide throughout New Jersey, One-Stop Career Centers assist with obtaining employment and training. The One-Stop Career Centers offer educational training programs at vocational and trade schools or on-site at the One-Stop, including on-the-job training with employers and apprenticeships in many fields.

NEW MEXICO

Department of Workforce Solutions
401 Broadway NE
Albuquerque, New Mexico 87102
E-mail: infodws@state.nm.us
www.dws.state.nm.us/index.html

The One-Stop System is intended to meet the needs of job seekers and workers through services such as access to job listings, career-planning resources, soft skills training, and training and education for high-growth industries. Workforce Offices are located throughout New Mexico.

NEW YORK

Department of Labor
Division of Employment and Workforce
 Solutions
State Campus, Building 12
Albany, New York 12240
518-457-9000
888-4-NYSDOL (toll-free)
E-mail: nysdol@labor.state.ny.us
www.labor.state.ny.us/workforcenypartners/
 osview.asp

At New York's One-Stop Career Centers, job seekers can learn resume writing and successful interviewing techniques, access apprenticeship training and training grants, search online job listings, and attend a job fair. Job seekers can research occupations on the Career Zone site and post customized resumes on Job Portfolio, part of the Job Zone section.

NORTH CAROLINA

Department of Commerce
301 North Wilmington Street
Raleigh, North Carolina 27601-1058
4301 Mail Service Center
Raleigh, North Carolina 27699-4301
919-733-4151
www.nccommerce.com/en/WorkforceServices/
 FindInformationForIndividuals/
 JobLinkCareerCenters/#map

The Division of Workforce Development oversees the chartering and operation of the state's JobLink One-Stop Career Centers and administration of the federal WIA. These centers combine a variety of state and local agencies in one location to provide job seekers and businesses with information, recruitment and placement, and training opportunities. JobLink One-Stop Career Centers are located throughout the state.

About Tools for America's Job Seekers

The U.S. Department of Labor ran a challenge to find the top-rated sites for job seeker tools on the Internet. Members of the public rated more than 600 online tools over a two-week period. The top tools in each of the six categories are available through http://www.careeron-estop.org/jobseekertools. The tools cover general job boards, niche job boards, career planning tools, career exploration tools, social media job search, and other job and career tools such as preparing for an interview, labor market data, and training grants.

NORTH DAKOTA

Job Service North Dakota
PO Box 5507
Bismarck, North Dakota 58506-5507
701-328-2825
www.jobsnd.com/

Job Service's online labor exchange system provides individuals with maximum flexibility in their job searches. Customers may use the online services exclusively, or they may consult with a Job Service employment professional who can assist them in a variety of ways. Job seekers may attend workshops to learn about resume writing, interviewing, and other job search techniques. They may work through an assessment of their interests and abilities to find an appropriate career path. If job seekers do not have the necessary skills to pursue their desired occupations, Job Service employment professionals offer guidance on ways to access funds for training. Fourteen full-service offices and two part-time offices are located in the state.

OHIO

Department of Jobs and Family Services (JFS)
Office of Workforce Development
PO Box 1618
Columbus, Ohio 43216-1618
614-644-0677
E-mail: Workforce@jfs.ohio.gov
http://jfs.ohio.gov/workforce/

In Ohio, there are thirty-one comprehensive, full-service One-Stop sites and fifty-nine satellite sites throughout the state's twenty workforce development areas, with at least one site in every Ohio county. The local workforce development areas are based on population, economic development, educational resources, and labor markets, and the One-Stop Centers tailor their services to meet local customer needs. Job-seeking customers can expect services like resource rooms, job-related workshops, supportive services, individual training accounts, and other activities that match job seekers to employment.

OKLAHOMA

Department of Commerce
900 North Stiles Avenue
Oklahoma City, Oklahoma 73104-3234
405-815-5125
800-879-6552 (toll free)
www.workforceok.org/locator.htm

Under the umbrella of Workforce Oklahoma, business leaders, educators, training providers, and employment professionals work together to achieve job growth, employee productivity, and employer satisfaction within the workforce system. A network of statewide offices integrates employment, education, and training to assist employers in finding qualified employees and to help workers find jobs, make career decisions, and access training opportunities.

OREGON

Employment Department
875 Union Street, NE
Salem, Oregon 97311
503-451-2400
800-237-3710 (toll-free)
http://findit.emp.state.or.us/locations/index.cfm

Through forty-seven WorkSource Center offices across the state, the department serves job seekers and employers by helping workers find suitable employment, providing qualified applicants for employers, supplying statewide and local labor market information, and offering unemployment insurance benefits to workers temporarily unemployed through no fault of their own. The department helps job seekers find jobs that match their skills and employers' needs, provides up-to-date information about trends in occupations and skills needed for success in the job market, and works with other agencies to direct workers to appropriate training programs and job experiences.

PENNSYLVANIA

Department of Labor and Industry

717-787- 3354

http://www.paworkforce.state.pa.us/portal/server
    .pt/community/contact_us/12950

The department prepares job seekers for the global workforce through employment and job-training services for adult, youth, older workers, and dislocated workers. The Commonwealth Workforce Development System (CWDS) is an Internet-based system of services for use by customers and potential customers of the PA CareerLink offices. CWDS provides online access to job openings; information about employers, services, and training opportunities for job seekers; and labor market information. The department administers a network of PA CareerLink centers around the state.

RHODE ISLAND

RI Department of Labor and Training

Center General Complex

1511 Pontiac Avenue

Cranston, Rhode Island 02920

401-462-8000

www.networkri.org/

Rhode Island's One-Stop Career Center System, netWORKri, is a partnership of professional, labor, training, and education organizations. The netWORKri Centers, located throughout the state, match job seekers and employers through high-quality employment programs and services.

SOUTH CAROLINA

Department of Commerce: Workforce
    Development

1201 Main Street

Suite 1600

Columbia, South Carolina 29201-3200

803-737-0400

800-868-7232 (toll-free)

www.sces.org/Individual/locations/1stoploc.htm

Matching the needs of businesses for skilled workers and training with the needs of individuals for education and employment, the Workforce Division seeks to provide customers with timely information and services. Through its One-Stop system, South Carolina's Workforce Division assists in finding appropriate training for adults and enables smooth coordination with industries, education, and economic development.

SOUTH DAKOTA

Department of Labor: Workforce Training

700 Governors Drive

Pierre, South Dakota 57501-2291

605-773-3101

http://dol.sd.gov/workforce_training/clcs.aspx

The South Dakota Department of Labor (DOL) offers a variety of training and education programs to ensure that employers have the skilled workforce they need and to help individuals realize their potential as employees. Some of these programs are geared toward helping target groups successfully overcome unique employment challenges, such as those for whom English is a second language or those who do not possess a high school diploma. The department also helps individuals assess their training and educational needs and identify options. Career Learning Centers (CLCs) work closely with the DOL to provide education and employment training services that meet the needs of local job seekers and businesses.

TENNESSEE

Department of Labor and Workforce
    Development

220 French Landing Drive

Nashville, Tennessee 37243

615-741-6642

E-mail: TDLWD@tn.gov

http://state.tn.us/labor-wfd/cc/

Tennessee has a network of Career Centers across the state where employers can go to find the workers they need and job seekers can get assistance and career information. In addition to job placement, recruitment, and training referrals, each center offers computerized labor market information, Internet access, workshops, and an online talent bank.

TEXAS
Employment and Labor
Texas Workforce Commission
101 E. 15th Street
Austin, Texas 78778-0001
800-832-2829 (toll free)
www.twc.state.tx.us/dirs/wdas/wdamap.html

The Texas Workforce Commission (TWC) is part of a local/state network of 240 Workforce Centers and satellite offices represented on a regional level by twenty-eight local workforce boards. TWC oversees and provides workforce development services to employers and job seekers. For job seekers, TWC offers career-development information, job-search resources, training programs, and, as appropriate, unemployment benefits. Customers can access local workforce solutions and statewide services in a single location, the Texas Workforce Centers. The TWC administers a comprehensive online job resource service at www.workintexas.com.

UTAH
Department of Workforce Services
PO Box 45249
Salt Lake City, Utah 84145-0249
801-526-WORK (9675)
E-mail: dwscontactus@utah.gov
http://jobs.utah.gov/regions/ec.asp

Utah's one-stop Employment Centers provide training information and job-search assistance. Job seekers receive assistance in determining their interests, abilities, and current skill levels; develop individual employment plans; and explore potential training options. The Department of Workforce Services sponsors access to online services through Utah's Job Connection Web site at http://jobs.utah.gov.

VERMONT
Department of Labor
5 Green Mountain Drive
PO Box 488
Montpelier, Vermont 05601-0488
802-828-4000
http://labor.vermont.gov/Default.aspx?tabid=285

Vermont's fourteen Resource Centers provide employers with interview space, assistance in posting jobs, and help with human resources issues. A Resource Room in each center provides job seekers with services and resources such as personal computers and access to the Internet. The centers are equipped with assistive technology for individuals with disabilities. Staff members are also available to provide specific resources for veterans. Vermont JobLink, www.vermontjoblink .com, is an online portal with access to resources for job seekers and employers alike.

VIRGINIA
The Virginia Employment Commission
703 East Main Street
Richmond, Virginia 23219
PO Box 1358
Richmond, Virginia 23218-1358
804-786-1485
http://www.vec.virginia.gov/vecportal/field/
    field_offices.cfm

The Virginia Workforce Centers provide one-stop access to workforce, employment, and training services of various programs and partner organizations. Each Virginia Workforce Center provides services required by federal legislation, plus services designed to meet the needs of the local community. The Virginia Workforce Connection at www.VaWorkConnect.com is an online job-seeker service that provides job search and career information, training opportunities, skill requirements, and labor market information, including wage data and industry and occupational trends.

WASHINGTON

Employment Security Department (ESD)
PO Box 9046
Olympia, Washington 98507
212 Maple Park Avenue SE
Olympia, Washington 98504
360-902-9500
E-mail: work@esd.wa.gov
https://fortress.wa.gov/esd/
    worksource/StaticContent.
    aspx?Context=WSDirectorySeeker

WorkSource is a partnership of Washington State's businesses, government agencies, community and technical colleges, and nonprofit organizations. It has become the cornerstone for improving access to employment and training services via One-Stop Career Centers in the state. WorkSource services are delivered to customers in a variety of ways, including self-directed efforts via the Internet or at so-called kiosks; group programs and activities, like workshops, one-on-one discussions, training programs, and business consultations.

WEST VIRGINIA

Department of Commerce
WORKFORCE West Virginia
Capitol Complex Building 6, Room 609
112 California Avenue
Charleston, West Virginia 25305-0112
304-558-7024
https://www.workforcewv.org/

WORKFORCE West Virginia, a consortium of partners, assists workers in finding suitable employment and employers in finding qualified workers. It seeks to match job seekers with employers in an efficient manner, help those in need become job ready, and analyze and disseminate labor market information. One-stop Workforce Centers are located throughout the state.

WISCONSIN

Department of Workforce Development (DWD)
201 E. Washington Avenue,
Madison, Wisconsin 53703
PO Box 7946
Madison, Wisconsin 53707-7946
608-266-3131
888-258-9966 (toll-free)
https://jobcenterofwisconsin.com/

JobCenterOfWisconsin.com, operated by the Wisconsin Department of Workforce Development and the Wisconsin Job Center system, is a Wisconsin-centered employment exchange, linking employers in all parts of the state and in communities that border Wisconsin with anyone looking for a job. The Wisconsin Job Center system delivers services through locations in fifty-seven communities throughout the state. The centers are part of the workforce system led by Wisconsin's eleven independently operated, regional Workforce Development Boards.

WYOMING

Department of Workforce Services
122 W. 25th Street
Herschler Building 2E
Cheyenne, Wyoming 82002
307-777-8728
http://wyomingworkforce.org/contact/offices.aspx

Wyoming's Department of Workforce Services (DWS) has a number of programs available for individuals seeking jobs throughout the state—whether laid off, disabled, otherwise unemployed, or simply wanting to change career direction. The DWS administers numerous education and training programs to meet a variety of needs and groups through its local Workforce Centers.

11 Tips for Saving Energy—and Money

Follow these tips for easy, low-cost, or no-cost ways to save energy in your home:

1. **Avoid "phantom power."** Unplug your electronic devices and appliances when you're not using them. While they're plugged in, they continue to draw power even after you switch them off. Phantom power, also known as vampire power and idle current, can account for about 10 percent of your home's electricity use, or about a month of electricity.

2. **Use a power strip to "unplug" electronic equipment.** Rather than manually unplug all your electronic equipment, plug everything into power strips and turn them off when you're finished with your equipment. A "smart" power strip will cut the phantom power automatically when you turn off a device, such as the TV or gaming system. You don't have to remember to turn off the power strip. Some smart power strips allow you to choose a primary device—say, your computer—to plug into an assigned place on the strip. When it detects that you've turned off that device, it shuts down power to peripheral devices, such as the monitor, printer, speakers, external hard drives, and so on.

3. **Replace your light bulbs with compact fluorescent light bulbs (CFLs) or light emitting diodes (LEDs).** Incandescent light bulbs are due to be phased out beginning in 2012. The Energy Independence and Security Act of 2007 calls for the transition to more energy-efficient lighting starting January 1, 2012, at which time 100-watt incandescent bulbs will no longer be sold. The following year, 75-watt incandescent bulbs will be phased out, and in 2014, sales of 40- and 60-watt bulbs will end.

4. **Wash only full loads of dishes.** Dishwashers consume lots of electricity and hot water, so running only full loads saves on both. If you absolutely have to wash less than a full load, do the dishes by hand; you'll still use hot water, but you'll save on electricity. Another way to save energy is to air dry your dishes instead of using the dishwasher's drying cycle.

5. **Wash laundry in cold water.** Heating water uses about 90 percent of the power a washing machine consumes, so the best way to save energy is to wash in cold water. It's actually easier on fabrics, too. Line drying is the most energy-efficient alternative to a clothes dryer—if you have the space. If possible, buy a clothes dryer powered by natural gas rather than electricity. Natural gas dries a load of laundry three times faster than an electric clothes dryer.

6. **Install a programmable thermostat to control your heating and air-conditioning systems.** Set it to a high of 68°F in winter and a low of 72°F in summer. Also set it to turn down automatically at night in the winter or when you are out of the house. In summer, set it to turn up automatically when you are out of the house so you aren't wasting energy cooling an empty house.

7. **Seal leaky windows and doors.** Caulking and weather stripping windows and doors are low-cost do-it-yourself ways to save on your energy bills. Even one leaky window or door adds to your energy costs.

8. **Replace windows with low-E coated windows.** If you are replacing windows or a patio door, consider ones with a low-E coating. This is an extremely thin, almost undetectable metal or metallic oxide layer deposited directly on the surface of the glass to reduce infrared radiation from a warm pane of glass to a cooler pane. Low-E coatings are usually applied during manufacture, but some are available for do-it-yourself homeowners. They save energy and money and were required for the federal energy tax credit for windows and glass doors.

9. **Keep your freezer between 0°F and 5°F. The refrigerator should be no lower than 37°F to 40°F.** Otherwise, you are using unnecessary energy—and losing money.

And two tips for saving on gas—

1. **Don't turn the car on to idle on cold mornings.** It takes only 30 seconds for the engine to warm up. It may take you longer to warm up, but consider the fewer carbon emissions your car will generate and the money in gas you'll save.

2. **Check your car's owner's manual for the proper pressure for your car's tires.** Keeping your tires inflated to the correct pressure saves gas—and money.

PART IV

APPENDIXES

APPENDIX A

ENERGY JOBS BY INDUSTRY

ENERGY SECTORS

Biofuels
- Biofuels Processing Technician
- Biofuels Production Manager
  - Biodiesel Production Manager
  - Biodiesel Plant Manager
  - Biodiesel Plant Operations Engineer
  - Biodiesel Plant Superintendent
  - Biofuels Plant Manager
  - Biofuels Plant Operations Engineer
  - Biofuels Plant Superintendent
  - Ethanol Production Manager
  - Industrial Production Manager
  - Quality Control Systems Manager
- Biofuels Technology and Product Development Manager
  - Biodiesel Technology and Product Development Manager
  - Engineering Manager
- Biomass Plant Technician
  - Assistant Plant Technician, Biomass
- Biomass Production Manager
  - Biomass Operations Manager
  - Biomass Plant Engineer
  - Biomass Plant Manager
  - Biomass Plant Operations Engineer
  - Biomass Plant Superintendent
  - Industrial Production Manager
  - Quality Control Systems Manager
- Methane Capturing System Engineer
  - Landfill Gas Engineer
  - Senior Landfill Specialist
  - Project Engineer
- Methane/Landfill Gas Collection System Operator
  - Gas Operations Manager
  - Gas Plant Manager
  - Gas Plant Supervisor
  - Landfill Gas Operations Manager
  - Landfill Manager
- Methane/Landfill Gas Generation System Technician
  - Gas Operations Specialist
  - Gas Plant Technician
  - Methane Capturing System Installer
  - Methane/Landfill Gas Collection System Technician

Electric Power
- Electric Power-Line Installer and Repairer
  - Lineman

- o Journeyman Lineman
- o Electrical Lineworker
- o Power Lineman
- Electric Power Plant Operator
  - o Auxiliary Operator
  - o Control Operator
  - o Operations and Maintenance Technician (O&M Technician)
  - o Unit Operator
  - o Control Center Operator
  - o Control Room Operator
  - o Operations and Maintenance Gas Turbine Technician
  - o Plant Control Operator
- Energy Broker
  - o Account Executive: Energy Sales
  - o Energy Consultant
  - o Energy Sales Consultant
  - o Energy Sales Representative
- Power Plant Distributor and Dispatcher
  - o System Operator
  - o Load Dispatcher
  - o Transmission System Operator
  - o Electric System Operator
  - o Control Operator
  - o Distribution Operations Supervisor
  - o Distribution System Operator
  - o Power System Dispatcher
  - o Control Area Operator
  - o Power System Operator
- Smart Grid Engineer
  - o Distribution Engineer—Smart Grid Protection
  - o Electrical Engineer
  - o Lead Smart Grid Test Engineer
  - o Senior Engineer, Smart Grid AMR/AMI (Automated Meter Reading/Advanced Metering Infrastructure)
  - o Smart Grid Software Engineer
  - o Smart Grid Test Engineer
  - o Systems Engineer
  - o Transmission Services Engineer

Geothermal Power
- Geothermal Production Manager
  - o Geothermal Electrical Engineer
  - o Geothermal Project Manager
  - o Geothermal Operations Engineer
  - o Geothermal Operations Manager
  - o Geothermal Resource Manager
- Geothermal Technician
  - o Geothermal Installer

Hydroelectric Power
- Hydroelectric Plant Technician
  - o Controls and Electrical Technician (ICE Technician)
  - o Hydroelectric Plant Installation Technician
  - o Instrumentation Technician
- Hydroelectric Production Manager
  - o Engineer Manager
  - o Engineer Supervisor
  - o Hydroelectric Operations Supervisor
  - o Operations Manager
  - o Plant Manager
- Hydrologist
  - o Dam Designer
  - o Hydraulic Engineer
  - o Hydrologic Engineer
  - o Project Manager—Hydro Licensing and Water Resources
  - o Senior Hydrologist
  - o Supervisory Civil Engineer/ Hydrologist

Nuclear Power
- Nuclear Engineer
  - o Criticality Safety Engineer
  - o Engineer
  - o Generation Engineer
  - o Nuclear Reactor Engineer
  - o Nuclear Design Engineer
  - o Nuclear Licensing Engineer

- o Nuclear Process Engineer
- o Resident Inspector
- o System Engineer
- Nuclear Equipment Operations Technician
  - o Nuclear Equipment Operator
  - o Nuclear Auxiliary Operator
  - o Nuclear Plant Equipment Operator
  - o Licensed Nuclear Operator
  - o Auxiliary Operator
  - o Nuclear Station Plant Equipment Operator
  - o Radiation Protection Technician (RPT)
  - o Systems Operator
- Nuclear Power Reactor Operator
  - o Reactor Operator (RO)
  - o Nuclear Control Room Operator
  - o Nuclear Power Reactor Operation
  - o Nuclear Station Operator
  - o Nuclear Operator
  - o Nuclear Plant Operator (NPO)
  - o Nuclear Control Operator
  - o Unit Reactor Operator
  - o Control Room Supervisor
  - o Nuclear Control Room Nonlicensed Operator

Solar Power

- Solar Energy Installation Manager
  - o Foreman
  - o Project Manager
- Solar Energy Systems Engineer
  - o Commercial Project Engineer
  - o Director of Engineering and Operations
  - o Principal Electrical Engineer—Solar PV
  - o Principal Systems Engineer—Solar Systems
  - o PV Power Systems Engineer
  - o Senior Renewable Energy Systems Engineer—Solar
  - o Solar Energy Engineer

- o Solar Energy Systems Design Engineer
- o Solar PV Systems Engineer
- o Solar Systems Designer
- o Solar PV Utility Manager
- Solar Fabrication Technician
  - o Journeyman Sheet Metal Worker
  - o PV Fabrication and Testing Technician
  - o Sheet Metal Apprentice
  - o Sheet Metal Layout Mechanic
  - o Sheet Metal Mechanic
  - o Sheet Metal Worker
- Solar Photovoltaic Installer
  - o Solar Field Service Technician
  - o Solar Installation Electrician
  - o Solar Installation Technician Commercial
  - o Solar Installation Technician Residential
  - o Solar and PV Installation Roofer
- Solar Sales Representative and Assessor
  - o Account Manager
  - o Assistant Sales Manager
  - o Director, Regional Sales
  - o Independent Sales Representative, Solar
  - o Outside Solar Energy Sales Representative
  - o Outside Solar Sales Representative
  - o Outside Sales Representative, Residential Solar
  - o PV Sales Representative, Commercial
  - o Senior Account Executive
  - o Solar Account Executive
  - o Solar PV Sales Representative
- Solar Thermal Installer and Technician
  - o Solar Field Service Technician
  - o Solar Installation Technician Commercial
  - o Solar Installation Technician Residential

Wind Power
- Wind Energy Engineer
  - Civil Engineer, Wind Energy
  - Electrical Engineer, Wind Farm
  - Wind Energy Electrical Engineer
  - Wind Farm Design Manager
  - Wind Farm Electrical Systems Designer
  - Wind Projects Development Engineer (Civil)
- Wind Energy Operations Manager
  - Assistant Operations Manager
  - Assistant Site Manager
  - Operations Manager
  - Wind Power Plant Project Engineer
  - Wind Project Site Manager
  - Wind Farm Site Manager
  - Wind Site Manager
- Wind Energy Project Manager
  - Director of Wind Development
  - Projects Development Director
  - Project Manager, Development
  - Senior Wind Energy Consultant
  - Wind Project Developer
- Wind Turbine Machinist
  - Machinist
  - Tool Room Machinist
  - Machine Operator
  - Machine Repair Person
  - Gear Machinist
  - Maintenance Specialist
  - Set-Up Machinist
  - Utility Operator
- Wind Turbine Service Technician
  - Lead Wind Technician
  - Lead Wind Turbine Technician
  - Senior Wind Plant Technician
  - Wind Services Technician
  - Wind Turbine Technician

TRANSPORTATION INDUSTRY

Vehicle Design, Development, Manufacture, and Maintenance
- Automotive Engineer
  - Automotive Power Electronics Engineer
  - Powertrain Control Systems and Software Engineer
  - Hybrid Powertrain Development Engineer
  - Diesel Retrofit Designer
  - Electrical Engineer
  - Electronics Engineer
  - Emissions Researcher
  - Mechanical Engineer
  - Quality Engineers
- Automotive Engineering Technician
  - Automotive Testing Technician
  - Electrical Engineering Technician
  - Engineering Technician
  - Aeronautical and Aerospace Engineering Technician
- Automotive Specialty Technician
  - Electric Vehicle Electrician
  - Electric Vehicle Conversion Specialist
  - Automotive Master Mechanic
  - Automotive Service Technician and Mechanic
  - Air Conditioning Technician (A/C Technician)
  - Alignment Specialist
  - Automobile Radiator Mechanic
  - Automotive-Cooling-System Diagnostic Technician
  - Automotive Technician (Auto Technician)
  - Automotive Technician Specialist
  - Brake Technician/Brake Repairer
  - Carburetor Mechanic

- o   Drivability Technician
- o   Front-End Mechanic
- o   Fuel-Injection Servicer
- o   Spring Repairer
- o   Tune-Up Mechanic
- o   Trim Technician
- o   Undercar Specialist
- Diesel Service Specialist
  - o   Bus and Truck Mechanics and Diesel Engine Specialist
  - o   Certified Mechanic
  - o   Commercial Transport Mechanic
  - o   Diesel Engine Mechanic
  - o   Diesel Mechanic
  - o   Diesel Retrofit Installer
  - o   Diesel Retrofit Manufacturing Plant Worker
  - o   Diesel Technician
  - o   Fleet Mechanic
  - o   Heavy Duty Mechanic
  - o   Heavy Equipment Service Mechanic
  - o   Heavy Equipment Service Technician
  - o   Journeyman Bus Mechanic
  - o   Medium/Heavy Truck Mechanic
  - o   Mobile Equipment Mechanic
  - o   Transit Mechanic
  - o   Transportation Mechanic
  - o   Aircraft and Avionics Equipment Mechanic
  - o   Aircraft and Avionics Equipment Service Technician
- Electromechanical Engineering Technologist
  - o   Electromechanical Technician
  - o   Electrical Engineering Technician
  - o   Electronic Engineering Technician
  - o   Mechanical Engineering Technician
  - o   Mechatronics Technician

- Mechatronics Engineer
  - o   Computer Hardware Engineering
  - o   Controls Engineer
  - o   Electro-Mechanical Engineer
  - o   Manufacturing Engineer
  - o   Mechanical Design Engineer
  - o   Mechanical Modeling and Simulation Manager
  - o   Powertrain Simulation Engineer
  - o   Systems Engineer
  - o   Technical Engineer
- Mechanical Engineer
  - o   Electromechanical Engineer
  - o   Lead Mechanical Engineer
  - o   Lead Process Engineer
  - o   Mechanical Handling Engineer
  - o   Process Design Engineer
  - o   Project Manager
  - o   Projects Control Manager
- Mechanical Engineering Technologist
  - o   Design Engineer
  - o   Engineering Fitter (Machine Fitter)
  - o   Engineering Lab Technician
  - o   Engineering Technician
  - o   Engineering Technical Analyst
  - o   Equipment Engineer
  - o   Mechanical Engineering Designer
  - o   Mechanical Engineering Technician
  - o   Metal Turner
  - o   Operations Mechanic
  - o   Process Technician
  - o   Research and Development Technician
  - o   Toolmaker
- Nanosystems Engineer
  - o   Nanotechnology Engineer
  - o   Nanotechnology Researcher
  - o   Metamaterials Scientist

- Nanotechnology Engineering Technologist/Nanotechnology Engineering Technician
    - Nanotechnology Machinist

Fuel Cell Development and Applications
- Fuel Cell Engineer
    - Battery Product Development Specialist
    - Fuel Cells Application Engineer
    - Lithium-Ion Battery Cathode Materials Specialist
    - Mechanical Engineer
    - Structural Analysis Engineer
- Fuel Cell Technician
    - Fuel Cell Field Technician
    - Fuel Cell Maintenance Technician
    - Fuel Cell Manufacturing Technician
    - Laboratory Technician: Test Monitor

Transportation Systems
- Civil Engineer
    - City Engineer
    - Civil Engineering Manager
    - Design Engineer
    - Geotechnical Engineer
    - Project Engineer
    - Project Manager
    - Structural Engineer
    - Railroad Design Consultant
    - Research Hydraulic Engineer
    - Water/Wastewater Engineer
- Supply Chain Manager
    - Logistics Analyst
    - Logistics Engineer
    - Logistics Manager
    - Demand Planner
    - Project Manager
    - Supply Chain Analyst
    - Vendor Manager Inventory Analyst
    - Senior Consultant
    - International Logistics Manager
    - Master Production Scheduler
    - Purchasing Manager
    - Sourcing Manager
    - Transportation Manager
    - Director of Operations
    - Director of Transportation
    - Vice President of Global Logistics
    - Vice President of Supply Chain Management
- Transportation Engineer
    - Highway Engineer
    - Traffic Engineer
- Transportation Planner
    - Aviation Planner
    - Campus Transportation Planner
    - Environmental Planner
    - Transportation Environmental Planner
    - Transit Operations Analyst
    - Urban and Regional Planner
    - Urban Planner

Vehicle and Transit System Operations
- Truck Driver, Heavy and Tractor-Trailer
    - Delivery Driver
    - Feeder Driver
    - Flatbed Truck Driver
    - Industrial Truck and Tractor Operator
    - Long Haul Driver
    - Over the Road Driver (OTR Driver)
    - Road Driver
    - Truck Driver, Light and Delivery Services
- Dispatcher
    - Aircraft Dispatcher
    - Airline Flight Dispatcher
    - Bus Dispatcher
    - City Dispatcher
    - Dispatch Manager
    - Dispatch Supervisor

- o Dispatcher
- o Motor Coach Supervisor
- o Rail Operations Controller
- o School Bus Dispatcher
- o Train Dispatcher
- o Truck Dispatcher
- Freight Forwarder
  - o Cargo Agent
  - o Documentation Clerk
  - o Drop Shipment Clerk
  - o Forwarder
  - o Forwarding Agent
  - o Freight Agent
  - o Freight Broker
  - o Intermodal Dispatcher
  - o International Coordinator
  - o Load Planner
  - o Logistics Coordinator
  - o Logistics Service Representative
  - o Ship Broker

CONSTRUCTION INDUSTRY

- Architect
  - o Architectural Engineer
  - o Architectural Engineering Consultant
  - o Architectural and Engineering Manager
  - o Architectural Project Manager
  - o Design Architect
  - o Project Architect
  - o Project Manager
  - o Green Building and Retrofit Architect
  - o Industrial Green Systems and Retrofit Designer
- Construction Carpenter
  - o Rough Carpenter
  - o Helper, Carpenter
  - o Construction Laborer
  - o Carpenter
  - o Lead Carpenter
  - o Assembler
  - o Finish Carpenter

- o Construction Worker
- o Custom Stair Builder
- o Installer
- o Trim Carpenter
- o Concrete Carpenter
- Construction Manager
  - o Project Manager
  - o Construction Superintendent
  - o Construction Area Manager
  - o Construction Foreman
  - o General Contractor
  - o Job Superintendent
  - o Project Superintendent
- Electrician
  - o Journeyman Electrician
  - o Commercial Electrician
  - o Maintenance Electrician
  - o Inside Wireman
  - o Journeyman Wireman
  - o Electrician Technician
  - o Electrical Systems Installer
- Energy Auditor
  - o Energy Rater
  - o Energy Consultant
  - o Home Energy Rater
  - o Home Performance Consultant
  - o Building Performance Consultant
- Energy Engineer
  - o Energy Efficiency Engineer
  - o Energy Manager
  - o Distributed Generation Project Manager
  - o Environmental Solutions Engineer
  - o Industrial Energy Engineer
  - o Measurement and Verification Engineer
  - o Test and Balance Engineer
- Facilities Manager
  - o Building Manager
  - o Building Operations Manager
  - o Maintenance and Operations Manager
  - o Maintenance Engineer

- o Maintenance Manager
- o Energy Manager
- Heating, Air Conditioning, and Refrigeration Mechanic and Installer
  - o Air Conditioning Technician (AC Tech)
  - o Commercial Service Technician
  - o Field Service Technician
  - o Heating, Air Conditioning, and Refrigeration Mechanic and Installer
  - o HVAC Installer (Heating, Ventilation, and Air Conditioning)
  - o HVAC Specialist (Heating, Ventilation, and Air Conditioning)
  - o HVAC Technician (Heating, Ventilation, and Air Conditioning)
  - o HVAC/R Service Technician (Heating, Ventilation, and Air Conditioning/Refrigeration)
  - o Refrigeration Mechanic and Installer
  - o Refrigeration Operator
  - o Refrigeration Technician
  - o Service Manager
  - o Service Technician
- Insulation Worker: Floor, Ceiling, Wall
  - o Insulation Installer
  - o Installer
  - o Insulation Estimator
  - o Retrofit Installer
  - o Insulation Mechanic
  - o Insulation Worker, Mechanical
- Weatherization Installer and Technician
  - o Weatherization Field Technician
  - o Weatherization Crew Chief
  - o Residential Air Sealing Technician
  - o Window/Door Retrofit Technician
  - o Weatherization Operations Manager

POLICY, ANALYSIS, ADVOCACY, AND REGULATORY AFFAIRS

- City and Regional Planning Aide
  - o Community Planner
  - o Development Technician
  - o GIS (Geographic Information Systems) Technician
  - o Planning Aide
  - o Planning Assistant
  - o Planning Technician
  - o Transportation Planning Assistant
  - o Zoning Technician
- Compliance Manager
  - o Compliance Administrator
  - o Compliance Analyst
  - o Compliance Associate
  - o Compliance Engineer
  - o Compliance Inspector
  - o Compliance Officer
  - o Compliance Program Manager
  - o Compliance Team Manager
  - o Regulatory Compliance Manager
  - o Compliance Director
  - o Chief Compliance Officer
- Construction and Building Inspector
  - o Electrical Inspector
  - o Green Building Inspector
  - o Home Inspector
  - o Mechanical Inspector
  - o Plan Examiner
  - o Plumbing Inspector
  - o Public Works Inspector
  - o Specification Inspector
  - o Structural Inspector
- Paralegal
  - o Judicial Assistant
  - o Legal Assistant
- Public Relations Specialist
  - o Public Affairs Specialist
  - o Public Information Officer
  - o Public Information Specialist
  - o Communications Director

- o Communications Specialist
- o Public Relations Coordinator
- o Press Officer
- Urban and Regional Planner
  - o Airport Planner
  - o Building, Planning and Zoning Director
  - o City Planner
  - o Community Development Planner
  - o Community Development Director
  - o Community Planning and Development Representative
  - o Neighborhood Planner
  - o Planning Director
  - o Regional Planner

GREEN JOB BOARDS

ABOUT GREEN JOB BOARDS

Once upon a time, just a few years ago, if you were looking for a job, you'd read the want ads in the newspaper or in trade and association publications. Today, most job listings have migrated to the Internet where you will find hundreds of job boards. How do you decide which ones to search and what to look for? Here are a few ideas to help you concentrate your search in the best places.

Remember that job boards are not just for searching when you are looking for a job. They can be helpful when you are deciding on a career to pursue. Analyzing job titles related to your interests; the regions of the country where particular jobs are most common, for example, the Plains states and the Southwest for wind power jobs; types of employers such as public or private, nonprofit, small companies or large corporations; and salaries can help direct your career choice.

Where to Look?

Major Internet sites for jobs are monster.com, careerbuilder.com, and hotjobs.yahoo.com. Type in your job area such as "architectural designer" and see what jobs come up. You can search for jobs in a specific city or nationwide. Monster.com has a green careers section. Green For All and Yahoo! Hotjobs have partnered to create a Green Jobs page at hotjobs.yahoo.com. Green For All is not a job board, but it is a great resource for information about green-collar jobs for skilled workers, especially for those in urban centers and returning veterans.

You will also find job boards that are specific to green energy jobs, such as

- www.careersinwind.com (sponsored by the American Wind Energy Association)
- www.cleantech.org
- www.jobsinsolarpower.com
- www.renewableenergyjobs.com
- www.renewableenergyjobs.net
- www.renewableenergyworld.com
- www.simplyhired.com (not just for energy, but lists many green energy jobs)
- www.solarjobs.com

There are also a number of job boards that post a variety of green jobs. Type "green job boards" into a search engine and more than two dozen will pop up. The following are ones that came up in researching this book:

- http://careercenter.usgbc.org/home
- www.americangreenjobs.com
- www.brightgreentalent.com
- www.careeronestop.org (sponsored by the U.S. Department of Labor)
- www.cleanedgejobs.com
- www.ecojobs.com
- www.environmentalcareer.com
- www.greenbiz.com

- www.greendreamjobs.com
- www.greenjobs.net
- www.greenjobsalliance.org
- www.greenjobsearch.org
- www.sustainlane.com/green-jobs
- www.veteransgreenjobs.org

Other Sources for Job Boards

Also, look at the Web site of the professional organizations and trade associations that you belong to. Many of them have job boards, and their postings will be the most closely aligned with the group's specialties.

Don't overlook your college or university career counseling or job placement office. Many schools today offer their services to alumni and alumnae, not just to seniors and graduate students. If you graduated from a large university, your department may have its own career services link on its Web site or may have links to other job boards.

"GREEN" YOUR VOCABULARY FOR A SUSTAINABLE FUTURE

Just about everywhere you turn these days, you see and hear the lingo of the new green economy: *biofuel, carbon footprint, geothermal, LEED,* just to name a few. Understanding what these words actually mean will certainly help you in your green job search—and in your everyday life. Here's a list of some key green terms and their definitions to get you started on your way to a sustainable future.

alternative energy/renewable energy: energy derived from natural resources that aren't used up over time, such as wind and sun

biodegradable: able to decompose by natural forces and without harming the environment

biodiesel: fuel made from vegetable oils, animal fats, or recycled grease that are chemically processed and blended with petroleum diesel fuel

biofuel: fuel that is produced from renewable biological resources such as plant biomass and treated municipal and industrial waste; for example, ethanol produced from sugarcane or corn

biogas: fuel made from a combination of methane gas and carbon dioxide created by the bacterial degradation of organic matter

biomass: a wide range of materials that have uses other than as food or in consumer goods such as agricultural waste, wood, treated municipal waste, and energy crops such as corn and soybeans

cap-and-trade: system of pollution credits established by the government and based on the amount of air pollution created in a region that enables a company that doesn't use all its pollution credits to sell unused ones to companies that pollute more than the credits allotted to them by the government

carbon emissions: carbon dioxide and carbon monoxide gases released by motor vehicles and industrial production that pollute the atmosphere

carbon footprint: a way to measure the impact of human activity on the environment; uses units of carbon dioxide to calculate amount of greenhouse gases produced

carbon neutral: not adding to carbon dioxide emissions

carbon trading: process by which companies can sell their unused pollution credits; see *cap-and-trade*

clean tech: economically competitive and production technology that uses fewer resources and/or energy, generates less waste, and causes less environmental damage than traditional fuels such as oil and coal

ecotravel: traveling responsibly in terms of the environment, especially to natural areas in a way "that conserves the environment and improves the well-being of local people" (The International Ecotourism Society)

energy audit: assessment of energy use to determine ways to conserve energy; first step in *weatherization*

energy efficient: denotes a product that is as good as or better than standard products, but uses less energy and costs less to operate

Energy Star: U.S. Department of Energy and EPA joint program to increase the energy efficiency of household appliances and electronic devices; adopted by other nations including the European Union

ethanol: alternate fuel made from corn or sugar cane

Fair Trade: agreement by countries in international trade to live up to standards for the fair and just treatment of labor and the environment in the production of goods; goods manufactured and sold under the agreement

feedstock: raw materials such as corn and sugarcane used to produce biofuels

geothermal: energy source; uses heat from the Earth as a clean, renewable source of electricity

global warming: increase in the average temperature of the Earth's atmosphere resulting in climate change

green-collar career/job: a career/job that promotes stewardship of the environment now and for the future

green design: creating materials, products, buildings, services, and experiences that are energy-efficient and environmentally friendly

hybrid: motor vehicle that runs on gasoline and an electric battery

LEED: acronym for Leadership in Energy and Environmental Design, a Green Building Rating System developed by the U.S. Green Building Council (USGBC); "LEED certified" denotes that new construction, renovation, building operations, etc., meet the USGBC guidelines for building sustainability

methane: colorless, odorless, flammable gas that is a constituent of natural gas and a source of hydrogen; can be produced from the decomposition of landfills; LFG (landfill gas)

organic: product made solely from natural ingredients; farming without the use of synthetic pesticides and fertilizer

New Urbanism: urban design movement that encourages the development of walkable neighborhoods with a range of housing and jobs

photovoltaic cell: device that turns sunlight directly into electricity

PCW: stands for Post Consumer Waste; denotes product made from recycled materials

retrofit: to add new technology to an existing structure or system

solar energy system: one of two types of power systems: photovoltaic uses sunlight to produce electricity directly, and the solar water heating system uses sunlight to heat water that is used to provide electricity

solar panel/solar array: device that collects the heat of the sun for use in various types of solar energy systems

solar thermal collector: device that uses energy from sunlight to heat substances like water for use in heating

solar thermal power: energy produced by using sunlight to heat water; also known as concentrated solar power (CSP)

STARS: acronym for Sustainability Tracking Assessment & Rating System for colleges and universities, established by the Association for the Advancement of Sustainability in Higher Education, a consortium of U.S. colleges and universities

sustainability: efforts to "create and maintain conditions under which [humans] and nature can exist in productive harmony, and fulfill the social, economic, and other requirements of present and future generations of Americans" (U.S. Environmental Protection Agency)

sustainable design: the designing of objects and structures according to principles of economic, social, and environmental sustainability; also known as *green design*

VOC: stands for volatile organic compounds; carbon-based molecules that vaporize as gases and enter the atmosphere; ingredient in paint, paint thinners, paint strippers, furniture, and household cleaning products that causes the odor

waste audit: assessment of the amount of waste generated at a home or business

waste reduction: reusing materials, reducing or eliminating the amount of waste at its source by buying less, reducing the amount of toxicity in waste by using environmentally safe products

wastewater recycling: treatment of wastewater for recycling for industrial uses and agriculture

weatherization: improving the energy efficiency of a building by sealing off air leaks

wind turbine: device for harnessing the wind to create electricity